The Arguments of the Philosophers

EDITOR: TED HONDERICH

The purpose of this series is to provide a contemporary assessment and history of the entire course of philosophical thought. Each book constitutes a detailed, critical introduction to the work of a philosopher of major influence and significance.

Plato	J. C. B. Gosling
Augustine	Christopher Kirwan
The Presocratic Philosophers	Jonathan Barnes
Plotinus	Lloyd P. Gerson
The Sceptics	R. J. Hankinson
Socrates	Gerasimos Xenophon Santas
Berkeley	George Pitcher
Descartes	Margaret Dauler Wilson
Hobbes	Tom Sorell
Locke	Michael Ayers
Spinoza	R. J. Delahunty
Bentham	Ross Harrison
Hume	Barry Stroud
Butler	Terence Penelhum
John Stuart Mill	John Skorupski
Thomas Reid	Keith Lehrer
Kant	Ralph C. S. Walker
Hegel	M. J. Inwood
Schopenhauer	D. W. Hamlyn
Kierkegaard	Alastair Hannay
Nietzsche	Richard Schacht
Karl Marx	Allen W. Wood
Gottlob Frege	Hans D. Sluga
Meinong	Reinhardt Grossmann
Husserl	David Bell
G. E. Moore	Thomas Baldwin
Wittgenstein	Robert J. Fogelin
Russell	Mark Sainsbury
William James	Graham Bird
Peirce	Christopher Hookway
Santayana	Timothy L. S. Sprigge
Dewey	J. E. Tiles
Bergson	A. R. Lacey
J. L. Austin	G. J. Warnock
Karl Popper	Anthony O'Hear
Ayer	John Foster
Sartre	Peter Caws

SPINOZA

The Arguments of the Philosophers

R. J. Delahunty

LONDON AND NEW YORK

First published 1985 by Routledge

This edition reprinted in hardback 1999, 2000, 2001 (twice), 2002 (twice)
by Routledge
2 Park Square, Milton Park,
Abingdon, Oxon, OX14 4RN

Simultaneously published in the USA and Canada
by Routledge
270 Madison Ave, New York NY 10016

Routledge is an imprint of the Taylor & Francis Group

Transferred to Digital Printing 2009

© 1985 R. J. Delahunty

All rights reserved. No part of this book may be reprinted or reproduced or utilized in any form or by any electronic, mechanical, or other means, now known or hereafter invented, including photocopying and recording, or in any information storage or retrieval system, without permission in writing from the publishers.

British Library Cataloguing in Publication Data
A catalogue record for this book is available from the British Library

Library of Congress Cataloguing in Publication Data
A catalogue record for this book has been requested

ISBN 0–415–20392–9 (set)
ISBN10: 0–415–20360–0 (hbk)
ISBN10: 0–415–48764–1 (pbk)

ISBN13: 978–0–415–20360–9 (hbk)
ISBN13: 978–0–415–48764–1 (pbk)

Publisher's Note
The publisher has gone to great lengths to ensure the quality of this reprint but points out that some imperfections in the original may be apparent.

May not a man silence his awe or his love and take to finding reasons, which others demand? But if his love lies deeper than any reason to be found? Man finds his pathways.
George Eliot, *Daniel Deronda*, c.XL

Contents

	Life	page ix
	Abbreviations	xiii
	Preface and Acknowledgments	xv
I	Geometrical Method and Philosophic Doubt	1
	1 *The method of ethics*	3
	2 *The* diallelus	12
	3 *The tool analogy*	21
	4 *Philosophical doubt*	25
II	Error and the Will	31
	1 *The grammar of assent*	32
	2 *Close encounters*	36
	3 *The nature of error*	46
III	Knowledge and Imagination	55
	1 *The varieties of knowledge*	56
	2 *Knowledge from signs*	59
	3 *Vagrant experience*	67
	4 *Experience in science and metaphysics*	70
	5 *Common notions*	74
	6 *The distinction between reason and intuition*	78
	7 *Intuition and the attributes*	85
IV	Substance and Attribute	89
	1 *Substance defined*	89
	2 *Three notions of substance*	96
	3 *In itself and conceived through itself*	101
	4 *Monism and pluralism*	104
	5 *Substance: one or many?*	108

CONTENTS

	6 *Problems of the attributes*	116
	7 *Monism revisited*	123
V	God or Nature	125
	1 *Pantheism*	125
	2 *The Divine mind*	131
	3 *God and omnipotence*	136
	4 *The beginning of the Universe*	143
	5 *God and free will*	147
	6 *Freedom and necessity*	155
	7 *Final causes*	165
VI	Minds and bodies	176
	1 *Cartesian man*	177
	2 *Interactionism*	181
	3 *The critique of interactionism*	183
	4 *Dualism*	190
	5 *The order and connection of ideas and of things*	197
	6 *Beasts and machines*	205
VII	Morality and the Emotions	213
	1 *Cartesian passions*	213
	2 *Action and passion*	215
	3 *The concept of endeavour*	220
	4 *Egoism*	223
	5 *Value*	227
	6 *The passions*	231
	7 *The laws of feeling*	236
	8 *Of human bondage*	241
	9 *The conquest of the passions*	247
VIII	Freedom and Reason	255
	1 *Liberation through knowledge*	255
	2 *Freedom and resentment*	260
	3 *Virtue*	268
	4 *The contemplative life*	275
IX	Eternity and Immortality	279
	1 *Immortal longings*	279
	2 *Eternity*	282
	3 *Omnitemporality*	284
	4 *The proof of the mind's eternity*	295
	5 *The survival of the fittest*	300
	Bibliography	306
	Index	312

Life

The facts of Spinoza's life can be recited briefly. He was born in Amsterdam in 1632, the son of a prosperous Portuguese (or Spanish) Jewish merchant, who had come to the Netherlands as a refugee. From 1639 to 1650, Spinoza was an outstanding student at the new Spanish-Jewish school in Amsterdam, where he learned Hebrew. Among his teachers may have been the learned author Manasseh Ben Israel (1604–57), a friend of Rembrandt and of Grotius, who negotiated with Cromwell and the revolutionary English government for the return of the Jews to that country. Another teacher may have been the rabbi, apologist, and Talmudic scholar Saul Morteira (1596–1660), who later served as a member of the *bet din* which excommunicated Spinoza. A third early influence may have been less orthodox: this was the freethinker and philosopher Uriel da Costa (1585–1640), twice excommunicated by the synagogue and publicly whipped before the Amsterdam Jewish community in 1640. Da Costa had taught that the doctrine of the immortality of the soul was both questionable in itself and unsupported by the Scriptures, that a Divine sanction for the Mosaic law was doubtful, and that all religions were man-made. In the early 1650s, while working (with notable success) in the family business, Spinoza seems to have joined the circle of young intellectuals around the Marrano doctor Juan de Prado (1615–70), who had come from Spain to Holland, where he proclaimed himself a Jew. Prado's orthodoxy was suspect, however. In 1656 he was charged with public criticism of the Scriptures, denial of the distinctiveness of the Jewish people, disrespect for rabbinical authority and a wrongful doctrine of Natural Law. To avoid condemnation, Prado recanted his heresies; nevertheless, he was excommunicated in 1657. His friend and follower Spinoza, who had fallen under similar suspicions, was also made to suffer for his beliefs. There is a story that a fanatic from the synagogue tried to assassinate him in 1656, attacking him one evening with a knife; Spinoza is said to have preserved his torn coat for the rest of his life. However that may be, he was formally excommunicated on 27 July 1656 for 'abominable heresies' and 'monstrous acts'.

Little is known with certainty of Spinoza's activities in the years immediately following his excommunication. He may have spent some time studying at the University of Leiden; he may also have learned the craft of optical instruments (in which his work was reputedly excellent). The Spanish Inquisition issued arrest warrants for him and for Prado in 1659: the Inquisitors' report describes them as denying the Mosaic Law and the soul's immortality, and as maintaining that God exists only in a philosophical sense.

In 1660 or thereabouts, Spinoza left Amsterdam for Rijnsburg, near Leiden, and changed his given name from the Hebrew 'Baruch' to its Latin equivalent 'Benedictus'. A small philosophical club in Rijnsburg formed around him: Jarrig Jelles, Peter Balling, Simon de Vries became his pupils, assistants, friends. Spinoza's *Short Treatise on God, Man and his Well-Being* dates from this period. In 1663, with the editorial assistance of Ludovicus Meyer, Spinoza published his *Principles of the Philosophy of René Descartes* in Latin; Meyer wrote an introduction, and added an Appendix containing Spinoza's *Metaphysical Thoughts*.

The early 1660s saw the writing (but not the publication) of a *Treatise on the Improvement of the Intellect* and the start of Spinoza's master work, the *Ethics*. During this time, his reputation grew. In July 1661, Spinoza received the first of many distinguished visitors to come to his door: this was Henry Oldenburgh (1620–77), the Secretary of the newly founded Royal Society of London, who subsequently initiated an active correspondence with him on scientific and philosophical matters. In 1663, Spinoza moved to Voorburg, a suburb of The Hague; there he became friendly with the leading statesman and Grand Pensionary of the Netherlands, Jan de Witt. Spinoza became closely associated with the de Witt interest (he may have composed his first political treatise at de Witt's request), and accepted a modest pension from that source. De Witt's advocacy of republicanism and of tolerance, and his opposition to Calvinist fanaticism and the claims of the House of Orange, won him Spinoza'a perfect sympathy. Spinoza's concerns with Biblical criticism and with government (which were intertwined more closely then than now) were expressed in his *Tractatus Theologico-Politicus*, which appeared (unsigned) in 1670. An attack on revealed religion and a defence of liberty of thought, the book created a scandal and was banned everywhere. Spinoza's authorship was suspected, and the denunciations of the Reformed clergy forced him to suppress the projected Dutch edition; indeed, he may have removed to The Hague itself in 1670, in order to escape the worst fury of the pastors' sermons. (The reaction against the book was not confined to Protestant ranks: in 1671, Spinoza wrote a long letter to the Jewish leader Orobio de Castro, in which he rebutted the charge of atheism.) Spinoza lived in The Hague until his death, boarding with the Van der Spick family. He sustained himself by lensmaking and pursued his speculations in philosophy. We are told that he would occasionally take a little wine, or smoke a pipe with his landlord.

On 20 August 1672, in the wake of the French invasion of the Low Countries, an Orange mob, with the silent approval of the authorities, murdered Jan de Witt and his brother in the street. Spinoza was beside himself with grief and rage. As he later told Leibniz (who came as a visitor), he had made up a placard with the legend 'Ultimi barbarorum', intending to display it to the murderous mob, and was only prevented when his landlord, fearing that Spinoza too would be killed, locked him inside the house. This outburst of almost suicidal passion, on the part of a philosopher who had always taught control of the emotions, suggests that he was a more troubled and rebellious spirit than is often supposed.

Soon afterwards, in May 1673, Spinoza was summoned to Utrecht by the commander of the French army, the Prince of Condé. The purpose of the visit remains unclear: was it a purely private matter, or an undercover peace mission? Perhaps naively, Spinoza accepted the invitation and went; but the Prince and the Philosopher never met. Members of the Prince's entourage did, however, suggest to Spinoza that a pension awaited him if he dedicated a new work to Louis XIV. Spinoza rejected the proposal and returned home, where he was accused of being an enemy agent.

Another titled personage was also taking an interest in Spinoza. In early 1673 he was invited by the Elector Palatine to take up the Chair of Philosophy at the University of Heidelberg. He was to be given complete liberty to philosophise – providing he did not disturb the established religion. In an exquisitely courteous reply, Spinoza declined any offer conditioned on such a term.

The last years of Spinoza's life, spent in the shadow of the hated Orange rule, were perhaps unhappy ones. His efforts to have the *Ethics* published in 1675 met resistance from the theologians, and after a visit to Amsterdam he abandoned the project. This did not put a stop to his literary activity, however: in addition to his correspondence, he began work on a *Hebrew Grammar* for his Christian friends, and undertook his only scientific book, a *Treatise on the Rainbow*. His last work, completed not long before his death, was a major new study of government, the *Tractatus Politicus*. He died, probably of an occupational illness, on 21 February 1677. After his death some of his later writings, including the *Ethics* and the unfinished *Treatise on the Improvement of the Intellect*, were published as the *Opera Posthuma*.

Spinoza's admirers have been as unstinting in their praise of his character as his detractors were in criticism of it: he has been described (by Russell) as the noblest and most loveable of the great philosophers. More revealing are the testimonies from the humble people among whom he lived, who knew him best, and who clearly admired and esteemed him. His calmness, gentleness, modesty and tact are evidenced in many accounts. He may have won the good will of ordinary people by showing their deepest beliefs the tolerance which he sought for his own. There is a story that his landlady once asked him if she could be saved in her religion; he is said to have replied, 'Your religion is good, and you ought not to look for another nor to doubt that you will find salvation in it, if you attach yourself to piety and at the same time lead a tranquil life.'

Another story told of Spinoza (one hopes unreliably) shows a less pleasing aspect of his character. It is said that, in order to divert himself, he would set spiders to battling one another, or would drop flies into a spider's net, and laugh to see the struggle. Did he delight to find self-assertion run so far down in the scale of things? Or did some of the resentment for the wrongs he had suffered seek release in the spectacle of the tiny combatants? So far as we know, he bore poverty, odium and isolation without other signs of malice or bitterness.

Whether or not he was (as some maintain) a secular saint, Spinoza was certainly a very good man, independent-minded, humane, without pretensions. But what we chiefly remember is not the man but the thinker – as he himself wished. To the thinker we must now turn.

Abbreviations

Spinoza's works

G	*Opera*, in 4 vols, ed C. Gebhardt, Heidelberg, 1925.
CM	*Cogitata Metaphysica* (*Metaphysical Thoughts*), G I, pp. 243ff.
DIE	*Tractatus de Intellectus Emendatione* (*Treatise on the Improvement of the Intellect*), G II, pp. 29ff.
E	*Ethica* (*Ethics*), G II, pp. 41ff. (References to the *Ethics* indicate (i) part, (ii) number of axiom, definition, postulate or theorem, (iii) where appropriate, corollary, demonstration or scholium.)
Ep.	*Epistolae* (*Letters*), G IV, pp. 1ff. (All translations from the Letters are taken from A. Wolf, *The Correspondence of Spinoza*, London, 1928.)
PPD	*Principia Philosophiae Renati Des Cartes* (*Principles of the Cartesian Philosophy*), G I, pp. 122ff.
ST	*Korte Verhandeling van God, de Mensch, en des zelfs Welstand* (*Short Treatise on God, Man and his Well-being*), G I, pp. 19ff. (All translations from this work are taken from A. Wolf, *Short Treatise, etc.*, London, 1910.)
TP	*Tractatus Politicus* (*Political Treatise*), G III, pp. 269ff.
TTP	*Tractatus Theologico-Politicus* (*Theologico-Political Treatise*), G III, pp. 1ff.
Wernham	*The Political Works of Spinoza*, ed and trans. A. G. Wernham, Oxford, 1958. (This translation has

ABBREVIATIONS

been regularly used for the two preceding treatises.)

Descartes' works

A.G.	*Descartes: Philosophical Writings*, ed and trans. Elizabeth Anscombe and Peter Geach, Edinburgh, 1954.
A.T.	*René Descartes: Oeuvres*, in 12 vols, ed Ch. Adam and P. Tannery, Paris, 1897–1913.
Cottingham	*Descartes' Conversation with Burman*, ed and trans. J. Cottingham, Oxford, 1976.
H.R.	*The Philosophical Works of Descartes*, in 2 vols, ed and trans. E. Haldane and G. R. T. Ross, Cambridge, 1911.
Kenny Letters	*Descartes: Philosophical Letters*, ed and trans. A. Kenny, Oxford, 1970.

Preface and Acknowledgments

The object of this book is to provide an account of the main parts of Spinoza's philosophy. The first three chapters deal with his epistemology; the second three, with his metaphysics and theory of mind; the final three, with his psychology, ethics and doctrine of immortality. I have not attempted to be comprehensive: I have left some parts of his philosophy (e.g., his theory of politics) to those who are more competent in such questions than myself; while other parts (e.g., his analysis of sense-perception) have been omitted either because there seemed to me little value in them, or because I felt, after persistent study, unable to understand them. Nevertheless, I have tried at least to touch on every major issue in Spinoza's thinking.

In writing this book, I have been guided by the principle which underlies the series in which it appears; that is, I have attempted to present Spinoza's *arguments* as fully and as rigorously as possible. Spinoza himself, who condemns as 'confused ideas' any reasoning in which the conclusions appear divorced from their premisses, would of course have applauded this aim. I have also taken very seriously the platitude that Spinoza was a seventeenth-century philosopher, not a thirteenth- nor a twentieth-century one. In particular, I have read him against the background of Cartesianism, which was the dominant philosophy of the period, and with which he was intimately familiar. In locating him securely within the context of his own time, I do not of course mean to suggest that his ideas are lacking in interest or relevance for us. We are still, to an extent which we have only recently begun to realise, the children of the seventeenth century.

This book was begun at St Andrew's University in Scotland; continued at Carleton College, Ontario and at Oriel College,

PREFACE AND ACKNOWLEDGMENTS

Oxford; brought to near completion at the University of Durham; and finally revised at St John's College of the University of Queensland in Australia. In the course of writing it, I have acquired many intellectual debts; and the pleasantest part of the writing is to acknowledge some of them.

I would like to thank Mr Ted Honderich, the general editor of the series, for his kindness and patience in waiting for the final version, and Professor G. H. R. Parkinson, the reader from Routledge & Kegan Paul, for his very valuable comments on an earlier typescript, from which I learned much. My former tutor, and later colleague, Mr Jonathan Barnes, set me a daunting example of scholarly exactness and analytical precision which I hope this book, however inadequately, may reflect. Mr Michael Inwood of Trinity College, Oxford has also taught me much good philosophy; I thank him particularly for his comments on Chapter II, which was read to the Philosophical Society at Oxford. Professor Wolfgang von Leyden of the London School of Economics has been abundantly generous to me, not least in sharing his enviable knowledge of Spinoza. My thanks go also to my former colleagues at the University of Durham, especially to the late Colin Grant, who commented on parts of the book. My good friends Dr James Krauss and Mr Andrew Solomon have taught me, in many conversations, to look at Spinozism in ways I find novel and exciting. Most of all I must thank my friend, the Reverend Dr J. L. Morgan, Warden of St John's College, for providing the ideal opportunity and facilities for finishing my work on Spinoza, and my employers, Messrs Sullivan & Cromwell, for allowing me leave of absence from my legal duties while I was a Visiting Scholar at St John's. My thanks go also to Jenny and Andrew Tosio, who have taken such care and pains in preparing the final typescript. Finally I must thank the President and Fellows of Harvard College and the Harvard University Press for permission to quote from H. A. Wolfson's *The Philosophy of Spinoza*, and Doubleday & Company, Inc. for permission to cite passages from their anthologies *Spinoza*, edited by Marjorie Grene and *Leibniz*, edited by Harry G. Frankfurt.

I dedicate this book to my mother, and to the memory of my father.

R. J. Delahunty,
St John's College,
University of Queensland,
Queensland, Australia

I

Geometrical Method and Philosophic Doubt

Misleadingly styled an Age of Reason, the seventeenth century was torn between dogmatism and doubt. The problem of authority was its torment and its joy: authority in knowledge, as Galileian dynamics and Copernican astronomy destroyed the traditional picture of nature; authority in religion, as the wars between the sects brought discredit on them all; authority in law and politics, as the absolutist state took form, releasing men from outworn allegiances; authority in morals, as the virtues of medieval Christendom proved unsuited to the needs of the competitive market economy. The demise of the old order left a vacuum, which many new philosophies offered to fill. Some, like Montaigne, cultivated a modest scepticism and a taste for the quiet life: the rediscovery of Sextus Empiricus suited the temper of those grown weary of contending religious fanaticisms. Others, like Pascal, turned the weapons of reason against itself, in defence of the waning orthodoxy: the tragic art of Port-Royal glimpsed a design in the universe, but not one men can fathom. A complex and enigmatical figure like Descartes combined in himself the sceptical impulse and the dogmatic dream, mastery of the new knowledge and deference to the old pieties.

Spinoza, trained in the Jewish schools, remained complicatedly loyal to the tradition; but in subjecting even the Bible to the rule of reason, he carried the war on supernaturalism into the most sacred places. His scientific work, while inferior to that of Descartes or of Leibniz, is nonetheless impressive: he experimented with nitre, fluidity, water pressure; he corresponded with the newly founded Royal Society in London; he read and admired Bacon; he composed a treatise on the rainbow; he studied the habits of insects. More significantly than this, he possessed a comprehensive knowledge of one developed science –

the science of optics. The great Dutch sea-borne trade had stimulated the demand for fine optical instruments: the craft by which Spinoza earned his living made possible the astonishing discoveries of van Leeuwenhoek, and influenced the luminous art of Vermeer. On the theory of sovereignty, too, Spinoza left his mark. Like Plato and Leibniz, he took an active part in the life of his Commonwealth, and was sought out by leading statesmen, for whom he wrote treatises. Like his predecessor Hobbes, he saw rulership as justified only by contract, and sought to draw his fellows into the habits of peace and acquisition. But above all else, his interests were metaphysical and moral. In this early period, the alliance (or misalliance) between natural science and philosophical empiricism had not yet been formed. For Spinoza, as for other continental thinkers, the ideal of a unified science remained Aristotelian, setting forth the common notions of reason, and deducing from them the essences of things in a clear and distinct sequence. Hence we find that, for all his practical and experimental activity, Spinoza is primarily the theorist: the deepest secrets of Nature can be wrung from her in one brief, tremendous struggle. These metaphysical successes would in turn pour over into medicine and morals, the care of the body and the cure of the soul: the solitude and midnight studies of the Faust of Part One would prepare for the engineering and construction projects of the Faust of Part Two (*Spengler*, I, p. 354).

Here we touch on the affinities between Spinoza and that other Faustian-souled thinker, Descartes. Descartes had written that philosophy was like a tree, whose roots were metaphysics, whose trunk was physics, and whose branches were all the other sciences, of which the chief were medicine, mechanics, and morals – the moral science which constituted the highest degree of wisdom. This bold image reverberates in Spinoza's thought. Descartes is indeed the central figure in Spinoza's intellectual career – the sceptic to be confuted, the dogmatist to be corrected, the physicist to be modified, the psychologist to be superseded. Spinoza's first published work was a brilliant 'geometrical' exposition of Descartes, more successful than Descartes' own effort in the genre, in which skilful and sensitive commentary is leavened by unobtrusive criticism. This early fascination with the Cartesian philosophy did not fade. (Here again local influences were at work: Descartes himself lived and wrote in the Netherlands, out of reach of the Roman clergy; and his doctrine was studied closely in the universities of that nation. Cartesianism became as much a Dutch philosophy as a French one.) But let us not overstate the case: Leibniz was wrong to describe Spinozism as 'un Cartesianisme outré' (*Theodicée*, Pt III). Spinoza is too original, too many-sided, too equivocal a figure to have been the acolyte of another master. Perhaps more than any other, he is a comprehensively *European* thinker, with his Iberian-Jewish ancestry, his Dutch upbringing and culture, his youthful involvement in Protestant sectarianism, his international correspondence, his links to Bacon, Bruno, Machiavelli, Leibniz, Hobbes, his command of several languages, his familiarity with the works of Latin and Spanish literature. Many streams of thought are tributary to him: it is fitting that, in Wolfson's great book on Spinoza, there are copious references to Greek, Latin, Arab, British, French, Spanish and Dutch writers. His influence has also been great. Leibniz and Berkeley studied him; Hume and Voltaire mocked him; Goethe esteemed him; Renan paid him homage; Nietzsche hails him for denying free will, purposes, the moral world order, the unselfish, and evil; Plekhanov acclaims him as a proto-Marxist. To the extent that our world is still liberal, secular, tolerant, and protective of free thought, he must be reckoned among its chief creators.

1 The method of ethics

I begin with two questions which arise as soon as one studies Spinoza: Why does he call his main work an *Ethics*? And why does he pursue a 'geometrical order'? The latter question arises if only because Spinoza's decision to write *more geometrico* makes his book so very hard to read: the exposition is not only, as he admits (*E* IV, 18S), inconveniently prolix, but tedious, rebarbative and confusing. Spinoza is often a graceful writer, expressing abstract ideas lucidly and in memorable phrases; and he achieved success in several philosophical forms, including the dialogue. But Part I of the *Ethics*, bristling with axioms and definitions at the outset, and encased in theorems, demonstrations, corollaries and scholia, is all too apt to disconcert and discourage the reader. Time and again we have to peep behind the façade of formal demonstrations in order to discover how his mind was actually working; time and again we have to translate, or rather decode, the unfamiliar jargon, strain to identify the adversary at whom a proof is directed, or eke out an elliptical assertion with passages from other works or authors. Spinoza himself seems to realise the straitjacketing effect of his method. He interrupts his relentless demonstrations with long, illuminating notes or scholia, which serve to clarify, develop, reinforce or illustrate the argument. Leibniz once remarked impatiently that Spinoza had no head for a demonstration (*Leibniz*, p. 202); and while this is unfair and absurd, there is no doubt that the real work of arguing is often done in the informal expositions rather than the formal proofs. Spinoza was of course anxious to communicate his ideas; but, not unreasonably, he demanded perseverance, attention and good will from his readers. In view of the common culture of his audience, these expectations were not unrealistic. Trained in mathematics and theology, in Euclid and the Scriptures, they would have grasped the calculated resemblance of the *Ethics* to both types of literature. Like both, it professes to reveal knowledge which lies hidden beneath the surface of things; like both, it can be esoteric; like both, it requires concentrated study. It will give revelation, but within the limits of reason alone; its substance may be sacred, but its method is profane.

The title of the *Ethics* intimates, however, that Spinoza's central concerns are as much human and practical as speculative and Divine. Of the five parts of the *Ethics*, one is explicitly devoted to God, four to Man. (Even the brief excursus into physical science in Part II is plainly subordinate to the overriding aim of understanding *human* nature: we are told just enough about body in general to enable us to understand the workings of the human brain and body; and of those workings we are told no more than we need in order to understand the human mind.) This concern with human conduct determines two lines of inquiry. There is the question of shaping and improving conduct; but prior to that, there is the question of understanding and explaining it (*cf. Hirschman* (1), pp. 12–15; pp. 20–21). The traditional moralists distribute praise and blame, exhortation and invective, without considering the true natures of those whom they address: like clumsy craftsmen, they do not study the properties of the material they would shape, and cut against the grain. To change human nature, we must first understand it:

> In order to investigate the topics pertaining to this branch of knowledge with the same objectivity as we generally show in mathematical inquiries, I have taken great care to understand human actions, and not to deride, deplore or denounce them. I have therefore regarded human passions like love, hate, anger, envy, pride, pity and other feelings that agitate the mind, not as vices of human nature, but as properties which belong to it in the same way as heat, cold, storm, thunder, and the like belong to the nature of the atmosphere. Inconvenient though they be, such things are necessary; they have definite causes through which we try to understand their nature; and a true

understanding gives the mind as much satisfaction as does the apprehension of things pleasing to the sense. (*TP* I, 7; Wernham, p. 263)

His other works reflect the same desire to obtain an exact, scientific account of human actions and emotions. Spinoza's very early work, the *Short Treatise on God, Man and his Well-being*, plainly shows this; more significant are the remarks at the beginning of his *Tractatus de Intellectus Emendatione*, which seem intended, from their dramatic weight and placing, to have prefaced a much longer treatise than the one we now possess (Joachim (1), pp. 14–15). There he confesses his aim of showing men the true way to discovering spiritual blessedness, which he says consists in 'the knowledge of the union existing between the mind and the whole of Nature' (*G* II, p. 8). If men are to gain a true view of their chief good, and of the means to attain it, they must devise a regimen for the intellect, in order to cure and purify it, rendering it fit to apprehend things easily, without error, in the best possible manner (*DIE*, *G* II, p. 9). The treatise prescribes such a regimen, and for this reason Joachim suggests that we translate its title as *On the Purification of the Intellect*. The medical associations of the image are happy: medicine aims both at theoretical understanding and at a practical good, and so does Spinoza's book. The medical analogy was extended to the *Ethics*: Leibniz had learned of an early and unfulfilled plan of the *Ethics*, and wrote that it was to contain a *de medicina mentis* and a *de medicina corporis* (*cf.* McKeon, p. 12).

Another aspect of the work is hinted at by the designation *Ethics*. It is not far-fetched to suppose that that title alludes to another famous work of the same name, Aristotle's *Nicomachean Ethics*, which in many respects Spinoza's *Ethics* resembles. Both books contain what we would now distinguish as meta-ethical analysis and substantive ethical opinion; both weave together 'philosophical' issues and 'empirical' – chiefly psychological – matter; both display certain pictures or ideals of human excellence. There is, moreover, a large overlap in the topics studied: the emotions, the virtues and vices, the nature of happiness, figure prominently in each. But the resemblances are overlaid by at least three massive differences, which we must now consider.

First, there is a disagreement about the nature of the subject matter of ethics. In a famous passage Aristotle advises us not to demand of a subject a greater degree of precision than it can admit of. A carpenter and a geometer both deal with the right angle; but as their interests in it differ, so too their investigations of it may vary in accuracy and definiteness (*Nicomachean Ethics*, 1094b11–22; 1098a25). This remark may be understood to make a weak or a strong claim (*Barnes* (1) II, pp. 219–220). Weakly, Aristotle is saying that the common rules of morality – that is, the rules we are first taught, and generally continue to operate with – are only rough and ready, and do not always hold true. ('Stealing is wrong' is a sound rule for most purposes, but a man may steal to save the life of a child.) Understood in this way, Aristotle is implicitly making a point about the costs of information. Rules which were more nuanced than the common ones would be too complicated to teach, absorb and apply with reasonable convenience. (Of course, information costs are variable. If we have world enough and time, we can supplant generality with detail, and forgo pithiness for exactitude. A developed legal system creates incentives to move in that way: a judge who wants to do equity will designedly complicate the rules of law, trading off certainty of application against justice in the particular case.) Aristotle may, however, be contending for a more radically sceptical claim – one which touches, not only the *common* rules of morality, but moral rules *as such*. He may be saying that there are no true and exceptionless rules in ethics at all, no general theorems of the form 'Φing is always good (bad, right, wrong, virtuous, vicious)' (*cp. Nicomachean Ethics*, 1137b13; b30). (Somewhere short of this is the view that there are no truths of that form which, *at any humanly feasible cost*, we could discover or formulate.) At best, then, we can hope to say that *in general* something is vicious or forbidden, mandatory or fit to be encouraged. But in individual cases, 'the decision rests with perception'. (*Nicomachean Ethics* 1109b23; 1126b4; *cp.* Mill, *A System of Logic*, VI, 8, ii).

While Spinoza would fall in with the first of these claims, he would certainly reject the stronger of them. In his view, you cannot rest with propositions holding only 'for the most part' in the theory of ethics, any more than you can in pure geometry. Rough approximations to the truth are legitimate in practical matters, such as applied geometry; and, analogously, rules of thumb, broad generalisations, wise saws and modern instances are useful, even indispensable, in the common conduct of life (*Ep.* 56). But at a higher level of theory and reflection, we can attain knowledge which is strictly universal (*Lachtermann*, pp. 72–3). Spinoza also recognises an intermediate stage, at which we drill ourselves in these universal ethical rules, without quite seeing how to derive them from reason; but this condition is contrasted to the more perfect one, in which the grounds of the laws are made plain. 'The best thing we can do *so long as we lack a perfect knowledge of our affects* is to conceive a right rule of life, or sure maxims (*dogmata*) of life, to commit these to memory, and constantly to apply them to the particular cases which frequently meet us in life, so that our imagination may be pervasively affected by them and that they may be always ready to hand' (*E* V, 10S). The 'maxims' we rely on in this way can ideally be transformed into items of reasoned knowledge, displayed in their necessity and universality: thus the 'maxim' Spinoza actually quotes at *E* V, 10S ('Hatred is to be conquered by love or generosity, not by reciprocal hatred') is a consequence of a theorem in Part IV (*E* IV, 46), which itself is derived from the universal proposition that 'Hatred can never be good' (*E* IV, 45). Where such reasoned, demonstrated knowledge of the affects is wanting, we shall be forced to make shift with maxims which either fall short of universality, or which, though universal and necessary, are not perceived to be so. But this deficiency can be overcome, for it is possible to construct a morality which is less porous and less uncertain. What we can and must strive after is the knowledge of the nature and properties of our soul.

Spinoza thinks that Aristotle frustrates the pursuit of ethical knowledge in a second way. Aristotle tells us that 'we must not demand the cause in all matters alike; it is enough in some cases that the fact be well established' (*Nicomachean Ethics*, 1095b6). But Spinoza denies that we can ever rest satisfied with the 'fact' and not the 'cause': *vere scire est scire per causas* (*E* I Axiom 4; *DIE*, G II, p. 32). Where matters of fact are not known through their proximate causes, they are not truly known at all (III, 1; VI, 5). Furthermore, when Aristotle does begin to look for the starting point of ethical knowledge, he mislocates it. If we are trying to formulate a true and reasoned general view, Aristotle says, we must start with common or received opinions, especially those of the wise: 'we must set the observed facts before us and, after first discussing the difficulties, go on to prove, if possible, the truth of all the common opinions about these affections of the mind or, failing this, of the greater number and the most authoritative' (*Nicomachean Ethics*, 1145b2). But from assumptions which, however probable or well-accredited, fall short of rational certainty, we can only reach hazardous and shifting conclusions. In the *Rules for the Direction of the Mind*, Descartes had urged us to discard 'all modes of knowledge that are merely probable (*tantum probabiles*), and resolve to believe only that which is perfectly known, and in respect of which doubt is not possible'. (*Kemp Smith* translation, pp. 6–7; *cf. H.R.* I, p.3). Spinoza would certainly have endorsed this Cartesian thesis: opinions which are backed up only by authority belong to hearsay knowledge', the lowest mode of perception, which is in fact a form of error and imagination (*E* II, 40S2; *vide* III, 2). In the Preface to Spinoza's book on the Cartesian philosophy, his friend, disciple and collaborator Ludovicus Meyer condemns the Aristotelians on precisely this score: they 'do not prove with demonstrative arguments what they put before the public, but only heap up verisimilitudes and probable arguments' (*PPD*, Preface). This was undoubtedly also Spinoza's opinion: Meyer's introduction had passed through his hands, and been approved by him (*Ep.* 151; *cf.* also *Offenberg*).

Aristotle's misconceptions concerning method lead to deformations in his doctrine; in particular, the method dictates that its conclusions should leave the central core of conventional morality intact (*Nicomachean Ethics*, 1145b2–6; 1172b36–1173a1). But Spinoza is prepared to welcome shocking results, if they seem to him rationally demonstrable. Reason cannot be shackled by conventional opinion, in morality or in anything else. To grasp Spinoza's radicalism on this point, we need only glance at a few propositions from Part IV of the *Ethics*. For example: 'A man who lives according to the dictates of reason endeavours as much as possible to prevent himself from being touched by pity'. 'Humility is not a virtue; that is to say, it does not spring from reason'. 'Repentance is not a virtue; that is to say, it does not spring from reason; on the contrary, the man who repents of what he has done is doubly wretched or impotent', (*E* IV 50C; 53; 54). Whether we accept these startling conclusions or not, we cannot fail to be impressed by the boldness and consistency of the mind which drew them: as Father Parmenides said to the young Socrates, such daring is the mark of the true philosopher (*Parmenides* 130de).

So much then for the first two of Spinoza's main disagreements with Aristotle. The third is connected with them: a divergence in understanding the subject matter, and the method appropriate to it, is accompanied by a difference in manner of exposition and presentation. Euclid is to be the model, not Aristotle; the syllogistic order is to be superseded by the geometrical one. Meyer contrasts the typical procedure of the scholastics, 'in which definitions and divisions are interwoven and occasionally interspersed with questions and explanation', with the practice of mathematicians 'in investigating and propounding scientific matters by demonstrating conclusions from definitions, postulates and axioms'. It is the latter, he claims, which provides 'the best and surest means of searching out and teaching the truth'. I take it that the practice of the mathematicians helps us to *search out* the truth because it inculcates the knowledge of a 'rule of truth' (*E* I, Appendix) and tells us how rightly to order our ideas; and it assists us in *teaching* the truth because its successive inferences, when valid, ineluctably compel our assent.

Of course the choice of an expository style does not guarantee the correctness of one's doctrine: Spinoza himself expounded Descartes in the geometrical manner, even while rejecting many of his views. Equally, philosophical truth can be conveyed in other literary forms: Spinoza scarcely supposed that his numerous letters, treatises and dialogues, which corroborate, amplify or correct the *Ethics* on many points, could not be true because they were differently composed. But although he would have agreed that these other presentations were frequently more insinuating, charming or persuasive, those very qualities would, in his view, have unfitted them to be methods of securing rational conviction. Pascal spoke for many of his contemporaries when he said, in his little book *De l'esprit géometrique,* that he 'could not make better understood the procedure one ought to follow in rendering a demonstration convincing than to explain that which geometry observes' (*Pascal* (1), p. 121). Hobbes' conversion to geometry is recounted in the unforgettable story by Aubrey in his *Brief Lives*:

> He was 40 years old before he looked on Geometry; which happened accidentally. Being in a Gentleman's Library, Euclid's Elements lay open, and 'twas the 47 *El. libri* I. He read the Proposition. *By G*——, sayd he, (he would now and then sweare an emphaticall Oath by way of emphasis) *this is impossible!* So he read the Demonstration of it, which referred him back to such a Proposition; which proposition he read. That referred him back to another, which he also read. *Et sic deinceps* that at last he was demonstratively convinced of that truth. This made him in love with Geometry.

The craze for Euclid was not universal (*Lakatos*, II, pp. 84–5). When Mersenne and his colleagues asked Descartes for a Euclidian demonstration of the *Meditations*, he obliged them, but grudgingly. In his *Reply* to their *Second Set of Objections*, he makes a distinction between two aspects of the 'geometrical mode of writing' – *order*, and *manner of demonstration*. *Order*, as he conceives it, does not require the Euclidian apparatus of axioms, postulates and definitions; it consists in putting forward just those things which can be known without the aid of what follows, and in so arranging subsequent matters that they are demonstrated solely by those which have preceded them. Descartes claims to have followed that order in the *Meditations*: in demonstrating God's existence in the *Third Meditation*, for instance, he starts from things which were antecedently known, to wit, certain facts concerning the contents of his own mind (*Delahunty*, p. 35). As for the *manner of demonstration*, he distinguishes two kinds: the *analytic* and the *synthetic*. 'Analysis displays the true way by which a thing was methodically discovered, and makes known how the effect depends upon the causes': the cosmological proof of the *Meditations* is presumably analytic, in that a cause (the existence of God) is exhibited through one of its effects (the idea of Him in the mind). Analysis, though it has many merits, 'is not suited to convince prejudiced or inattentive readers, for if one fails to notice the least thing which it puts forward, the necessity of the conclusions will not appear; and it does not as a rule state with full explicitness things which are clear enough of themselves, although they are ordinarily the very things of which one should take special notice'. The procedures, merits and disadvantages of *synthesis* are described as follows:

> Synthesis on the contrary employs a wholly distinct procedure, and so to say examines the causes by their effects – though the proof which it contains here too is often from causes to effects. It demonstrates clearly what is found in its conclusions, and avails itself of a long series of definitions, axioms, theorems and problems, so that if someone denies some of the consequences, it makes clear how they are implied by their antecedents. Thus it pulls the reader to consent, however obstinate and prejudiced he may be; but unlike analysis, it does not give complete satisfaction to the minds of keen learners, because it does not teach them the method by which the thing was discovered.

The manner of demonstration adopted in the remainder of the *Reply* is synthetic, as Mersenne had requested: it advances from premisses which are taken as evident ('causes') to conclusions which demonstrably follow from them ('effects'). Although Descartes preferred the analytic manner, he is willing to allow that his results can be cast in the alternative form; what he did reluctantly and unthoroughly in his *Reply*, Spinoza did systematically and well in the *Principles of the Cartesian Philosophy*.

There is a very great deal in Descartes' remarks which calls for comment and explanation (*cf. Lakatos* II, pp. 70–103; *Buchdahl* III, section 2; *Hintikka* (1)); but for our present purpose it is enough to note that his account of synthesis confirms Meyer's judgement of its value as a pedagogic instrument. The reader is 'pulled to consent' by the irresistible force of the deductions: like Hobbes in the gentleman's library, he is 'demonstratively convinced', despite his initial 'obstinacy and prejudice'. Spinoza's belief in its effectiveness for teaching purposes is surely evidenced by his use of it to expound Descartes. He succeeded brilliantly there, and his success must surely have influenced his choice of the same form for his own masterpiece. What is more, we have his encomium on Euclid in the *Tractatus Theologico-Politicus*, which reveals another merit in this manner of writing. 'Euclid', he says, 'who only wrote of matters very simple and easily understood, can readily be comprehended by anyone in any language; we can follow his intention perfectly, and be certain of his true meaning, without having a thorough knowledge of the language in which he wrote' (*TTP*, c. VII; *G* III, p. 97). Because of the simplicity and diaphanousness of the language used, the student does not fear that his conviction may rest on the emotional colouring and associations of the author's words; nor will he feel that he has been bullied into submission by obscure technicalities or uncouth neologisms. The literary form of the *Ethics* and the language in which it was written complement one another. It is not strange that Spinoza regarded the late, arid Latin of his century, in which all educated Europe wrote, as a very pure medium of expression. Its terms seemed to have acquired a standard and unequivocal meaning from long use; it lacked the vivid imagery and disturbing concreteness of the livelier vernacular languages. Friedrich Waismann once objected to the claims of philosophers to have given proofs as compelling as mathematical ones:

> There is . . . another task looming before [the philosopher] when it comes to developing the consequences: can he be sure how to operate with the terms? . . . The ordinary rules of logic often break down in natural speech – a fact usually hushed up by logic books. The words of common speech are so elastic that anyone can stretch their sense to fit his own whims . . . 'If I believed that I should be very silly indeed': does this, or does this not, entail that I don't believe it? (*Waismann*, pp. 22–3)

Whether Waismann is right or not about the failure of logical rules in ordinary speech, his objection would count for little with Spinoza: the language Waismann refers to is not the purified, stable, imageless, uncoloured language in which Spinoza wrote.

2 *The* diallelus

Thus far I have tried to explain why Spinoza named his great project an *Ethics*, to indicate where he disagreed with Aristotle about the nature and method of ethics, and to suggest some reasons for his choice of a geometrical style of presentation. From what I have said, it may appear that the geometrical form of his work is inessential, and that he could have poured his ideas into a different mould. The implied view seems close to that of commentators like Parkinson, who merely find the geometrical order 'not wholly inappropriate to what Spinoza wanted to say' (*Parkinson* (1), p. 89), and to differ from that of Joachim, who believed that 'the form of Spinoza's exposition is essential to its matter ... The subject matter as he conceives it demands [geometrical] treatment' (*Joachim* (2), p. 13).

Now Joachim is wrong; for Spinoza both expounds his own ideas *non*-geometrically, and presents ideas which are *not* his own in a geometric form. Nevertheless, a suspicion lingers that the character of Spinoza's thought somehow calls for a distinctively geometrical manner of expression. That suspicion, I believe, is well-founded; and I want to argue that Spinoza's choice of form springs from his strategy for refuting scepticism. More precisely, it is the natural outcome of his solution to a sceptical problem, raised by Sextus Empiricus in antiquity and revived in the rediscovery of the Pyrrhonist philosophy by writers such as Montaigne. The problem goes by the name of the *diallelus*, or 'The Wheel'. Here is Montaigne's version of it, as paraphrased by Roderick Chisholm:

> To know whether things really are as they seem to be, we must have a *procedure* for distinguishing appearances that are true from appearances that are false. But to know whether our procedure is a good procedure, we have to know whether it really *succeeds* in distinguishing appearances that are true from appearances that are false. And we cannot know whether it does really succeed unless we already know which appearances are *true* and which ones are *false*. And so we are caught in a circle. (*Chisholm*, p. 3; the original text, which appears in Book II, chapter 12 of Montaigne's *Essays*, is given by Chisholm in a footnote *ad loc.*)

Montaigne's point can be illustrated by the analogy Descartes suggested beween the mind and a basket of apples. There is a basket containing both good and bad apples. We want to sort out the good from the bad. Similarly, in our minds there are good, or

GEOMETRICAL METHOD AND PHILOSOPHIC DOUBT

true, beliefs, and bad, or false, ones; and again we want to be able to separate the two, retaining the good and discarding the bad. In the case of the apples, we know how to proceed: the good apples have a distinctive colour, taste, odour and feel; so too the bad. In other words, we have a criterion for classifying apples. But with beliefs it is seemingly different. How *are* we to distinguish good beliefs from bad ones? If we happened to know, with respect to some of our beliefs, that they *were* good, or that they *were* bad, we might be able to pick out characteristics belonging to them, in virtue of which they were good or bad; and, having found out what their good-making or bad-making characteristics were, we could go on to look for those features in the remainder of our beliefs. If we could do this, we would be operating with a criterion of truth, which enabled us to certify some beliefs as good, and to withhold that certification from others.

The trouble with this hopeful suggestion is of course its presumption that we already know how to grade some of our existing beliefs. It is from such knowledge that we are expected to derive a general method for distinguishing good beliefs from bad ones in other cases. But according to the sceptic, we must be in possession of such a method *before* we can tell the goodness or badness of *any* of our beliefs. According to him, we cannot legitimately start from the assumption that certain specific beliefs are good (bad); in the absence of a procedure for establishing them to be so, we are not entitled to ascribe those qualities to them.

If, on the other hand, we try to begin by adopting a good method, and then sorting out beliefs in accordance with it, we run up against another sceptical difficulty, for obviously there are both good and bad methods. It does not, for example, seem to be a good method for assessing beliefs to accept them if and only if the Delphic oracle has pronounced them to be true. How can we know whether any candidate method is a good one or not? Seemingly we cannot, unless we invoke some reliable, higher-order method for selecting from among the various possible lower-order methods. But if we need a higher-order method to make that choice, we will need a method of a higher-order still, to enable us to pick from among the original set of higher-order methods; and then we are embarked on a vicious infinite regress.

Let me try to set out this sceptical argument more fully and more carefully (following *Rescher* (1), pp. 13–14). The sceptic makes four assumptions:

(1) If x is to be entitled to claim that 'p' is true, then x must

have established that '*p*' satisfies a criterion of truth;
(2) A criterion of truth must take the form: Whenever '*p*' meets the requirement *R*, then '*p*' is true –

(p) (Rp ⊰ Tp);

(3) To *establish* a proposition with reference to a criterion of truth is to give a sound deductive argument of the form –

$$\frac{(p)\ (Rp \multimap Tp)}{Tp;} \\ Rp$$

(4) A sound argument contains premises which (a) validly imply its conclusion and (b) are true. (No argument can therefore qualify as sound unless its premises have been established to be true. 'Soundness', in this sense, outruns 'validity'.)

(One note: in the case of what Rescher calls an 'authorising', as distinct from a 'guaranteeing', criterion, the form of the criterion would be such as to invoke some other relation than strict implication; for example, it might have the form '*(p) (if Rp then it is confirmed that Tp)*'. But let us concentrate only on the sceptical argument which demands a more stringent type of criterion.)

The sceptic's argument then proceeds as follows. Assume that *x* is entitled to claim that a certain proposition '*p*' is true. It follows by (1) that *x* has established that '*p*' satisfies a criterion of truth. It follows thence by (3) that *x* has given a sound argument of the form prescribed in (3). Now by (4), *x*'s argument qualifies as sound only if the truth of both of its premises has been established. But how is the truth of its premises – and especially the first or major premiss – established? There seem to be only two possibilities: (a) the criterion is self-validating; (b) the criterion is not self-validating, but is established in some other way. In the first case, if the criterion is self-validating, then it must itself be established by a sound argument of the form:

$$\frac{(p)\ (Rp \multimap Tp)}{T\ (p)\ (Rp \multimap Tp)} \\ R\ (p)\ (Rp \multimap Tp)$$

But for *this* argument to be reckoned to be sound, all of *its* premises would have had to be established antecedently, and we have not yet established the premiss of form '*(p) (Rp ⊰ Tp)*'. Rather, to establish it is precisely what we were setting out to do. Thus the first possibility is eliminated.

In the second case, if the criterion is non-self-validating, then if it is established at all, it must be established by reference to yet another criterion. Let us assume that there is such a criterion. Then our original criterion will have to be derived as the conclusion of a purportedly sound argument of the form:

$$\frac{(p) (R_1 p \dashv3 Tp)}{R_1 (p) (Rp \dashv3 Tp)}$$
$$T (p) (Rp \dashv3 Tp).$$

But where does the first premiss in *this* argument come from? Either it is self-validating, or it is not. If the former, then we re-encounter the difficulty considered previously in connection with the first alternative. If the latter, then it has to be established by yet another criterion; and the credentials of this criterion will then be open to question. With that, we are well launched upon a vicious infinite regress, leaving the original criterion still unestablished.

From this argument, the sceptic draws the conclusion that no-one is ever entitled to claim that any proposition is true: there is thus no rational assent, no knowledge. That frightening conclusion haunted the minds of many seventeenth-century thinkers, Descartes, Hobbes and Spinoza among them. The attempt to answer it inspired some of their best philosophical activity.

According to Chisholm, who re-introduced the *diallelus* into recent philosophical discussion, there have been two classic anti-sceptical replies to it. In his nomenclature, these are *methodism* and *particularism*. In Chisholm's view the empiricists, and notably Locke, tended to be methodists; the rationalists, or at least Descartes and Spinoza, were inclined to particularism. There is, however, no necessary connection here; Chisholm thinks that an empiricist could be a particularist, and a rationalist a methodist. Chisholm's terms need explaining.

A *methodist* believes that we have a criterion of truth, and that we can apply it to determine which of our beliefs are true. In response to the sceptic, he will deny that one must always have established a proposition by reference to a criterion in order to be entitled to assert that proposition; for the criterion of truth is itself the unique (non-mathematical) exception to that rule. That is, the criterion is itself a proposition which we can rightly claim to *know*, but which we neither can nor must establish by reference to anything else. In the case of the (alleged) methodists who were also empiricists, the criterion was, roughly, conformity to experience. On their view, a given (non-mathematical) proposition (*sc.* other than the criterion itself) was true if and only if that proposition could be found to match or correspond to experience (whether perceptual or introspective).

The *particularist*, like the methodist, agrees in rejecting the first step in the sceptic's reasoning. He differs from the methodist in two ways. First, he does not think that there is only a *single* non-mathematical exception to the rule which the sceptic advances. (Descartes, for instance, who can plausibly be seen as a particularist, claimed to have knowledge of *many* non-mathematical truths, even though he had not antecedently established them by reference to a criterion. As he said to Burman, 'Regarding the common principles and axioms, e.g. "it is impossible that one and the same thing should both be and not be" . . . if people were to think about these propositions in the abstract, no-one would have any doubt about them; and if the Sceptics had done this, no-one would have been a Sceptic' (*Cottingham*, p. 3). Again, according to Descartes, I know criterionlessly that I think, that I exist, what the words 'mind' and 'soul' mean, and many other such things.) Second, the particularist does *not* include a criterion of truth among those things of which we have criterionless knowledge. Again Descartes illustrates the position. Consider a passage near the start of the *Third Meditation*, which occurs directly after he has listed all the things he thus far knows:

> Now I will consider more carefully whether there may be other things in me that I have not yet discovered. I am certain that I am a conscious being. Surely then I also know what is required for my being certain about anything? In this primary knowledge all I need is a clear and distinct perception of what I assert; now this would not be enough to make me certain as to the truth of the matter if it could ever happen that something clearly and distinctly perceived in this way should be false; so it looks as though I could lay down the general rule: whatever I perceive very clearly and distinctly is true (*A.G.*, p. 76)

In this passage, Descartes is starting from a particular item of (criterionless) knowledge, viz., that he is a conscious being; he then picks out a feature of his state of mind when he is attending to that proposition (that it is a state of clear and distinct perception); he infers that it is the possession of this feature which causes his state of mind to be one of knowledge; and he is tentatively extrapolating the general rule that *any* conscious state which exhibits the mark of clear and distinct perception will be knowledge. (In the last step, he seems covertly to assume the causal axiom that if a state is Φ because it is Ψ, then any Ψ-state will also be Φ.)

GEOMETRICAL METHOD AND PHILOSOPHIC DOUBT

What Descartes is doing, then, is to work *towards* the knowledge of a criterion of truth *from* his knowledge of particular things, and from an examination of his state of mind when he attends to those things. The criterion can itself be known, but it is neither self-validating nor established by reference to a higher-order criterion. It is true that Descartes does not press the demonstration of his criterion further; he will only claim to have proved it *after* he has shown the reality of a veracious God, who insures that the criterion of clarity and distinctness is correct. However, I believe that, if he were willing to announce the causal axiom which is latent in his reasoning, and were prepared to claim that it was something evident, then he could cut his work short and go directly to the criterion, without making the theological circuit.

Where does Spinoza belong? Should we see him as a methodist, as a particularist, or as neither? Certainly he seems to have been aware of, and interested in, the sceptical difficulty posed by the *diallelus*. He clearly signals the dangers in the sceptic's line of argument when he says in the *DIE*:

> We must take care not to commit ourselves to a search going back to infinity – that is, in order to discover the best method for finding out the truth, there is no need of another method to discover such a method; nor of a third method for discovering the second, and so on to infinity. By such proceedings we should never arrive at the knowledge of the truth (*G* II, p. 13)

This little passage proves three things: (i) that Spinoza was familiar with the sceptic's puzzle; (ii) that he had rejected the sceptic's conclusion (since he implies that we *do* have knowledge); (iii) that he saw the hopelessness of appealing to a higher-order criterion in the effort to establish a first-order criterion of truth. By itself, however, the passage does not commit him either to methodism or to particularism; it does not even rule out the possibility that he erroneously opted for the view that some first-order criterion was self-validating. His agreement with the particularists, and especially with Descartes, only becomes clear when we inspect subsequent passages in the *DIE*. I shall quote them, interweaving commentary with them.

> (a) In order to know, there is no need to know that we know <i.e. *there is no need to have established, by the use of a criterion, that the thing we are claiming to know is true*>; still less is there need to know that we know that we know <i.e. *to have established the reliability of the first-order criterion by*

17

reference back to itself, or to another criterion> ... (b) The contrary is the case: in order to know, that I know, I must first know <i.e. *in order to work out a criterion, I must first know particular propositions to be true*> ... (c) It is evident that, for the certitude of truth, no further sign is necessary beyond the possession of a true idea. ... The truth needs no sign <i.e. *we do not in general have to have shown that 'p' satisfies the appropriate requirement, say that of being clearly and distinctly perceived, in order to know that 'p' is true; for 'p' may be known directly, without having been established from a criterion*>. (G II, p. 15)

I hope that these passages can be taken to prove that Spinoza believed that the *diallelus* argument could be answered, and that the answer he espoused was particularism, not methodism. He does, indeed, search for a criterion; but the search gets underway only because we already possess knowledge which will guide and inform our selection of one. His position, then, resembles that of Descartes at the outset of the *Third Meditation*: he knows certain things, and on the basis of that knowledge aims to discover a general criterion of truth, by means of which he can extend the knowledge he has.

But what *is* the general criterion which Spinoza eventually adopts? I suggest that, with some reservations, he embraces what Rescher calls an 'intuitionistic theory of truth' (*Rescher* (1), p. 10). According to a theory of this type, there are two, and only two, sorts of proposition which can be rationally certified as true: (a) those whose truth is recognised by some non-discursive process, which might be named 'intuition', and (b) those whose truth can be derived by some kind of inference (ideally, logical deduction) from the truths of the first group. The statement of these conditions comprises a general criterion of truth.

On this interpretation, it appears that the *Ethics* will be intended to consist wholly or mainly of propositions which are certified in accordance with the requirements of such a criterion. (Since some of the deductions in it depend upon postulates, not axioms, and since postulates *may* fall short of intuitive certainty, it is arguable that not everything in the *Ethics* would be held to satisfy the criterion.) Thus Spinoza will confidently assert: 'I do not presume that I have found the best philosophy, but I know that I think the true one. If you ask me how I know this, I shall answer, in the same way that you know that the three angles of a triangle are equal to two right angles' (*Ep.* 76). He has discovered the true philosophy because he has applied the correct method –

that of making only truth-preserving deductive inferences from premisses which are known to be true. The choice of an admittedly cumbersome geometrical form goes hand in hand with an intuitionistic theory of truth; for with no other presentation will the flow of truth from premisses to conclusions be so manifest and so incontestable. The reader will ideally resemble a 'spiritual automaton': since his 'perceptions' in thinking will be rightly 'ordered', and will put first the essence of the universal cause, his mind's activity in working through the consequences will mirror the true order of causes in Nature (*DIE*, *G* II, p. 32; *cf*. III, 6; VI, 5; IX, 5).

So far, then, our account of Spinoza's answer to the sceptic seems warranted: the facts have fallen neatly into place. But as so often with Spinoza, a closer look will reveal obscurities in what had seemed a clear picture. There are two complications, a trivial one and one that is deeply unsettling. The trivial point is that the word 'intuition' (*intuitus*) has a special use in Spinoza: he reserves it for what he calls the third and highest form of knowledge. We therefore cannot say that he would have held the basic assumptions of the *Ethics* to have been known by 'intuition' in his special sense; there is, as we shall see, abundant evidence to the contrary (*vide* III, 6). In characterising him as an 'intuitionist', we must not prejudge the issue of how his starting points are supposed to be known; all we can say is that their truth must be taken to be patent (*cp*. III, 4). But this admission brings us up against our second difficulty. What exactly *is* the status of Spinoza's basic assumptions, and how *are* they known? It will help here if we note three of the axioms from Part II of the *Ethics*:

Axiom 2. Man thinks.
Axiom 4. We perceive that a certain body is affected in many ways.
Axiom 5. No individual things are felt or perceived by us excepting bodies and modes of thought.

Note also the solitary axiom of Part IV:

There is no individual thing in nature which is not surpassed in strength and power by some other thing, but any individual thing being given, another and a stronger is also given, by which the former can be destroyed.

Now certain aspects of these axioms deserve comment. First of all, they appear to state propositions which are contingent rather than necessary. Even if it is characteristic of men to think, there might not have been any men; it may be contingent that I am united to a single body, rather than to none or several; Spinoza can give no reason for our inability to perceive modes belonging to unknown attributes other than Thought and Extension; there is no guarantee that Nature should not contain one or more beings, than which none is more powerful. Contingency, however, does not disqualify a proposition from serving as the starting point of a rationalistic system: Descartes began with the claim 'I think', which was contingent. Yet Spinoza's axioms do not seem to possess the salient features of the Cartesian *cogito*: Descartes' premiss was allegedly both *incorrigible* (i.e. true if believed) and *evident* (i.e. believed if true); but Spinoza's axioms are neither evident nor incorrigible (*Williams* (1), p. 306). On the other hand, Meyer's *Preface* to the *PPD* asserts that 'postulates and axioms – or the common conceptions of the mind – are such clear and perspicuous statements that no-one who has merely understood the words aright can in any way refuse to assent to them'. Spinoza himself assured a correspondent that the axioms of an early draft of the *Ethics*, whether they were common notions or not, were *true*, and could be seen to be true if the definitions which accompanied them were studied attentively (*Ep.* 4); and at *E* V, 36S, he characterises a typical demonstration of the First Part as 'legitimate and placed beyond the possibility of doubt (*legitima . . . et extra dubitationis aleam posita*)'. This is pitching his claims high: it is not as if he were merely to say that his axioms are incontestable, in the way it is incontestable that there are a lot of dogs about, or that many men wear shoes (*Geach* (1), p. 151). What is the solution?

I think we are forced to go in one or the other of two ways (*cp.* III, 4). (i) In *On Certainty*, Wittgenstein maintained that 'the *questions* that we raise and our *doubts* depend on the fact that some propositions are exempt from doubt, are as it were like hinges on which these turn' (section 341). Wherever a doubt is entertained, a claim to know established, or a linguistic performance understood, there are propositions which are and must be taken for granted. Without the assumption of these propositions, we should not have our present concepts of knowledge, error, truth, falsity or doubt. These propositions form a system: 'All testing, all confirmation and disconfirmation of a hypothesis takes place already within a system. And this system is not a more or less arbitrary and doubtful point of departure for all our arguments: no, it belongs to the essence of what we call an argument. The system is not so much the point of departure, as the elements in which arguments have their life' (section 105; *von Wright* (1), p. 52). It is not implausible to say that Spinoza's axioms might be seen as propositions belonging to such a system. Certainly some of them resemble the propositions which Wittgenstein had in mind, e.g., that time is real, or that there is an external world, or that selves exist (*von Wright* (1), pp. 48–9). Unfortunately, however, Wittgenstein denied that the *Vor-Wissen* (as von Wright calls it) constituted propositional knowledge. In his view, it was incorrect to say that such propositions were *known* to be true, that there was *evidence* in support of them, that they could be used to *prove* conclusions: 'Giving grounds, however, justifying the evidence, comes to an end; – but the end is not certain propositions striking us immediately as true, i.e. it is not a kind of seeing on our part; it is our *acting*, which lies at the bottom of the language-game' (section 204). Spinoza could not admit any of this concerning his axioms: if a Wittgensteinian defence of them is given, then Spinoza's mathematical paradigm is grotesquely misleading.

(ii) The alternative is to say that Spinoza was a fully-fledged intuitionist *in aspiration*; that he took himself to be one *in fact*; but that (oddly, as it seems to us) his intuitionism was laced with a strong dose of 'experience'. We are accustomed to the idea that statements of contingent fact (apart from the special class represented by the 'Cogito') cannot withstand sceptical doubt; but need that have been Spinoza's view? Did he perhaps, like Galileo, believe in a category of '*reasoned* facts', which yielded – at least – *more* certainty than the 'facts' of uncriticised experience (*Lakatos* II, pp. 70–103)? If so, did he also think that such 'reasoned facts' could serve as axioms for the special sciences of *Ethics* II and IV, if not for the metaphysical science of *Ethics* I? (Note that only a demonstration from Part I is said by *E* V, 36S to be 'placed beyond the possibility of doubt'.) There are hints of some such view (*vide* III, 4 *infra*); and it may even be that, *if* Spinoza regarded these concessions to contingency as unfortunate, he imagined that they could be blotted out as our understanding of Nature grew. At any rate, the mere presence of contingency in some of his axioms need not prevent us from thinking him an 'intuitionist'.

3 The tool analogy

I want now to test my interpretation further by setting it against a crucial passage in the *DIE*. If I am right, a correct reading of the passage will confirm that Spinoza advances a 'particularist' reply to the *diallelus* argument. The passage develops an analogy between the acquisition of knowledge and the manufacture of tools. It reads as follows:

> In order to work iron, a hammer is needed; and to have a hammer, it is necessary to make one. For that one needs another hammer and other tools, in order to have which there is need of other tools, and so on to infinity; in this manner someone might vainly attempt to prove that men lack the power of forging iron. But in the beginning men, with natural tools (*innatis instrumentis*) succeeded in making certain very easy objects, albeit laboriously and imperfectly; when these had been created, they created other more difficult ones with less labour and more perfectly; and thus gradually progressing from the most simple works to tools, and from tools to other works and tools, they arrived at accomplishing many difficult things with little labour; in the same manner the intellect, by its own native force, makes itself intellectual tools thanks to which it acquires other powers for other intellectual works; and thanks to these works it acquires other tools, that is, the power of searching farther; and so stage by stage it progresses, until it attains the summit of wisdom.' (*G* II, pp. 13–14)

I think that this analogy is intended to make two points. First, it brings out the folly of the sceptic's attempt to show that there is no knowledge: there is a precise fit between *his* infinite regress and an infinite regress argument purporting to prove that men lack the power to forge iron. Of course men must have tools to forge iron; and since those tools are apt to be sophisticated, we must have other tools by which we make the tools we use in forging iron; but it would be ludicrous to conclude from these facts that men lack the power to forge iron, for nothing could be plainer than that they do have that power. Similarly, Spinoza is arguing that it is true, as the sceptic claims, that we could only establish a non-self-validating criterion of truth by appealing to a higher-order criterion, and this (if it is non-self-validating) by appeal to another, and so on to infinity; but it does not follow, and would be absurd to suppose, that we must lack all power to gain knowledge of truth. The sceptic's argument, being strictly parallel to an unsound argument, is itself unsound.

Second, Spinoza wants to liken the intellect to a workman who uses natural tools (most obviously, his hands – which Arisotle called the tool of tools (*De Anima* 432a1) – and his body) in order to perform certain rudimentary tasks, among them the manufacture of primitive tools, and who then employs these manufactured tools in executing more complex tasks, which will result in the creation of still more complex instruments. As I construe this analogy, its terms are as follows: (i) the innate tools of the workman = the native power ('*vis*') of the intellect; (ii) the first simple tasks laboriously performed by the workman = the discovery with difficulty of a few simple truths by the intellect; (iii) the first primitive tools devised by the workman = the augmented powers of the mind, enabling it to push its inquiries farther; (iv) the more complicated tasks carried out by the use of the new tools = the discovery of more esoteric truths with the aid of the new powers; (v) the later and more sophisticated tools = the remoter and less simple truths.

Now it might be objected that the analogy, as I have set it out, is intolerably askew; for it pairs off the native and earliest *tools* with *powers*, and the later and more sophisticated *tools* with *truths*. Surely tools should be paired off consistently with items of the *same* type? And, if so, surely we should look for a correspondence between all the sorts of tool which the analogy mentions (native, rudimentary, and developed) and rules or criteria for accepting propositions? Pursuing that line of thought, we should have to conclude that Spinoza was, after all, a 'methodist'; for it will commit him to holding that the intellect is endowed with an innate criterion of truth which it uses from the outset.

I reject that criticism: as a reading of Spinoza, it departs too far from his actual words. It is true that Spinoza likens a workman's tools and hammers to criteria of truth in order to vindicate the *first* of his two main points in the paragraph. However, he tacitly discards that comparison when he comes to make his *second* point, and quietly moves on to a distinct and more elaborate comparison between the different sorts of tool on the one hand, and powers or truths on the other. And in any case, the counter-proposal is philosophically absurd: for if Spinoza was a *methodist* and believed that men had a built-in criterion for selecting truth, why should he have multiplied that criterion indefinitely many times over, as the analogy would then oblige him to do? The original reading is both saner in itself and closer to the texts; and if it is right, it removes the suspicion that he is not a particularist.

As to the other main part of my case, that Spinoza was an *intuitionist*, the 'hammer' analogy proves little. But in one respect it helps us to understand better what Spinoza's 'intuitionism' is like, if that really is his view. The workman is said to perform his first tasks only laboriously; and that suggests that the intellect must experience difficulty in discovering its first few intuited truths. This may mean that the intellect cannot easily hit upon the truths which are really primary and simple; but it could also mean that it may fail to recognise their truth, even when they have been brought to its notice. Certainly Spinoza thinks that philosophy is beyond the abilities of the common people (*Ep.* 19); and so he ought to agree that, even if his axioms are in some way incontestable, they will not be 'incontestable' to every mind which is invited to consider them.

A brief word concerning *innate ideas* is in order here. Spinoza's position in this controversy distinguishes him both from his fellow rationalists and from their empiricist critics. Descartes had classified his ideas into the innate, the acquired and the fictitious, regarding the first as contributed by the mind itself, and the latter two as deriving in some manner from experience. But from Spinoza's standpoint, this classification must be untenable. Since all ideas are modifications of the attribute of Thought, and since no interaction between Thought and Extension is possible (*cf.* VI, 2), no idea can be caused by the workings of bodies; hence it follows that no idea can be 'derived' from experience; hence *all* ideas are innate. On the other hand, every idea is necessarily correlated with some state of the body or mode of extension; so no idea is any less adventitious than any other (*Allison*, p. 109). The motives which inspired Descartes to make his distinction would, however, have won Spinoza's sympathy. In the *First Meditation*, Descartes entertains the thought that 'the things which appear in sleep are like painted representations, which cannot have been formed except in the likeness of real objects': I cannot dream of a head or a hand without having experienced heads or hands. Behind this thought lies a crude empiricist assumption, captured in the scholastic tag '*Nihil est in intellectu nisi prius in sensu*': I cannot have the idea of Φness unless I have been acquainted with something Φ. Apart from the obvious difficulty created for this doctrine by the fact that some of my ideas are fictitious – I do not have to have seen sirens or hippogriffs to be able to conceive of them – there is the deeper problem that my ideas of secondary qualities are not 'formed in the likeness of real objects': though I perceive a piece of wax as cold, white, and honey-scented, in itself it is destitute of temperature, colour and odour. Cartesian innatism is bound up with the rejection of the Aristotelian doctrine of sensible forms, and the 'realistic' view of secondary qualities which accompanies it (*cf. Adams*). Spinoza joins forces with Descartes in waging that fight, but he does not use the weapon of innatism.

GEOMETRICAL METHOD AND PHILOSOPHIC DOUBT

4 *Philosophical doubt*

I have been arguing that Spinoza's choice of the geometric method was the natural outcome of his adoption of an 'intuitionistic' theory of truth, and that the acceptance of a theory of that type was in turn a response to the sceptical problem of the *diallelus*. Now Spinoza's insistence that certain truths could be discovered by the native power of the mind, his rejection of the *diallelus*, and his confidence that a general criterion of truth could be found, all suggest the conclusion that he saw little need to worry further about philosophical scepticism. Surely he would stigmatise sceptical doubt as foolish or obstinate or uncomprehending or insincere? We do indeed find flashes of dogmatic impatience in him: 'are there not people so enamoured of contradiction that they laugh at geometrical demonstrations themselves? Sextus Empiricus and the other sceptics you mention say that it is false that the whole is greater than the part, and think the same of the other axioms' (*Ep.* 56). In general, however, his treatment of scepticism is more patient and more discerning: the sceptic is not turned back at the door without a hearing. Let us look at Spinoza's general account of doubt, and then see how it influences his critique of scepticism.

In the *DIE*, Spinoza marks a distinction between 'real doubt in the mind' and 'verbal doubt' (*vide* II, 2). Of the two kinds of doubt, the former is, he thinks, the more interesting philosophically, and consequently he devotes much more attention to it. Concerning real doubt, he says:

> There is no doubt existing in the soul through the thing itself, concerning which the doubt arises; that is, if there were only a single idea in the soul, then whether it were true or false, there would be no doubt, nor yet certainty, but only a certain sensation. For it is in itself nothing other than a certain sensation; but it will exist on account of another idea which is not so clear and distinct that we can conclude something certain from it about the thing which is doubted of; that is, the idea which throws us into doubt is not clear and distinct. (G II, pp. 29–30)

There are several things here. One point is that if my doubt whether p is 'genuine' or 'real', then there must be an assignable reason for it: I must doubt whether p because I accept, or am inclined to accept, that q. Second, my grounds for doubt must themselves be insufficient to settle the question they provoke: if I doubt whether p because I surmise that q, then 'q' must appear to be consistent both with 'p' and with '*not-p*'. The first of these clarifications should help to explain why Spinoza says that if there were only a single idea in the mind, there would be no doubt, for I could not have real (or rational) doubt concerning 'p' unless I had the quite separate thought that 'q' might be the case. The second clarification is intended to shed light on his comment that the doubt-creating idea must not be clear and distinct enough to permit a sure conclusion to be drawn.

Spinoza illustrates his claims with reference to the case of a peasant. The peasant has never troubled his head with doubt as to the size of the sun; it looks to him smaller than the earth, and he accepts appearances at their face value. (His condition, Spinoza says, is simply that of having a certain sensation.) The peasant is astonished to be told that this is not in fact the case, but that the sun is many times larger than our planet. (It is significant that Spinoza says that he is *told* this: for although the rustic has now got hold of a scientific fact, he has only knowledge of the most inferior grade, viz., hearsay knowledge.) The peasant's doubts may be aggravated when he is invited to reflect that our senses do often deceive us as to the size of remote bodies. (If he engages in such reflection, then 'knowledge from wandering experience', as Spinoza calls it, will come into play, deepening his perplexity.) In his earlier, uncritical state, the peasant had 'only a single idea in his mind'; and hence he felt neither doubt nor (rational) certainty, but only blind confidence. (Spinoza reserves the term 'certainty' for a different use, as is clear from E II, 44S and E II, 49S1). Doubt only enters in when the peasant acquires some further information which he is inclined to credit. This disturbing evidence, however, has been obtained only from sources which are inherently unreliable – the senses; thus the peasant does not yet have the clear and distinct perception of the truth of what he has been told. Such a perception would eradicate his doubt and overthrow his prior belief: without it, he can only weigh the sense-impressions he originally had, and still continues to have, against both the testimony of his informant and his own recollection of past experiences of deceitful sense-appearances. In order to resolve his doubt, Spinoza says, the rustic must come to learn precisely *how* the senses deceive us, i.e., he must gain 'true knowledge of the nature of the senses and of how they function in the perception of things at a distance'. Only if his confused and inadequate knowledge is transformed into clear, distinct, scientific knowledge will his bewilderment cease.

With this account of doubt in the background, let us now approach Spinoza's refutation of the sceptic. The key passage reads as follows:

It follows that we cannot call true ideas into doubt on the grounds that there perhaps exists a deceiving God, who makes us go wrong even in the most certain things, unless for so long as we have no clear and distinct idea of God; that is to say, if we attend to the knowledge which we have concerning the origin of all things, and find nothing in it which teaches us that He is not a deceiver – and that by the same sort of knowledge which, when we consider the nature of the triangle, we discover that its three angles are equal to two right angles. But if we have such a knowledge of God, then all doubt is dispelled. And just as we can arrive at the knowledge of the triangle, even though we are not certain that a supreme deceiver is not misleading us, so we can arrive at a knowledge of God even though we do not certainly know whether there is a supreme deceiver. But if we possess such a knowledge, it will suffice, as I have said, to eliminate all doubt we can have concerning clear and distinct ideas. (*G* II, p. 30)

It is plain that Spinoza is engaged with a form of scepticism which is stated near the end of the *First Meditation*. The correct interpretation of Descartes' text at that point is very arguable; I will state my own view of it dogmatically.

Descartes never casts doubt upon the truth of what he clearly and distinctly perceives, as long as he is clearly and distinctly perceiving it. Thus, for instance, he does not doubt that a square has four sides, or that 2 and 3 add up to 5. But he does doubt the reliability of mathematical operations he performs, even very simple ones: 'may not God cause me to go wrong whenever I add 2 and 3, or count the sides of a square?' (*A.G.*, p. 64). To be more precise still: for as long as he attentively considers a proposition under a form of words which reveal it in clarity and distinctness, he cannot doubt. But, in a way, even what is clearly and distinctly perceived can be doubted. If, for example, I refer to the proposition that 2 and 3 add up to 5 as 'the proposition inscribed on the blackboard in the next room', then I can doubt that proposition. I cannot truly say 'I doubt whether 2 and 3 add up to 5', but I can truly say 'I doubt whether the proposition inscribed on the blackboard in the next room is true'. Again, I might take refuge in *generality*, and say 'Perhaps even what I clearly and distinctly perceive is not true'. If I clearly and distinctly perceive that 2 and 3 make 5, then that proposition, together with many others, will in a manner fall under doubt. If the sceptic (so to say) 'screens off' the idea that 2 and 3 make 5 in either of these ways – by presenting it under a form of words which does not reveal it clearly, or by bringing it under a general doubt affecting all propositions of a certain kind – then he can perfectly well succeed in making it dubious. 'Clarity' and 'distinctness' are thus *relational* notions: a proposition is clear and distinct *for* a person, *under* a form of words, *for as long as* he considers it attentively.

When Descartes advances the hypothesis that there might be a deceptive God, he is introducing it, I think, in support of the very general and radical doubt expressed by the formula 'Perhaps even what I clearly and distinctly perceive is untrue'. And I believe that Spinoza is following him here, both in assigning that radical doubt to the sceptic, and in supposing that, if the veil of generality were lifted, so that simple truths were confronted head on, no doubt would be possible concerning them. He then attempts to show that the grounds which the sceptic gives for his doubt are demonstrably inadequate. The sceptic's reason for doubting *appears* to be a good one, since it raises the possibility of a Being with the demon-like will to deceive us and the god-like power to accomplish His design. If there *were* such a Being, He would thus be willing and able to perpetrate deception on the comprehensive scale which the radical doubt envisages. Furthermore, at the point in the *Meditation* where the supposition is brought in, the Cartesian thinker is credited with having only 'hearsay' knowledge of God ('there has been *implanted* in my mind the old opinion that there is a God who can do everything'); he has not yet framed a clear and distinct idea of Him, though it lies in his power to do so.

Now Spinoza's prescription for removing doubt in the case of the peasant is meant to be good for curing the sceptic of more sophisticated anxieties. (Note that *his* doubt counts as *real*, not *verbal*.) The reason which supports the doubt is insufficient to settle the question: the bare *possibility* that there is a deceitful Deity proves neither that our clear and distinct perceptions are shot through with error, nor that they are wholly free from it. So if the doubt is to be removed, and a clear decision arrived at, it is essential to discover additional facts bearing on the question. There are such facts, and we have them in our hands: for, says Spinoza, 'reflection on the idea of the origin of all things teaches that God is not a deceiver'. When we consider the description which the sceptic gives of the Being whose possible existence rationalises his doubt, we can perceive that it is a *contradictory* one: *no* being could at once possess the qualities of unlimited power and unmitigated malice. (This is also assumed by Descartes in the *Third Meditation* (A.G., pp. 89–90), and may be regarded as a theological form of the doctrine of the inseparability of the Virtues.) Since the description cannot, in the nature of the case, apply to any existing thing, it follows that a deceitful Deity, far from being possible, is in fact an impossible entity. This removes the prop on which the sceptical doubt rested. If the sceptic persists in his doubt, then willy-nilly he alters its character: failing further reasons in support of it, it will become *verbal*, a sign of obstinacy or prejudice, beyond the corrective power of the true method (*DIE*, G II, p. 29). Indeed, Spinoza might press the attack harder at that stage: since verbal doubt is both unsupported by plausible reasons, *and* unexpressed in practical (non-verbal) conduct, the sceptic's utterances make no discernible claim at all: his audience cannot interpret what he is saying (*Doney*, p. 634). Scepticism concerning clear and distinct ideas, in the form it has assumed in the discussion, can fairly be dismissed.

In Descartes' case, the refutation of scepticism was still more complete. For he claimed to have shown that there actually is a Being who conforms to our clear and distinct idea of the Deity, and who therefore will not permit us to go wrong in any of our clear and distinct perceptions. We are thus in a position to affirm, not only that there are not worthy reasons to indulge in radical doubt, but that there is compelling reason to accept the general rule that whatever we clearly and distinctly perceive, is true. Spinoza once seems to be arguing in this way (*CM*, II, 9, iii); but this cannot be his final view, because 'veracity' is an attribute which he believes we can apply to God only for so long as we have a defective, anthropomorphic conception of Him.

Spinoza's argument against the sceptic presumes that reflection upon the idea of God will render it clear and distinct. What he says about that might be compared with some remarks of Wittgenstein's, in which he discusses the effects of proving the impossibility of trisecting the angle. Wittgenstein says:

> We should be inclined to say that the proof of the impossibility of trisecting the angle with ruler and compasses analyses our idea of trisection, one which we didn't have before the proof constructed it. The proof led us a road *which we were inclined to go*; but it led us away from where we were, and didn't just show us clearly the place where we had been all the time. (Wittgenstein, *The Blue Book* (2nd edn), p. 41)

In advance of an impossibility-proof, we may well believe that the operation of trisecting the angle can be performed; and we may build various other supposals on the assumption of that possibility. But once the impossibility-proof is produced for us, two things happen: the supposals we had entertained are seen to be groundless, and our concept of 'trisecting an angle' has been transformed. We may say, as Wittgenstein does, that we have been provided with a new concept; or we may say that our earlier, confused concept has been made clear and distinct. This is exactly what Spinoza claims will happen with the sceptic's assumption that a deceiving God is possible. Various other conjectures and supposals are made to rest on that assumption; but the sceptic's concept is inherently confused, and when it is clarified, those supposals lie in ruins. The clarification of the idea is the death of a philosophical illusion.

II

Error and the Will

The method of doubt has a dual role in the working out of the Cartesian project. First, it filters out false beliefs; second, it abets the discovery of knowledge. It is chiefly in this second goal that Cartesian scepticism differs from other varieties of doubt: mere error-avoidance, though desirable, must be coupled with truth-finding. Not all truths, however, are of equal interest or importance; and it is an essential feature of the Cartesian method of doubt that it claims to lead us to truths which are peculiarly deep, fecund and powerful. In particular, under the pressure of the most extreme version of the sceptical hypothesis, we are forced to make explicit to ourselves the idea of a veracious God, the master concept which enables the sceptical hypothesis to be overcome. From the idea of God we are able to derive the general rule that all our clear and distinct perceptions are true; and equipped with that rule, we can proceed to extend the domain of what is known without exposing ourselves to the rise of error.

Lurking in the method of doubt are substantive implications for our view of the mind and its functions. The sceptic's doubts fasten on the weakness and imbecility of the mind: its tendency towards error. The refutation of scepticism exhibits the mind at the peak of its performance: deduction of certainty from certainty. The very enterprise of doubting carries with it a conception of the *will*: it presupposes that we can stand back from, disengage from, whatever we have previously believed, if we merely choose to do so. On the other hand, the refutation of scepticism conveys a certain picture of the *intellect*: it appears as a sort of automaton, inherently tending to centre on deep-lying truths, and primed to work smoothly through their consequences. Obviously these conceptions are in conflict; and the tension between them comes out in Descartes' account of *error*. For reasons we shall soon consider, Descartes traces the origin of error back to the workings of the will. At the same time, the very possibility of error, on his assumptions, is problematic: for if the mind naturally tends towards truth, then what explains its chronic malfunctioning?

The conception of the will implicit in the method of doubt interlocks with other basic notions in the Cartesian scheme. It meshes with a certain understanding of freedom, of the personality, of the possibility of a science of man. On all these questions, Spinoza's views differed radically from Descartes', and were developed in opposition to them. Most of this book is concerned with mapping out those differences. Hampshire has written that 'this point of difference in the philosophy of mind between Descartes and Spinoza' – meaning their disagreement over error and the will – 'is one of the greatest importance in the assessment of human powers and virtues: indeed it is one of the dividing lines of philosophy' (*Hampshire* (1), p. 155). In this chapter, I examine the controversy between the two thinkers, and begin to probe some of its larger implications.

1 The grammar of assent

In the *First Meditation*, Descartes asks himself whether God may not cause him to go wrong even when he performs so simple an operation as adding two and three together; and he acknowledges that, despite the fact that God is called good, 'it seems foreign to His goodness to allow me to be deceived sometimes' (*A.G.*, p. 64). The difficulty recurs in a more pressing form in the *Fourth Meditation*, which is largely addressed to answering it. Indeed there is not one problem here, but several. First, there is a theological issue: God being held to be creator of all there is, omnipotent, and perfectly good, how then can He have made me intrinsically liable to err, without being to blame for the errors I commit? Second, there is a specifically epistemological problem: since, for Descartes, knowledge is self-intimating – if I know that p, then it follows that I know that I know that p – how is it possible that I should mistakenly think that I know something, when I do not (*cf. Popper*, p. 7)? Then the theological and epistemological problems are intertwined. I can rely on my clear and distinct perceptions because, but only because, God vouches for their truth; but if God has made me intrinsically liable to err, His veracity may be placed in doubt.

The solution propounded in the *Fourth Meditation* is, at any rate, ingenious. Summarily, it is as follows. Human error arises through the misuse of free will. The human intellect is finite; there are limits on what it can intelligibly be supposed to understand. The human will, however, is finite: for any 'p' whatever, I can choose or decide that p, although my decision may not bring 'p' about. If it is objected that there *are* limitations on the will – that I cannot, for example, decide to have been at the sack of Troy, or choose to voyage to Venus – the answer comes back that these limitations are not due to any incapacity of the will, but merely to unfavourable external constraints. Error arises when the finite intellect imperfectly grasps a proposition to which the will then rashly and precipitately assents. Whenever this happens, it has been in my power to have withheld assent, and so to have avoided error; hence in accepting what I did not understand, the fault was mine alone. The avoidance of error is always possible: in order to be clear of it, I should make it my rule never to assent to anything which I have not first understood completely.

Spinoza's motives for rejecting this theory were various. For one thing, he considered the theological 'problem' which it purported to answer to be spurious. For another, he denied the reality of the free and indifferent will which the theory postulates (V, 5; VIII, 1). For a third, he believed the theory to rest on a mistaken understanding of the nature of the mind's activity, and of how the mind is related to its own ideas. We can begin by exploring this third objection, and by asking what it is that the mind does when it 'assents' to a proposition.

Spinoza's account of assent, riddlesome and dark, may be illuminated by some suggestions of Peter Geach's concerning *assertion*. Following the lead of Frege, Geach has observed that there is in general 'no expression in ordinary language that regularly conveys assertoric force' (*Geach* (2), p. 261). If I say 'Queen Anne is dead', or even 'It is true that Queen Anne is dead', the fact that I am making an assertion is not signalled by any expression or sign within the sentence I use. It would be possible to prefix an 'If . . .' to either sentence without altering its grammatical structure, phrasing or sense; and yet by inserting it into an 'If . . .' clause I destroy its assertoric force. How then is it shown that my use of the sentence is assertoric, if its grammar, phrasing and sense do not reveal that fact? The answer seems to be that the utterance of a sentence in the indicative mode is, so to say, naturally assertoric: 'one might say that 'p' automatically says that p unless you obstruct it from doing so' (*Bell*, p. 120, citing Wiggins). There is an analogy to mathematics here: just as all free-standing, unembedded propositions in a direct proof are assertoric logically, so all unqualified utterances are assertoric pragmatically (*Bell. ibid.*). (It is not however correct, *pace* Geach, to assume that every unembedded proposition is logically assertoric: *cp. Bell*, p. 91, p. 127, discussing premisses in indirect proof.) But although the utterance '*p*' may be naturally or presumptively assertoric, it is not *inevitably* so: the circumstances in which '*p*' is uttered may strip it of the assertoric force which would otherwise accrue to it. Thus the actor who declaims 'Paris is burning' does not cause the journalists present to rush to the telephones.

How do these facts bear on the notion of *assent*? Geach makes the suggestion that Spinoza takes assertion to be the public and outward analogue to the private and inner mental act of assent. He suggests that we might find in him the idea that 'a thought is assertoric in character unless it loses this character by occurring only as an element in a more complicated thought' ((2), p. 262). This is not quite right, for as I have just remarked, an unembedded proposition can fail to be assertoric, preventing the assimilation of the mental to the logical. Nor is the view Geach discerns in Spinoza correct if it implies that there is no distinction between barely 'entertaining' a proposition and assenting to it, for 'surely one can simply grasp a thought, without necessarily asserting it' (*Bell*, p. 127). Nevertheless, Geach's point is extremely valuable. He directs us to a passage in the *Ethics* (II, 49S) where Spinoza gives the example of a boy whose mind is wholly occupied by the idea of a winged horse, but who lacks the background adult knowledge which rules out the possibility of winged horses. In such a case, Spinoza says, the boy would 'regard the winged horse as present, nor would he have any reason for doubting its existence, nor any power of refusing assent to it'. That is to say, the boy entertains the proposition that there is a winged horse; at the same time he perceives no reason to think there are no winged horses; and so it *follows* that he assents to the proposition 'entertained'. Assent is, on this view, automatic: it is not something that requires or consists in an act of will supervening on the entertaining of a proposition. Assent equals the entertaining of a proposition plus the failure to see reason to doubt it. It is bound up with the presentation of an idea in the mind, as assertion is bound up with the declaration of a sentence in speech. That is what Spinoza means when he says (in the same scholium) that it is mistaken to treat ideas as 'mute pictures on a tablet', and that if we so regard them we shall not see that 'an idea, insofar as it is an idea, involves affirmation or negation'.

ERROR AND THE WILL

This theory is a bold one, but it goes too far. It is wrong in maintaining that when a thought occurs which is not part of a more complex thought, then that thought must inevitably be assented to. Just as I can recite the verses of Empedocles without also asserting them, so I can concentrate my mind wholly upon them without also assenting to them. But the theory is right in that the occurrence of an 'unembedded' thought is naturally or inherently assertoric, i.e., it will usually require an extra act or state to nullify its assertiveness. 'Judgements are phenomenologically basic; and the formulation of a hypothesis, or the suspension of judgement as to the truth of a given claim, these are to be regarded as subsequent, modificatory acts' (*Bell*, p. 127).

From Spinoza's view that assent is not an act or exercise of will, it follows that it is not an act or exercise of *free* will. This consequence, fatal to the Cartesian theory, can be reached on other grounds. 'The will', Spinoza says 'is a universal, or the concept by which we explain all individual volitions, i.e., that which is common to them all' (*E* II, 49S). In other words, since the will is simply a capacity for making affirmations and denials, manifested equally in each such individual act, it cannot be invoked to *explain* any individual affirmation or denial: you cannot attribute my assenting to '*p*' to my capacity to assent to it, since I might both have that capacity and yet not assent to '*p*' (*Curley* (1), p. 168). Indeed, the entire Cartesian distinction between intellect and will is ultimately unfounded. To have a will is simply to affirm or deny, accept or reject, ideas and proposals; and to affirm or deny, accept or reject, as we have just seen, is nothing other than to *have* ideas, to think. But although Spinoza would deny that free will enters into assenting, he would nonetheless allow an important sense in which it remained true that assent could be called free or unfree. For when I am drawn to affirm that *p* by an adequate perception of the truth of '*p*', I am maximally free, since true freedom is nothing other than to be determined to a certain response by the perception of compelling rational justification for that response (VIII, 1).

Spinoza would thus agree with that part of Descartes' doctrine which is hardest to reconcile with the rest of it: for Descartes says of the decision to believe or to act that 'the more I am inclined one way – either because I clearly understand it under the aspect of truth or goodness, or because God has so disposed my inmost consciousness – the more freely do I choose that way' (*A.G.* p. 96). (This is apparently contradicted in the letter to an unknown addressee found in *Kenny Letters*, p. 159 (*cf. Williams* (1), pp. 180–1)). But whereas Descartes would have gone on to say that it

35

was *also* an instance of free choice when he affirmed what he did not clearly perceive – albeit a case of the 'lowest grade' of freedom – Spinoza would deny that to be a free act, or a freely willed act, at all. If I do not clearly and distinctly perceive that p, but do nevertheless affirm that p, then my response – like every response – must have been determined; and in the present type of case it will have been determined by factors which are more or less irrelevant to the truth of 'p' – by idle wishes or regrets, perhaps, or by stray and disconnected thoughts, or by garbled reports concerning the matters in hand. In erring, I show myself not merely fallible, but unfree.

2 Close encounters

Thus far we have viewed the controversy between Descartes and Spinoza from a lofty perspective – in an aerial reconnaissance, as it were, of trenches and battle-lines spread out below. But now we must shift the perspective, and examine the patient, detailed reasoning in which Spinoza grapples hand-to-hand with his great antagonist. Most of Spinoza's critical points – I shall discuss five of them – are embedded in the long scholium at E II, 49S, which the reader should consult. Although Descartes is not named (Spinoza disliked personalising a controversy: *Ep.* 2), he is unmistakeably the target of most of Spinoza's thrusts (*Gueroult* II, p. 496). By studying the finer execution of his moves against Descartes, we can gain a more sensitive understanding of Spinoza's views on six crucial topics: ideas, doubt, error, knowledge, freedom, and the will.

(i) Spinoza first warns his readers to distinguish carefully between ideas and, on the one hand, images, on the other hand words. 'It is because these three things, images, words and ideas, are by many people (*a multis*) either altogether confounded or not distinguished with sufficient accuracy or, finally, with sufficient caution, that such ignorance exists about this doctrine of the will.'

The criticism of those who confound ideas with images is obscure; we must note that by 'images' (*imagines*), Spinoza seems to mean, not what we would style *mental images*, but rather 'those affections of the human body whose ideas represent to us external bodies as present' (E II, 17S). (In the scholium to the preceding theorem, he has explicitly distinguished ideas from 'the images which are formed at the back of the eye, or, if you please, in the middle of the brain'.) Descartes may well have been guilty of this error, since in the *Treatise of Man*, he describes material images imprinted on the pineal gland by the animal spirits as 'ideas' (*A.T.*, XI, p. 174; *T.S. Hall*, p. 86; cf. *Gueroult*, II, p. 496); but why should this have encouraged him to believe in freedom of the will? Spinoza explains: 'Those who think that ideas consist in images which are formed in us from the encounter with bodies persuade themselves that those ideas of things of which we cannot form a resembling image are *not* ideas, but only fictions (*figmenta*) which we invent (*fingimus*) by the free decree of the will; accordingly, they look upon ideas as dumb pictures on a tablet'. The suggestion seems to be that our freedom of the will is proved by the fact that, if we choose, we can invent representations of things and situations, the like of which we have never experienced. (For the activity of invention, Spinoza uses the word '*fingere*', not the word '*imaginari*': cf. the *Pléiade* edition of his *Oeuvres*, p. 377, n. 1.)

I do not know whether this argument for freedom is maintained anywhere by Descartes, but there is some discussion of what seems to be a related view in the *DiE* (G II, p. 23). Spinoza's primary object there is to show that 'the mind, in paying attention to a thing hypothetical or false, so as to meditate upon it and understand it, and derive the proper conclusions in due order therefrom, will readily discover its falsity'. The mind, in reasoning hypothetically, has a natural tendency to correct false starting points. This position is defended against unnamed opponents who believe that 'fiction is limited by fiction, and not by understanding (*fictio fictionem terminat, sed non intellectio*)'; and that opposing view is spelled out as follows:

> In other words, after I have formed some fictitious idea (*postquam finxi aliquid*) and have affirmed of my own free will (*ex mea libertate*) that it exists under a certain form in nature, I am thereby precluded from thinking of it under any other form. For instance, when I have feigned (to repeat their argument) that the nature of body is of a certain kind, and have of my own free will desired to convince myself that it actually exists under this form, I am no longer able to hypothesise (*fingere*) that a fly, for example, is infinite. (G II, p. 23)

I think we must take this view to have three parts. First, it is implied that I have the power freely to invent speculative possibilities or imaginary situations; and the existence of this power reveals, and springs from, a free and indifferent will. Second, my power of free invention is, so to say, self-limiting: if I feign that p, then if I perceive that 'q' is inconsistent with 'p', it is no longer in my power, so long as the original assumption persists in my mind, to feign that q. Third, my power of free invention is *not* similarly limited by the intellect: it is *not* the case that, given that I understand that p, I cannot feign that q, where I perceive 'q' to be inconsistent with 'p'.

Spinoza confronts his opponent with a choice: either we have understanding, or we do not. If we do, then it must be able to 'limit' free invention, if free invention can limit itself. If it is asserted that we do not, then the view collapses into an extreme scepticism, which need not trouble those of us who 'know that we know'. Woven into this reply is another strand of argument: if we have a free and indifferent will, then the actions of our mind do not have causes; but reasons are causes, and so it will follow that the mind does not act from reasons. But the admission that the power of free invention is self-limited conflicts with that conclusion; for the opponent himself assumes that 'after it has formed a fictitious idea, and has given its assent thereto, it cannot think or feign it in any other manner, but is constrained by the first fictitious idea to avoid inconsistency therewith (*ut prima fictio non oppugnetur*)'. The conclusion of free will, drawn from the first of the opponent's theses, is inconsistent with the second thesis he advances. Thus not only is the adversary mistaken in his third claim (which it is here Spinoza's main object to show), but his position is self-contradictory, and goes no way towards demonstrating free will.

The controversy I have tried to reconstruct may seem shadowy, remote and unfamiliar, but some of the points which Spinoza is touching on in these discussions relate to issues raised by the work of that modern Cartesian and libertarian, Noam Chomsky. In the spirit of Chomsky, we might mark a distinction between those utterances consisting of a simple form of words ('Hello!' or 'Pass the salt') which we are drilled to produce in certain standard and recurring types of situation, and utterances which combine words in novel and unanticipated fashions, which are not stereotyped responses to recurrent features of the environment, and which may express situations which are only possible or imaginary. Then we might argue that stimulus-response theory is inadequate to explain the occurrence of utterances of the latter type, and that the creativity we exhibit in at least some of our language use attests to our powers of freedom. (I do not say that Chomsky propounds this argument, but only that it might be derived from his work.)

Against this, however, it might be said that while language-use is not a complex conditioned reflex, it still does not follow that the creativity we display in it proves that we are metaphysically free; that even those utterances which provide the paradigms of language-use for the stimulus-response theorist partake of the character of spontaneity and creativity; but that both the facts stressed by Chomsky, and those emphasised by the behaviourist school, are capable of a deterministic explanation. The parallel or analogy to Spinoza's argument against the Cartesian is exact: the Cartesian's 'figments' will answer to Chomsky's novel and unprogrammed sentences; the 'images' of the Cartesian, to the stock sentences-responses featured by the behaviourist; the dangerous conflation of ideas with images, to the tendency to underestimate the innovative aspect even of standardised responses; and the inference to free will from the facts of invention, to the argument for freedom from the facts of creative language-use.

So much then for the idea/image confusion; what of the idea/word confusion, and its place in the controversy over free will? Here Spinoza writes: 'those who confound words with an idea, or with the affirmation which the idea itself involves, think that they will contrary to what they feel (*sentiunt*), because they affirm or deny something in words contrary to that which they feel'. The point here may be that the Cartesian overlooks a notable difference between outwardly asserting, and inwardly assenting, and tries to exploit a spurious similarity between them. For there is no harm in supposing that someone has said or asserted what he does not take to be true; but it is contradictory to suppose that someone has assented to something, without taking it to be true (*cp. Curley* (1), p. 177). Descartes alleges that our power to withhold assent from what we customarily believe exhibits our freedom of the will (*Synopsis of the Second Meditation*, A.T., VII, p. 12; *Principles* I, 39; *cf.* Spinoza, CM, II, c. 12). But against this Spinoza may be observing that, whatever we *profess*, we cannot in fact withhold assent from our previous opinions, or cannot at any rate do so at will.

Spinoza's point is an interesting one, with obvious bearings on the scope and the character of Cartesian doubt. In his view, it is simply false that we can genuinely doubt, whether at will or by a conscious effort, many of the things which Descartes professes to doubt. In the *De Intellectus Emendatione* (G II, p. 20), he writes: 'If there is some God, or something omniscient, He could not make suppositions (*nihil fingere*) at all. For, even as far as we are concerned, after I know myself to exist, I cannot suppose myself either to exist, or not to exist; nor too can I imagine an elephant which can go through the eye of a needle; nor can I, after I know the nature of God, suppose Him to exist or not to exist; the same must be understood of a chimera, whose nature implies it cannot exist (*cujus natura existere implicat*)'. These examples seem to point to the general conclusion that once I know that p, I am unable to doubt whether p. (This is not the truistic 'It cannot be that both: I know that p, and I doubt whether p', but the stronger 'If I know that p, then it cannot be: that I doubt whether p'.) Doubt is possible only where there is reason to doubt: if I believe that p, I cannot doubt it, unless I come to believe or suspect that q, where 'p' and 'q' are in conflict (*vide* I, 4). If the Spinozistic view of doubt is correct, then Cartesian doubt is far less extensive than Descartes himself supposed; and where doubt does not really extend, but only purports to, there cannot be a question of the will's freely withholding its assent.

There is an apparent difficulty for my interpretation of this passage in the *DIE*, arising out of the fact that Spinoza does not enunciate the general conclusion towards which I have steered him, but instead concludes that 'it is plain from these things that . . . supposal does not affect the eternal truths'. By an eternal truth, he explains, he means a proposition which never alters in truth value: 'God is' and 'There is no chimera' are eternal truths; 'Adam thinks' and 'Adam does not think' are not eternal truths (*vide* IX, 2–3). Now the problem is this: the explanation given for saying that I cannot doubt whether I exist, or whether God exists, or whether an elephant can go through the eye of a needle, or whether there are no chimeras, is *not* that I *know* these propositions to be true, but that they are *eternally* true. The problem, however, is surmountable: for the reason Spinoza gives for our being unable to doubt an eternal truth, at least once we have grasped its sense, is simply that in grasping its sense we cannot fail to see that it is true. It is this fact, that such truths are known as soon as we endeavour to doubt them comprehendingly, that renders it impossible to doubt them other than in words: 'although many say they doubt whether God exists, they nonetheless have nothing beside the name (*sc.* "God") or else imagine something which they call "God" '. There are in fact really *two* senses in which such 'doubt' deserves Spinoza's epithet 'verbal': it is a state caused by an imperfect grasp of the sense of *words*, and it is a state which we *profess* to be in, but are not in. To contrast such doubt with 'real' doubt (*vera dubitatio in mente*), as Spinoza does, could be either to emphasise the cause, or the character, of the 'doubt'.

(ii) Returning now to the scholium at *E* II, 49, we may take up the second of Spinoza's criticisms of the Cartesian theory. He argues here that it is not true that the will extends itself further than the intellect, and is therefore distinct from it. His criticism falls into three parts.

(a) Like Kenny ((1), p. 12), Williams ((1), 182–3) and others, Spinoza notes that there is a crucial ambiguity in Descartes' terms *'intellectus'* or *'entendement'* (but contrast *Wilson*, p. 142). 'I grant that the will extends itself more widely than the intellect, if by "intellect" we mean only clear and distinct ideas; but I deny that the will extends itself more widely than the perceptions, or the faculty of conception.' It is true, he admits, that we affirm things by the will which we do not understand with the intellect – providing, that is, that 'understanding with the intellect' means 'perceiving clearly and distinctly'. But it is not true that there are things we will to affirm but fail to understand, if by 'understanding '*p*' ' we simply mean 'making sense to ourselves of '*p*' '. Now Descartes seems to maintain that the will can freely withhold assent from anything it understands: but this is true only if 'understanding' is taken to mean, not 'clearly perceive', but 'make sense of'. On the other hand, he seems also to insist that the will can freely give its assent to what it does not understand, and that is true only if 'understanding' does *not* mean 'make sense of', but 'clearly perceive'.

(b) To this he adds the somewhat puzzling consideration that if the will is infinite, then so is the faculty of feeling (*sentiendi*), which would appear to be that of sense-perception. Just as we can affirm infinitely many ideas, he alleges, so we can feel or perceive an infinite number of bodies. The thought here may be that the faculty of feeling was a part of, or involved in, its workings, the faculty of 'perceiving truths', or the understanding; so that if I am able to sense infinitely many bodies, I must be capable of making an infinity of perceptual judgements, and hence must possess an intellect capable of grasping infinitely many propositions. It may be that Spinoza thinks of 'contemplating external bodies', not as a matter of peering at mental pictures, but as a matter of making sensory judgements (*E* II, 17S; *Parkinson* (2), p. 37); his 'ideas that represent external bodies to us' are perhaps not meant to be 'representative ideas' of the Lockean or Cartesian variety. The intimate connection he sees between *perceiving* and *understanding or affirming* is revealed by his remark later in the scholium: 'What is it to perceive a winged horse, other than to affirm wings of a horse?'. Descartes, too, had lumped together sense-perception, imagining and pure understanding as modes of perceiving, opposing that faculty to the faculty of willing (*Principles* I, 32; *Brentano*, p. 29); and it may be that Spinoza thought he had found a means of proving that both faculties were infinite, in that each comprised the power to perform an infinity of operations.

(c) He seems however to recognise that this last criticism may evade the issue: for in denying that the intellect is infinite, Descartes may be saying, not that it cannot make infinitely many judgements, but that however many judgements it can make, there will always be others that it cannot make. But to this Spinoza's answer is devastatingly apt: if we cannot grasp, or even formulate to ourselves, certain ideas, then equally we are in no position to affirm them – the alleged limitations on our intellect themselves impose corresponding limitations on the will.

(iii) Of the main critical points, the third, to which I now advert, concerns the nature of the 'suspension of belief'. In reporting Descartes' view of the matter, Spinoza says: 'Experience seems to teach nothing more clearly, than that we can suspend our judgement, so as not to assent to the things we perceive . . . experience therefore seems to teach nothing more clearly than that the will or faculty of assenting is free and is distinct from the faculty of understanding'. Against this, Spinoza argues that suspension of judgement simply *consists in* perceiving that we do not see the truth adequately. It is not that, finding the available reasons too inconclusive to support a verdict, we *decide* not to assent to either of two inconsistent propositions before us; rather, there is nothing more to suspending judgement than seeing that the matter itself is undecided. Suspension of judgement is not an act of the will at all, and consequently is not an act of the free will; it is itself a judgement, dictated by a view of the case. If you ask me whether the number of the stars is even or odd, I cannot decide, although I may give you an answer; the state of the evidence does not permit a decision, as of course I see; I therefore cannot assent, or make myself assent, to either alternative. Suspending judgement is not the only *sensible* course, it is the only *possible* course. Descartes has thus idly projected a decision to adopt a mental attitude onto an attitude which is already present and accounted for. I take it that Spinoza regards these points not as contingencies, open to falsification by experience, but as conceptual truths. (For a criticism of him, *cf. Wilson*, p. 146).

Descartes' argument drew upon 'experience', that is, upon phenomenological data; and Spinoza, rightly appreciating the force of such considerations, attempts to answer it with a phenomenological argument of his own (or rather, with a sort of *reductio* of Descartes, based on the kind of data a Cartesian would admit). He reasons as follows. I can in fact suspend judgement while I am dreaming. For if I dream that p, I am confusedly thinking that p; and because of the inherently assertoric character of thoughts, I am therefore at least inclined to accept 'p'. But this tendency to believe 'p' will be checked, and my judgement concerning 'p' will be suspended, if – as sometimes happens – I should happen to dream that I am dreaming. For if that should happen, then I must be inclined to deny that I am actually perceiving or witnessing 'p'; and that in turn will counteract the tendency to accept 'p'. One inclination will thus cancel out the other, leaving my judgement in suspense: I will neither accept nor reject 'p'. Yet, Spinoza says, no-one will really suppose that he can exercise the power of freely withholding his assent while he is asleep. (Descartes, to be sure, did make this claim in the *Discourse* (A.G. p. 37), but to that Spinoza's response is incredulity.) Hence the suspension of judgement need not result from the exercise of free will; the data of experience may be explained in a way less objectionable to philosophy, as reflection on those very data will show.

(iv) The fourth of Spinoza's anti-Cartesian points is wrapped up in some obscurity. Nevertheless, I think that it too can be made more or less intelligible. The Cartesian is alleged to hold that the distinction between intellect and will is revealed by the fact that a greater power of mind is displayed in assenting to a true proposition than in assenting to a false one; for every affirmation, considered strictly in itself, requires exactly the same degree of mental power as any other, so where the differences in the powers displayed are found, they must be attributed to the activity of a faculty other than that by which we form ideas, and that can only be the will. In effect, Spinoza argues in reply that every idea is an affirmation and, considered abstractly, every affirmation is as much an affirmation as any other; but it does not follow, as the Cartesian supposes, that every affirmation is equally *real*. On the contrary, *how* real an affirmation is, is determined precisely by *what* affirmation it is: it is the propositional *content* of an idea, not the operation of the will upon it, which accounts for the variable degree of reality comprised in affirming it.

A more straightforward reply, which accompanies the one just outlined, seems to run as follows. To speak of the will as a separate faculty or power is to fall prey to an illusion fostered by language, to be guilty of an illegitimate abstraction (*cp. Spengler*, I, p. 263; p. 302). In reality, the phrase 'The Will' refers to nothing at all; in using the phrase, we are speaking compendiously of a characteristic common to all thoughts, which is their tendency to be assertoric. To say that the greater power of mind exhibited in the affirmation of a piece of knowledge derives from the involvement of the will is to speak what is strictly nonsensical: 'the Will' has no power to impart (*cp.* V, 1).

It is not immediately clear why Spinoza holds that a true affirmation expressing knowledge should reflect greater power of mind than a false affirmation. The answer, or a part of it, is given in the *Short Treatise* (II, c. 15): 'From this, then, we see the perfection of one who takes his stand upon truth, as contrasted with one who does not . . . Since the one changes easily, while the other does not change easily, it follows therefrom that the one has more stability and essence than the other has'. The man who has true knowledge, whose affirmations express rational certainty, is in a state of mind which does not alter as new facts or suppositions are put to him, or as persuasion is practised on him to influence his opinions. Being in possession of the truth, and knowing that he is, he judges these novel ideas in the light of the ideas already in him, and admits the possibility of their correctness only if they are consistent with his existing views. The man who affirms what is untrue is, by contrast, in a state of mind which is specially precarious and vulnerable (*cp.* I, 4). The inadequacy of his reasons (if he has any) is apt to be exposed by the least criticism from others, or by the discoveries he himself makes; he is liable to succumb to the pressures, whether rational or non-rational, which are brought upon him to make him change his mind; he remains secure in the state of false belief only so long as no contrary evidence or disagreeing opinion chances to arise for him. (For example, consider the case of the man who fears in ignorance, at *E* IV, 1S.) It is the greater *rootedness* of knowledge which, in Spinoza's view, accounts for its making the mind more powerful and more perfect.

(v) I come, finally, to the fifth and last of Spinoza's objections to the Cartesian view. In this place, he considers the problem traditionally known as 'the ass of Buridanus' and its bearing on the nature of the will (for an excellent discussion, *cf. Rescher* (2)). Spinoza had previously examined the case, from a Cartesian point of view, in his *Cogitata Metaphysica*. In that work, he presented the argument in this manner: a man who is hungry and thirsty is situated between two equally accessible and enticing supplies of food and drink. There is nothing in the situation to incline him to take the food rather than the drink (or conversely), and yet it would be madness to dither indecisively between them, and die rather than make an arbitrary choice. But since nothing in the circumstances themselves, or in his own beliefs and desires, determines him to one choice rather than the other, it follows that if he chooses, it is *he himself* who determines the choice, and hence that there is in him a will by which he may be freely determined in his choices. Spinoza has already tried to meet this argument, by pointing out that since *either* outcome could have been willed, it explains nothing to attribute the actual outcome to the working of *the will*; but at the present juncture, instead of repeating himself, he merely *denies* that the man would make any choice at all. To the objection that someone who permitted himself to die in such circumstances would not be a man, but only the statue of a man, Spinoza answers that he does not know how to describe such a creature, any more than he knows how to describe suicides, children, fools or madmen: in all these cases, I suppose, we have to do with human beings, or beings akin to men, who nevertheless perform acts *clearly* opposed to rational self-interest (*vide* VIII, 1).

The problem Spinoza raises for the Cartesian is strikingly close to one pressed more recently by Bernard Williams. Endeavouring to prove that there are, after all, internal limitations on the power of the will, Williams asks, 'What of a man who has conceived of various courses of action, knows that they are all possible for him, and just cannot decide between them? He, surely, "cannot choose" in a straightforward sense – he can do the actions, and the thing he cannot do is, precisely, to choose between them. He experiences a "felt obstacle" to the act of choosing itself' ((1) p. 173). The man of Spinoza's example exemplifies this sort of condition, in which the obstacles to action come, not from without, but from within. Williams envisages two possible replies Descartes could make. '(Descartes) might say that, in some cases at least, the situation really is that the man's reasons for not choosing this or that are extremely evenly balanced, and hence that it is not . . . any defect in his will as such, that he cannot make the choice. Or, again, in some cases, he might say that the man can strictly speaking make the choice, but cannot produce the slightest effect thereby even within his own body: this is the situation that Descartes supposes to arise when the will is in conflict with the bodily passions, because the inertial force of the "animal spirits" which are moving in the body prevent the soul operating upon it' (*Williams* (1), p. 173). But of these two replies, the first, though relevant to the case in hand, is inconsistent with Descartes' actual views, while the second is simply inapplicable to the situation we are imagining, which is not one of conflict between the will and bodily passion, but between one bodily passion (thirst) and another (hunger). The first reply is unavailable, because it is precisely what Descartes contends *for* and Spinoza contends *against*, that the man whose reasons are evenly balanced should be able, by an exercise of the will, to effect a decision. The second reply is inapplicable, because if the man is unable to *act* (but remains statue-like), this cannot be explained as the result of forces connected with the bodily passions resisting contrary forces emanating from the will: what we have to do with here are *two* movements of the 'animal spirits', presumably of equal force, operating on the pineal gland and preventing it from moving; and each movement is connected with a bodily passion (*vide* VI, 3). If the will can then come in, and exert a force of its own on the pineal gland, then this superadded force should cause the gland to move, with the result that the limbs are set in motion, and action takes place. It follows that if – as Spinoza alleges – the man in the dilemma does *not* act, then the will cannot have any force *of its own* to add. It seems that Descartes must say, not only that the man can choose between the food and the drink, but also that his choice must be an efficacious one, leading to action. Williams and Spinoza agree in finding that contention doubtful; and it is hard not to sympathise with them.

3 *The nature of error*

To this point, I have concentrated on the expository tasks of describing Spinoza's view of assent and the suspension of judgement, of stating his reasons for denying the Cartesian theory of error, and of elucidating his account of the will, and of the will's role in the formation of belief. The stage has been set for the last and most formidable task: that of explaining Spinoza's own theory of error.

Traditionally the problem of error, like the problem of sin, has had two solutions. The first consists in attributing sin and error to the misuse of free will; the second denies that sin and error are finally real. Spinoza firmly rejected the first solution, but it has appeared to many of his students that he embraced the second. In *Ethics* II, 32 and 33, Spinoza announces that 'all ideas, insofar as they are related to God, are true', and that 'in ideas there is nothing positive, on account of which they are called false'. These statements have been taken to imply that error is sheerly illusory. Joachim, for example, in his commentary on the *Ethics*, paraphrases Spinoza's meaning as follows: 'The form of evil, error, and crime does not consist in anything which expresses essence or being, and therefore God cannot be called its cause. "Sins and evil are nothing positive"'. And he continues,

' "Falsity" and "evil" . . . *do not "belong" even to partial knowledge and partial or finite being.* They are mere negations and defects which attach to partial knowledge *which poses as* complete (or completer than it is), and to imperfect forms of humanity which yet *claim to be* human' (Joachim (2), p. 250, p. 251) *cf. Evans*, pp. 136–40).

If that is really Spinoza's view of error, then it is readily rebutted, as indeed Joachim saw. His criticism is so effective that I must quote a part of it: 'Illusion, error, and evil are "facts" in some sense real, and facts which will not come into harmony with Spinoza's conception of the general nature of Reality. Absence of knowledge becomes "error", imperfection of human nature becomes "sin", only when the one *poses* as complete, the other *claims* to be human. The *pose* and the *claim* constitute the distinctive characters of error and sin; and they are not mere "negations". . . . [T]his *pose* and *claim*, which constitute the distinctive nature of error and evil, can neither be grounded in Reality as Spinoza conceives it, nor be dismissed as mere illusions. For the former alternative would bring imperfection and defect into the nature of God, whilst the latter would leave the illusion itself as inexplicable as the "facts" it was intended to explain' (Joachim (2), p. 253; p. 254).

This appears to me to be philosophical criticism of a very high order; and if Joachim's interpretation is correct, then we do not need to pause long over this part of Spinozism. But while Spinoza's language may certainly bear that interpretation, I believe that is is possible to devise a formulation which is at once more congruent with his actual statements and more satisfying philosophically.

My starting point is theorem 35 of *Ethics* II. The theorem states that 'Falsity consists in the privation of knowledge which inadequate, that is, mutilated and confused, ideas involve'. It is apparent that by 'falsity' Spinoza means, not a property of propositions, but a certain state of mind, which elsewhere he calls 'error'. In characterising this state as a 'privation', he wishes to express two things. First, it is only *minds* which can properly be said to err or not to err; the body, though in a certain sense it lacks knowledge, is categorially the wrong type of thing to commit an error. Error is not simply an 'absolute' privation of knowledge, but the absence of knowledge in a subject of a particular sort, just as blindness is not the bare absence of sight, but the absence of sight in a living animal (*E* II, 35 D; *Ep.* 21). Second, error must be differentiated from the state of complete *ignorance* in which human minds often find themselves. For a man to be in error, he must have been concerned with a question in the first place – the issue must somehow have arisen for him (*E* II, 35 D). But apart from these two things, there is a more substantial implication in the thought that error is a privation. This is the notion, found also in Descartes (*Williams* (1), p. 165), that error is a condition which calls for special explanation in a way that knowledge does not, that it is something which in some sense ought *not* to have happened, and whose existence implies a failure of the mind to work as it may be expected to work. (Williams nicely describes the view in question as 'a significant Cartesian presupposition' to the effect that 'the human mind . . . is a rational instrument effortlessly embodying the truth'.)

Spinoza identifies error as 'an inadequate knowledge of things' or as a matter of having 'inadequate and confused ideas'. To be in error, then, is to be in a condition in which one has ideas concerning a given subject, which require to be supplemented or corrected by further ideas relating to the same subject. In *E* II, 28 D, Spinoza dilates on the nature of 'confused' ideas: he says that they are plainly analogous to 'conclusions detached from their premisses'. His thought seems to be that my idea that p is confused if and only if I accept that p but am unable to explain, or explain in a certain manner, why it is that p. Thus to be in error regarding 'p' is to accept that p, without possessing knowledge of the facts which would explain why it was true that p.

This notion of error is correlative to a certain view of knowledge, which we need to examine more closely. In the *De Intellectus Emendatione*, Spinoza expressed his agreement with the 'ancients' that what is truly called knowledge 'proceeds from cause to effect' (*G* II, p. 32); and it seems clear that he had in mind the paradigm of a demonstrative science which is delineated in Aristotle's *Posterior Analytics*. To say that knowledge advances from cause to effect is to say that what we know must be capable of being exhibited in a system of propositions in which every theorem is ultimately derivable from certain principles which neither admit of, nor require, justification (*Parkinson* (2), pp. 49–50); *cf*. VI, 5). But there is a further point of comparison with the ancients: for just as Plato relegates beliefs, even true beliefs, to the lowly spheres of conjecture, opinion, or intelligence if they cannot be derived from an 'unhypothesised beginning', and promotes them to the rank of knowledge if they are connected to such a starting point, so Spinoza deprecates forms of belief which are not derived from axioms or common notions, and brands them as 'confused' and 'mutilated' ideas.

If I have grasped the theory aright, it is nicely illustrated by the case of the boy who has been told of a winged horse. The boy's mind is naturally credulous, in that it tends to assent to what is put before it, unless inhibitions or contrary perceptions check the impulse. Since the boy lacks the adult knowledge which would show him that horses cannot fly, that such a creature would contravene the laws of anatomy and of dynamics, the impulse is not restrained, and he lapses into error. His state of mind is doubly defective: he cannot explain adequately why there should be a flying horse, relying only on hearsay for corroboration of his belief; and he does not understand that the thing is in any case impossible.

It is a consequence of Spinoza's view that *any* state of mind which falls short of knowledge, including the state of true belief, must be reckoned to be error (a point appreciated by some of the commentators: *Parkinson* (2), p. 45; *Hampshire* (2), p. 106). For him, the difference between a false belief and a belief which, though true, is inadequately grounded, is a slight and inessential one. Thus although he is prepared to say that a merchant who has learned by rote that 6 is to 4 as 3 is to 2 has hearsay *knowledge* (*E* II, 40S2), he immediately goes on to say that this *soi-disant* knowledge is 'the unique cause of falsity' (*E* II, 41). By that he means that the lowest grades of 'knowledge' comprise the *formal* cause of 'error', i.e. are precisely what 'error' consists in (*Parkinson* (2), p. 46). To call these states of mind 'knowledge', as of course is vulgarly done, is to exhibit once again the inexactness of ordinary speech, and the careless habits of mind to which it attests (III, 2, *Words*).

Like Descartes, Spinoza connects our liability to error with the fact that we are *embodied* (*E* IV, 1S); and so what he says about error is illuminated by his views concerning the imagination – which is peculiarly the property of *embodied* minds (*E* V, 21). In *Ethics* II 17S, he tells us that 'the imaginations of the mind regarded in themselves (*in se spectatas*) contain nothing of error, nor does the mind err in that it imagines, but only insofar as it is considered to be lacking in an idea which implies the non-existence of those things which it imagines as present to itself'. Spinoza conformed to the regular, but pernicious, practice of the philosophers of his period in bringing such multifarious states and activities as perceiving, dreaming, hallucinating, experiencing illusions, devising phantasies, feigning, hypothesising, and even thinking, under the general heading of the imagination. The result is that it is far from clear what he means to be saying when he alleges that 'imaginations regarded in themselves are free from error'. I think at least three possibilities suggest themselves.

First, he could be distinguishing the 'content' of sensory or quasi-sensory states from the 'interpretation' we put upon them, and then be claiming that the question of truth and falsehood, knowledge and error, only arises for the latter. (One difficulty for this interpretation is that it invokes the idea that the quality of our experiences is independent of their linguistic expression – an idea which is very disputable: *cf. Feyerabend*, pp. 71–3). Second, he may mean to contrast imagining that *p*, in the sense of *feigning* or *hypothesising* that *p*, with affirming that *p*, and to be remarking, correctly, that the latter introduces the possibility of error, as the former does not. But third and most interestingly,, he may be saying that if the mind only 'imagined', it could not be said either to have knowledge or to err; the possibility of knowledge, as also that of error, only emerges when the mind begins to reflect critically upon itself and its imaginations, to discern logical and evidential connections between some ideas or imaginations and others, to look for a means of systematising them, and making them cohere. In Kantian terms, knowledge and error can only come in with 'the synthesis of perceptions' (*Gueroult* II, pp. 212–13).

This third interpretation fits in well with a passage of the *De Intellectus Emendatione* which we have already encountered (*vide* I, 4) (*G* II, p. 30). Recall the case of the peasant who looks at the sun and forms the idea that it is vastly smaller than the earth. So long as only that single 'idea' or 'sensation' is present in his mind, he can neither strictly doubt, nor yet be certain, that the sun was of lesser extent than the earth. It is only when someone tells him that his senses may mislead him – only, that is, when a second, and conflicting, idea enters into his mind – that he can begin to doubt whether the sun is smaller; and it is only when the conflict is overcome that he can attain *certainty*, as against the naive, unquestioning *conviction* of the purely 'imaginative' level. Doubt, certainty, and error are mental attitudes, so to speak, of a higher order; they presuppose that one's 'imaginations' have been unsettled, and that one has stood back from them, or reflected upon them.

If this is what Spinoza really meant, then a serious contradiction within his views threatens to emerge. On the one hand, he must treat *all* ideas, including the rustic's 'imagination' of the sun, as inherently assertoric; and from this it follows that the rustic is not merely supposing the sun to be small, but actually affirming that it is smaller than this globe. But if he makes that affirmation, it is surely in place to speak of error on his part. (In fact, although his choice of terms may be unguarded, Spinoza does seem to describe the bare '*imaginatio*' as itself an 'error': in *E* IV 1S, he says that when ignorance is removed, '*tollitur quidem error*'.) On the other hand, the fact that the rustic is only at the level of unquestioning conviction, and has not yet begun to reflect on his idea (or 'sensation'), forced us to assume that his state of mind was too rudimentary a kind to amount to a positive error. Thus we must both proffer, and fail to proffer, the charge of error: which is absurd.

The difficulty I have tried to expose arises for Spinoza even on an alternative construction of his theory of error. In *The Nature of Truth*, Joachim argued that Spinoza had made it a necessary condition of being in error that one should take one's state of non-knowledge for one of (indubitable) knowledge (*Joachim* (3), p. 138; p. 142; p. 144; seconded by *Evans*, p. 142). Error is indeed, on this view, something 'higher-order': it involves one in adopting not merely an attitude towards a proposition, but an attitude towards that attitude. From this account it follows that the rustic's 'imagination' of the sun, and perhaps too the boy's 'perception' of a winged horse, are not after all errors. But as I have just remarked, that cannot be right. Furthermore, Joachim's exegesis creates a separate problem for Spinoza. Spinoza repeatedly insists that truth is its own standard ('*verum index sui*'), and by that he seems to mean that reflection upon the 'intrinsic denominations' or non-relational properties of certain ideas will make the truth of those ideas manifest (*DIE*, *G* II, p. 26). Knowledge is self-intimating: if I know that p, it follows that I know that I know it (*E* II, 43D). Similarly, falsehood will, after reflection, inevitably reveal itself for what it is: if I tried to think through the false idea that, say, men are suddenly turned into beasts, I would be unable to discover any connection between the subject and the predicate, so that it would become apparent to me that I was entertaining a fiction (*DIE*, *G* II, p. 24). But if both knowledge and error are recognisable in this way, how is it possible that I should mistake a state of non-knowledge for one of knowledge? And how could error be an especially precarious and unstable state, if the man who was in error took himself to be certain of the truth? The only reply I can envisage is that it requires some pains and attention to discover whether our state of mind is one of knowledge or of error: though these characteristics are manifest, they are not *immediately* manifest.

I come, finally, to what seems to be the most fundamental weakness of all in Spinoza's theory: it makes error at once eradicable and ineradicable. The eradicability of error is emphasised when Spinoza thinks of the mind as primarily an *intellect*;

its ineradicability is stressed when he remembers that the mind includes an *imagination*.

The *eradicability* of error is connected with a feature of Spinoza's concept of knowledge already known to us: falsehood is self-disclosing (*E* II, 43S). In any sequence of hypothetical reasoning, if we start from assumptions which include what is false, then providing we attend to our ideas, we cannot fail to note the falsehood and expel it (*G* II, p. 24 and *G* II, p. 37). The lack of 'connection' between the subject and predicate in the judgement that men are suddenly turned into beasts will alert us to the absurdity of that idea. Indeed, it can almost be said that Spinoza thinks error to be, not merely eradicable, but impossible to any mind endowed with adequate ideas (as all minds are: *E* II, 38C). For Spinoza believes that the relation between the ground and the consequent of an argument is mirrored by the relation within the reasoner's mind between the apprehension of the ground and the apprehension of the consequent (*E* II, 7; *E* V, 4S; *cf*. VI, 5; IX, 5). In virtue of this 'mirroring', the acceptance of an adequate idea must be a causally sufficient condition for the acceptance of any idea which is a logical consequence of it. Thus it follows that if I have any ideas at all, I must have complete knowledge of their entailments: if I have the common notions pertaining to bodies, I must accordingly possess an adequate idea of the causes of the affections of my own body. It is therefore much too weak to say, as Spinoza does at *E* V, 4, that there is no affection of the body of which we *cannot* form a clear and distinct conception (*clarum et distinctum conceptum*); rather, he ought to claim that there is no bodily affection of which we *do* not have a clear conception. But if so, then we cannot be in error regarding these things – a consequence which spells ruin, not only for Spinoza's account of perception, but for his theory of the passions (*vide* VII, 8).

The features of Spinoza's concept of knowledge which lure him into these consequences are not superficial ones, removable by some mild cosmetic surgery. The concept of knowledge, as shaped by a rationalist like Spinoza, seems to be one whose general character is well exhibited in the system of epistemic logic invented by Jaakko Hintikka. There are two theorems in particular which should be noted in this connection. First, Hintikka maintains that knowledge is self-intimating: if x knows that p, then x knows that x knows that p (*Hintikka* (2), pp. 104–6). This, of course, is also accepted by Spinoza, and is assumed in his refutation of the sceptic (*cf*. I, 2). And more relevantly to our immediate purpose, it is a theorem that I have knowledge of all the deductive consequence of anything I know: if x knows that p, and 'p' entails 'q', then x knows that q (pp. 30–1).

Hintikka is of course aware that this result appears to be wholly incredible: a man might know the axioms of some sophisticated mathematical theory but not know all their remote consequences (p. 31). His theorems 'tell us something definite about the truth and falsity of statements only in a world in which everybody follows the consequences of what he knows as far as they lead him . . . They are applicable to actual statements only in so far as our world approximates one of the "most knowledgeable of possible worlds" ' (p. 36). But for all that, there *is* a tendency, exploited by rationalist thinkers, to suppose that in some sense we already 'know' what we could have arrived at without being given extra factual information – to think that this is already one of the most knowledgeable of possible worlds. So it was that Plato maintained that Meno's slave-boy had always known the square of the diagonal of a square to be twice the original square (p. 38, note 11). It appears that Spinoza shared that Platonic view.

The *ineradicability* of error, on the other hand, follows even more plainly from Spinoza's assumptions. We are part of the 'common order of nature', subject to its laws, and incapable of functioning independently of the things which interfere with us (*E* III, 2). In particular, 'the human mind, when it perceives things in the common order of nature, has no adequate knowledge of itself nor of its own body, nor of external bodies, but only a confused and mutilated knowledge' (*E* II, 29C) – that is, it must be in error concerning them. The mind of Paul will necessarily be caused to form and assent to a representation of the body of Peter which reflects the constitution of Paul's body rather than the true nature of Peter's (*E* II, 17S); and in giving its assent, Paul's mind will err. Even the acquisition of a true idea concerning a given matter need not eradicate error concerning it: at *E* IV, S1, Spinoza admits that we will retain an 'idea' of the sun as a body only 200 feet away even after we know its true distance. But if 'ideas' are propositional, and not merely mute pictures, then it follows that inconsistent judgements on the sun's distance are unavoidable.

The problem is quite general, moreover, and not confined to sense perception. Men must (*'debeant'*) devise for themselves the notions of good, evil, order, confusion, heat, cold, beauty and deformity, wherewith to explain nature (*E* I, Appendix). Yet those notions do no more than indicate our own reactions to what surrounds us, not the intrinsic character of the things themselves. The notions are not, so to say, valid as metaphysical categories, but they are necessary and valid within the limits of human life (*Joachim* (2), p. 250). 'The mind is determined to this or that volition by a cause, which is determined also by another cause, and this again by another, and so on *ad infinitum*' (*E* II, 48). But among the things that determine our volitions, and so our assent and dissent, must be the haphazard concourse of external bodies (*E* II, 29S). That inescapable source of belief destines us to falsehood. If we were angelic intelligences, our minds might operate without such hindrances and distractions, but we are not; we are not even (as Spinoza insists) ghosts in a machine. In the *Sixth Meditation*, Descartes seems forced to concede that the soul's union with the body renders error inevitable; and for a strikingly similar reason, Spinoza thinks that the vagaries and illusions of the imagination cannot finally be overcome. To err is human.

III

Knowledge and Imagination

Cartesianism fought war on two fronts. On one side, it wanted to extinguish the doubts raised by scepticism, while accepting the sceptical imperative that error was to be avoided. On the other side, it assailed dogmatism, and subverted the Aristotelian world view. Descartes' own subversive activity was largely confined to science and metaphysics; Spinoza broadened the conflict, attacking orthodoxy in religion, ethics and politics. In trying to understand his theory of knowledge, we do well to see him as an agitator and propagandist, eager to demolish an obsolete scheme of ideas, and urging a new set of doctrines on his fellows.

His enemies included both the vulgar and the learned. The uncritical confidence in the reliability of the senses, the willingness to credit second-hand reports, however fantastic or unfounded, the mindless acceptance of religious myth and political drivel, all earned his scorn. (Living as he did in the interstices of society, he was painfully sensitive to the evils of gossip, rumour, prejudice.) But equally the canting of the educated, their show of erudition tricked out in hard words and empty jargon, seemed to him so much rubbish, needing to be swept away. In taking these views, of course, he was not alone. Philosophers from Plato onwards had taught that the senses were liars; sceptics from Epicurus to Montaigne had ridiculed the gibberish of the Schools. But the motives for Spinoza's attacks, though not peculiar to him, had not been common. First of all, the emergence of analytical geometry and of Galileian physics had undermined the claim of the senses to reveal the world in its intrinsic character. To understand the Universe as it actually was, men had to pierce the beguiling veil of colour, sound, savour, fragrance and warmth in which it concealed itself, and contemplate the bare, abstractible essences which lay beneath. Nature is the measurable: the concepts of geometry, eked out perhaps with a few others (duration, position, matter), were sufficient for the understanding of physical reality (*Wedberg* II, p. 10). The ancient Pythagoreans had been fascinated by observing that the pitch of a tone was functionally dependent on the length of a vibrating string, but now the speculation was put forward that all sensory qualities were expressible in terms of shape, and ultimately of number. (Insofar as the secondary qualities were not so expressed, they could be consigned to a residual category, the Mental.) Spinoza's theory of knowledge is an attempt to vindicate that speculation.

Spinoza had another motive for offering his new view of knowledge – a spiritual, as well as a scientific, one. For he held that it is chiefly in knowledge that human blessedness consists: it is knowledge that cools the fevers of passion, that dissipates egoism, that infuses tranquillity, that leads to salvation.

The two motives, superficially distinct, may in fact be connected at a deeper level. Describing the emergence of the Galileian world picture, Husserl said:

> The phenomena are only in the subjects; they are there only as causal results of events taking place in true nature, which events exist only with mathematical properties. If the intuited world of our life is merely subjective, then all the truths of pre- and extra-scientific life which have to do with its factual being are deprived of value. (*Husserl*, p. 54)

It may be that Spinoza thought, not only that the new knowledge portended the loss of meaning and value, but also that it provided the materials for their recovery. In the origin of the problem lay the means to its solution.

1 *The varieties of knowledge*

In the *Short Treatise*, the *De Intellectus Emendatione* and finally in the *Ethics*, Spinoza presents an inventory of kinds of knowledge ('*genera cognitionis*'). In doing so, he has contrived to exasperate later students and commentators. His several formulations differ from one another; the examples he provides to illustrate his meaning only serve to obscure it; and his other comments on the topic seem inconsistent with his leading pronouncement. The root of the trouble, I suspect, is that Spinoza never really got clear about the different purposes he wanted the classification to serve, and as a result put it to inconsistent uses. Part of the time it seems designed to demarcate the *sources* of knowledge, so that we can assess the validity of knowledge-claims by asking *how* the matter in question has come to be known. On other occasions, it seems intended to mark a division between whole *bodies of knowledge*, sorting them into those which are genuine and those which are sham. (Thus a physics of sensible forms counts as bogus knowledge, and a physics derived from 'common notions' is true knowledge.) Finally, it seems also to be envisaged as a ranking of *mental processes or states*, classified by reference to their desirability or the desirability of their effects. (This purpose, recessive elsewhere, emerges in *E* V.)

At *E* II, 40S2, the doctrine is set out as follows:

From what has been already said, it clearly appears that we perceive many things and form universal ideas:

I. From individual things, represented to us by the senses in a confused and mutilated manner, and without order to the intellect (*E* II, 29C). These perceptions I have therefore been in the habit of calling knowledge from vagrant experience (*cognitionem ab experientia vaga*).

II. From signs; as for example when we hear or read certain words, we recollect things and form certain ideas similar to them, through which ideas we imagine things (*E* II, 18S). These two ways of looking at things I shall hereafter call knowledge of the first kind, opinion or imagination.

III. From our possessing common notions and adequate ideas of the properties of things (*E* II, 38; 39 and its corollary; 40). This I call reason and knowledge of the second kind.

Besides these two kinds of knowledge, there is a third, as I shall hereafter show, which we shall call intuitive science. This kind of knowing advances from an adequate idea of the formal essence of certain attributes of God to the adequate knowledge of the essence of things.

The three-fold division in the *Ethics* (the corresponding division in the *DIE* has four parts: *G* II, p. 10) is probably meant to mirror the overall design of the work. Imagination or opinion, the lowest kind of knowledge, corresponds to the state of bondage to the passions (*E* III); reasoned knowledge answers to the state of human freedom, or liberation from the passions (*E* IV); intuitive science matches up with blessedness, or the intellectual love of God (*E* V). Spinoza himself draws attention to these correspondences in an elliptical passage from the *Short Treatise* (II, 2):

We shall say that from the first proceed all the passions which are opposed to good reason; from the second, good desires; from the third, true and sincere Love, with all its offshoots.

Spinoza's classification is prefigured in two authors he studied attentively, and it helps in understanding him to compare their views with his. The first author is Descartes, the second Maimonides.

In the letter to Picot which prefaces his *Principles of Philosophy*, Descartes wrote that 'all the knowledge we now possess' belongs to four types: (i) 'those notions which are of themselves so clear that they may be acquired without any meditation'; (ii) 'all that which experience of the senses teaches us'; (iii) 'what the conversation of other men teaches us'; and (iv) 'the reading of books . . . written by persons who are capable of conveying good instruction to us' (*H.R.* I, p. 205). Spinoza's 'knowledge from vagrant experience' corresponds to Descartes' knowledge through the experience of the senses; and his knowledge 'from signs', which arises when we 'hear or read certain words', answers both to Descartes' 'conversation of other men' and 'reading of books'. But the Cartesian 'clear notions that may be acquired without any meditation' seem to have undergone a curious mitosis, and divided into intuitive science and reasoned knowledge.

Maimonides' discussion in the *Guide for the Perplexed* also has echoes in Spinoza. In Maimonides' scheme, there exist (i) imaginative knowledge, belonging to ordinary folk in their transactions with the word; (ii) scientific or philosophical knowledge; (iii) prophetic knowledge. Each type of knowledge has its proper and distinctive range of objects: imaginative knowledge takes in particular corporeal things; scientific knowledge extends to universal and incorporeal ones; prophetic knowledge goes to incorporeal particulars. As in Spinoza, intellect and imagination are sharply contrasted. Imagination 'only perceives the individual, the compound, in that aggregate condition in which it presents itself to the senses; or it combines things which exist separately, joins some of them together, and represents them all as one body or as a force of the body'. Intellect is held to be 'a faculty entirely distinct from the imagination, by which the necessary, the possible and the impossible can be distinguished from each other' (*Guide for the Perplexed*, I, 73, Tenth Proposition). Both faculties are surpassed by prophecy, which has the noblest range of objects, more certainty than the imagination, and a less discursive manner of operating than the intellect. The prophet 'tells things which men could not discover by reason or ordinary imagination alone'; he 'conceives ideas which are confirmed by reality, and are as clear to him as if he deduced them by means of syllogisms'; he is able to 'pass over all . . . causes, and draw inferences . . . very quickly, almost instantaneously' (*Guide*, II, 38).

Maimonides' 'imagination' is plainly cognate to Spinoza's 'knowledge of the first kind'; and his 'intellect' is cousin to Spinoza's 'knowledge of the second kind'. Maimonides' 'prophecy' seems to foreshadow Spinoza's 'intuitive science'; but as we shall see, Spinoza ultimately treats prophetic knowledge as reducible to hearsay and to vagrant experience (III, 2).

Before turning to a closer examination of the kinds of knowledge, we must recall a point made earlier (*cf*. II, 3). Despite Spinoza's statements that he is treating of 'knowledge', 'perception', and the formation of 'universal ideas', it is obvious that imagination and opinion are not, for him, forms of knowledge at all. The two theorems which follow *E* II, 40S make it abundantly plain that these states of mind are really nothing but error. 'Knowledge of the first kind alone is the cause of falsity', he writes; 'knowledge of the second and third is necessarily true'. In saying that opinion and imagination are the sole cause of falsity, he means that they comprise the *formal* cause of falsity – they are what falsity consists in (*Parkinson* (2), p. 46). And 'falsity' here refers, not to a property of propositions, but to what he elsewhere calls 'error', i.e. belief which, whether true or false, falls short of knowledge. So the first kind of knowledge is only 'knowledge' by courtesy; or rather, the fact that these states of mind (or bodies of doctrine) are *called* knowledge merely underscores the confusions of ordinary speech (*G* II, p. 33).

2 Knowledge from signs

In the *Ethics*, Spinoza talks of knowledge 'from signs; as for example when we read or hear certain words, we recollect things'; but in the *De Intellectus Emendatione*, he had spoken instead of perception arising from hearsay ('*ex auditu*') or from arbitrary ('*ad placitum*') signs (G II. p. 10). In the later version, 'hearsay' seems to have become one species in the broader category of knowledge 'from signs'.

Hearsay

Spinoza gives us a few examples of what he means by hearsay. He tells us that 'by hearsay I know the day of my birth, my parentage, and the like; concerning which matters I have never had any doubt' (*DIE*, G II, p. 10). Another example involves the so-called 'Rule of Three': 'Let there be three numbers given through which a fourth is to be derived which will be to the third as the second is to the first. Merchants do not hesitate (*non dubitant*) to multiply the second and the third together, and divide the product by the first, because they have not yet forgotten the things which they heard from a teacher (*magistro*) without any proof' (*E* II, 40S2). His most interesting example comes in Chapter XIII of the *Tractatus*, when he considers the popular conception of God:

> If any man tell us that it is not necessary to understand the divine attributes, but that we must believe them without proof, he is plainly trifling. . . . The repetition of what has been heard on such subjects no more indicates or attains to their meaning than the words of a parrot or a puppet speaking without sense or signification. (G III, p. 156)

To characterise a piece of 'knowledge' as hearsay is to cast doubt on its reliability. That is why the Cartesian sceptic uses the description to weaken our attachment to our previous beliefs. In the *First Meditation*, Descartes says that 'what I have so far accepted as true *par excellence*, I have got either from the senses or by means of the senses' (*A.G.*, p. 61). Pressed by Burman to explain this distinction, he is reported to have said that it amounted to a distinction between knowledge from sight and knowledge from hearing (*Cottingham*, p. 3). The explanation is confused, but we can see plainly enough what Descartes was getting at. He obviously intended to mark the difference between knowledge at first-hand, and knowledge at second- (or later-) hand. However, knowledge can be first-hand even if obtained by hearing (I hear the crack of a gun); and it can be secondhand even if acquired through sight (I read a newspaper account of a massacre in Afghanistan).

'Hearsay', as Spinoza understands it, is much wider than the forensic notion used by the lawyers. In common law jurisdictions, at any rate, hearsay consists of statements not made at trial by the witness who is testifying, and introduced as evidence for the truth of the proposition asserted (*Cowen and Carter*, p. 1). So if witness W testifies that declarant D stated that p, W's testimony need not be hearsay, if, e.g., it is offered in proof, not of 'p', but of the claim that D *stated that p*. It seems, however, that whether we concluded that p, or merely that D had stated that p, Spinoza would say that we had only hearsay knowledge in our grasp.

Does Spinoza think that what is known by hearsay cannot be

known in any other way, and so cannot be an object of genuine knowledge at all? Curley has suggested this, pointing out that 'it is difficult to see how Spinoza could know on what day he was born or who his parents were in any other way than by report' (*Curley* (2), p. 30). On the other hand, the 'trifler' in the *Tractatus* whose knowledge of God's attributes is entirely second-hand can be brought to form an adequate idea of God, and so to have reasoned knowledge of something he had previously known only through hearsay.

Although Spinoza does not use the notion of 'hearsay knowledge' polemically, it follows directly from his views that most of our religious 'knowledge' is only a matter of hearsay, and so utterly unreliable. The place to focus on first is Chapter II of the *Tractatus*, entitled 'Of Prophecy'. There Spinoza tells us that the 'natural knowledge' of God and His decrees is accessible to all men alike. What then of the knowledge of God claimed for the Biblical prophets, on whose authority *our* claims to knowledge of Him may depend? Do these prophets enjoy a special faculty or mode of awareness, lacking in the rest of us, by which they can discover things not apprehended by 'natural knowledge'? Setting apart (disingenuously) the case of Jesus, Spinoza maintains that the prophets neither had, *nor declared that they had*, any extraordinary power of cognition. As (he claims) they themselves assert, Divine revelation was communicated to them only through words or sounds that they heard, or visions that they saw, or phenomena of both kinds occurring together. Only ordinary sense-modalities and mental operations were involved, only ordinary objects of perception and thought.

These views of Biblical prophecy link up with Spinoza's theory of knowledge (though he himself does not exhibit the connections). Insofar as popular beliefs about God rest on the authority of the prophets, they comprise only hearsay knowledge. The prophet, Spinoza says, is an 'interpreter' or intermediary: the reports of his encounters with God, which we hear of or read in the prophetic books, are intrinsically no more credible than any other reports. Moreover, not only is *our* religious knowledge defective (insofar as it is only 'hearsay'), but *their* knowledge is often no better. Even the philosopher ('*philosophus*') Solomon, whose opinions Spinoza esteems highly (G III, p. 81), was ignorant of the ratio between the circumference and diameter of the circle and, 'like the generality of workmen, thought it was as three to one' (G III, p. 22); why then accept the report of the dimensions of his Temple, assumedly revealed to him by God? Here we have hearsay enfolded within hearsay; and in general,

Scripture justifies its assertions only by (vagrant) 'experience' (*G* III, p. 63) Finally, the accounts we have of the revelations to the prophets are badly corrupt, since doubtful readings and mutilated passages have crept in (*G* III, p. 121); and, more importantly, the *authors* of the accounts were frequently not the prophets themselves, but persons living much later, who could not have witnessed the reported events.

The critical case here is the authorship of the Pentateuch: 'casting doubt on whether Moses was in fact the author of the Pentateuch, the foundation on revealed Scripture, was taken as tantamount to doubting that the Law was revealed' (*Strauss*, p. 142). Spinoza, who discusses this question at length in the *TTP* (cs VIII and IX), and whose excommunication may have been due to his views on it (*Strauss*, p. 292, n. 177), concludes that the Pentateuch is mainly the work of Ezra, 'a man of only average intelligence' (*Strauss*, p. 293, n. 179), and hence not attributable directly to a figure with the authority of Moses (*Strauss*, p. 141). The Pentateuch is thus itself hearsay, retailed by a mediocre mind, and the validity of the Mosaic law is wholly undercut.

From signs

Hearsay knowledge is classified together with knowledge 'from signs' (*E* II, 40S2) or perception arising 'from some sign which they call arbitrary' (*DIE*, *G* II, p. 40).

In describing some signs as 'arbitrary', Spinoza alludes to the tradition, reaching back to Aristotle, of contrasting 'arbitrary' with 'natural' signs (*Joachim* (1), p. 26). He may also have in mind Hobbes' chapter 'Of Names' in the *De Corpore* (a book in Spinoza's private library). Hobbes distinguished between 'natural' signs, such as the clouds which mean that rain is to follow, and 'arbitrary' signs, which are 'those we make at our own pleasure, as a bush hung up, signifies that wine is to be sold there . . . and words so and so connected, signify the cogitations and motions of our mind' (*Hobbes*, p. 33). Although Spinoza drops the reference to 'arbitrariness' in the *Ethics*, it seems that even there his knowledge 'from signs' is specifically connected with non-natural signs.

What is knowledge 'from signs', and why is it a 'cause of falsity'? Spinoza's answers are not clear. He illustrates this kind of knowledge by pointing to the fact that 'when certain words are heard or read, we remember things, and from certain ideas of them similar to them, through which we imagine the things' (*E* II, 40S2).

KNOWLEDGE AND IMAGINATION

Contrary to Spinoza's preferred usage (*E* II, 43S; *cf.* II, 1), 'ideas' here are not assertoric, but rather mental pictures or mental images. This is so because (i) they are said to be 'similar' to things (and so are pictorial rather than assertoric), and (ii) they are described as the means or vehicles through which we imagine the things (and so must be mental entities, not the 'images' printed on our bodies: *cf.* II, 2).

It is hard to see what point Spinoza is making. (a) We might think of 'ideas' such as the idea of *cold*, which Descartes tells us, is 'materially false', in that it misrepresents the quality or power in bodies to which 'coldness' really refers (*A.G.*, p. 84; *cf.* Cottingham, p. 11). But if the idea of cold is materially false, that is only because it is *not* similar to the underlying quality in bodies which coldness really is; and Spinoza says of the ideas involved in knowledge from signs that they *are* similar to things (i.e. presumably, to the things they are ideas *of*). (b) He may be referring back to the end of the preceding scholium at *E* II, 40S1, where he has remarked that those who have been frequently struck by a particular sensible characteristic of a thing (e.g. the posture of men, or their risibility, or rationality, or two-footedness and featherlessness) will understand by the name of the thing ('Man') a being which has that characteristic. Here we may suppose that the 'ideas' (or mental pictures) which come to be formed *are* 'similar to the things', in that the idea-picture presents a likeness of its subject matter. One who has such an idea will say, e.g., that man is a featherless biped, and that statement might reasonably be called a piece of 'knowledge from signs', insofar as it is merely the speaker's resolve to use the word 'man' in a certain way. (c) The point might cut a little deeper. Statements like 'Man is a featherless biped' purport to give the essence of man, and the reason why they fail in that regard may precisely be that the 'ideas' associated with them *are* similar to the things represented. Less obscurely: the essence of a physical complex such as man cannot be rendered in terms of the characteristics of the thing which are most salient to the senses (and which could figure in 'ideas' of the thing, causing those ideas to be 'similar' to it). The essence of a complex thing must be stated in terms of its fine structure and the relations among its minute parts. (Thus a purported account of the essence of a physical complex, if couched in terms of the sensorily obtrusive features of it, would turn out to be at best a triviality, indicating only how the speaker employed a certain word (*cf.* III, 3).)

After illustrating 'knowledge from signs' in this cryptic way, Spinoza exacerbates the difficulties by sending us back to the long scholium at *E* II, 18S. Part of that scholium deals with *words*:

> Hence we can clearly understand why the mind from the thought of one thing falls to thinking of another which bears no resemblance (*similitudinem*) to the former; for example, from the thought of the word '*pomum*' a Roman will immediately fall to thinking of the fruit, which bears no resemblance to the articulate sound '*pomum*', nor has anything in common with it, save that the body of the man was frequently affected by these two things, i.e. the man has frequently heard the word '*pomum*' when he has seen the fruit; and so everyone is led from one thought to another, as habit has ordered the images of things in his body.

But despite the reference here to words, the passage is simply irrelevant to 'knowledge from signs'. Its point is merely that the perception or thought of X (here, as it happens, the hearing or thinking of the word '*pomum*') will trigger in A the thought of a dissimilar object Y (here, an apple) if A's body has been affected by X and Y together. The same thesis could readily be illustrated by an example in which words did not feature at all.

The scholium at *E* II, 18 goes on, however, to make a further point, though one which fits in more neatly with the analysis of 'vagrant experience' than with 'knowledge from signs'. A soldier seeing a hoof-mark in the sand, Spinoza says, will immediately think of a rider, and then of war; a farmer, seeing the hoof-mark, will think of a ploughman and a field. The same sensory stimulus will set in train different sequences of thought in the two minds, because of an underlying difference in the two bodies, which have become conditioned to distinct sequences of image-formation. Spinoza might be taken here to be warning against certain (inductive) inference patterns, by which we fallaciously conclude that when one of a group of features is present, another is present as well ('Since that is a hoof-mark, a rider has passed by'). Knowledge-claims based upon such an inference-pattern would have to be discounted (*cf.* III, 3); but there is no reason to say that such 'knowledge' prominently involved signs of an arbitrary kind. (The passage is also interesting in that it shows Spinoza defying his own pronouncement that mind and body do not interact (*cf.* VI, 3), and has him locating the source of error in the fact of our embodiment (*cf.* II, 3).)

Words

Although the nexus between language and 'knowledge from signs' proves hard to trace, Spinoza's observations on words are not confined to that topic. It may be instructive to take brief note of them.

The *DIE* contains a sombre warning against words:

> Since words are part of the imagination – that is, since we form many conceptions just as they are arranged at random (*vage*) in the memory from some dispositions of the body – so it may not be doubted that words, equally with the imagination, can be the cause of many serious errors, unless we guard carefully against them. (*G* II, p. 33)

As an example of the deceptiveness of language, Spinoza argues that concepts which are really affirmative are rendered by negative words (e.g. 'infinite'). Spinoza is right in saying that one cannot determine whether a concept is affirmative or negative by seeing whether its expression contains a negative particle (as Frege also was to observe: *cf. Kenny* (2), p. 135). But if that test is inadequate, how *is* the distinction to be drawn?

In characterising certain ideas or concepts as affirmative, Spinoza may be putting forward a claim about the *origin* of such ideas: in some sense, they are *a priori*. Consider the idea of infinity, as applied to God (or what Robert Nozick calls 'the unlimited': *Nozick*, p. 600). For the empiricist Hume, that idea is a complication of several 'simple' ideas, each of which is acquired by abstracting from experience; by 'magnifying, compounding, augmenting and diminishing' these simple ideas, the idea of infinity is formed (*Enquiry Concerning the Human Understanding*, I, 2 xiv). Descartes by contrast denied in the *Third Meditation* that the idea of infinity (*sc.* of this type of infinity) can be concocted in any such way:

> I must not think that my conception of the infinite has come about, not through a proper idea, but by a denial of the finite – as I conceive of rest and darkness by way of the denial of motion and light; on the contrary, I clearly understand that there is more reality in an infinite than in a finite substance, and that therefore in a way my primary concept (*perceptionem*) is rather of the infinite than of the finite – rather of God, than of myself. (*A.G.*, p. 85)

Ordinary language, then, may be held to be misleading insofar as it assigns negative names to affirmative ideas, and so encourages a mistaken theory of how such ideas originate in us.

A word may camouflage, not only the origins of an idea, but its inner *content*. Spinoza claims that words are devised 'according to the pleasure and notions of the common people, so that they are nothing more than the signs of things as they are in the imagination, and not as they are in the understanding' (*G* II, p. 33). One of his examples is the word 'immortal', also negative in form, and surrounded by a penumbra of associations with ideas of 'life' and 'dying'. In speaking of immortality, we may be led to confound the eternity of the mind, of which we are obscurely conscious, with mere unending duration or continuance of existing (*E* V, 34CS; *cf.* IX, 3).

Words may betray us, not only as to the sources and contents of our ideas, but as to the range of the *possible*. We can devise sentences which are grammatically acceptable and which do not have the form of a contradiction, even when the situation the sentences purport to describe cannot obtain in reality. 'When we know the nature of body, we cannot imagine an infinite fly; when we know the nature of the soul, we cannot imagine it as square, *though anything may be expressed verbally*' (*DIE*, *G* II, p. 22).

The *Ethics* also emphasises that we must consult the 'nature of things', and not mere words, if we are to avoid *self-deception*. In the Definitions of the Affects in *Ethics* III, Spinoza analyses *favour* ('*favor*') as 'love towards one who has benefited the other' (Definition 19), and *indignation* ('*indignatio*') as 'hatred towards one who has injured the other' (Definition 20). In the 'Explanation' which is tacked on the Definition 20, Spinoza adds:

> I know that these names (*nomina*) mean something else in common use. But my purpose is not to explain the meaning of words, but the nature of things, and to indicate them by words whose usual meaning is not wholly averse to the meaning I want to put on them.

Spinoza does not say in what respects his use of 'indignation' differs from the customary one, and comes closer to the 'nature' of the phenomenon. But three possibilities suggest themselves:

(a) Indignation is not normally reckoned to be a species of *hatred*, but only of some milder emotion.

(b) Indignation is regarded as a vicarious or disinterested attitude: we do not think that if A is indignant at B's conduct towards C, that A must feel some sentiment or attachment towards C (even if only that of judging himself similar to C), or some dislike or aversion towards B. But, Spinoza claims, the science of the mind shows that such an attitude is impossible (*E* III, 22S).

(c) The ordinary idea of indignation carries with it a distinction between appropriate and inappropriate instances to the reaction. If A discovers that B is not

KNOWLEDGE AND IMAGINATION

'responsible' for his conduct towards *C*, then *A*'s indignation against *B* is out of place. For Spinoza, however, this whole scheme of ideas is a gigantic mistake (*E* III, Preface; *cf.* VII, 8; VIII, 2). Indignation can be righteous, but it cannot be rightful.

3 Vagrant experience

We can distinguish between 'having experience' and 'having *an* experience'. To have an experience is, roughly, to be in a certain (conscious) state, or (consciously) to undergo some happening. To have experience is, still more roughly, to be possessed of a store of memories, usually acquired in and connected with a practical activity. (Sadly, 'experience' is contrasted not only with inexpertness, but also, routinely, with innocence.) The Aristotelian notion of *empeiria* links up with 'having experience'; the positivist notion of *experience* goes to 'having (an or some) experience(s)'.

Spinoza uses *experientia* and its cognates in both ways. When he says (*E* V, 23S) that we feel and experience ('*experimur*') that we are eternal, the first (phenomenological) sense is uppermost in his mind. When he says in the *Tractatus Politicus* (I, 2; *Wernham*, p. 261) that statesmen have produced better work in political theory than philosophers because 'with experience as their mistress, they taught nothing that was inconsistent with practice', he plainly invokes the second (pragmatic) sense.

What is meant by calling experience (in either sense) 'vagrant' or 'fluctuating'? Commentators have regularly maintained that the description is lifted from Bacon's *Novum Organon*. In Aphorism *c* of Book I, Bacon says:

> For experience, when it wanders in its own track is, as I have already remarked, mere groping in the dark, and confounds men rather than instructs them. But when it shall proceed in accordance with a fixed law, in regular order, and without interruption, then may better things be hoped of knowledge.

Bacon is making two points. One is that unless 'experience' is somehow ordered and systematised, it will be a source, not of knowledge, but of error. The other point is that 'experience' does admit of such ordering and systematisation, and can be made to yield knowledge (*cf.* III, 4).

The bare reference to Bacon does not succeed, however, in pinning down what Spinoza meant. I suggest that he may have had some or all of the following points in view:

(a) He could mean that the propositions we accept on the basis of 'experience' are subject to change in truth-value, and hence are cognitively undependable. ('Proposition' here has the sense preferred in *Geach* (3), p. 25) In *Ep.* 56, Spinoza says that what can be contradicted is more akin to a falsehood than to a truth. I may firmly hold the proposition 'Peter is alive' to be true, he says, because of having seen Peter yesterday; but if you report having seen Peter unconscious yesterday, and say that you believe him to be dead, then 'Peter is alive' becomes dubious. A proposition known, not by hearsay or perception, but by reason, is in contrast not subject to a change from truth to falsehood: it is necessarily and eternally true (*E* II, 44, with C2).

(b) Bacon was impressed by the 'dullness, incompetency, and deceptions of the senses', and may have communicated these misgivings to Spinoza. Pointing out that the human sense organs are too insensitive to detect the workings of the minute ingredients which make up grossly observable bodies, Bacon lamented that we miss 'the more subtle changes of form in the parts of coarser substances, which men commonly call alteration, though it is in truth local motion through exceedingly small spaces' (*Novum Organon* I, Aphorism 1; *cf.* II, xxxviii). Now Spinoza, skilled in the craft of lensmaking, was well aware that these native deficiencies can be compensated for by optical (and other) instruments. So sense-experience can be said to 'wander' in that its range can be varied by the use of tools.

(c) More generally, the character of our conscious experience (in the phenomenological sense) notoriously depends on the nature, disposition, and aptitudes of our bodies, and on the surrounding conditions in our environment. Descartes had recited some of the common sceptical cases in the *Meditations*: thus, a tower may look round when seen from afar, but square when viewed closer up (*A.G.*, p. 113). Spinoza went so far as to say that the ideas we have of external bodies 'indicate the constitution of our own bodies rather than the nature of external ones' (*E* II, 16C2). This might seem to mean that the sensory reports of 'normal' perceivers in 'normal' environments are bound – just because our bodies are parties to the transaction – to be erroneous (but *cf.* III, 5). On a better reading, Spinoza is noting that our constitutional infirmities cause us all to misapprehend other bodies systematically in certain respects (e.g., we must perceive them as bitter, sweet, pungent or insipid, when they are none of these things (*E* I, Appendix)) and that the episodic derangements to which we are all subject may cause us to misapprehend even the characters with which (other) bodies may truly be endowed.

This gives another sense in which experience – or at least *sense-experience* – may be said to be 'vagrant'.

(d) Experience (in the 'pragmatic' sense) can be crystallised in adages, rules, and generalisations. But these formulas will not comprise scientific knowledge insofar as they hold only 'for the most part' (*cf.* I, 1). Spinoza, as we have seen, concedes the necessity for such rough-hewn 'truths': 'Man would perish of hunger and thirst if he would not eat or drink until he had obtained a perfect proof that food and drink would do him good' (*Ep.* 56). Nevertheless, they 'wander' in that they cannot be counted as stable, scientific knowledge.

Some of these inescapable, if unscientific, generalities are precepts or rules of *conduct*; others are (at least on the surface) inductively grounded statements of *fact*. Among the precepts, consider the rule laid down by Jesus: 'if a man strikes you on the right cheek, turn to him the left also'. In thinking over this rule, Spinoza says, we must take into account 'who the speaker was, what was the occasion, and to whom were the words addressed' (*cp. Nicomachean Ethics*, 1106b4). If we do, we can see that Jesus' rule applies only within certain limits: it is fitted 'to men who were oppressed, who lived in a corrupt commonwealth on the brink of ruin, where justice was neglected' (*G* III, p. 89). As to the inductive generalisations: if I have seen only short-tailed sheep, I will draw the conclusion that sheep have short tails. But then I shall be astonished when I first see the long-tailed Moroccan sheep (*ST* II, 3, ii). When (as here) I make an inductive extrapolation which is based on a small, localised, or untypical sample, I reason by what Bacon disparagingly called 'induction by simple enumeration' (*Novum Organon* I, Aphorisms lxix,cv). Spinoza probably thought that 'induction by simple enumeration' was pervasive in ordinary life: the soldier who infers a rider's presence from seeing a hoof-mark, the farmer who concludes from the same shape that a ploughman has passed by (*E* II, 18S; *cf.* III, 2), may both be guilty of reasoning in this way.

There are some hints in Spinoza of a theory which would *assimilate* generalisations through simple enumeration *to* precepts and prescriptions. Under the heading of 'vagrant experience', Spinoza enters such propositions as 'The dog is a barking animal' and 'Man is a rational animal'; and having done so, he implies that these items are pieces of *practical* knowledge (*DIE, G* II, p. 11). Elsewhere, discussing universal terms such as 'dog' and 'man', he says that the principal function of such words (or of the ideas they signify) is to expedite classification and recall: these are 'certain modes of thought for retaining things more firmly and easily, and for calling them into our minds when we wish, or for keeping them in mind' (*CM* I, 1, iii). Because these 'modes of thought' are practical devices, we have to distinguish them from 'ideas' in a more honorific sense, i.e. from the 'conceptions of the mind, which it forms because it is a thinking thing' (*E* II, Definition 3). (When modes of thought arise, not through the mind's autonomous activity, but in part through the seepage of *bodily* influences, 'ideas' in this strict sense are not found: *cf.* II, 3; III, 2). Spinoza tells us that these modes, in that they are not 'ideas', cannot be *true* or *false*, but only *good* or *bad*: thus the choice between Plato's definition of man as a featherless biped, and Aristotle's definition of him as a rational animal, is a question of convenience, not of knowledge (*CM*, I, 1, viii; *cf.* III, 2). In effect, then, Spinoza treats these 'definitions' as rules of conduct: 'The dog is a barking animal' means something like 'If you hear a bark, expect a dog'. If (other) inductive generalisations (from simple enumeration) are like this, then (i) they cannot provide the materials for knowledge, since they do not even rise to the level of truth-or-falsehood; (ii) they are 'vagrant', in that as practical precepts they are of limited and unreliable use.

4 Experience in science and metaphysics

Bacon, as we have seen, takes a harsh but not a despairing view of experience: if corrected and regularised, it can become a source of knowledge. This is part of the meaning of one of his delightful parables. There are three kinds of philosopher: one is like the ant, which gathers and heaps up grain bit by bit; another is like the spider, which spins its web out of its own entrails; the third and wisest is the bee, which takes its materials from without, but transforms them within itself, and so creates honey (*Novum Organon* I, xcv). Bacon condemns the naive empiricism of the ant, and the dogmatic rationalism of the spider. Query: was Spinoza spider-minded?

The quick answer is that he *was*: he declares that 'vagrant experience' falls to the lot of 'imagination', and that 'imagination' is the cause of error and falsity. So how can experience yield knowledge? On the other hand, 'experience' does seem to find (at least) a tolerated place in his philosophy. He often invokes it to support conclusions which he claims to have proven by reason alone; and if 'experience' could *only* give inadequate ideas, how could it corroborate theorems which reason has shown to be true (*Fløistad*, p. 47)?

A closer look at his description of 'vagrant experience' is

needed. In the *DIE*, Spinoza speaks of 'vagrant experience which is not determined by the intellect (*experientia, quae non determinatur ab intellectu*)' (G II, p. 10). Syntactically, this is ambiguous. Is the relative clause restrictive or explicative? That is: (a) does the sentence mean that *all* experience is vagrant, undetermined by the intellect? or (b) does it mean that there *is* experience which is of this kind (but also, impliedly, experience which is *not*)? Bacon marks an emphatic distinction between 'simple experience' and 'experience duly ordered and digested, not bungling or erratic' (*Novum Organon* I, Aphorism lxxxii). Does Spinoza go along with this?

At first sight, it seems not. Spinoza minimises the importance of experience in philosophical and scientific matters in an early letter to Simon De Vries (*Ep.* 10):

> We only need experience in the case of whatever cannot be deduced from the definition of a thing, as for instance the existence of modes; for this cannot be deduced from the definition of a thing. But we do not need experience in the case of those things whose existence is not distinguished from their essence, and therefore follows from their definition. Indeed, no experience will ever be able to teach us this: for experience does not teach us the essence of things; the utmost it can do is to determine our mind so that it thinks of certain essences of things only.

Experience is given two assignments here. It alone informs us of the existence of contingent things – of those beings whose existence cannot be deduced from their essence. And it can 'determine' the mind to think of 'certain essences', without, however, teaching what those essences are. The notion seems to be that certain observations may, with luck or insight, point us to general scientific truths. By observing the parabolic path of a cannonball in flight, we might discover that the motions of small bodies near the earth's surface follow mathematically expressible patterns, normally concealed from us by the apparent randomness of natural motion. Experience alone could not tell us this, and even in describing the path of the ball as parabolic, we are abstracting from the irregularities of real motion (*cf.* Descartes, *Principles* II, 37; *A.G.*, p. 216; *Caton*, p. 87). Furthermore, the mathematical formula we have arrived at goes beyond the senses in other ways: it is inherently general, applying to indefinitely many cases beside the one we had witnessed; and it might assert a systematic connection between properties of bodies – say, acceleration and mass – which experience would find to be only coincidentally joined.

Thus far, then, experience seems to work only at the margins of knowledge. But in fact Spinoza awards it a more important, though not perhaps an exalted, position. For one thing, he invokes it in support of conclusions which he takes himself to have demonstrated on other grounds. A case in point is the scholium to *E* III, 2, in which Spinoza admits that his refutation of the doctrine of mind/body interaction will not carry conviction 'unless I prove it by experience'. He refers to such commonplace facts as that 'if the body be sluggish the mind is then not fitted for thinking'. Again, at *E* IV, 35S, experience is summoned to confirm the theorem that 'insofar as men live in conformity with the guidance of reason, thus far only do they always necessarily agree in nature'. Experience also figures in the destruction of rival views: at *E* IV, 39S, Spinoza cites it in order to refute the notion that a man dies only when his body becomes a corpse.

The relations between experience on the one hand, and science and philosophy on the other, are not uncomplicated. Spinoza requires that scientific postulates which are self-consistent but not self-evident should be established by ('*constare*') experience (*E* II, 17 CDS). But experience is only pertinent if it does not support beliefs which are inconsistent with philosophically demonstrated results. In refuting Zeno's arguments against motion, Spinoza repudiates the example of Diogenes, who appealed to the fact that we see things move (*PPD* II, 6S): the work of unravelling the sophisms must be done by reason alone.

Finally, in political theory, experience of the kind which is practical knowledge is extremely valuable; we learn more about the governance of men from Machiavelli than from Plato (*TP* 1, 2; *Wernham*, p. 261; *cp. Nichomachean Ethics*, 1181a1–18).

In various ways, then, Spinoza admits that experience can make a contribution to knowledge in science, philosophy, and the study of human nature. But is this all? There is reason to think it may not be: like Cinderella, experience seems to emerge from obscurity in order to play a dazzling and unexpected role. The crucial text to look at is from the *Tractatus Theologico-Politicus*:

> Anyone who wishes to make men believe or disbelieve anything which is not self-evident (*per se notum*) must win their assent by deducing his doctrine from common ground, and appealing either to experience or to reason; i.e. either to their sense-experience of what happens in nature (*ex rebus quas per sensus experti sunt in natura contingere*) or to self-evident

intellectual axioms. The appeal to experience may convince a man; but unless the experience is such as to be understood clearly and distinctly, it will not itself be able to influence his understanding and dispel its doubts as effectively as a deduction of the doctrine from intellectual axioms alone . . . especially if the question is a spiritual one and outwith the sphere of the senses. (*TTP*; *Wernham*, pp. 99–101)

What we have to consider is whether the *a posteriori* proof of God's existence attached to *E* I, 11, is a case in which sense-experience, clearly and distinctly understood, is invoked to assist the understanding of a spiritual matter. Spinoza relies on the fact that finite things exist (or, more specifically, that *we* exist) in order to prove the reality of an absolutely infinite being. In calling the proof *a posteriori*, he might mean only that it proceeds from premisses which involve an 'effect' (our existence) to a conclusion which states the cause of that effect (God's existence). This would not commit him to any view about the type of knowledge which was involved in asserting the premiss. But he could also mean that the premiss was *known a posteriori*, unlike the premisses employed in his other demonstrations of God's existence; and to say that it was *known* in that way would be to suggest that it was derived from experience. But that 'experience' would presumably answer to the description given in the *Tractatus*.

If we take the latter view, then we will be able to see a great deal of the *Ethics* as consisting of empirical knowledge. If it is known *a posteriori*, or through experience, that we *exist*, then surely it must be known in the same way that man *thinks*, or that each of us feels that a certain body is affected in many ways, or that we perceive nothing except bodies and modes of thought. But these facts, as we have noted (I, 2), are all laid down as axioms in *Ethics* II. Perhaps Spinoza believed that the manner of verifying these axioms through experience was of such a kind as to qualify them as certainties. For example, the claim that finite modes exist could be based on the fact that the proposition 'I exist' can never be thought or uttered without being true (*DIE*, G II, p. 20, note *u*). Or again, take the proposition that 'Man thinks'. This might be held to be indubitable, in that no sceptic could pointfully doubt or deny it to an audience, without assuming that those whom he addressed were thinking beings like himself. The axiom that we feel a certain body to be affected in many ways is equally easy to prove: anyone who reads the words in which it is printed, or hears them spoken aloud, is acquainted with experiences of the kind which make the axiom true. Finally, the claim that we can only experience things as modes of thought or of extension is rendered certain by the impossibility of imagining things as perceived in any other forms. In all these ways, Spinoza could try to defend as rationally certain what he also would admit to be empirically known.

The position just sketched in is highly speculative, and it is hard to see how Spinoza could dogmatise so confidently if he himself thought that his system rested largely upon empirical knowledge. The passage from the *Tractatus*, after all, *contrasts* experience with deductive knowledge, and admits only that 'clearly and distinctly understood' experience will suffice, like a proof from intellectual axioms, to quiet doubt and to win conviction. There is no hint that the 'intellectual axioms' might express 'clear and distinct' experience themselves. Nor, as I have pointed out, is it necessary to assume that the '*a posteriori*' proof at *E* I, 11 relies upon empirically obtained information: that description of the proof can bear another meaning. Finally, even if it seems obvious to us that the axioms of Spinoza's system are not necessary or self-evident, it cannot be assumed that he observed this himself (*cf*. I, 2). The fact is, I believe, that Spinoza was prepared to find an honourable place for experience within his scheme, and thought that when its findings were criticised and corrected, they need not yield only inadequate ideas. But he would have recoiled from the suggestion that even clear and distinct experience provided the starting points of his theorising. He is not altogether the spider; but he is more the spider than the bee.

5 *Common notions*

'Knowledge of the first kind' is, or is deeply tainted with, error, but 'knowledge of the second kind' or 'reason' is a thing of a different order. In the *Ethics*, Spinoza tells us that this kind of knowledge derives 'from our possessing common notions and adequate ideas of the properties of things' (*E* II, 40S2). Since the business of reason has to do, at least partly, with 'common notions', we can begin by asking what 'common notions' are.

The term, as Spinoza was well aware, can be applied to axioms generally: Euclid's axioms were traditionally accorded that name. But Spinoza seems to give it a more restricted sense when he first speaks of 'common notions' at *E* II, 38. There he characterises common notions as ideas of that which is common to everything, and which is equally in the part and in the whole. The demonstration which ensues makes it clear that he is referring to the characteristics which are common to all *bodies*, whether simple or compound. Though the sensory perception of external bodies is generally distorted, and reflects the constitution and temper of the perceiver's body rather than an outer reality (*E* II, 16C2; *cf.* III, 3), Spinoza considers that this is not the case when, as here, the perceived characteristic is common both to external bodies and to the bodies of those who perceive them. Given that perceptions of this class are exempt from distorting influences, the ideas we form of the underlying common characteristics cannot fail to be adequate. The ubiquity of these characteristics implies also that our 'notions' of them are 'common' in another way: since all bodies 'agree' in certain respects, *all* thinkers must have adequate notions of them (*E* II, 38C).

In Lemma 2 to Axiom 2 of the second set of Axioms in Part II of the *Ethics*, Spinoza mentions some of the characteristics, the ideas of which are common notions. All bodies are modes of *Extension*; all bodies can move more *quickly* or more *slowly*; all can be *moved* or come to *rest*. It is plausible to assume that both this and the next set of axioms are Spinozistic 'common notions'. Connected with them, and also among the sources of knowledge of the second kind, are the 'adequate ideas of the properties of things' (*E* II, 40S2), by which Spinoza apparently means ideas of the characteristics which belong specifically to *human* bodies and to certain external bodies which routinely interact with them (*E* II, 39). As Parkinson points out (*Parkinson* (1), p. 165), these 'adequate ideas' seem to concern only certain systems *within* Nature, and not Nature as a whole; thus they belong, not to physics as such, but to the special sciences such as physiology.

This brief description of the common notions gives rise to three questions about the nature of reasoned knowledge. First, are the common notions *a priori* or not? Second, since the common notions seem to relate only to Extension, and since reason proceeds from common notions, how can there be reasoned knowledge of Thought, as there appears to be in *Ethics* II and III? Third, how can the knowledge imparted in *Ethics* I be reasoned, as Spinoza suggests it is, when it has nothing specifically to do with the natural sciences (*Fløistad*, pp. 54ff.)?

(1) The concepts involved in framing the common notions are plainly not innate in any crude sense: if Spinoza cannot exactly say that experience *induces* us to form them (since that would contravene his denial of interaction: VI, 3), he would still have to concede that the experience of outer bodies *occasions* these ideas to arise in us. There is thus an empirical element in the common

notions. More, our knowledge of these notions is (startlingly) said to be 'clearer' than our knowledge of such philosophical truths as the infinity and eternity of God, (*E* II, 47S). Our power to visualise bodies (a power stemming from the imagination, and ultimately from the fact that we ourselves are embodied) makes it easier for us to grasp the most general features of bodies; whereas God's infinity and eternity, being essentially undepictable, can be seized only by the intellect (which holds itself aloof from the body: II, 3).

These considerations do not, however, lead Spinoza to say that our knowledge of the common notions is empirical. The truth of at least some of them is assumed to be evident, known through itself: after attempting to prove the Law of Inertia, Spinoza remarks that in any case it is *per se notum* (*E* II, Lemma 3C; *cf.* Curley (2), p. 52). Since this Law is presumably to be numbered among the common notions, Spinoza must suppose that like it, they too are known through themselves. (Thus, as before (I, 2), he sees incontestable knowledge where others discern only empirical truth or falsehood.) Yet if that is his assumption, then he owes us an explanation of the fact that error concerning the common notions has arisen. How is such error possible, given that the common notions are *per se nota* (*Curley* (2), p. 54)? And how can it be that men continue to reject the truth about Physics, even after it has been thrust upon them? This cannot be explained merely as the effect of 'prejudice' or the 'imagination', since *every* sensory experience is supposed to bring these ideas home to us in their full adequacy (*cf.* III, 4). Spinoza fails both to explain how the common notions are known, and to account for the fact that we can go wrong about them (*Caton*, p. 136; *cf.* II, 3).

(2) If there were 'common notions' relating to Thought and its modes, then they would figure in a scientific psychology exactly as the other common notions figure in physics. Spinoza clearly believes in (and thinks he has discovered) a science of the mental, which would treat ideas and affects, actions and appetites, as subject to determinate laws. These phenomena, he avers, should be studied by the psychologist in the way that the physicist investigates the causes and properties of bodies (*E* III, Preface). But where are the principles of psychology to be found? *Ethics* II, which is devoted to 'the origin and nature of the mind', begins with certain *axioms* which ostensibly give such general psychological principles; and *Ethics* III, which works out the laws governing the affects, adds a number of *postulates* which seem to be co-ordinate with the physical postulates set forth after the 13th proposition of *Ethics* II. Assuming that these are meant to be the

starting points of Spinoza's science of Psychology, would he have them described as 'common notions', discoverable by 'reason'? It seems so. True, he implies at *E* II, 38D that the 'common notions' pertain only to the natural sciences; but that implication arises only because he is focusing narrowly on the natural sciences at that point. There is no need to suppose that he would wish to deny that psychology had its own proprietary 'common notions'. *E* II, 40S1 notes that 'there are other axioms *or common notions*' than those which are peculiar to Extension; and the comment at *E* II, 44C2, that common notions 'explain *(explicant)* those things which are common to everything', may contain an oblique reference to common notions of *both* types (Fløistad, p. 56).

This conclusion leaves open the question whether Spinoza envisaged the scientific psychology he was presenting as a general science of Life or Sentience, or as a more circumscribed science of the Human Mind (*Parkinson* (1), p. 77). Under the attribute of Extension, he seems to discern both a general physics of 'the Infinite Modes of Motion-and-Rest' and 'the aspect *(facies)* of the whole Universe' (*Ep.* 64), and subordinate to that, a special science of physiology. Are the principles of his psychology supposed to be analogous to those of his physics, or to those of his physiology?

In entitling *Ethics* II 'Of the Nature and Origin of the *Mind*', Spinoza may be implying a distinction between the *mind* (which is peculiarly human) and the *soul* (which is not) (*cf. Ep.* 2; Descartes, *H.R.* II, p. 53, p. 210; Leibniz, *Monadology*, section 82). In the brief foreward to *Ethics* II, he reinforces this suggestion by saying that the chapter will concentrate on those things which 'can lead us, as if by the hand, to the knowledge of the *human* mind and its highest blessedness'. And if we inspect the Axioms of *Ethics* II themselves, we find that the first, second, fourth and fifth obviously concern *human* beings, while the third, which speaks of 'affects of the *spirit (animus)*', rather than of the *soul (anima)*, readily lends itself to that construction.

Against this, however, is the evidence of *E* II, 13S, which says that the demonstrations made 'to this point *(hucusque)*' – that is, the first 13 theorems of *Ethics* II – do not pertain more to men than to other individuals, 'which are all, although in different degrees *(diversis gradibus)*, animate *(animata)*' (i.e. ensouled).

If on the strength of *E* II, 13S, we turn back to the preceding demonstrations, expecting to find that they outline a Psychology of Life or Sentience, we shall be disappointed. Some of the propositions set forth there could encompass both human and non-human life-forms (e.g. *E* II, 7); but others are explicitly about the human mind (e.g. *E* II, 11). On balance, it seems to me that Spinoza neither has, nor purports to have, a general science of psychology: he cares neither for brutes nor angels, but only for humankind (*cf*. VI, 6). The result is, however, to leave a curious gap in his scheme:

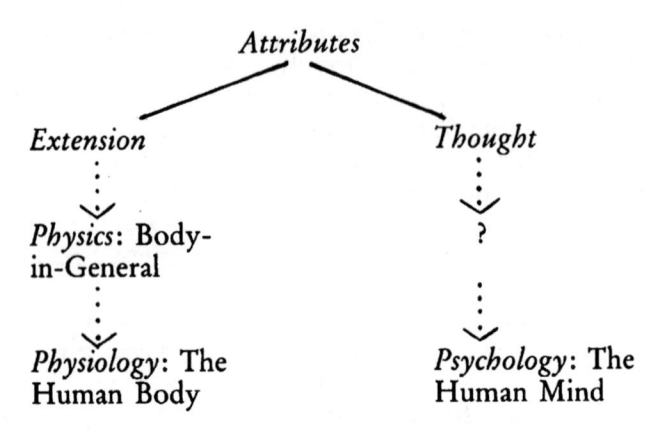

```
                       Attributes
                      /          \
               Extension          Thought
                  ⋮                 ⋮
                  ⋎                 ⋎
          Physics: Body-             ?
          in-General
                  ⋮                 ⋮
                  ⋎                 ⋎
          Physiology: The    Psychology: The
          Human Body         Human Mind
```

(3) Whatever may be the case with *Psychology*, is *Philosophy* also known, or known only, by Reason? The argument is made that the 'common notions' which Reason is said to exploit are too lowly to be the servitors of philosophy: if physics and psychology are in the charge of Reason, then philosophy cannot have been committed to it (*Fløistad*, p. 57). Against this we have Spinoza's statement at *E* V, 36CS that the First Part of the *Ethics* consitituted knowledge of the second kind. Admittedly, *E* II says that Reason deals with 'common notions'; admittedly too, *E* II seems to restrict the 'common notions' to the principles of non-metaphysical science. But if we bear in mind that there was traditionally a more ample sense of 'common notion' (as e.g. at *G* III, 252–3) which is certainly generous enough to take in metaphysical and non-metaphysical axioms alike, we will not be deterred from concluding that Philosophy can be known by Reason.

The passage at *E* V, 36CS on which this answer rests is, however, very controversial. In particular, it raises the troubling issue of Spinoza's distinction between Reason on the one hand, and intuitive science on the other. That will be our next topic.

6 *The distinction between reason and intuition*

There are really three issues here: the nature of the distinction in the *DIE*; the nature of the corresponding distinction in the latter

Ethics; and the relationship between the two pairs of distinctions (*Carr*, p. 243). My concern in this section is selective: what is the teaching of the *Ethics* on this matter? Is Spinoza rightly said to have offered there a distinction between knowledge of 'truths of a general nature' versus 'insights into the essence of individual things' (*MacIntosh*, p. 47)? (On this construral, Spinoza's 'reason' is close cousin to Maimonides' 'prophecy'. Because both distinctions would turn on the difference in the range of objects covered by the terms distinguished, we can call this the 'range' interpretation.)

The 'range' interpretations

While some considerations support this theory, the preponderence of the evidence is against it.

Consider first *Reason*. At *E* V, 36CS, Spinoza speaks of 'universal knowledge, which I have said is of the second kind (*cognitione universali, quam secundi generis esse dixi*)'. Why is Reason 'universal'? One suggestion is that it is called 'universal' because its objects are laws, and laws are universal in form (*Curley* (2)). We have been told at *E* II, 40S2 that Reason connects with 'common notions' and 'adequate ideas of the properties of things'; and these might reasonably be equated with the 'laws' which the *DIE* says are 'inscribed' in the attributes and infinite modes 'as if in their true codes', (and) according to which 'all individual things take place and are arranged' (*G* II, p. 37).

As for *intuitive science*, *E* V, 36CS describes that as 'the knowledge of particular things, which I have called intuitive, or of the third kind (*rerum singularium cognitio, quam tertii generis appellavi*)'. In *E* II, 40S2, this kind of knowledge is said to 'proceed from an adequate idea of the formal essence of certain attributes of God to an adequate idea of the essence of things (*rerum*)'. The knowledge that the human mind depends on God, cited at *E* V, 36CS as a specimen of what can be known by intuition, may be a case of insight into the essence of an 'individual' or 'particular' thing.

One objection to this attempt to demarcate separate spheres for reason and intuition relies on an example given in the *DIE* and repeated at *E* II, 40S2. This is the case, already encountered, of the Rule of Three (III, 2). Spinoza says:

> I shall explain all these things (*sc.* the kinds of knowledge) through the example of one thing. Let there be three numbers given, through which a fourth is to be derived which will be to

the third as the second is to the first. Merchants do not hesitate to multiply the second and third together, because they have not yet forgotten the things they heard from a teacher without any proof, or because they have often experienced it (*experti sunt*) in the most elementary numbers, or from the power of the demonstration of the 19th theorem in the 7th Book of Euclid, that is from the common property of proportionals. But in the most elementary numbers there is need of none of these things. For example, given the number 1, 2, 3, no-one fails to see that the fourth proportional number is 6, and this much more clearly, because from that ratio which in a single intuition (*uno intuito*) we see the first has to the second, we conclude (*concludimus*) the fourth.

Whatever else this passage may be saying, it certainly commits Spinoza to the claim that some things can be known by reason and by intuition alike (*Carr*, p. 244). (It need not, however, commit him to holding that '6 is to 3 as 2 is to 1' is knowable in both those ways.) The same result holds elsewhere as well. In the *First Dialogue* of the *Short Treatise* (G I, p. 28), 'Intellect' (which stands in for 'intuition') makes only one pronouncement: 'I, for my part, consider Nature only in its totality as infinite, and supremely perfect, but you, if you have any doubts about it, ask Reason, and she will tell you'. And 'Reason' obligingly sets out a metaphysical proof of what 'Intellect' has seen non-discursively. Most significantly of all, *E* V, 36CS makes it clear that reason and intuition have overlapping spheres of objects: 'although in the First Part I have shown in general that all things (and consequently too the human mind) depend on God with respect both to essence and to existence, that demonstration, albeit legitimate and placed beyond the risk of doubt, does not affect our mind in the same way as when *the conclusion in question* (*id ipsum*) is derived from the very essence of some particular thing which we say depends on God'. (To the same effect is *E* II, 47S.)

Accepting this, how then do we explain the apparent contrast made at *E* V, 36CS between (reasoned) *universal* knowledge and (intuitive) knowledge of *particulars*? This proves to be a complex question; possible answers are outlined later in this section, and in the one which follows (7).

The 'ordering' interpretation

Another view, advocated recently by Carr, denies that the *Ethics*' distinction between reason and intuition hinges on a contrast

KNOWLEDGE AND IMAGINATION

between their objects. Instead it emphasises those passages in which Spinoza insists that true knowledge always advances from cause to effect. Carr puts his interpretation this way:

> What is important about knowledge is that it is rooted in causes and moves towards effects. Since the ultimate cause of everything is to be found in substance, or God, intuitive knowledge must have its source in attributes of God. Rational knowledge arises when we infer from the nature of dependent things and not from the nature of substance. It starts at the wrong place and it moves in the wrong direction. . . . Intuitive knowledge is an *advance from* the formal essence of an attribute *to* the adequate knowledge of the essence of things. . . . There is adequate knowledge arising from our ideas of things; but this knowledge is less than the ideal, according to which 'true science' will always move from cause to effect, from the independent to the dependent, from substance to mode, and from God to finite things. (*Carr*, p. 246)

The 'reason/intuition' distinction, on this view, depends on the nature of the premisses from which the knower starts. Either kind of knowledge may be discursive; both will result in the possession of adequate ideas; some propositions can be known in both ways; together Reason and intuition will be contrasted with imagination, in that they alone comprise knowledge rightly so-called.

The main, and in my view fatal, difficulty with this account is that it compels the conclusion that the philosophical knowledge found in *Ethics* I is not reasoned but intuitive. But that conclusion seems to fly in the face of E V, 36CS, which we have taken to imply the contrary view (III, 5). Expanding on this, we can see three interlinked objections to the 'ordering interpretation':

(a) In Carr's view, E II, 40S2 should imply that rightly-ordered (i.e. intuitive) knowledge of a particular proceeds from an adequate idea of the formal essence of an attribute, to the knowledge of the essence of the particular. And E V, 36CS, which illustrates intuitive knowledge of a particular by citing our knowledge of the conclusion that the human mind is dependent on God, should answer to this general characterisation. But it does not: the conclusion that the human mind is God-dependent seems in E V, 36CS to derive from the knowledge of the *mind's* essence, not from the knowledge of the formal essence of the attribute Thought. In other words, the intuitive knowledge of *that* particular proceeds from the knowledge of the essence of a

81

finite *mode*, not from that of an *attribute's* essence. Moreover, the intuitive knowledge cited in *E* V, 36CS results in the discovery of a *property* of a finite mode (the mind's *dependency*), and not, as Carr would have to say, in the discovery of the *essence* of a finite mode. Thus there is a mismatch between (what Carr takes to be) Spinoza's implicit account of intuitive knowledge of particulars, and (what Carr takes to be) Spinoza's illustration of that general account.

(b) Carr denies our assumption that *E* V, 36CS marks a contrast between reasoned and intuitive knowledge as such. As he reads the passage, it merely contrasts intuitive knowledge *of particulars* with reasoned knowledge *of particulars*, to the detriment of the latter. Hence the statement at *E* V, 36CS tying *Ethics* I to reasoned knowledge can be explained to mean that insofar as *Ethics* I gives knowledge *of particulars*, that knowledge is not intuitive, but only reasoned. This permits us to claim, as Carr wants to do, that *Ethics* I, being rightly ordered, provided *intuitive* knowledge; for we need only add the qualification that the intuitive knowledge found there is *universal*, and does not go directly to particulars.

Such an account leaves it unclear why Spinoza should have wanted to contrast the reasoned knowledge obtained in *Ethics* I with the intuitive knowledge found in *Ethics* V. Presumably Carr would say that, although *Ethics* I provided intuitive knowledge, it failed to give intuitive knowledge of such particular matters as the mind's dependency on God, and yielded (at best) a reasoned knowledge of them. But if in *Ethics* I Spinoza has an intuitive grasp of God and the Divine essence (as the 'ordering interpretation' must assume), then what prevented him from proceeding immediately to particular things as seen in relation to God, and so from acquiring intuitive knowledge of them? Why must intuitive knowledge of particulars wait until *Ethics* V to be discovered, and why must any knowledge of particulars in *Ethics* I be (at best) reasoned? The more natural reading of *E* V, 36CS forces no such question upon us: Spinoza really does seem to be saying that *Ethics* I consists *in its entirety* of reasoned knowledge (reasoned *because* 'universal'); and he really does imply that the particular conclusions we draw out of this knowledge (themselves presumably items of reasoned knowledge) affect our minds far less powerfully than when we attain them by intuition.

(c) Finally, *Ethics* I does not really conform to the guidelines which (Carr thinks) 'rightly ordered' knowledge must follow. In particular, it does not start from the idea of God, or of the formal essence of a Divine attribute. This should not be surprising, in view of Spinoza's statement in the *TTP* that the existence of God is not self-evident to human minds. (*Cp.* also the obscurity in our idea of God noted at *E* II, 47S: III, 5.) The *TTP* warns us that in order to conceive the nature of God clearly and distinctly, we must 'attend to certain very simple notions, which we call common, and must concatenate with them those things which pertain to the divine nature; and then for the first time it will be clear to us that God necessarily exists, and is everywhere, and then at the same time it will appear that everything which we conceive involves the nature of God in itself, and is conceived through the same, and finally that all those things are true which we adequately conceive' (*TTP*; G III, pp. 252–3).

That seems a likely description of the procedure actually followed in *Ethics* I. The necessary existence of God is deduced from a set of axioms or common notions, 'concatenated with' a group of definitions, at least some of which invoke notions which 'pertain to the Divine nature'. But all this meshes far more tightly with *E* II, 40S2's account of *Reason* (as proceeding from 'common notions and adequate ideas of properties') than with what is said there about *intuition*.

A synthesis?

It seems, then, that neither the 'range' interpretation nor the 'ordering' interpretation can reconcile all of Spinoza's statements (or even all those in the *Ethics*) on the 'reason/intuition' distinction. Can a synthesis of the two views do better than either? What follows is an attempt to find such a synthesis.

On this view, the core of truth in the 'range' interpretation is that Reason gives knowledge of universal facts, but does not convey truths about the essences of particular things. (There is thus a real point to the description of reason as 'universal' knowledge, and intuition as 'knowledge of particular things'.) But that is not to say that Reason prescinds from particularity: for while it cannot reach to particular *essences*, it can and does take hold of the *properties* of particulars. On the other hand, the central insight of the 'ordering' interpretation will also be correct: Reason and intuition differ, not in the conclusions they can attain, but in the premisses from which they depart. Thus, if Reason works towards a conclusion about the properties of some particular, it will start from universal truths, in the form of common notions; while if intuition goes in search of the same result, its point of departure will involve a premiss about the essence of a particular thing.

This synthetic interpretation is partly borne out by a reading of *E* II, 44C2D, *E* II, 47S and *E* V, 36CS. The first of these citations holds that the common notions from which Reason starts cannot 'explain the *essence* of any particular thing'. The second avers that the consequences which can be derived from *Ethics* I, 15 ('all things are in, and are conceived through, God') will form ('*formare*') intuitive knowledge. Finally, *E* V, 36CS indicates that the conclusion 'the human mind follows from, and continually depends upon, the Divine nature' – a result which must be taken to state a *property* of a *particular* thing (viz., the human mind) – can be derived *either* from the general theorem at *E* I, 15, *or* from the knowledge of the *essence* of the human mind. If the conclusion is drawn from *E* I, 15 (and so, ultimately, from the common notions which underpin it), then there is *reasoned* knowledge. If on the other hand the conclusion stems from a premiss about the mind's essence (itself *underivable* from common notions, as *E* II, 44C2D declares), then there is *intuitive* knowledge. The implications of a theorem such as *E* I, 15 can then be said to 'form' intuitive knowledge (as *E* II, 47S dictates), in that reflection on them could lead us to perceive alternate bases, 'particular' rather than 'universal', for inferring them (*E* V, 38).

But although this 'synthesis' weaves many strands together, the fabric is soon torn. (a) If intuition goes from knowledge of the essence to knowledge of the properties of a particular, then why is it said at *E* II, 40S2, and again at *E* V, 25D, to proceed from the knowledge of the formal essence of a Divine attribute? (b) If Reason is held to be competent to reach knowledge of *properties* of 'particulars' such as 'the human mind', then why is it unable to acquire knowledge of the *essences* of such things, given that the latter, no less than the former, is expressed in propositions which are law-like and universal in form? (c) Why should the reasoned knowledge found in scientific psychology (which, like any other, draws on common notions (III, 5)), not encroach on the knowledge of the human mind's essence? (This last point is reinforced when we consider that *E* V, 36CS *itself* deduces the 'essence' of this 'particular' from *E* I, 15 and *E* II, 47S – that is, from items of reasoned knowledge.)

Spinoza's confusions seem to me ineradicable, but I think we can do something to mitigate them. Our attempt at synthesis brings out this much: that Spinoza's 'universal/particular' contrast does (*at least*) double duty, and that the problems of understanding him can largely be traced to that fact. What he seems to have done is to have run together (i) the distinction between propositions which are *universal* in form, and propositions which are *singular* in form, and (ii) the distinction between propositions which are *general*, and propositions which are *specific*. The first of these distinctions is illustrated by the pair (i) 'The human mind depends on God' and '*This* human mind depends on God'; the second underlies the difference between (ii) 'All things depend on God' and 'The human mind depends on God'. In *denying* that Reason can know the essences of 'particulars', Spinoza must mean that propositions such as 'The essence of mind *M* is . . . ' cannot be known in that way. In implying that Reason *can* go to 'particular' essences, Spinoza must be holding that Reason is equipped to discover the truth of, e.g., 'The essence of *the human mind* is . . . '.

So much for Reason; but what about intuition? In describing it as the 'knowledge of particular things', Spinoza *could* be awarding it either the discovery of certain *particular* facts ('This mind's essence is . . .') or of certain *specific* facts ('The mind's essence is . . .'). That obscurity is bad enough, but what are we to make of the further suggestion that intuition 'proceeds from' the adequate idea, or knowledge, of the formal essence of a Divine attribute? How can *this* description be fitted together with the (ambiguous) characterisation of intuitive knowledge as going to 'particulars'? Here we begin to broach large issues in Spinoza's metaphysics (issues which will form the subject of the next three chapters); but metaphysical and epistemological issues are so intertwined at this place that it is impossible to try to separate them. In what follows, I want to argue that intuitive knowledge can *both* 'proceed from' the Divine attributes *and* be 'of particular things', providing we assume, as Spinoza encourages us to do, that the Divine attributes are (at least sometimes) concrete universals.

7 *Intuition and the attributes*

We have just seen that Spinoza's 'universal/particular' contrast ravels up two distinctions. Now I want to suggest that it also implicates a third – the distinction between *universals* (e.g. shagginess) and their *instances* (this shaggy pelt).

From Plato onwards, philosophy has seen many efforts to explain (or undo) the contrast between universals and their instances; but one theory – the theory of *concrete universals* – is particularly relevant to our present purpose. Here is Quine's sketch of such a theory for the universal term 'red', which in effect treats it like the singular term 'Caÿster':

By pointing and saying 'This is Caÿster' at various times and places, we progressively improve our listener's understanding as to what portions of space-time we intend our 'Caÿster' to cover; and by pointing and saying 'This is red' at various times and places, we progressively improve our listener's understanding as to what portions of space-time we intend our word 'red' to cover. The regions to which 'red' applies are indeed not continuous with one another as those are to which 'Caÿster' applies, but this surely is an irrelevant detail; 'red' surely is not to be opposed to 'Caÿster', as abstract to concrete, merely because of discontinuity in geometrical shape. The territory of the United States including Alaska is discontinuous, but it is none the less a single concrete object; and so is a bedroom suite, or a scattered deck of cards . . . So why not view 'red' quite on a par with 'Caÿster', as naming a single concrete object extended in space and time? From this point of view, to say that a certain drop is red is to affirm a simple spatio-temporal relation between two concrete objects; the one object, the drop, is a spatio-temporal part of the other, red, just as a certain waterfall is a spatio-temporal part of the Caÿster. (*Quine* (1), p. 69)

The suggestion then is that Spinoza's Divine attributes, like Quine's red, are concrete universals (*cf. Unger*, p. 129). Take the attribute of Extension. On the proposed view, Extension (like red) is a concrete particular (though unlike red, not confined to *portions* of space-time). But Extension (like red) is also universal in the sense that to be extended (red) is to be a *part* of Extension (red). Spinoza says that the 'finite modes' can neither be nor be conceived without the attributes (*DIE*, G II, p. 37). This translates into the claims that (a) a finite body cannot be without Extension, in that it must be a part of it, and (b) a finite body cannot be conceived without Extension, in that to characterise it as extended is to relate it to that whole (*cp.* IV, 3). The puzzle why Spinoza uses abstract nouns like 'Extension' to refer to what he plainly regards as concrete and dynamic individuals falls away (*Geach* (4)). Yet Spinoza will be free to describe the attributes as 'universals' (as in fact he does) without denying that they fall to intuitive science, the 'knowledge of particular things'.

Viewing the attributes as concrete universals enables us to make sense of such otherwise baffling passages as that in the *DIE* on the right ordering of thoughts (*G* II, pp. 36–7). Spinoza turns to this topic after having considered the rules for defining an uncreated thing, and tells us 'to deduce our ideas from physical things, or real entities, so far as may be, according to the series of causes from one real entity to another, never passing over to abstractions and universals' (*G* II, p. 36). The 'universals' derided here, like those condemned at *E* II, 40S1 or again at *E* II, 49S, are either the universals of Plato or of Aristotle, or certain universal propositions associated with them (*cp. Ep.* II; and *vide* III, 3). What are the 'physical things or real entities' to which these bad 'universals' are contrasted? Spinoza explains: 'by the series of causes and real entities I do not mean the series of mutable particular things, but rather the series of fixed and eternal things', as, for example, motion and rest. Particular mutable things 'depend so intimately and so essentially upon fixed things, that they can neither be nor be conceived without them. Whence these fixed and eternal things, *although they are particular, will be to us as it were universals*, on account of their presence everywhere, and their very wide power'. These 'fixed and eternal' things, which are also 'physical and real', which though 'particular' function as 'universals', and which feature in the rightly ordered deduction of scientific ideas, are of course the attribute of Extension and what are elsewhere identified as its infinite modes (*Ep.* 64). The various claims Spinoza makes about these 'fixed and eternal' things, at first sight uncombinable, fit together if they are seen as concrete universals.

We can thus safely reject the notion that intuitive knowledge in the *Ethics* 'includes adequate knowledge of the essences of singular things, i.e. finite modes, but . . . does not include adequate knowledge of the essences of the Divine attributes. Knowledge of the nature of an attribute . . . is knowledge of something universal, of something common to all bodies' (*Curley* (2), p. 57). The attributes are *at once* abstract and concrete, universal and particular. The *Ethics* specifically and repeatedly says that intuition 'proceeds from' them (*E* II, 40S2; *E* V, 25D); and we should take it at its word. It may even be said that Spinoza's claim that intuition has a distinctive 'excellence and utility' (*E* II, 47S) turns on these facts. In some sense which he found desperately important, but also desperately hard to explain, Spinoza thought that intuition sees the universal *in* the particular, a world in a grain of sand.

Our long review of Spinoza's theory of knowledge is now ended. We have seen how he tried to answer scepticism, and traced doubt back to the confusion of ideas. We have discussed his treatment of error, which is also attributed to 'confusion', and perhaps ultimately to the importunities of this too, too solid flesh. We have seen why he believes 'experience' to be shot through with error, and why he took 'reason' for his guide, relying on it in physics, metaphysics and the study of the human mind. Finally, we have grappled with his difficult theses about reason and intuition – or knowledge as such, in the only forms he recognises. That examination will at least have convinced us that, however else intuition may excel reason, it does not outstrip it in the certainty it can impart; it may also have persuaded us that reason and intuition can overlap, though they may not coincide, in the range of objects they survey. The forms and categories of knowledge now lying bare, the means to it being seized, and all doubts concerning it being overcome, we must consider what Spinoza claims for it: what can be known about the Universe?

IV

Substance and Attribute

The Universe which Reason delineates is one which consists of a single substance in infinite attributes. With the attributes we are already slightly acquainted (III, 7), but substance is as yet unknown. In this chapter, substance will loom large: the first section inspects Spinoza's definition of it; the second investigates three notions of it; the fifth and seventh sections expound Spinoza's demonstrations of its properties.

1 Substance defined

The idea of substance lies at the crossroads of several philosophical paths. We can begin by asking where the paths originate, and why they intersect.

For Descartes, the notion of 'substance' discharged two tasks. It entered into the problem of creation, and it had a place in the theory of predication (*Hacking*, p. 140). On the one hand, he connects the idea of substantivality with that of being self-caused: 'By substance, we can understand nothing else than a thing which so exists that it needs no other thing in order to exist. And in fact only one single substance can be understood which clearly needs nothing else, namely, God' (*Principles of Philosophy*, I, 51). On the other hand, he asserts that 'it is a common notion that nothing is possessed of no attributes, properties or qualities' (*Principles* I, 52; this 'common notion' features in some versions of the *Cogito*). Hence 'when we perceive any attribute, we therefore conclude that some existing thing *or substance* to which it may be attributed, is necessarily present' (*ibid.*). Since created things have properties, they too must be accounted substances, introducing a secondary meaning of the word (*Principles* I, 51). In the next section, we shall see how these two senses tend to come together.

The Empiricists, while inheriting from Descartes an interest in the problem of predication, were not content with his solution to it. (Their difficulties were interestingly prefigured by Gassendi: *H.R.* II, p. 147). Let Hume speak for them:

> I wou'd fain ask those philosophers, who found so much of their reasonings on the distinction of substance and accident, and imagine we have clear ideas of each, whether the idea of *substance* be derived from the impressions of sensation or reflexion? If it be convey'd to us by our sense, I ask, which of them; and after what manner? If it be perceiv'd by the eyes, it must be a colour; if by the ears, a sound; if by the palate, a taste; and so of the other senses. But I believe none will assert, that substance is either a colour, or sound, or a taste. The idea of substance must therefore be deriv'd from an impression of reflexion, if it really exist. But the impressions of reflexion resolve themselves into our passions and emotions; none of which can possibly represent a substance. We have therefore no idea of substance, distinct from that of a collection of particular qualities. (*Treatise of Human Nature* I, 1, vi)

The reasoning is simple. (i) All ideas come ultimately from experience; (ii) we experience only qualities, not substances; hence (iii) we have no idea of substance. The Cartesian, believing in innate ideas, will deny the first premiss; the Aristotelian, having a different view of the content of experience, will deny the second. Yet the Empiricist thesis retains a hold: Russell has declared it to be the result of a mere accident of language that subject/predicate logic and substance/attribute metaphysics have shaped our civilisation (*Russell*, p. 330). There is some plausibility in Russell's position, if it is cut loose from epistemology and soldered to logic. Russell's Theory of Definite Descriptions and Quine's programme for eliminating singular terms suggest that there could be a (workable) natural language which dispensed with names for particular things; and if substance is what can (only) be named, not predicated, why then posit substances (*Anscombe* (1), p. 7)?

In Spinoza's thought, by contrast, the notion of substance prospers. If the Empiricists have it that nothing is a substance, Spinoza avers that everything is, or is a part of, a single substance. If we wish to chart the course of his thinking, we must begin with the definitions of substance, and of the related notions of attribute and mode. These read as follows:

By substance, I understand that which is in itself and is conceived through itself; in other words, that, the concept of which does not need the concept of another thing, from which it must be formed.
By attribute, I understand that which the intellect perceives of substance, as constituting its essence.
By mode, I understand the affections of substance, or that which is in another thing, through which also it is conceived. (*E* I, Definitions 3, 4, 5).

The question of what these definitions *mean* can only be answered if we know what, in offering definitions like them, Spinoza wanted to *do*. And there is no doubt that on the subject of definition, Spinoza can be very perplexing. The very form in which he casts the definitions of *Ethics* I gives rise to several queries. Richard Robinson points to one problem in them:

Spinoza, who is thoroughly realistic in his view of definition, nevertheless expresses his most important definitions by such phrases as: 'By substance I understand that which . . . (*Per substantiam intelligo id quod* . . .).' This phrase means nothing unless the word 'substance' is taken to be here meant in inverted commas, as the name of itself. But then it is about a word, not about a thing. One can understand something by a word; but one can understand nothing by a thing, unless it is a symbol or a pair of spectacles or something of that sort'. (*Robinson*, pp. 157–8; *cp. Gueroult* I, pp. 20–1)

If the definitions of *Ethics* I are intelligible, they must be nominal (i.e. of words), not real (i.e. of things). But Spinoza declares elsewhere in the *Ethics* (I, 8S2) that true definitions are of *things*; and the form of words he adopts at the outset of the First Part indicates that it is *substance*, not '*substance*', which is being defined.

The question whether Spinoza's definitions there are real or nominal must be distinguished from the question whether they are truth-valued or not. And here too the answer is not clear. There are good reasons to think that the definitions of *Ethics* I are stipulative; and if they are stipulative, then they are non-truth-valued. Two things at least suggest that we take them as stipulations: their form and their role. Their form is that which was traditionally used by mathematicians to announce what a given word was to mean in the course of the work, or to request the reader to take it in a certain sense (*Robinson*, p. 59; *Pascal* (1) p. 122). And the Euclidean programme of the 'trivialisation of knowledge', which Spinoza appears to be following, calls for definitions at the start which cannot be contested, and which reduce the definer's truth-commitments to the minimum (*Lakatos*, II, pp. 4–5). The Preface to the *PPD*, which received Spinoza's *imprimatur*, encourages this view of definitions: 'Definitions are simply the clearest possible explanations of the terms and words by which the matters to be discussed are designated'. And it is no objection to the view that Spinoza's definitions are stipulative, to point out that he deduces consequences from them (*pace Gueroult* I, p. 21): for if I stipulate that 'triangle' is to mean a three-sided rectilinear area, it then becomes tautologous (and hence true) for me to say 'A triangle is a three-sided rectilinear area' (*Robinson*, p. 158). Nevertheless, Spinoza's *desiderata* for a good definition are hard to reconcile with the supposition that the definitions of *Ethics* I are purely stipulative (*DIE*, G II, pp. 35–6). For instance, he lays it down that once the definition of an uncreated thing is given, there must be no room for the question whether it exists (G II, p. 35). And of course, any reason we have for thinking that his definitions are real rather than verbal will be a reason to deny that they are stipulative (*Robinson*, p. 19).

The questions which perplex us were also felt by Spinoza's contemporaries and disciples. One of them, Simon De Vries, wrote to Spinoza, asking for his view of the nature of definition. The reply, which is given in *Epistle* 9, sheds light on the issue.

The letter distinguished two types of definition. In one type, the existence of the thing defined is given, and only its essence is problematic; in the other, the definition is put forward only to be examined. The distinction is then explained by considering the case of two descriptions of temples. (It is not plain whether the descriptions are offered as *instances* of each type of definition, or whether the case depends on an *analogy* between descriptions of different sorts and definitions of different sorts.)

If I am asked for a description of Solomon's Temple, Spinoza says, then I must describe it truly, i.e., 'give its essence' in at least the sense of saying what the Temple really is or is like. But I may also construct a plan for some temple in my head; and then my description need not be true, or correspond to any existing temple. (Indeed, he implies that the definition will be 'false' in that no object actually corresponds to it.) Since *this* 'definition' need not be true, there is no asking for a demonstration of it, as with a theorem, nor of likening it to an axiom. (As he puts it, such a formula is not conceived of '*sub ratione veri*'.) Nevertheless, he maintains that it will be possible to draw certain conclusions from it, as with an axiom or theorem: if I describe or define a temple of such-and-such dimensions, then it follows that it would have to have foundations to such-and-such a depth, or would consist of such-and-such a quantity of stones. The first sort of definition makes a thing known 'as it exists outside the understanding'; the second makes a thing known 'as it is conceived or can be conceived by us'.

Spinoza mentions an important constraint upon definitions of the second type. If I say, 'By (an) X I understand (a) Y which is Z', then it must be conceivable, and so possible, that there should be such a thing as (a) Y which is Z. For instance, if I say that by God I understand a being which is absolutely infinite, then my definiton is good ('*bona*') only if it is conceivable that there is an absolutely infinite being. This is not the example given in *Epistle* 9, but it makes the point. Spinoza's own illustration comes from the geometer Borelli. Suppose it is said: 'Let two lines enclosing a space be called a figure'. This definition is not valid if the term 'straight line' continues to be used in its ordinary sense; for in that sense, two distinct straight lines can meet in, at most, a single point, and hence the form of words 'space enclosed by two straight lines' does not express anything conceivable. If, however, the term is understood to mean, say, what is normally meant by 'curved line', then the definition is thus far acceptable. In short, it is a condition for the acceptability of a definition that it should be consistently conceivable; and whether it is or not, can sometimes be determined by considering the sense which the terms used to state the definition have for the author who proposes it.

Definitions of the second kind, then, (i) do not imply either the existence or the non-existence of the thing defined; (ii) are not conceived '*sub ratione veri*', i.e. are non-truth-valued; (iii) can be assessed as good or bad; (iv) do in a sense carry consequences; and (v) will be good only if it is possible to think them through without inconsistency. Aside from the fact that Spinoza speaks of defining *things* and not *words*, his characterisation of this type of definition seems well suited to *stipulative* definitions. And he gives as an instance of a definition of this type, a formula which resembles those of *Ethics* I, viz., 'By substance I understand that which consists of only one attribute'. (The *content* of course differs from his own definition of substance, but the *form* is identical.) It seems, then, that if we follow the letter to De Vries, we must treat the definitions of *Ethics* I as stipulative.

Several problems still remain. The *DIE* insists that the definitions of uncreated things should leave no doubt as to the existence of what they define. *Epistle* 2 asserts that Spinoza has given the *true* definition of God, from which His existence is easily proved; *Epistle* 60 adds that the definition of God in *Ethics* I expresses His (internal) efficient cause, thus permitting all His properties to be deduced. These facts suggest that the definitions of the uncreated things (God, substance, attribute) belong to the first, not the second, type distinguished in *Epistle* 9. Confirmation may be sought in *E* I, 8S2: 'Now since it pertains to the nature of substance to exist (as we have shown in this scholium) its definition must involve necessary existence (*debet ejus definitio necessariam existentiam involvere*), and consequently from its definition alone its existence must be inferred'. All this encourages the view that the definitions of *Ethics* I are not stipulative. Hampshire thinks they are 'certainly not arbitrary; they are not offered as one set of alternative possible and convenient definitions of Substance, Cause and God, but as the only possible or consistent set of definitions' (*Hampshire* (2), pp. 30–1).

I do not find this case persuasive: the definitions at the start of the *Ethics* are undoubtedly stipulative. It does not follow that they are arbitrary, if that means that they are unmotivated; but it does follow, and Spinoza admits in *Epistle* 9, that alternative definitions of the same terms are possible. Insofar as they are stipulative, they cannot be assessed '*sub ratione veri*'; nevertheless, they may well allude to the efficient causes of the things named by the words they define, and in that way be deductively more powerful than any other proposed stipulations. They are to be contrasted, as the rubric which they follow implies, with the definitions collected at the end of *Ethics* III, which are plainly both *real* and *truth-valued*, and which reveal the essences of the things they define (*E* III, Definition 20, 'explanation'). It must therefore be confessed that they do not meet the requirements laid down in the *DIE*, or for that matter in *E* I, 8S2, if these are interpreted strictly. The definition of substance, for example, does not 'involve' the necessary existence of substance, if that means that it *states* that it pertains to the nature of substance to exist necessarily; nor is it the case that the necessary existence of substance can be inferred from that definition taken *alone*. It is only when the definition is conjoined with theorems (in the present case, with *E* I, 6C), and ultimately with axioms, that the nature of substance can be concluded from it.

Although the definitions may seem defective when measured by these strict standards, it is necessary, from Spinoza's own point of view, that they should be so. *The Port-Royal Logic*, which Spinoza kept in his library, remarks that real definitions which analyse the essences of things 'do not depend on us, but on that which is included in the true idea of the thing, and must not be taken for starting points (*'principles'*), but must be considered as propositions which have frequently to be confirmed by reason, and which can be combated' (*E* II, 16). If Spinoza had advanced real definitions purporting to be true at the outset of the *Ethics*, they would indeed have been combated by many of his readers: as Leibniz was later to remark, men commonly conceived of substance as that which was in itself but *not* conceived through itself (*Leibniz*, p. 196). Real definitions are, as Arnauld and Nicole say, like 'propositions' or theorems; they cannot be starting points; they must frequently be reviewed and re-proved. But the definitions which head the *Ethics* must be uncontentious, like those of a mathematical treatise; and that can only be guaranteed by converting them into requests that words be understood with a certain meaning. Spinoza is then in a position to move, by way of these definitions and his axioms, to theorems which *do* really affirm the essences of uncreated things. At this stage, but not before, it becomes possible to codify the results in a set of real definitions, as was to be done in *E* III; and the definitions so obtained would exactly meet the standards of the *DIE*. So, for example, the third definition of *E* I in effect stipulates that the *word* 'substance' be used in a certain way; it does not state that substance is that, to whose nature pertains necessary existence. But from the permissible stipulation which is laid down, the contentious result can be derived in a few steps as a consequence. When it *is* derived, it is possible to assert as a real definition, capable of proof, that substance necessarily exists; and of course, that definition will foreclose the question whether there is substance or not. Stipulative definitions are appropriate for acquiring knowledge of essences, truth-valued real definitions are suited to displaying the knowledge so acquired.

I have two further comments to make concerning Spinoza's definitions. The first is that while Descartes introduced the term 'substance' with the admission that it was not univocal, Spinoza shows no sign of noticing any other sense than the one he defines it to have; and univocity is a feature of geometrical definitions. Pascal explained:

> Here is a geometrical definition then; after having clearly designated a thing – say, every number divisible into two equal parts – one gives it a name *which we strip of every other sense*, if there be any, in order to give it that of the designated thing.
> (*Pascal* (1), p. 122)

Those who think that Spinoza's method determined his conclusions have this much to say in their own defence: the geometrising procedure implies that 'substance' has a unique sense, and this predisposes anyone who uses it against a Cartesian view of substance.

The other point is this. It is clear that, in several of Spinoza's definitions, he was intentionally giving words a meaning which was different from their ordinary one. That was not sheer perversity on his part; it was a canny exploitation of one of the advantages of stipulative definition. A word or phrase can imply a proposition or belief: the word 'simultaneous' used to imply that the temporal relation of any two events is independent of all spatial relations (*Robinson*, p. 71). And what a word implies may be false – as it was found to be with 'simultaneous'. If we want to preserve the word, giving it a true meaning allied to the original false one, we can stipulate that it is to be understood in a new sense: as Einstein did for 'simultaneous' (*Robinson*, p. 64). What Einstein was to do for physics, Spinoza attempted to do for metaphysics.

2 *Three notions of substance*

In the *Categories* (c. 2), Aristotle distinguishes four basic kinds of things. 'Of things themselves, some are predicable of a subject, and are never present in a subject . . . Some things, again, are present in a subject, but are never predicable of a subject . . . Other things, again, are both predicable of a subject and present in a subject . . . There is, lastly, a class of things which are neither present in a subject nor predicable of a subject.' To the first class belong things which a given subject can be, but cannot have: *man* is such a thing, since Socrates may be a man (*man* is predicable of Socrates) but cannot have a man. To the second belong those things which a subject may have but cannot be: a *particular item of knowledge* may be had by Socrates' mind, but the mind 'is' not that point of knowledge. Into the third box go those things which subjects can both have and be: e.g. *knowledge*, which the mind may have, and which grammatical knowledge or literacy *is*. Fourth and finally, there are things which no subject either has or is: *this man, this horse*. Of course, the knowledge that *mensa* means *table* just *is* that knowledge, as Socrates just *is* Socrates; but that knowledge can also be had, or predicated of something, whereas Socrates cannot be. Perhaps Aristotle's classification is best understood, not as establishing four different kinds of *thing*, but as marking the distinctions, within things *verbal*, between the abstract and the concrete, singular and general (on all this, see *Prior* (1), pp. 61–2). No matter, for it also gives us the notion of a (first) *substance*. A (first) substance, in brief, is an item of the fourth kind.

Spinoza's notion of substance is related to Aristotle's notion of a first substance, but how? Jonathan Bennett notices the problem:

> In the traditional concept of substance there are two main strands which I shall distinguish by subscripts. A substance$_1$ is a thing which has qualities. A substance$_2$ is something which can be neither originated nor annihilated by any natural process, i.e. which is, barring miracles, sempiternal. These two have often been conflated, if not identified; yet is is not obvious that they are even extensionally identical . . . How did one word come to be used in two such different senses? (*Bennett* (1), p. 182)

Bennett's 'substances$_1$' are clearly meant to do duty for Aristotle's first substances (or for Descartes' 'substances' in the secondary sense). (But the fit is not exact, for Aristotle's substances not only *have* qualities, but are not *themselves* qualities. There are qualities of qualities: sorrow is bitter, remorse useless.) And Bennett's 'substance$_2$' seems to be tailor-made to be Spinoza's 'substance' (or Descartes' 'substance' in the *primary* sense). How was the Spinozistic substance evolved from the Aristotelian one? Why believe that every substance$_1$ is a substance$_2$? Bennett explains:

> It has been said, as far back as Aristotle, that while an attribute or quality can be part of the world's furniture only if there is a substance$_1$ to which it belongs, a substance$_1$ is not in the same way required to 'belong' to something else. Substances$_1$, we might say, exist *independently* of anything else. Now, if we give this a causal rather than a logical force, it says that the continued existence of a substance$_1$ does not depend causally upon the behaviour of anything else. Something which needs no outside help in order to continue existing cannot be annihilated by anything else; thus, if we hurry past the question of origination, it is sempiternal as far as natural processes go; and so it is a substance$_2$. Perhaps then, substance$_2$ became accrued to substance$_1$ through an innocent exploitation of words like 'independently'. This suggestion is confirmed in Spinoza's writings. His doctrine that the Universe is the only indestructible thing was expressed in his monistic thesis that the Universe is the only substance; and the terminological decisions to which this led him could be summed up by saying that the Universe is the only thing which is not adjectival upon

something else. So Spinoza made 'substance' do the work both of 'substance$_1$' and of 'substance$_2$'. This is not surprising. Since he believed that causal necessity is a kind of logical necessity, Spinoza could not allow a distinction between the logical independence of substances$_1$ and the causal self-sufficiency of substances$_2$. I suggest that he was covering the old route from one sense of 'substance' to the other, but with his eyes open. (*Bennett* (1), pp. 182–3)

If I understand Bennett aright, Spinoza proceeded consciously along the following route. (i) The Universe alone is indestructible. So (ii) the Universe alone is a substance (=substance$_2$). So (iii) the Universe alone is independent. So (iv) the Universe alone is not adjectival upon something else. So (v) the Universe alone is a substance (=substance$_1$). Hence (vi) whatever is a substance$_1$ (that is, the Universe alone) is also a substance$_2$.

The suggestion scarcely reflects credit on Spinoza's powers of reasoning. The move from (i) to (ii) is invalid: as Bennett notes, it brushes past the question of origins. The move from (ii) to (iii) is valid only if 'independence' is construed causally, while that from (iii) to (iv) holds good only if it is taken logically. The conclusion at (vi) remains as bizarre as it ever was. If Spinoza had been a somnambulist, he could have done no worse than he is said to have done with open eyes.

Bennett's account of Spinoza amounts to a libel on his reputation; we do better to dismiss it. That leaves us with a choice between alternatives. Either we can dissociate Bennett's (highly plausible) conjecture as to how 'substance$_1$' developed into 'substance$_2$' from his (implausible) conjecture as to how Spinoza's mind worked, and say that Spinoza did not contribute to that conceptual development (whether consciously or not); *or* we can invent a better story as to how Spinoza reasoned his way to the conclusion that every substance$_1$ was a substance$_2$. There is a great deal to be said for the first alternative. When we look hard at Spinoza, we do not seem to find a trace of substance$_1$; if there has been development from that notion, then Spinoza's writings appear to encode it rather than recapitulate it. Spinoza begins with, and adheres to, substance$_2$; the grammatical notion of substance$_1$ seems remote to him. That is not remarkable, after all: he is far more gripped by the issue of creation than by that of predication. But there is also something to be said for tracing a line of argument by which he could have defended the identification of substance$_1$ with substance$_2$. Bennett in fact expounds how the argument would go; the trouble is that he attributes it to Kant rather than to Spinoza. Kantian it may be; but it could conceivably have served Spinoza as well. In brief, the idea is that anything which can undergo an existence-change, whether or not it figures in our thinking as a substance$_1$, ought not to have such a place; but only the Universe cannot undergo an existence-change; hence only the Universe is a substance$_1$.

To get at this, we need first to follow Bennett and Kant in distinguishing an *alteration* in a thing from an *existence-change* affecting it. An object X undergoes an alteration if, having been Φ, it ceases to be Φ whilst not ceasing to be; it undergoes an existence-change if it ceases to be *simpliciter* (*cp. C.M.* II, 4, i). Now it appears that substances$_1$ can undergo existence-changes (or at least, that it is coherent to suppose that they do). How else, Bennett asks, can we interpret the following story:

> I produce, and submit to general inspection, a porcelain pig and a handful of coins; we find the weight and volume of the pig; watched by the bystanders, I place the coins in the pig, and put the pig inside a glass case which is then tightly sealed; finally, I put the case on a balance which I bring level by means of weights on its other arm. Then, as we watch, the porcelain pig disappears, the coins clatter to the bottom of the case, and the arm of the balance holding the case swings up; when we remove weights from the other arm, equivalent to the weight of the pig, the balance comes level again; when we unseal the glass case, the volume of air which hisses in is equal to that of the pig; and at no stage is there an explosion such as would occur if a few ounces of matter were converted into energy? (*Bennett* (1), p. 189)

According to Bennett, Kant 'would say that if a pig were annihilated . . . this would show only that it was not a substance$_1$ after all but just a complex of properties of the glass case, the coins, the balance, the bystanders, etc.'.

How does Kant defend that reply? Crucially (Bennett says) he assumes that if Y's existence-change can be known only through X's alteration, then Y's existence-change *is* X's alteration, and Y is therefore a property or 'determination' of X (*Bennett*, p. 190). And that assumption in turn is based, Bennett believes, on arguing that if (i) X's alteration is not merely evidence of Y's existence-change, then (ii) it is possible to hold that X's alteration *is* Y's existence-change, and thus that (iii) Y is a state or property of X (p. 191). In the case of the porcelain pig, one might argue that if a certain set of statements about the alterations in the glass case, the coins, the observers, and so forth, gave all the evidence there could possibly be for the pig's annihilation, then that set of statements would not only be evidence for the pig's annihilation, but would be equivalent to the statement that it had gone clean out of existence. This could in turn lead to the conclusion that the sum of alterations *was* the existence-change of the pig, and finally to the position that the pig was a property of the glass case and other items.

Bennett takes Kant to have shown that we *can* deny substantivality$_1$ to the porcelain pig, but not that we ought to. 'One good reason for treating something substantively is that it is conceptually efficient to do so . . . We can concede something to Kant: the phrase "the porcelain pig" would be much less useful if the pig had lasted for only a few seconds. But even if we grant that moderate durability is required for something to count as a substance$_1$, it is a far cry from this to saying that only the sempiternal is entitled to substantival treatment. Kant's all-or-nothing habit of thought has here carried him to an unreasonable extreme'. (p. 198)

Spinoza, not less than Kant, has an all-or-nothing habit of thought, and he would gleefully have seized upon the Kantian materials so ably fashioned by Bennett. The case of the porcelain pig shows that we connect the idea of substance$_1$, the idea of a thing which can *bear* qualities, with the idea of that which persists *through* changes in the qualities which are borne. Thus a sneeze, which is something ephemeral, does not count with us as a substance$_1$, although predications can be made of it ('a mighty sneeze'), for it does not last long enough to survive through more than a few changes. We take a sneeze to be, not substantial$_1$, but qualitative – an event, that is, a quality-instance. A porcelain pig, however, is – on the human scale – a relatively enduring thing. Not only can predications be made concerning it, but we can treat it conveniently as something of which many contradictory predications may, successively, be true. Let us call 'that which is subject to many changes, through which it persists' substance$_3$ (*Hacking*, p. 139). Then we can say that the thesis 'Every substance$_1$ is a substance$_3$' is one which generally recommends itself to us. Can we now take the further step of saying that 'Every substance$_3$ is a substance$_2$'? Here is where the 'all-or-nothing' move can be made. That which is most a substance$_3$, or most indubitably a substance$_3$, is that which is also substance$_2$ – the things least pervious to change are, tritely, the things which are indestructible. A porcelain pig, which purports to be a substance$_3$ (as well as a substance$_1$), though the survivor of many changes, cannot endure *unlimited* change – at the breaking-point, we are forced to admit that it can go clean out of existence. This fact tempts us to deny that the pig is, after all, a substance$_3$. Nothing less than the Universe as a whole, it might seem, can be regarded as safely, or fully, a substance$_3$.

Taking the two steps together, we reach the conclusion that 'Every substance$_1$ is a substance$_2$'. But we do not reach it by means of any specifically Spinozist doctrines, as that causality is a form of logical necessity, still less by an equivocation on 'dependence'. On the contrary, we start from the endemic tendency to base substantivality$_1$ upon identity through change, or substantivality$_3$. The conceptual tie is not a philosopher's invention, but a fact of ordinary thinking. And we then collapse the notion of substantivality$_3$ into that of substantivality$_2$ – what truly survives change, it is held, is what cannot be destroyed. *That* connection is less fixed in ordinary thought, and a philosophical turn of mind may insist that the connection be pressed and tightened. But the progression seems at each stage plausible: the problem of predication hooks onto that of identity through change, and that in turn onto the problem of creation.

3 *In itself and conceived through itself*

Spinoza's definition of substance speaks of it as what is both *in itself* and *conceived through* itself; his definition of mode characterises it as *in another, through which also it is conceived*. What exactly do these definitions mean? And is Spinoza prepared to say that, in addition to what is in itself and what is conceived through itself, or what is in another and conceived through another, there is also that which is itself but *not* conceived through itself? Or that some things are *not* in themselves, but are nonetheless conceived through themselves (*Parkinson* (3), p. 26)?

It is interesting to compare the four possible types of thing which Spinoza's scheme seems to admit with the four types of thing recognised in Aristotle's *Categories* (IV, 2). If 'to be present in a subject' corresponds to 'being in another', and 'not to be in a subject' to 'being in itself', and if 'to be predicable of a subject' answers to 'to be conceived through another', while 'not to be predicable' goes with 'to be conceived through itself', then Spinoza's *substance* will correspond to the first substances (this man, that horse) which Aristotle countenances, and Spinoza's modes will correspond with Aristotelian (universal) qualities, such as knowledge or literacy. Arguably, Spinoza does not acknowledge things which are in another but conceived through themselves (*Parkinson* (3), p. 29); and if that is right, then he will have nothing which parallels Aristotle's quality-instances. However, he will have things which match Aristotle's second substances (such as man) – namely, the *attributes*, which will be in themselves but conceived through another. The suggestion has pleasing consequences. The relation between Spinoza's substance and its attribute(s) is mirrored by the relation between Aristotle's first substances (Socrates) and second substances (man), and the relation between substance and modes (which, for Spinoza, are concrete things such as bodies: *E* I, 25C; II, Definition 1) can even be assimilated to that between first substances and universal accidents. But the relation between Aristotle's universal accidents and his second substances (e.g. literacy and horse) does not seem to answer in any way to that between Spinoza's modes and his attributes. It is not safe to interpret Spinoza's terms as if they meant the same thing as the corresponding terms in Aristotle.

Parkinson follows a different approach. Starting with the definition of *mode*, he remarks that 'to say of a mode that it is in *X* seems to mean that it is predicated of *X*' ((3), p. 27). On this view, a mode such as a porcelain pig is reckoned to be a property, and to speak of a porcelain pig is to predicate something of matter. (We have seen in IV, 2 how Spinoza might defend that paradoxical view.) But what is added by saying that a mode is *conceived through* that in which it exists? Parkinson answers:

> If . . . to be in X is to be predicated of X, then it follows that Spinoza must say that, for example, the colour green is 'in' a leaf. It does not seem likely, however, that he would say that green is a mode of the leaf, for a leaf is certainly a mode, and Spinoza does not speak of modes of modes. The reason for not regarding green as a mode of a leaf seems to be that green is not *conceived through* a leaf; that is, in forming the concept of green we do not require the concept of a leaf. On the other hand, a leaf is a mode of matter in that it is not only in matter, in the sense explained earlier, but also the concept of a leaf is one into which the concept of matter enters – in thinking of a leaf, we have to think of it as matter. ((3), p. 27)

Can we generalise from Parkinson's leaf case? If so, we must say that *X* is conceived through *Y* if and only if in thinking of *X* one must think of it as *Y*. Now this proposal is not wholly satisfactory: 'conceived *per se*' and 'conceived *per aliud*' seem to contradict each other; but a leaf must be thought of, not only as a bit of extended matter, but as a leaf; and substance is to be regarded, not only as substance, but as thinking and extended. That seems to make the leaf conceivable *per se*, substance conceivable *per aliud*, which is doubtful.

Perhaps we should equate the 'in itself/in another' distinction, not with 'impredicable/predicable', but with 'independent/dependent'; and reserve 'impredicable/predicable' for the pair 'conceived *per se*/conceived *per aliud*'. Then Spinoza's double-barrelled point about substance will be that it is both independent and impredicable; while of mode he will be saying that it is to be predicated of what it depends upon. Attributes will be a special case, for sometimes Spinoza implies that they *are* substance (at e.g. *E* I, 4D, I, 19), and sometimes he says that they *characterise* substance (*E* I, 10S: '*tribuere*'). Insofar as they can be identified with substance, they must be held to be *independent*; insofar as they characterise it, they must be conceivable '*per aliud*'. (That result may be seen as a reflection of the fact that they are at once concrete and universal: III, 7.) This consequence will directly oppose the view of Parkinson, who believes that 'an attribute is conceived through itself but is in something else' ((3), p. 30). And on this matter, Parkinson can bring to bear the testimony of Spinoza himself, for *E* I, 10 affirms that each attribute must be conceived *per se*.

Three proposals, then, have come to grief. But before we despair of recovering Spinoza's meaning, we ought to explore a fourth possibility. Like the previous suggestion, this equates 'in itself/in another' with 'independent/dependent'; but it differs in linking 'conceivable *per se/per aliud*' to 'self-explanatory/non-self-explanatory'. On this view, both *substance* and *attribute* will be (as they should be) conceivable *per se*, in that their natures or essences explain the fact of their existence; while mode will be conceived through that in which it exists, in that it will be necessary to account for modal existence by referring outside the mode, to the substance on which it depends (as is confirmed by *E* I, 6 D2, which implicitly connects 'being conceived through another' with 'being *known* through a *cause*'). This is, I think, the most satisfactory reading on offer. But it does have one strange consequence: if substances are to be regarded as '*in se*' (*Gueroult* I, p. 48: *Curley* (3), p. 17; contrast *Parkinson* (3), p. 30, pp. 38–9), then there will be nothing to distinguish substance from the attributes which it is elsewhere said to *have*.

Finally, let me note a fifth possibility (*cp. Donagan* (1), p. 165). When Descartes introduces the topic of attributes and modes, he writes:

> Any attribute gives us knowledge of substance; but every substance has a principal property that constitutes its essential

nature, and all others are reduced to this. Extension in length, breadth and depth is what constitutes the very nature of corporeal substance; consciousness is what constitutes the very nature of a conscious substance. For any other possible attribute of body presupposes extension and is, so to say, a mode (*modus*) of an extended thing; and likewise whatever is found in the mind is merely one mode or another of consciousness. For example, shape is not conceivable except in an extended thing, nor motion except in an extended space; whereas imagination, sensation and will are inconceivable except in a conscious being. But on the other hand extension is conceivable apart from shape or motion, and so is consciousness apart from imagination and sense; this is clear to anyone on reflection. (*Principles*, I, Art. 53; *A.G.*. p. 192)

In this passage, modes are not concrete things, but full-blooded properties like *doubting, willing, being square, having such-and-such a shape*, and they are related to their attributes as determinates to determinables (*Prior* (1), p. 63). The attributes themselves do not fall under any higher determinable as determinates; on the contrary, they are the most utterly general features of substance, to which all other properties of substance may be 'reduced'. They are, in effect, the highest genera, of which the 'modes' of thought and extension are species. This Cartesian conception of mode and attribute is not unknown to Spinoza: not only does he speak of properties like *love* and *desire* as modes (*E* II, Axiom 3), but he asserts that, in explaining the attributes, we need 'no genus, or anything through which they might be understood or explained', whereas for modes we must mention the attribute 'through which, as their genus, they must be understood' (*ST* I, 7, ix–x; *cf. Curley* (3), p. 35). Here then we have a fifth sense for the 'conceived *per se/per aliud*' contrast: the attributes are conceived *per se*, in that no higher genus or determinable includes them; the modes are conceived *per aliud*, in that they do fall under a higher genus or determinable. In this sense, and in it alone, substance is *not* conceived *per se*.

4 Monism and pluralism

In the First Dialogue of the *Short Treatise*, Reason addresses Desire in the following words:

What you say, O Desire, that there are different substances, that, I tell you, is false; for I see clearly that there is but One, which exists through itself, and is a support to all other attributes. And if you will refer to the material and the mental as substances, in relation to the modes which are dependent on them, why then, you must also call them modes in relation to the substance on which they depend: for they are not conceived by you as existing through themselves. And in the same way that willing, feeling, understanding, loving and so on are different modes of that which you call a thinking substance, in which you bring together and unite all these in one, so I also conclude, from your own proofs, that both Infinite Extension and Thought together with all other infinite attributes (or, according to your usage, substances) are only modes of the One Eternal Infinite Being, who exists through himself; and from all these we posit, as stated, An Only One or a Unity, outside which nothing can be imagined to be. (*Wolf* translation, pp. 33–4; *G* I, p. 27)

William James says somewhere that the essence of any philosophical system can be inscribed on the back of a postage stamp, and the passage from the *Short Treatise* is an excellent postage stamp summary of Spinoza's position. To round out the description: there is ultimately only a single substance, which is divine. That substance is characterised by infinitely many attributes, each infinite in its own kind; of these attributes, only two are known to us – Thought and Extension. Each attribute comprehends a variety of modes: Thought comprehends willing, feeling, understanding and so forth; Extension includes being square, being in motion, being at rest, and so forth. There is another use of the term 'mode' in which we speak, not so much of modes *of*, as of modes *in* substance: modes so spoken of are concrete individuals, like particular minds or bodies. Modes are both finite and infinite; if they are infinite, then they are either immediate or mediate. The infinite immediate modes of Extension is Motion-and-Rest; its infinite mediate mode is 'the face of the whole universe'. The infinite immediate mode of Thought is the absolutely infinite intellect; its mediate mode is left unspecified (*Ep.* 64).

That quick tour may give us some sense of the scenery; now let us retrace our steps, and pause a little over one of the prominent sights. Spinoza holds that there is only one substance (*E* I, 14), but he also admits at least a duality of attributes (*E* II, 1 and 2). He is usually called a monist on the basis of the first claim, but the second claim entitles him to be considered a dualist as well. The truth is, of course, that the contrast between monism and pluralism is not a single, straightforward thing: not one, but as many as three, contrasts can be seen here. The lesson is well expounded in *Broad* (1), pp. 21–7, from whom I borrow freely.

We have seen Descartes asserting that, among the various attributes of a substantial thing, there will always be one attribute which is its 'principal property', and to which all the others may be 'reduced'. This principal 'property' is an 'attribute' in the stricter sense, defined by Spinoza at *E* I, Definition 4. Now it is possible to maintain that there is only a single attribute, which constitutes the essence of whatever substance(s) there may be; and it is also possible to believe that there are more attributes than one. The former view is *attributival monism*, and latter, *attributival pluralism*. It is arguable that Hobbes and Leibniz were monists in this sense, the first taking materiality, the other mentality, to be the sole attribute belonging to all things whatsoever. Bradley, too, may have been an Attributival Monist, if Broad is right in saying that the Absolute is wholly mental or experiential. Descartes and Spinoza, by contrast, were certainly pluralists. Attributival Pluralism, however, comes in several varieties, of which we may note *Compatibilism* and *Incompatibilism*. The first of these asserts that more than a single attribute may belong to a given substance; the other holds that no more than a single attribute may belong to a single substance. For the most part, Descartes is an incompatibilist, Spinoza a compatibilist. ('For the most part', because although Descartes says that the attributes of Thought and Extension exclude each other (*Kenny Letters*, p. 107), he has a special problem about God Who, whilst being a substance, contains *both* Thought and Extension 'eminently', i.e. in a manner suitable to His nature as a being of a higher type than His creatures (*Kenny Letters*, pp. 238–9; *Gueroult* I, p. 276, n. 40).)

As against this, we have *Substantival Monism* and *Pluralism*. Here Descartes and Spinoza part company: Descartes believed in a plurality of (created) substances; Spinoza rejected the distinction between created and uncreated substance, holding there to be only one, uncreated substance. There have been many substantival pluralists, few true substantival monists. Aristotle was plainly a pluralist, taking every individual in the category of first substance to be substantial; Hume was an extreme substantival pluralist, holding that (on the traditional definition of 'substance') 'everything which can possibly be conceived' counted for one (*Treatise* I, 4, v). Strawson's *Individuals* can be read as advocating substantival pluralism of an interesting sort – if *one* substance is known to fall under the attribute 'person', then other substances *demonstrably* come under it. On the other hand, Parmenides is commonly, if perhaps wrongly, regarded as a substantival monist, but the Eleatic Melissus appears really to have been one (*Barnes* (1) I, pp. 204–7). Broad ascribes substantival monism, not only to Spinoza, but to Bradley (*Broad* (1), p. 26).

These distinctions cut across one another, giving four possible positions. One can be a substantival monist and an attributival monist (Bradley). One can be a substantival monist and an attributival pluralist (Spinoza). One can be a substantival pluralist but an attributival monist (arguably, Hobbes and Leibniz). And finally, one can be both a substantival and attributival pluralist (Descartes).

I have said that three things were bundled up in the 'monist/pluralist' contrast; so far we have inspected two of them. The third contrast arises out of the fact that every substance possesses its attributes in some specific form. 'No material substance is *just* a bit of matter; it has the Oxygen properties, or the Hydrogen properties, or the Silver Chloride properties, and so on. Similarly, no mind is *just* a thinking substance; it has the characteristic properties of an oyster's mind, or of a dog's, or of a man's, or of an angel's, and so on' (*Broad* (1), p. 24). The features which distinguish the main natural kinds which fall under a common attribute are (let us say) *'specific properties'*. Now with regard to the specific properties of substances, all of which fall under a certain attribute, one can say that there is some single specific property to which all the others in the group may be reduced, or one may maintain that there are at least two specific properties within the group which are irreducible to any others within it. The former position is *Specific Property Monism*, the latter *Specific Property Pluralism*. (It is of course possible to be a Specific Property Monist with respect to the properties associated with one attribute, and a Specific Property Pluralist with respect to those associated with another attribute.)

Descartes may have been a Specific Property Monist with regard to the attribute of Extension: he seems to have believed that the apparently various kinds of matter (which, for him, *is* extension) were merely differences in size and shape of the parts of a single homogeneous stuff. In the *Principles* he classifies matter into three kinds: the fiery, the celestial or airy, and the earthy (*A.T.* VIII, pp. 100–5; *cf. Dijksterhuis*, pp. 409–11). But in his correspondence, he expresses the belief that ultimately only one kind of matter exists, differentiated into variously shaped and arranged corpuscles (*Kenny Letters*, p. 205). On the other hand, Broad asserts that Descartes was a Specific Property Pluralist with respect to the attribute of Thought, for 'he certainly held that

God's mind differs in kind from human minds' ((1), p. 25).

Broad's distinctions are immensely serviceable: they can help us to understand many things better. Here for instance is a passage from the *Leviathan* on which our new instruments can operate:

> The World (I mean not the Earth onely, that denominates the Lovers of it Worldly Men, but the Universe, that is, the whole masse of all things that are) is Corporeall, that is to say, Body; and hath the dimensions of Magnitude, namely, Length, Breadth, and Depth: also every part of Body is likewise Body, and hath the like dimensions; and consequently every part of the Universe, is Body; and that which is not Body, is no part of the Universe: And because the Universe is All, that which is not part of it, is Nothing; and consequently no where. Nor does it follow from hence, that Spirits are nothing: for they have dimensions, and are therefore really Bodies; though that name in common Speech be given to such Bodies onely, as are visible, or palpable; that is, that have some degree of Opacity. (Chapter 46)

Hobbes' belief that the Universe is corporeal suggests Attributival Monism; his statement that it is Body implies Substantival Monism. That latter thought is immediately cancelled out, however. The comment that every part of Body is likewise Body, together with the view that every body is a substance (*Third Set of Objections*, A.G., p. 129), point rather to Substantival Pluralism. His description of two specific properties of body, coarseness and subtlety, leaves open the question of Specific Property Monism or Pluralism, for he says nothing here as to whether these are irreducibly distinct. But his notion that spirits are really only subtle bodies helps him to combat both Attributival Pluralism of the kind that treats Thought as an attribute, and Substantival Pluralism of the kind that takes Minds to be substances.

5 Substance: one or many?

Spinoza's demonstrations of substantival monism are arid, abstract, over-compressed, hard to understand. Here, if anywhere, he is served badly by his strictly deductive method, his aversion to controversy, his tendencies to ellipsis, to brevity, to allusion. It is only too easy to regard the arguments as an empty verbal game, the manipulation of unmeaning symbols. To infuse life into his words, we have to set them against the words of others. Spinoza's thought does not move in a void, sealed off from all contaminating influences. What he is *for*, is often understood by seeing what he is *against*. There is no Open Sesame to unlock the doors of the cave and reveal the treasures within; but there may be no better way to enter it than the one I propose to follow.

In the first place, then, Spinoza is out to refute the Aristotelian and scholastic idea that individual, nameable things, and primarily *men*, are substances. That view of things is nervously argued against Spinoza by his correspondent Henry Oldenburgh:

> The more I consider (the axioms), the more I am overwhelmed with doubts about them. For against the first proposition, I submit that two men are two substances, and have the same attribute, since both are endowed with reason; whence I conclude that there do exist two substances with the same attribute. (*Ep.* 3)

Spinoza is also taking aim at the Cartesian view. Setting apart God, who for Descartes is substance in the primary sense, there are two types of substances in the Cartesian scheme: thinking and extended. Descartes believes in a plurality of thinking substances., but he acknowledges only a single extended one, which is the whole of the physical universe. These commitments come out in the *Synopsis* to the *Meditations*:

> Whereas body taken generally (i.e. taking body collectively, as meaning matter), is a substance, and therefore can never perish, the human body, insofar as it differs from other bodies (i.e. taking 'bodies' in the plural, thereby meaning material things), is composed entirely of a certain configuration of members, and other similar accidents, while the human mind is not constituted of accidents of any kind whatever, but is a pure substance. For though all the accidents of the mind suffer change, though, for instance, it thinks of other things, wills others, and senses others, it is yet always the same mind. The human body, on the contrary, is no longer the same, if a change takes place in the structure of some of its parts. (*Kemp Smith translation*, pp. 193–4; the interspersed comments, with which I agree, are by Kemp Smith)

The view that the mind, the soul or the self is a substance is repeated and insisted upon (*Cottingham*, p. 17; *Discourse on Method*, A.G., p. 32). But that the human body, or any particular body short of the whole of matter, is *not* substantial, is equally clear. 'Particular bodies are not each substances as are separate minds . . . [Descartes'] doctrine of physical existents, strictly formulated, requires them to be *modes*, not substances – modes of a single *substance* that is all matter, i.e. the whole natural world tri-dimensionally extended in one substance. So much is plain in places where he writes more carefully' (*Keeling*, p. 130, n. 1, citing *Principles* I, 53; II, 21–2; II, 25. But contrast *Lachièze-Rey*, pp. 54–7). There is thus a perceptible asymmetry in the Cartesian system, which tilts lopsidedly towards the substantiality of individual *minds*, and away from that of individual *bodies* (as noted, perhaps, in *Kenny Letters*, p. 235). Spinoza departs from this scheme thrice over: (a) bodies and minds are put on the same footing as modes; (b) substantiality is assigned peculiarly to the uncreated, rather than awarded derivatively to the created as well; (c) Thought and Extension become attributes, not of separate and creaturely things, but of a single, uncreated thing.

How does Spinoza achieve these bold results? According to one writer, he takes the goal in two broad strides:

> We are all aware of the distinction between substances which stand alone and the properties which depend upon or inhere in them. Thus the blueness of the eye cannot exist apart from the eye which is a substance. But if we really think the matter through we soon see that the eye itself is only relatively able to exist alone, and that it in turn is dependent for its existence upon the whole organism or is in Spinoza's terminology a mere mode. (*Wild*, p. xxvii)

That is the first stride: a thing like the eye, which appears to be a substance$_1$, is held to be dependent on some other thing, exactly as a property like blueness is dependent upon it. The confusion between the (causal) sense in which the eye is dependent on the body and the (predicative) sense in which blueness is dependent on the eye is overlooked; and the proximate conclusion is drawn that the eye is not really a substance$_1$. Next:

> And then if we consider the human individual, he turns out to be obviously dependent upon the existence of other organisms, which are dependent upon the sun, which is dependent upon the motions of the other stars *et cetera*, until we reach the whole Universe. Only then do we seem to have a reality truly self-dependent. (*Wild, ibid.*)

The second stride is easier: since only what is (causally) independent is truly a substance$_1$, and since nothing short of the whole Universe is independent (or substantial$_2$), only the Universe is a substance$_1$.

SUBSTANCE AND ATTRIBUTE

Any such account, I believe, will be too gross (*cf.* IV 2); Spinoza simply does not reason in this way. The conclusion that there is exactly one substance is reached by stages, and only emerges fully at *E* I, 14C1, which declares that 'it follows with the greatest clearness firstly that God is one, that is to say (Definition 6) in Nature there is but one subtance, and it is absolutely infinite'. That there is exactly one substance in Nature is shown, first by proving that there is *at least* one substance (which is done at *E* I, 7), and then by proving that there is *at most* one substance (which is done through the mediation of the notion of *infinity*, introduced at *E* I, 8). The proof that there is *at least* one substance seems to depend on two assumptions: that no substance is caused to exist by another substance, and that nothing exists without a cause (*E* I, 7D). From those assumptions it is concluded that substance is self-caused, or that it exists of necessity. That nothing exists without a cause is regarded by Spinoza as so obvious that he does not trouble to state it (but *cf. E* I, 8S2; I, 11, Second Demonstration; *E* I, Axiom 3). But that no substance can be produced by another requires proof, and this is intended to be given at *E* I, 6. That proof draws upon the preceding theorems of the *Ethics*, and it is necessary to examine closely how it works.

Proposition 5 lays down the very thesis to which Oldenburgh objected: it asserts that in nature there cannot be two or more substances of the same nature or attribute. Proposition 3 maintains a thesis concerning causality: if two things have nothing in common with one another, one cannot be the cause of the other. Now if two substances differ in their attributes, Spinoza claims, they have nothing in common; hence they cannot be causally related; hence one cannot produce the other – which gives us *E* I, 6. In this demonstration, there are three main assumptions. (i) The notion that two substances which differ in their attributes have nothing in common (*E* I, 2) seems puzzling. But I think it can be explained if we bear in mind that, in the Cartesian scheme, the attribute of a given substance is *presupposed by* all its other properties, which are *reducible* to it; or again that the properties of a substance are *modes* of its principal property or attribute, as *being square* is a mode of *being extended*. Hence to say that substances having different attributes 'have nothing in common' is to say that the difference in attributes entails a difference in modes: something which is (simply) extended will have none of the modes of thought; something which is (simply) thinking will have none of the modes of extension. 'Can anyone conceive of a passion of a yard in length, a foot in breadth, and an inch in thickness?' (Hume, *Treatise* I, 4, v). Similarly, no body, *qua* body, can feel or think; no soul, *qua* soul, can be heavy, square or immobile. (ii) The causal principle, that two things which have 'nothing in common' cannot act upon each other, would also have met with general acceptance. Descartes himself, I shall argue (VI, 1), was committed to it. In defence of it, it may be said that it rests upon the view, inherited from Aristotle, that 'Like can only come from like'. If X is to bring it about that Y is Φ, then X itself must be, in some manner or to some degree, Φ. That is common coin: Descartes relies on this assumption in his cosmological proof; Berkeley quotes it as an 'old known axiom'; Spinoza invokes it, or a corollary of it, in his correspondence (*Ep.* 3) and in his refutation of interactionism (*E* II, 6; *cf.* VI, 3). Now the combination of (i) and (ii) will yield the consequence that if two substances differ in attributes, the one cannot be produced, or in any way be causally affected, by the other. But to get the starker conclusion, that no substance is produced by any other, we shall obviously need to show that (iii) no two substances fail to differ in their attributes. That, of course, is what Proposition 5 upholds. The demonstration of *E* I, 5 is puzzling, and it is well to set it out in full:

> If there were two or more distinct substances they must be distinguished one from the other by difference of attributes or difference of affections (*ex diversitate affectionum*) (by *E* I, 4). If they are distinguished only by difference of attributes, it will be granted that there is but one substance of the same attribute. But if they are distinguished by difference of affections, since substance is prior by nature to its affections (by *E* I, 1), the affections being therefore placed on one side (*depositis ergo affectionibus*) and the substance being considered in itself, or, in other words, truly considered (*in se considerata, hoc est, vere considerata*) (by *E* I, Definition 3 and Axiom 6), it cannot be conceived as distinguished from another substance, that is to say (*E* I, 4), there cannot be two or more substances, but only one possessing the same nature or attribute.

The problem is to see why two things falling under the same attribute could not be distinguished by the diversity of their 'affections' (a term Spinoza leaves undefined) and yet be substances. Spinoza leaves the point murky (*cf. Leibniz*, p. 199), but I suggest that we can see what he may be after if we connect *E* I, 5D with the famous case of the lump of wax in Descartes' *Second Meditation*.

There are several ways of understanding Descartes, some better, some worse (*Williams* (1), pp. 213–27), but we need consider only what Spinoza *might* have made of it. On any account of the 'wax' argument, Descartes will have observed that a particular lump of wax can change in respect of any of its sensible qualities, and still remain the same particular thing: it can lose its honeyed taste, its smell of flowers, its hardness and coldness, its power to give out a sound when rapped with the knuckle – and still not cease to be. What this might be taken to show (among other things) is that the lump of wax, considered in itself, is not fragrant, hard, scented, cold and so forth. The intent of the argument may be to uncover the nature of the inner core which persists through these sensible changes – to isolate the substance (=substance$_3$) of the wax (*Williams* (1), p. 220). And to get at that, Descartes will have to abstract from the manifest and sensible qualities of the wax. When he does, he will discover that the wax, considered in itself, is *body*: ' "Perhaps what I distinctly knew was what I am now thinking of: namely, that the wax was not the sweetness, nor the fragrance of the flowers, nor the whiteness, nor the shape, nor the sound, but body; manifested to me previously in those aspects (*modis*), and now in others." But what exactly am I thus imagining? Let us consider; let us remove what is not proper to the wax (*remotis iis quae ad ceram non pertinent*), and see what is left: simply, something extended, flexible and changeable' (*A.G.*, p. 72). Now if the lump of wax, considered in itself or as substance$_3$, is nothing other than body, then it is not distinguishable from another lump, or from a brass farthing or the planet Jupiter, when these things are considered in themselves. All these things, considered in themselves or as they appear to the intellect, are bodies – things extended in length, breadth and depth. They are substantially the same, despite the superficial differences in (sensible) 'affections'. And that will prove that they are only 'modally' distinct from one another – that is, they differ only as modes, or specifications, of the same substance$_3$, which is *Res Extensa*.

If Spinoza understood the 'wax' passage along those lines, then it is possible that he thought that that case proved that any two things falling under Extension or Materiality could not be distinguished by their affections and *also* count as substances. (More exactly, he might have taken it to show that two such things could not be distinct substances$_3$, and concluded that they therefore could not be distinct substances$_1$: *cf.* IV, 2, last paragraph.) And – departing radically now from Descartes – he may then have generalised this result, applying it also to things which fell under Thought. Human minds, differentiated only by their affections, could not be substantially₃ distinct: the mind of X is no more a substance₃ than X's body was. Just as X's body, considered by the intellect, had to be reckoned a mode of Extension, so X's mind, viewed from the same angle, had to be taken as a mode of Thought. To think of the self as substantival₃ (or, therefore, as substantival₁), would be to fall prey to the imagination, just as if one judged that different bodies were substantival₃,₁.

What emerges is that if X and Y are distinct substances₃,₁, then they cannot fall under a common attribute. To this it is necessary to add only the trifling observation that every substance₂ is a substance₃, and it will follow that no two substances (of *any* type) can fail to differ attributively. That gives Spinoza his premiss (iii); and if (iii) is added to (i) and (ii), it does indeed seem to follow that no substance is produced by another substance (*E* I, 6). If X and Y are genuinely distinct substances, then they must fall under different attributes, the one being F and the other G; but nothing G can be caused by anything F; hence Y cannot be produced by X.

That takes us as far as *E* I, 6, and *E* I, 7 purports to establish that there is at least one substance: 'It pertains to the nature of substance to exist'. The demonstration is too brief: 'a substance cannot be produced by another thing; it will therefore be the cause of itself' – so goes the gist of it. There are three puzzles here.

(a) 'Proposition 6 has shown only that one substance cannot be produced by another *substance*; it has not shown that a substance cannot be produced by another *thing*. Why should a substance not be produced by a distinct but non-substantial thing?' The answer Spinoza would give must appeal to a relic of scholasticism: a doctrine of degree of being or perfection (*cf.* Williams (1), pp. 135–6). According to this, there are only 'accidents', 'modes' and 'substances'. 'Accidents' depend upon 'modes', and are thus less real or perfect (CM I, 1, xi), 'modes' less real than 'substances', 'created substances' less real than 'uncreated' ones. This hierarchical ordering of reality is then combined with a causal principle, enunciated by Descartes, that 'it is contradictory that the more perfect should follow from and depend upon the less perfect' (*Discourse*, Part IV; *A.G.*, p. 33). The consequence is that substance cannot be produced by a mode (or accident); and since that leaves nothing other than a substance to produce a substance, the objection will be held to have failed.

(b) 'Even if a substance cannot be produced by another

substance, and still less by a mode, why should it have to be produced at all? Why should it not exist but be *uncaused*?' Spinoza's demonstration is technically incomplete in that it does not rule out the possibility of a substance whose existence was uncaused; but that is not, for him, a genuine worry. In a supplementary demonstration intended to confirm *E* I, 6, he posits that 'there is necessarily given for each existing thing a certain cause, on account of which it exists' (*E* I, 8S2; *cf. E* I, 11 '*Aliter*'). That assumption is, or is a corollary of, the thesis of universal determinism (on which see V, 6). Hume has made us dubious about the claim that this principle is a *necessary* truth (*Treatise* I, 3, iii); but Spinoza had not had the benefit of reading Hume.

(c) 'Even if substance is neither caused by another nor uncaused, it does not follow that it is self-caused; for it might not exist at all.' That, I think, hits the nail on the head. There is an ambiguity in the notion of 'being self-caused' which Spinoza appears not to have noticed. To say of *X* that it is self-caused might be to say that it exists and is the cause of its own existence, or it might mean only that *if X* exists it is the cause of its own existence. Even if we grant that Spinoza has shown that a substance is neither caused by another thing nor yet uncaused, it will follow that it is 'self-caused' only in the weaker sense, which leaves the question open whether any substance exists. Only by assuming the existence of substance or substances from the start can he reach the conclusion that substance is self-caused in the first and stronger sense. What he is entitled to is: for any *X*, if *X* is a substance, then *X* causes its own existence. But it does not follow, and he has no right to assume, that for some actual *X*, *X* is a substance. The demonstration is either worthless or otiose – either it does not prove that there is a substance, or it assumes that there is from the start. (Anscombe discerns a very similar fallacy in the Ontological Argument: *Anscombe* (2), p. 15.)

Spinoza's proof of substantival monism seems to fail, not because there are too many substances (although that may be true), but because he does not succeed in showing that there is even *one*. But the examination of his proof, or rather of the first long stretch of it, may have brought its own rewards. It has introduced us to some of his notions concerning causality, which will return to figure in his theory of the mind and in his ethics; and it has intimated some of his reasons for regarding the human mind and the human body as alike, non-substantival modes of some more encompassing thing. The second part of his monistic proof can only be considered after referring to the attributes (*cf.* III, 7) and the knotty problems they involve.

6 *Problems of the attributes*

Spinoza's doctrine of the attributes left behind a tangle of problems which some of his contemporary critics, and all of his subsequent critics, attempted to grapple with. The statement of three of these problems, and the effort to elucidate them, will occupy this entire section. But there is at least one matter on which agreement seems finally to have been reached, and which we can immediately get out of the way. This is the question whether the attributes are dependent upon the human mind.

'By attribute', Spinoza says, 'I understand that which the intellect perceives of substance as (*tanquam*) constituting (*constituens*) its essence'. Two cruces leap to the eye: what is the 'intellect' referred to – the infinite intellect of God, or the finite human intellect? And what is the force of '*tanquam*'? Does it mean 'as *if*', with the suggestion that the intellect does not perceive substance as it is in itself (*Parkinson* (3), p. 29)? Commentators from Hegel onwards have occasionally opted for the view that an attribute is 'only a subjective mode of thinking, expressing a relation to a perceiving subject and having no real existence in the essence' (*Wolfson* I, p. 146; defended by *Wolfson* at I, pp. 152–6; other 'subjectivists' are cited in *Gueroult* I, p. 50, n. 119). But there are ten facts which torpedo the 'subjectivist' or Hegelian view. (i) It is not forced upon us by Definition 4: we are free to understand '*tanquam*' as meaning 'as', not 'as *if*'. (ii) The fact that the definition says that the intellect *perceives* the attributes as constituting the essence of substance suggests that the intellect is *successful* in what it does. (iii) In *Epistle 2*, Spinoza criticises Bacon for supposing that, 'besides the deception of the senses, the human intellect is fallible by its very nature, and imagines everything after the analogy of its own nature, and not after the analogy of the universe, so that it is like an uneven mirror (turned) to the rays of things'. But if the 'intellect' referred to in Definition 4 is human, then Spinoza will himself be guilty of the error he condemns in Bacon. And if that 'intellect' is not human, he will be guilty of the graver error of implying that God's mind is fallible, and mistaken as to His own nature. (iv) In the *Short Treatise* he asserts that 'it is clearly manifest that the idea of infinite attributes in the perfect being is not fiction' (I, 1), and that the attributes '<constitute> a being which subsists through itself, and therefore makes itself known and reveals itself through itself' (I, 7; *cf. Kessler*, pp. 636–9). (v) At *E* I, 4D, Spinoza implies that the attributes, like substance, exist 'outside the intellect'. (vi) At *E* II, 7, he tries to prove that the order and connection of ideas is the same as the order and connection of things: this is plausibly taken to involve the consequence that our ideas, when rendered clear and distinct, do faithfully represent things as we conceive them to be (VI, 5). (vii) At *E* II, 44 he states that 'it is the nature of Reason to perceive things truly, namely as they are in themselves'; but 'Réason' is here equivalent to 'intellect' (*E* IV, Appendix iv). (*Parkinson* (3), p. 29, considers this reason alone to be decisive.) (viii) At *E* II, 47, he ascribes to the mind an adequate idea of the essence of God, but an adequate idea is a true idea (*E* II, Axiom 4). (ix) If the attributes were projections by the intellect, then they would depend for their reality upon something which is itself a mode of one of them (Thought); and that is absurd (*Gueroult* I, p. 50). (x) The intellect referred to in Definition 4 is the Divine intellect (*E* II, 75), for Spinoza believes that there are an infinite number of attributes (*E* I, 11), of which, however, the human intellect knows only two (*Ep.* 64; *cf. Parkinson* (3), p. 29). But if that intellect is Divine, then its perceptions cannot be delusive; and the attributes are in themselves what it takes them to be. (For further discussion of the controversy, *see Gueroult* I, Appendix 3.)

Two important features in Spinoza's doctrine of the attributes emerge from this discussion. First, Spinoza would repudiate the traditional view, sometimes called 'Nominalism', that 'this plurality of attributes does not arise from God (*ex parte Dei*), but from the different effects which our intellect variously knows and refers to God' (Thomas Aquinas, I *Sentences*, Dist. 2, q. 1, a. 3; *cf. Garrigou-Lagrange*, pp. 165–6). 'Nominalism' concerning the Divine attributes was current in Spinoza's period: according to Hobbes, the attributes of God 'cannot signifie what he is, but ought to signifie our desire to honour him with the best appellations we can think on' (*Leviathan* IV, c. 46). Spinoza, unlike Hobbes, does not think that God's nature is incomprehensible: here he is the more revolutionary of the two. Second, he denies not only 'Nominalism', but 'Negativism', i.e., the claim, defended by Maimonides, that the only attributes which can truly be predicated of God 'do not, as regards the essence of the thing which we desire to know, in any way tell us what it is, except indirectly' (*Guide for the Perplexed* I, c. 58). 'Extension' and 'Thought' pertain to, and express, the essence of God.

The interpretation of Definition 4 is, however, the least of the many difficulties in understanding Spinoza's view of the attributes: those that remain are far more intricate and unyielding. There are, I think, at least three related problems, not easy to distinguish; let me now try to state them.

(A) First, there is the problem of *simplicity*. Spinoza follows orthodoxy in holding that God is simple (*Ep.* 35) and indivisible (*E* I, 13). The belief that simplicity was a Divine perfection may have entered into orthodoxy from Neoplatonism (e.g., from Plotinus: *Enneads* V, 3, iii; V, 4, i). Simplicity can be opposed either to *compositeness* or to *complexity*: in Aquinas, to say that God is simple is to say (i) that He is not a body, made up of extended parts; (ii) that He does not differ from His own essence; (iii) that He cannot be subsumed under any genus or species; (iv) that He has no accidental qualities; (v) that He is not constituted of form and matter; (vi) that He does not differ from His existence (*Summa Theologiae* 1a, q. 3, a. 7, *responsio*). But while asserting that God is simple, Spinoza also believes that He is complex, at least in that He comprises infinite attributes, each of which expresses infinite and eternal essence (*E* I, Definition 6). (The problem of simplicity arises in a peculiarly acute form for Descartes: for he holds that the unity, simplicity and inseparability of all God's attributes is one of his chief perfections: *Third Meditation*, A.G. pp. 89–90.) On this view, the Divine simplicity is not only consistent with having a plurality of attributes, but actually entails it, and is itself a Divine attribute: *Geach* (3).

(B) Second, there is the problem of the *compatibility* of the attributes. This issue was raised in correspondence with Spinoza by his young friend and disciple, Simon De Vries. De Vries wrote: 'You, Sir, seem to suppose that the nature of a substance is so constituted that it can have many attributes, which you have not yet proved, unless you refer to the fifth definition of the absolutely infinite substance, or God; otherwise, if I may say that each substance has only one attribute and if I had the idea of two attributes, then I could rightly conclude that where there are two different attributes there are also two different substances' (*Ep.* 8).

As we have noted, Spinoza was a compatibilist in thinking that several distinct attributes could characterise the same substance. Descartes on the other hand was an incompatibilist, believing that at most one attribute could belong to a given substance (IV, 4). De Vries seems to be alluding to the view of Descartes, and demanding a refutation of it. That view is crisply stated in the *Notes against a Programme*:

> Of the attributes which constitute the natures of things, it cannot be said that those which are different, and of which

neither is contained in the concept of the other, are coexistent in one and the same subject; for that is equivalent to saying that one and the same subject has two different natures, and this involves a contradiction, at least so long as the subject in question is simple and not composite. (*H.R.* I, p. 436)

By a 'simple subject', Descartes means in this context a 'created substance' such as *the human mind*; by a 'composite subject', he means an entity such as a *man*, who from the Cartesian viewpoint is a compound thing, formed by an individual mental substance interacting with a body, or mode of the substance Extension. In the passage from the *Notes*, Descartes is glancing at the fact that both mental and physical predications can be made in respect of a composite (human) subject, but he denies that it follows that there is a single substance characterised both by a mental and by a physical attribute. He maintains that, on the contrary, any substance has only a single nature; but to impute more than one attribute to a substance is to imply that it has more than a single nature, since every distinguishable attribute is associated with a distinguishable nature (*cp.* Donagan (1), p. 180: the 'buried premiss' of a 'radical' restatement of De Vries' objection is 'that to every really distinct attribute there corresponds a really distinct essence').

(C) Third, there is the problem of the *real distinction* between the attributes. Spinoza says that the attributes 'constitute', 'express' and 'pertain to' the essence or nature of God. He also says that 'to the essence of anything pertains that which, being given, the thing itself is necessarily posited and which, being taken away, the thing is necessarily taken away; or that without which the thing can neither be nor be conceived, and which in its turn can neither be nor be conceived without the thing' (*E* II, Definition 2). Now the attributes of Thought and Extension pertain to God's essence; hence '*extensio* being given, an absolutely infinite being is also given; for *extensio* expresses an eternal and infinite essence, and whatever expresses such an essence is an attribute of an absolutely infinite being. Again if, *per impossibile*, *extensio* were taken away, there could be no absolutely infinite being . . . Parallel arguments obviously hold for *cogitatio*' (*Donagan* (1), p. 181). From this it follows that if a substance possesses an infinite and eternal attribute, then it must be an absolutely infinite substance; and if it is an absolutely infinite substance, then it must possess *every* infinite and eternal attribute. (This is, to speak loosely, a theological form of the Platonic doctrine of the Unity of the Virtues.) This reasoning ties in with *E* I, 9, which asserts that 'the more reality or being a thing possesses, the more attributes belong to it': a theorem whose brief demonstration merely refers us back to the definition of *attribute*. From *E* I, 9, it follows that if there is a God, an absolutely infinite substance which is maximally real (an *'ens realissimum'*), then He will combine in Himself all the attributes there can be; and furthermore that if it is *necessary* that there is a maximally real being, then it is *necessary* that all possible attributes coexist in it. In short, then, Spinoza seems committed to the view that the attributes are mutually implicative, and that each of them entails each of the others.

The problem is to reconcile this result with *E*I, 10S, which declares that the attributes are conceived of as *really distinct* from one another. For Descartes had laid it down, and Spinoza appears to have agreed, that 'two substances are really distinct when each of them can exist without the other' (*PPD* I, Definition 10). Similarly, it is clear that two *attributes* are really distinct if and only if it is possible that one should exist without the other – that is, two really distinct attributes are never necessarily coexistent in the same substance. (True, *E* I, 10S says only that the attributes are *conceived* as really distinct, not that they *are* so, but we have seen earlier in this section that as the intellect takes the attributes to be, so in truth they are. Again, it might be said that if the attributes were really distinct, then each would be a substance; but this very consequence is episodically suggested by Spinoza himself – at, e.g., *E* I, 4D, and perhaps again at *E* I, 19.)

The last problem, which appears to be the gravest of the three, may underlie the criticism once urged by Collingwood: 'In spite of the brilliant merits of Spinoza's cosmology . . . it failed because the two attributes of extension and force are held together in the theory, so to speak, by main force: there is no reason that Spinoza can give why that which is extended should also think, and vice versa; and consequently the theory remains at bottom unintelligible, a mere assertion of brute fact' (*Collingwood* p. 106). Collingwood may have meant that the demonstrations which would cement the attributes together, and show them to be reciprocally implied, were inadequate; or he may have meant that the admission of a real distinction between them made it impossible to account for their coexistence and parallelism.

The problem of the real distinction carries over directly into Spinoza's theory of the mind. The crucial theorem is *E* II, 7, which maintains that the order and connection of ideas and the order and connection of things are the same (*vide* VI, 5). It is clearly Spinoza's intention to deny the Cartesian view that, in man, mind and body are only accidentally conjoined, but are really or substantivally distinct (VI, 1; 5). But what does his denial come to? On one interpretation, he is upholding psycho-physical parallelism; on another, he has adopted a form of the identity theory. The former view, which commands some textual support (*E* II, 7S: '*duobus modis expressa*'), will have it that a mode of Thought, and the corresponding mode of Extension, whilst distinct things, are nevertheless connected to each other in some peculiarly intimate fashion (VI, 4). (The connection cannot be *causal*, for Spinoza denies that mind and body interact; but it might imaginatively be taken to be *functional*, so that corresponding states of the mind and the body are related as the temperature and volume or pressure of a gas: *Matson*, p. 574; *vide* VI, 3). The latter view, which emphasises the fact that Spinoza says that the corresponding modes are one and the same thing ('*una eademque res*': *E* II, 7S; III, 2S; *cf. Zac*, p. 97), insists that the relation between them is some form of identity (VI, 4). (It cannot, however, be strict or 'Leibnizian' identity, or else interactionism could not be denied.) The 'identity' interpretation, in order to be faithful to Spinoza's leading ideas, must apparently hold that the corresponding modes are 'one and the same' in that each is a necessary and sufficient condition for the other. Now this divergence in the interpretations of Spinoza's account of the mind/body relation in man reflects the difficulty of understanding his theory of the Thought/Extension nexus in God: the microcosm mirrors the macrocosm. If we stress the real distinctness between the attributes, we must incline to a 'parallelist' interpretation of the mind/body problem; if, on the other hand, we emphasise the fact that the attributes are necessarily co-inherent, we should favour the 'identity' interpretation.

I do not think that Spinoza appreciated how grave the problem of the real distinction was; possibly, he failed to disentangle it from the problem of simplicity and the problem of compatibility, to both of which he may have thought he had solutions. The nearest he seems to come to an answer to the third problem is in his reply to De Vries (*Ep.* 9):

You however wish me to explain by means of an example, which it is very easy to do, how one and the same thing can be called by two names. But, not to seem niggardly, I will supply two examples. First, I say that by the name Israel I mean the third Patriarch; I also mean the same by the name Jacob, since the name Jacob was given to him because he had seized his

brother's heel. Second, by plane I mean that which reflects all
the rays of light without any change; I mean the same by
white, except that it is called white in relation to a man who is
looking at the plane (surface).

Spinoza's remark has struck many readers as irrelevant:
Donagan complains that 'neither De Vries nor Descartes had
evinced the slightest difficulty in understanding how the same
thing could be designated by different names, when those names
designated different modes of it' ((1), p. 168). I think that that is
to misunderstand: Spinoza is employing an analogy to *illustrate*
his views. There are two points that he wants to make: first, that
the attributes are *relational* (*sc.* to the intellect); and second, that
one and the same substance can be conceived under distinct
attributes, each of which is conceived *per se*. In the analogy, the
third Patriarch corresponds to substance; the fact that the third
Patriarch may be correctly called *either* 'Israel' *or* 'Jacob'
corresponds to the fact that substance may be truly conceived
either as Thought *or* as Extension. 'What distinguishes an
Attribute from Substance is that it is the same but in a different
respect; and . . . this respect is respect to *intellect*' (*Hallett*, p.
138): to this answers the fact that Jacob *is* the third Patriarch, but
the name 'Jacob' (i.e. 'supplanter') is implicitly relational. That
each attribute is conceived '*per se*' is mirrored by the consideration that the names 'Israel' and 'Jacob' differ in sense; that
distinct attributes can nevertheless coexist in a single subject is
implied by the fact that 'Israel' and 'Jacob' refer to, and
characterise, the same individual. The analogy, like any analogy,
is imperfect. As Donagan observes, 'being the third Patriarch, and
grasping his brother's heel, are different modes of the man called
'Israel' and 'Jacob', and not attributes constituting his essence'
((1), p. 168). But the imperfection of the analogy does not prove
its irrelevance: in fact, Spinoza's example brings out his two main
points very aptly. The second example, of the plane white surface,
may be designed to correct and improve upon the first example in
one feature: for to call a surface 'white' is to describe it under a
mode of Thought, whereas to call it 'plane' is to bring it under a
mode of Extension; and yet it is one and the same thing that is
characterised in these alternative ways. So too, then, the analogy
implies, it is possible for Substance to be brought under the
attributes of Thought and Extension alike.

The real trouble with Spinoza's answer is not that it is
irrelevant to the criticism, but that it does not refute it. All he has
done is to reiterate the position under attack; he does nothing to

defend it. Whether or not *being Israel* and *being Jacob* are necessarily equivalent, it has not been shown that *having infinite and external extension* and *having infinite and eternal thought* are necessarily so; and whether or not 'Israel' and 'Jacob' differ in sense, it remains hard to see Thought and Extension, if necessarily bound together, can each be conceived *per se*. I say again: Spinoza did not see the size of the problem; he missed his chance to deal with it; and his uncertainty shows up again exactly where we would expect to find it – in his theory of mind.

7 Monism revisited

At the end of IV, 5, I argued that the first limb of Spinoza's proof of substantival monism had not worked: he has not shown that there was at least one substance in existence. The second limb of the proof, which tries to demonstrate that there was *no more than one* substance, was left unconsidered: that limb extended from E I, 8 to E I, 14. We are now equipped to understand that second argument.

In the reasoning which takes place in those theorems, Spinoza is guided by two basic assumptions. The first is 'his revolutionary idea . . . that the two attributes which Descartes had taken to express distinct finite essences, in fact each express an eternal and infinite essence' (*Donagan* (1), p. 172). The second is that any being, or substance, who possesses an attribute which expressed infinite and eternal essence, is itself an absolutely infinite being, or *ens realissimum*, and so possesses *all* the attributes which expressed eternal and infinite essence. Just as Descartes supposed that if God had any of the perfections, then He must have them all, so Spinoza believed that if God had any attribute, so He must have them all. And since he plainly believed that an *ens realissimum* was at least a *possible* being, he saw no real difficulty in De Vries' claim that a substance could fall under no more than one attribute (Problem (B) of IV, 6). The fact that God was, in his view, absolutely *infinite*, also suggested to him that there was no difficulty in admitting that He was simple and indivisible (Problem (A) of IV, 6). For although God was extended, His infinity ruled out any *real* division of parts within Him (E I, 15 and S; *cf. Bennett* (2), p. 44). (He might also have argued that God was 'simple', not only in being non-composite, but in being non-complex; for in Him, essence and existence were one, and the attributes were reciprocally implicated.) His two basic assumptions, in short, will have fitted him out with answers to (some of) the problems of the attributes, and will have enabled him to complete his proof of substantival monism.

It is not necessary to work through the consequences of these two principles in detail, for they – or at least the second of them – are easily challenged (*Dewey*, p. 255). Ever since Leibniz demanded a consistency proof for the notion that there was a being who combined all perfections in Himself, philosophers have been alert to the dangers of hidden contradiction in propositions such as Spinoza's definition of God as 'an absolutely infinite being, a substance consisting of infinite attributes, each one expressing eternal and infinite essence' (*E* I, Definition 6). Leibniz himself thought he could provide a consistency proof, and tells us that he had shown it to Spinoza, when they met at The Hague, who finally accepted it; but that proof relies on the problematic notion of an 'affirmative' property (on which see III, 2, *Words*), and is of little value. Spinoza's claim that God *must* hold together all the attributes is inconsistent with the claim that the attributes are *really* distinct; but it is also idle unless he can show first that God *can* combine all the attributes – and that he has left undone.

V

God or Nature

1 Pantheism

The Cartesian world was riven by the two great dualisms of God and Nature, and of Matter and Mind. Spinoza rejected both. In this chapter, I shall consider his attack on the first dualism and in the following chapter, I shall examine his criticism of the second.

In his correspondence, Spinoza bluntly declares that 'the Universe is God' (*Ep.* 43). The usual name for that doctrine is pantheism. Spinoza's pantheism has been acclaimed or reviled far more frequently than it has been understood. To his immediate successors, his 'hideous hypothesis' seemed a ruseful version of atheistic materialism, honeyed words coating poisoned messages; to the Young Germany of the Romantic period, and later to Arnold and Renan, it seemed the inspired vision of a God-intoxicated man, the last magnificent blaze of the Hebrew religious imagination. Both views are partial and distorted. Spinoza was deeply sympathetic to the scientific aspirations of his era, but he explicitly repudiates materialism. In *Epistle* 73, he condemns the misunderstanding of those who 'think that the *Tractatus Theologico-Politicus* rests on the view that God and Nature (by which they mean a certain mass, or corporeal matter) are one and the same'. And his metaphysical vision, though awesome and exalted, is not the work of poetical sensibility and fine feeling, but the patient elaboration of axioms, postulates and definitions. Spinoza knew that the novelty of his conceptions would bring incomprehension and controversy. He writes to Oldenburgh of his fears that the Christians may 'take offence and with their customary hatred attack me, who loathe quarrels' (*cf.*

Gueroult I, pp. 585–6), and he expects to incur their hostility because 'I could not separate God from Nature as all whom I have any knowledge of have done' (*Ep.* 6). This insistence on the oneness of God and Nature is present from his earliest work. In the *Short Treatise* (I, 8) he remarks: 'By *Natura naturans* we understand a being that we conceive clearly and distinctly through itself, and without needing anything beside itself . . . that is, God'. It reappears mutedly but unmistakeably in the *Ethics*: 'that eternal and infinite being, which we call God, that is, Nature (*Deus, sive Natura*)'.

To some minds, pantheism seems downright ridiculous. Swinburne parodies it as the doctrine that:

> One, who is not, we see:
> but one, whom we see not, is:
> Surely this is not that:
> but that is assuredly this . . .
> God, whom we see not, is:
> and God, who is not, we see:
> Fiddle, we know, is diddle:
> and diddle, we take it, is dee.

And Chesterton mocks the pantheist with the question, whether the Piccadilly Circus is God. But in Spinoza's hands, the theory has consequences which are only too comprehensible. In identifying God and Nature, he endows Nature with many qualities which had not been thought to belong to it, e.g., eternity, infinity and necessary existence; and he divests God of those (personal) qualities which orthodox theology and pious belief had joined in ascribing to Him ('omniscience', 'mercy', 'wisdom' and 'being the highest good' are mentioned in *ST* I, 8). And the consequences he deduces bear, not only on theology, but on science. By assigning the attribute of Thought to Nature, Spinoza establishes the possibility of a scientific psychology, which treats thought as a natural phenomenon, capable of being explained in terms of efficient causes. And by supposing Extension to belong to God, he relieves himself of the necessity of explaining how motion could have arisen in the first instance from a cause which was unmoved. Pascal had complained of Descartes: 'he would fain have managed to dispense with God throughout his philosophy; but he could not help letting Him give a fillip to get the world going' (*Pascal* (2), section 285). Whether or not that is just to Descartes, it could not be said of Spinoza (*Ep.* 40). Furthermore, by removing the Creator who got the world in motion, Spinoza also obviated the need to explain the world's workings by reference to that Creator's purposes. In short: if God is identified with Nature, then there can be a science of mind which parallels the science of body, and the study of bodies in motion can proceed without reference to minds and their aims.

Spinoza's pantheism has two main sides, both of which are seen at *E* I, 18, which asserts that God is the immanent, but not the transitive, cause of all things. In denying God to be the *transitive* cause of things, Spinoza is repudiating the idea that God stands apart from the world as a Platonic demiurge or Christian creator. 'The vulgar distinction, based on imagination and not on reason, between God and Nature has always been tied to the distinction between the Creator and his Creation; God is imagined as an artificer and Nature, including man, as his artifact' (*Hampshire*, (2), p. 40). Spinoza plainly wants to put paid to this. But what is meant in affirming that God is the *immanent* cause of things? We are given a hint at *Ep*. 43: 'it is the same, or not very different, to assert that all things emanate necessarily from the nature of God, and that the Universe is God'. A fuller, and perhaps a more intelligible, statement is given in the *First Dialogue* of the *Short Treatise* (*G* I, p. 30). Spinoza's spokesman, Reason, is trying to refute the claim of Desire that the cause of the universe must be distinct from its effect. Reason replies:

> You say this because you only know of the transeunt and not of the immanent cause, which by no means produces anything outside itself, as is exemplified by the Understanding, which is the cause of its ideas. And that is why I called the understanding (insofar as, or because, its ideas depend on it) a cause; and on the other hand, since it consists of its ideas, a whole. (*Wolf* translation, p. 34)

The suggestion is that God is both the cause of His creatures and the whole of which they are parts; His relation to them is thus analogous to the intellect's relation to its ideas.

When we work out the analogy, however, a striking and paradoxical conclusion emerges. As Desire points out to Reason, the idea of a 'whole' 'is a second notion, and nothing in Nature apart from human thought'. To say that the understanding is a 'whole' whose ideas are 'parts' suggests that the understanding is a logical being, an *ens rationis*. There is no faculty or power, distinct from ideas, which is exercised in producing them, and whatever we wish to say abstractly concerning the understanding (or will) we can say in terms of particular ideas (or volitions). (This we know to have been Spinoza's later view: *cp*. *E* I, 31S;

Ep. 2; *ST* II, 16, iv; *cf.* II, 2.) But if the intellect is an *ens rationis*, then how can we say that it is the *cause* of its ideas?

The only possibility I can see requires further analogies: we might say that the intellect is related to its ideas as a chess game is to the particular moves it embraces, or as a sine curve is related to the points which lie upon it. (*Vendler*, p. 187, argues that this conception of the mind is Cartesian; see also *Caton*, p. 140; p. 149.) In other words, the intellect supplies the principle which forms certain ideas into one unified and continuous thing. (It does not do that as an underlying substratum, distinct from the ideas which inhere in it, or on which they depend; and just as a chess game can be one, though divided into discontinuous phases, so an intellect can be one, without having to engage in thinking without intermission.) If the intellect can be said to 'cause' its ideas, it is not as something which brings about their existence, but as something which explains, in a certain way, why those ideas belong together and form a unity. (In the same way, the formula for the sine curve explains why precisely those points which lie upon it are picked out.) If this suggestion is correct, then we can reconcile the claim that the intellect and its ideas are as whole to part with the claim that they are as cause to effect. But the price is that we are then compelled to say that the intellect is a 'construct', and can we also say that of the thing to which Spinoza likens it – that is, of God?

Wolfson rebels against this consequence, offering a different explanation of God's 'immanent' causality in the world. He writes:

> When Spinoza . . . says that all things are in God he means exactly the same thing as when Aristotle says that man exists in animal as a species in a genus. And when he further says that all things are in God as parts are in the whole he means again exactly the same thing as when Aristotle says that the 'part is in the whole' . . . It is in this sense that God is the immanent cause of all things; He is their internal cause as the genus is the internal cause of the species or the species of the particulars and as the whole is the internal cause of its parts. (*Wolfson* I, p. 324)

Wolfson here indifferently equates the relation of God to His creation with the genus/species, the species/particular, and the whole/part relations, as if these were all the same. Furthermore, as he himself observes (pp. 324–5), Spinoza regards genera, species, and wholes as alike logical beings, *entia rationis*: and if God stands to the Creation as these things stand to what they include, then God must again be reckoned to be an *ens rationis* – which is what Wolfson denies. More precisely, Wolfson seeks to stave off the consequence to which his own interpretation points by admitting that Spinoza's God is an *ens rationis* 'only in the sense that [His] real existence can be discovered only by the mind, by the ontological proofs based upon the adequacy of the idea of God in our mind. In truth, however, God is an *ens reale*' (pp. 325–6). Now it is simply wrong to say that Spinoza thinks God's existence to be discoverable only by the ontological argument; he himself traces out a different route to that knowledge (*E* I, 11S). But in any case, Wolfson's 'solution' amounts to a verbal dodge: he invents a novel sense of the term *ens rationis*, not found in Spinoza's own writings, and asserts that it can be applied to God only in that meaning, without showing that it cannot be applied in its standard sense.

The paradox that Spinoza's God is a logical being ought to be disarmed rather than resisted. To say this of God is not to imply that He is a 'fiction' in the way that Mr Micawber is, or that His existence is in any sense 'mind-dependent'. After all, there *are* human understandings, just as there *are* ideas, and sine curves exist along with points. They differ in their 'mode of being' (or, if you like, the existential claims made on their behalves differ in 'logical grammar'). But that does not consign minds or sine curves to the realm of the illusory (*cp. CM* I, 1, ii, which distinguishes 'logical beings' from 'fictions' and from 'chimeras'). We may think of them as real, providing that we do not think of them as real in the way the ideas or points are. Spinoza's 'immanentism' thus far amounts to the claim that God is Nature, conceived as the totality of things (*Hampshire* (2), p. 32; but *cf. Curley* (3), p. 42).

The *Short Treatise* is not a self-consistent work, however, and it offers yet another elucidation of 'immanent causality'. If we attend to this alternative account, we shall have to conclude that God is the totality, not of *objects*, but of *facts*.

Theophilus, Spinoza's spokesman, has laid it down that the effect of the immanent cause remains united with its cause in such a way that together they constitute a whole. Erasmus, his opponent, objects that if this is so, then God cannot be an immanent cause: for if He and His effects together form a whole, then He will have more essence at one time than at another. Theophilus denies this consequence, and invokes the illustration of the idea of a triangle, i.e. of a construction which extends one of the figure's angles, so that the extended angle is equal to the two interior opposite angles. 'These, I say, have produced a new idea, namely, that the three angles of the triangle are equal to two right angles. This idea is so connected with the first, that it can neither be, nor be conceived without the same. Mark well now that although the new idea is joined to the preceding one, the essence of the preceding idea does not undergo any change in consequence; on the contrary, it remains without the slightest change' (*Wolf* translation, p. 37; G I, p. 32).

Following through on this, it seems that God's 'immanence' in Creation is like the relation between certain facts about the nature of the triangle to other facts about its *properties*. The nature of God, in other words, is a fact which entails (whether of itself or in conjunction with certain other facts) facts about the created order. God is a 'cause', in that His existence and nature entail certain consequences; He is 'immanent', in that these consequences are inescapable, given that He exists and has a nature of a certain kind; He is 'prior', in that the consequences do not in turn entail the facts concerning Him from which they can be deduced; He is 'total', in that *all* the facts pertaining to the created order follow from the relevant facts about Himself.

One problem in this interpretation may be mentioned. The *Short Treatise* draws a distinction between 'infinite and immutable things', of which God is said to be the 'proximate' cause, and 'particular things', of which He is 'in a sense the remote cause': I, 3, i. (This distinction is echoed in *E* I, 28S.) But the account which has just been sketched in implies that all 'things' – i.e. facts – follow from God in the same manner. An ingenious solution to this and other difficulties has been suggested by E.M. Curley (*Curley* (3), c. 2). Very briefly, Curley thinks that the totality of facts must be divided into general or nomological facts, and singular facts. God's attributes, or *Natura naturans*, are then taken to be basic nomological facts; the immediate infinite modes to be derivative but primary nomic facts; the mediate infinite modes to be derivative and secondary nomic facts; and the finite modes of *natura naturata* to be the singular facts. God's 'causal' relation to the world thus corresponds to the relations between basic natural laws and derivative laws, or to those between natural laws of the several kinds, and singular facts. This interpretation succeeds in giving a clear sense to the claim that God is 'immanent' in the world, whilst also allowing for the various ways in which His 'causality' affects facts of different types.

Summary

Let us review our progress thus far. We have seen that Spinoza's pantheism, for all its portentously metaphysical appearance, is a doctrine with very definite consequences, both for science and for theology. It involves him in saying that God did not 'create' the world, in any traditional and accepted sense, but it permitted him to hold that God was 'immanent cause' of the world. The type of causality in question here was unfamiliar and obscure, but with the aid of a pair of suggestions from the *Short Treatise*, we have been able to fix two possible interpretations. In calling God the immanent cause of all things, he may mean *either* that God is Nature as the totality of things, *or* that He is Nature as the totality of facts. If he really meant the latter, then his distinctions between infinite and finite (or, relatedly, between *Natura naturans* and *Natura naturata*), and his views concerning the modes of Divine causality, can be regarded – as Curley shows – as anticipating modern accounts of scientific explanation.

2 The Divine mind

Orthodoxy had separated God from Nature, but it did not interdict all commerce between them. On the contrary, it saw God's mind and power at work everywhere in the Universe. But the principle bond between God and the world, and the bond that made all other ties possible, was the fact that God was the *Creator* of Nature. Originating in the creation-narrative in *Genesis*, this view had been systematised and defended by many notable thinkers. But Spinoza, as we have seen, was committed to rejecting it. For him, as later for proponents of Darwinism, the belief in the *Genesis* account presented a massive obstacle to the advance of science and of reason. He devoted much effort to subverting it, as a reading of the *Short Treatise*, the *Cogitata Metaphysica*, and *Ethics* I will show. In what follows, I shall examine some of his most fundamental criticisms of Creationism. It is not too much to say that, in studying Spinoza's critique of this part of Theology, we can see the naturalistic world outlook struggling to emerge (*Strauss*, p. 127).

Let us try to state what Creationism held. As Spinoza represents it, it maintains that God brought the universe of minds and bodies into being *ex nihilo*, and not from any pre-existing matter. His creative act involved the exercise of the Divine intellect, which shaped His plan, and the Divine will, which ordained its execution. His will to create the Universe occurred freely and without constraint, and He acted for ends which were His own. The Universe therefore exists contingently, and the assumption that it is not contingent implies the denial of God's perfection and omnipotence. If we follow the standard calculations, we must date the origin of the Universe to approximately 4004 B.C.: at any rate, it had a beginning in time.

In Spinoza's criticism of this theory, nearly all the major themes of his philosophy are announced. In this and the sections which follow, I discuss five aspects of his critique. First, there are his objections to the claim that God has both an intellect and a will; second, there is his effort to reconcile belief in God's omnipotence with denial of the contingency of the Universe; third, there is the question whether the Universe had a beginning in time; fourth, comes the rejection of free will in God; and last, there is the attack on final causes, the denial that God acts for certain ends. Putting these together, we have one of the most determined assaults ever made on religion in the name of philosophy.

We begin with the first issue. In *E* I, 17S, Spinoza appoints himself the task of proving that 'neither intellect nor will pertain to the nature of God'. The promised demonstration appears later in the scholium, when he writes:

> To say a word, too, here about the intellect and will which we commonly attribute to God – if intellect and will pertain to His eternal essence, these attributes cannot be understood in the sense in which men generally use them (*aliud sane per utrumque hoc attributum intelligendum est, quam quod vulgo solent homines*), for the intellect and will which could constitute His essence would have to differ entirely from our intellect and will (*toto caelo differre deberent*), and could resemble ours in nothing except in name (*nec in ulla re, praeterquam in nomine, convenire possent*). There could be no further likeness than that between the celestial constellation of the Dog (*Canis, signum caeleste*) and the animal which barks (*canis, animal latrans*). This I will demonstrate as follows. If intellect pertains to the Divine nature, it cannot, like our intellect, follow the things which are its object (as many suppose), nor can it be simultaneous in its nature with them, since God is prior to all things in causality (*E* I, 16C1); but, on the contrary, the truth and formal essence of things is what it is, because as such it exists objectively in God's intellect. Therefore the intellect of God, insofar as it is conceived to constitute His essence, is in truth the cause of things, both of their essence and of their existence – a truth which seems to have been understood by those who have maintained that God's intellect, will and power are one and the same thing. Since, therefore, God's intellect is the sole cause of things, both

of their essence and of their existence (as we have already shown), it must necessarily differ from them with regard both to its essence and existence; for an effect differs from its cause precisely in that which it has from its cause (*nam causatum differt a sua causa praecise in eo, quod a causa habet*). For example, one man is the cause of the existence but not of the essence of another, for the essence is an eternal truth; and therefore with regard to existence they must differ. Consequently if the existence of one should perish, that of the other would not therefore perish; but if the essence of one could be destroyed and become false, the essence of the other would be likewise destroyed. Therefore a thing which is the cause both of the essence and of the existence of any effect must differ from that effect both with regard to its essence and with regard to its existence. But the intellect of God is the cause both of the essence and existence of our intellect; therefore the intellect of God, so far as it is conceived to constitute the Divine essence, differs from our intellect both with regard to its essence and its existence, nor can it coincide with our intellect in anything except the name, which is what we essayed to prove. The same demonstration may be applied to the will, as anyone may easily see for himself.

It is important to see that Spinoza is *not* conceding that intellect and will belong to the nature or essence of God in even a *remote* sense; it is stated roundly that 'neither intellect nor will pertain to the nature of God'; and the demonstration is designed to prove the *conditional* proposition that *if* they belonged to God's nature, then even so His intellect and will would have nothing in common with ours save the name (*Gueroult* I, pp. 562–3). If it is necessary that intellect and will belong to a thing's nature in order that the thing should be a person, then Spinoza's God is not a person:

> Was soll mir euer Hohn
> Uber das All und Eine?
> Der Professor ist eine Person,
> Gott ist keine.

How is this result proved? Assuming, of course, that intellect and will do pertain to God's nature, Spinoza says, it is the case that (i) the Divine intellect, insofar as it is conceived to constitute the essence of God, is the cause both of the essence and of the existence of all things. Consequently, (ii) it is the cause of the essence and existence of our intellect. But (iii) an effect differs from its cause precisely in that which it has from its cause. So (iv) the Divine intellect, conceived of as constituting the Divine essence, differs from our intellect in both essence and existence. And this, in turn, supports the conclusion that (v) the Divine intellect has nothing in common with our intellect except the name.

As so often in Spinoza, the implicit target of the argument is not easy to identify; I conjecture that it was Descartes. In the *Replies to the Second Set of Objections*, Descartes wrote that 'the idea which we have of the Divine intellect does not seem to me to differ from that which we have of our own intellect, save only as the idea of an infinite number differs from the idea of a binary or ternary number' (*H.R.* II, p. 36). (For Spinoza's related struggle with Maimonides, see *Strauss*, pp. 151-4.)

How effective is the reasoning? Premiss (i) can be taken to mean that an intellect which belonged to God's nature or essence would not be 'receptive', as human intellects are, but 'creative' (*Barker*, p. 115). And that in turn can be read to mean that if such an intellect belonged to God, then it would be the case that for any 'p' such that it is a fact that p, then 'p' because God's intellect understands that p. (This contrasts with the human intellect, of which it cannot be said that its understanding a fact causes that fact to hold.) Spinoza could have derived this premiss from Descartes himself who, in a letter of 2 May 1644, praises St Augustine's prayer, 'Truths are so because you see them to be so' (*Kenny Letters*, p. 151).

Suppose next that it belongs to our intellect to have essence F. Then we can deduce, by means of (i), that our intellect has essence F because God's intellect understands it to have F – or more loosely, that our intellect has F because of God's intellect. (In a similar way, we can deduce that our intellect *exists* because of God's intellect.) That gives us step (ii). But now, by (iii), it seems to follow that our intellect differs from God's in essence (and in existence) – which is what (iv) asserts. To reach (v), however, we need an extra, unstated premiss. It will not do to say that (vi) if X and Y differ in essence (and existence), then X and Y cannot both be 'Φ' in the same sense. For a man and a horse, Spinoza says, differ in (specific) essence (*E* III, 57S) – as, presumably, they do in existence; and yet both can unequivocally be called 'animal'. Instead of (vi), we need something like (vii): if it is the specific essence of X to be Φ, then if Y differs in specific essence from X, Y cannot be called 'Φ' in the same sense as X. And this will give us (v), or something very close to it.

Thus far, then, the reasoning appears to be successful. But let us turn our attention to the causal axiom announced in (iii). At a first approximation, this seems to mean that if X causes Y to be Φ, then X and Y differ in respect of Φness. But how do they differ? Not, surely, in that one is Φ and the other *not-*Φ: in the example Spinoza gives, both the man who imparts existence, and the man who receives it from him, are in existence. They 'differ' in that it is *possible* for one to cease to exist without the other's ceasing to do so (*cp.* VI, 3 (A)). Perhaps then (iii) might be formulated as: if X causes Y to be Φ, then if X is Φ, it is possible for X (Y) to cease to be Φ, without Y's (X's) also ceasing to be Φ.

On this construal, the claim that God's intellect differs from our in essence amounts to saying: if God's intellect has essence F, then it could cease to have F without our intellect's ceasing to have F, and conversely. But why should that show that the predicate '... *has essence F*' cannot be ascribed in the same sense to God's intellect and to ours? In the illustration, the one man 'differs' from the other in existence in just the way that God's intellect 'differs' from ours in essence, but it scarcely follows that the one man '*exists*' in a radically different sense from the other.

Premiss (vii), however, remains plausible. But that is only because it uses the phrase 'differing in essence' in a quite separate meaning. A river bank and the branch of Barclays in the Market Place differ in specific essence, and if both are *called* 'banks', that does not signify that they have a common nature – the term is just being used equivocally. If God's intellect differed in specific essence from ours, as the Tyne bank differs from the branch of Barclays, then indeed it would be only equivocally that the two things could be called 'intellects', or be said to have such-and-such an essence in common. But Spinoza has done nothing to prove the the Divine intellect and the human differ in specific essence. He has shown only that if God's intellect has the essence which it causes ours to have, then the one could cease to have that essence without necessitating that the other also ceased to have it. When Descartes compared the human and the Divine intellects to a binary or ternary and to 'an infinite number', he was assuming that the former, like the latter, were the same in specific essence. That may be untrue of infinite intellects, as well as of 'infinite numbers', but Spinoza has not *proved* it to be so. The fallacy which Spinoza committed may have been encouraged by his nominalism (*cf.* III, 2; III, 7). For although he himself uses the term 'essence (*essentia*)' to cover the same ground as 'specific essence' (as at *E* III, 57S), he wants to maintain that there are no common essences or natures, only individual ones. (Thus in *Ep.* 2 he denies that 'humanity' or 'human nature' is anything real.)

When he says that a begetter and his begotten differ in essence, what he asserts is true, if all essences are individual. But this difference in essence cannot entail that no specific terms can be applied to both without equivocation. If it did, then specific terms would effectively be banished from the language. For by that account, it would be invalid to reason: 'Abraham was a man; Isaac was a man; so there is something which both Abraham and Isaac were'. On the extreme nominalistic view, that would be like reasoning: 'That star is a Dog ("*Canis*"); Rover is a dog ("*canis*"); so there is something which both Rover and that star are'.

3 God and omnipotence

The scholium which we have just been studying divides into two complementary halves. One half, which we have examined, tried to refute the idea that intellect and will pertain to the essence of God. The other half, which we shall now consider, concerns the question of God's omnipotence.

At first sight these two topics might seem unrelated. But in fact, as Spinoza saw, the connection between them is very close. When we reflect on the Creation, it is natural to ask whether God could have made other things or better things than He has made. And two reasons for thinking that He could have are certain to be mentioned. The first is that even human beings can act otherwise than in fact they do: they possess a free will, which empowers them to do or to refrain from certain things. But if men possess this crowning attribute, how can it be denied to God? The other reason stems from the fact that God is omnipotent. If we supposed that His power to create was limited to the world He actually made, we would treat Him as a very paltry god, subject like Jupiter to Fate. Both reasons influenced Descartes, and led him to maintain that the world could have been otherwise than it is. Spinoza denied that God could have made other or better things, and consequently he was bound to repudiate the reasoning which had persuaded Descartes. In *E* I, 17S, we see part of his counter-argument. By denying that intellect and will belong to God's nature, he is subverting the claim that God has a *free* will (*cf*. *E* I, 32C1, C2). And in the other half of the scholium, he tries to reconcile God's omnipotence with the denial of the possibility of things' being otherwise.

I have implied that Spinoza's target is once again Descartes. That may not be true, or not the whole truth. Spinoza does not name the exponents of the view he criticises. He calls them 'enemies' or 'adversaries', but leaves us to guess who they were.

GOD OR NATURE

(Wolfson suggested that the unnamed opponent may have been Abraham Herrera (*Wolfson* I, pp. 313–14), but Spinoza had worthier foes.) The problem which Spinoza was analysing had had, when he wrote, a long history. Two of the greatest writers who had dealt with it were Descartes and Aquinas. Whether or not Spinoza actually had both of them in mind, it will illuminate his answer to treat it as if he had.

The Cartesian view is the simpler and the more extreme. It held that God, in virtue of His omnipotence, it able to do literally anything. Descartes stated his thesis forcefully, in a series of letters to Mersenne. 'The mathematical truths which you call eternal have been laid down by God and depend on Him entirely no less than the rest of His creatures. Indeed to say that these truths are independent of God is to talk of Him as if He were Jupiter or Saturn and to subject Him to the Styx and the Fates' (*Kenny Letters*, p. 11). 'In general we can assert that God can do everything that we can comprehend but not that He cannot do what we cannot comprehend' (*Kenny Letters*, p. 12). 'Just as He was free not to create the world, so He was no less free to make it untrue that all the lines of a circle to its circumference are equal' (*Kenny Letters*, p. 15).

Descartes' view is riddled with difficulties. If God can do anything, then He can lie (which overturns the claim that He cannot deceive us) and He can walk (which implies that He could have a body). Both of these consequences are inconsistent with theses which Descartes was bound to defend. Moreover, he himself seems to place a limit on God's power when he writes that 'it is not the case that God would be showing the immensity of His power if He made things which could exist without Him later on; on the contrary, He would thus be showing that His power was finite, since things once created would no longer depend on Him' (*Kenny Letters*, p. 116). But if God cannot bring it about that His creatures should be independent of him, then it follows that there *is* something which he cannot do. Nor are the difficulties peculiarly internal to the Cartesian system, for if God can do anything, then He can bring it about that p and not-p. But can God really create a self-contradictory state of affairs? Aquinas thought not, and consequently he defined omnipotence in such a way as to avoid that result. (In this respect he is typical of the medieval tradition: *Wolfson*, I, p. 312). Aquinas' view appears to be: God is omnipotent in that, for any 'p' such that it is 'absolutely' (i.e. logically) possible that p, then God can bring it about that p (*Summa Theologiae* Ia, q. 25, a. 3, *responsio*; *cf.* Kenny (3), pp. 91–2).

GOD OR NATURE

We have then two contrasting conceptions of omnipotence, either of which may have been before Spinoza's mind when he wrote *E* I, 17S. With these conceptions in the background, we may approach his own formulation of the 'adversaries'' view. It reads:

> They do not believe that He can bring it about that all those things which are in act in His Intellect should exist; for they think that thus they negate the power of God. 'If He had created everything which is in His Intellect,' they say, 'He would not have been able then to create any more'; and that they believe to contradict God's omnipotence.

In other words, Spinoza's antagonists argue from the denial of their own view of the scope of God's power, together with a certain thesis about the Divine omnipotence, to a conclusion which cannot be reconciled with the doctrine of omnipotence. That is they maintain that the contrary position – the position held by Spinoza – can be refuted by a reduction to logical absurdity. Now the *reductio* argument which Spinoza gives them is only adumbrated; but if we can make it out, we will have a fairly clear picture *both* of what they believed *and* of what Spinoza believed.

I think we can successfully reconstruct the *reductio* which Spinoza was describing. What Spinoza's enemies want to uphold is the notion that there are some states of affairs which are present in the Divine intellect – states, therefore, which God had the power to actualise – which in fact God failed to actualise. In their view, God could have made it happen that Bloody Mary had left living issue, or that Oswald's bullets missed Kennedy, but in fact He did not exercise those powers. Since that is what they want to *prove*, and since the argument they put up is a *reductio*, then it must be the *negation* of that opinion which provided their starting point. Accordingly, we must assume that the first premiss of the *reductio* is, or anyway implies:

> (i) There is no state of affairs '*p*' such that *both*: it was in God's power to bring it about that *p*, *and*: God did not bring it about that *p*.

There can, I think, be little real doubt that this is doctrine which the '*adversarii*' attacked and which Spinoza defended. But it is important to see that the Latin sentence in which he characterises this premiss is modally ambiguous. The proposition they reject, it tells us, is that God can bring it about that all those things which are in act in His intellect should exist ('*eum posse omnia quae actu*

138

intelligit efficere ut existant'). On one reading, this is plausibly construed by sentence (i); but on another, it is given instead by (ii):

(ii) It was in God's power to bring it about that, for any '*p*' such that God was able to bring it about that *p*, *p*.

It can be marginally useful to put these formulas into symbolism, so that their differences in logical form are more apparent. There is, so far as I know, no standard notation which is perfectly adequate to the job; but if we take '*M* . . .' to mean 'possibly . . .' and '*aD* . . .' to mean 'God brings it about that . . .', then untensed versions of (i) and (ii) can be rendered by:

(iii) $-(\exists p)(MaD{:}p \ \& \ -aD{:}p)$

and:

(iv) $MaD{:}(p)(MaD{:}p \rightarrow p)$.

(For the moment we can safely neglect (ii), although it will recur later in the analysis; it is (i) which features in the 'adversaries'' reasoning.)

Recollect that *two* premisses were needed. We have the first of them; the second will come from the adversaries' conception of God's omnipotence – a conception which Spinoza does not share, since he calls his own 'the more perfect' ('*hoc modo Dei omnipotentia longe, meo quidem judicio, perfectior statuitur*'). What is this defective conception? We are not expressly told, but I submit that it was either the one which Descartes defended – the extreme suggestion that God's omnipotence consists in His ability to actualise any state of affairs whatsoever; or that it was the more sensible idea found in Aquinas that God's omnipotence lay in His power to realise any logically possible state of affairs. Either conjecture will enable us to make sense of the *reductio*; but since the Thomistic view is the more plausible of the two, and since it is in any event implied by the radical proposal, it is the one which I shall attribute to Spinoza'a opponents. Thus we may take it that the second premiss of their argument reads:

(v) For any '*p*' – if it is logically possible that *p*, then it was in God's power to bring it about that *p*.

With that, the argument is launched. Suppose we take some – apparently – contingent state of affairs, say, that Adam sinned. We can agree that, in the actual world, this contingency did arise:

(vi) Adam sinned.

Furthermore, we must assume that whatever happens in the world, does so because God has made it happen (*E* I, 16):

(vii) For any '*p*' – if *p*, then it is because God brought it about that *p*, that *p*.

From these two uncontentious assumptions, it follows that:

(viii) God brought it about that Adam sinned.

Now premiss (i) is equivalent to:

(ix) For any '*p*' – if God brought it about that *p*, then God had no power not to bring it about that *p* (i.e. God necessarily brought '*p*' about).

The convertibility of (i) and (ix) ought not to surprise us, for (ix), being what the theologians are out to refute, is Spinoza'a own thesis; and in the form of (ix), that thesis is readily seen to be a statement of theological Necessitarianism, which is evidenced elsewhere: *E* I, 33. Next, from (viii) and (ix), we can collect:

(x) God necessarily brought it about that Adam sinned.

That gives us the first limb of the *reductio*: the rest is easy. From the fact that Adam's sinning is a *contingency*, it follows that his *not* sinning is a *possible* state of affairs, and so by (v) it follows that:

(xi) It was in God's power to bring it about that Adam did not sin.

But the conjunction of (x) and (xi), though not a *formal* contradiction, is nevertheless a perfectly genuine contradiction; and from that it is meant to follow that the assumptions in the argument – or, more specifically, proposition (i) – cannot be true.

There we have the theologians' reduction; undoubtedly, it looks persuasive. But Spinoza thought he had discovered the answer to it. *E* I, 17S says:

> In truth, I take myself to have shown with sufficient clarity (in Theorem 16) that from the sovereign power of God, or from the infinite nature, infinite things in infinite modes – that is, all things – have flowed necessarily, or do always follow with the same necessity, in the very way it follows from eternity and for eternity from the nature of the triangle that its three angles equal the sum of two right angles . . . And thus God's omnipotence was in act from eternity, and will remain in the same actuality for eternity. And in this manner the omni-

potence of God – in my own opinion, of couse – is stated to be the more perfect. What is more, my adversaries (permit me to speak openly) appear to deny the omnipotence of God. For they are forced to admit that God understands infinite creatable things, which nonetheless He will never be able to create. For otherwise, if He were to create all the things He could create, then on their view He would exhaust His omnipotence, and make Himself imperfect. Thus in·order that they may state that God is perfect, they are reduced to the point at which they are obliged to state at the same time that He cannot bring about all the things to which His power extends – and anything more absurd than that, or more inconsistent with the omnipotence of God, I cannot easily imagine.

The passage is not wholly transparent in its details, but the main features of the argument stand out clearly. Spinoza is putting forward a two-part response to his enemies – trying, as it were, to trap them by a pincer movement. First, he claims that he has produced a direct refutation of the theologians in the preceding theorem. (I shall not consider that claim.) He takes himself to have proved there that 'all things have flowed necessarily from the sovereign power of God', in the way in which geometrical conclusions follow demonstrably from their premisses. (In the terms of our analysis, this amounts to claiming that he has already proved (vii) and (ix). If so, then *cadit quaestio*: the axe of the *reductio* cannot fall on (ix), i.e. on (i).) Second, and more relevant to our current purpose, he seems to be saying that he has a *reductio* of his own, which will show the theologians to be wrong – an argument, that is, which cancels out the one they have advanced. (Gueroult seems to agree: *Gueroult* I, p. 273.) What is this counter-reduction?

The interpretation I shall offer originates with Geach (*Geach* (2), p. 11). According to it, Spinoza maintains that his opponents can be manoeuvred into the absurdity of admitting that 'God is unable to bring about all the things to which His power extends' (compare the earlier remark – 'they are forced to admit that God understands infinite creatable things which nonetheless He will never be able to create'). In these comments the smell of modal ambiguity is uncomfortably strong (contrast *Gueroult* I, p. 272). Does he mean that God cannot bring it about that everything He can cause to obtain, should obtain? Or is it rather that it is not the case that whatever God can bring about, He can bring about? The first item is:

(xii) It is not in God's power to bring it about that, for every

GOD OR NATURE

'*p*' such that it is in God's power to bring it about that *p*, then *p*,

while the second item is:

(xiii) It is not the case that for every '*p*' such that God can bring it about that *p*, God can bring it about that *p*.

Again it may be useful to clothe these formulas in symbolism. The difference between (xii) and (xiii) is, or rather is akin to, that between (xiv) and (xv):

(xiv) $-\mathrm{MaD}{:}(p)\ (\mathrm{MaD}{:}p \to p)$
(xv) $-(p)\ (\mathrm{MaD}{:}p \to \mathrm{MaD}{:}p)$.

Of these, it is obvious that (xiii) really is contradictory or absurd: there could not be a state of affairs such that God both was and was not able to bring about. But that absurdity does not infect (xii). Far from appearing contradictory, (xii) has the solid ring of truth: for while God was able to bring it about that the earth was flat, and was also able to bring it about that the earth was not flat, not even God was able to make an earth which was flat-and-not-flat. To bring about an impossible state of affairs is an impossible action, and an impossible action is one which God Himself cannot perform, nor cause to be performed.

Geach indicts Spinoza for muddling up (xii) and (xiii), and for shifting the absurdity which belongs to the latter onto the former. He seems to think that it was only because of this blunder that Spinoza took himself to have beaten the theologians. But a problem remains: why even so did Spinoza suppose that by rejecting (xii) he had got rid of the opposing view? Why should he have thought that the theologians had a stake in the truth of (xii)? Geach does not tell us; but I think that the answer is that Spinoza piled Pelion upon Ossa by adding one modal confusion to another. Not only will Spinoza stand accused of muddling up (xii) and (xiii); he must also have confused (i) and (ii). (Here, as promised, my earlier distinction comes into play.) Had Spinoza been utterly clear-headed, he would have ascribed only the denial of (i) to his opponents; but by a – surely comprehensible – lapse he converted their view into a negation of (ii) instead. He then compounded the error by smudging the difference between (xii) and (xiii), taking (xii) to be contradictory on the grounds that (xiii) was; and finally, seeing that the negation of (ii) is the affirmation of (xii), i.e. that the negation of (iv) is the affirmation of (xiv), he concluded that the theologians were involved in an absurdity.

My Geachian reading of Spinoza may be criticised on the grounds that it offends against Spinoza'a reputation as a reasoner. But I think that even the staunchest defender of Spinoza would agree that the Master *appears* to be caught up in modal confusions; and the story I have told fits those apparent confusions into a coherent account of how he came to his results. Moreover, if I impute several large howlers to Spinoza, it must be said that the howlers take some ingenuity to avoid: they are, so to say, respectable howlers. To accuse Spinoza of arguing fallaciously is not to treat the *Ethics* as a storehouse of exploded sophisms; it is to approach it in the spirit which it demands, and which it helped to create.

4 The beginning of the Universe

The claims that God has both an intellect and a will, and that He need not have willed to make the world He actually made, are the legs on which Creationism stands. But the trunk and body of the doctrine is the idea that the world He willed was made from nothing, and came into being a finite time ago. We would expect to find Spinoza dealing directly and explicitly with this issue in the *Ethics*, and not only because it is so clearly central to Creationism. For the problem of the beginning of the Universe had come to be seen as setting the limit of philosophy, and as the proof to reason of reason's own incapacity. Such at least was Maimonides' view (*Strauss*, p. 149), and it is directly opposed by Spinoza's epistemic theory (*E* II, 47). Nevertheless, the *Ethics* does not appear to discuss the issue, although some theorems may bear on it (e.g. *E* I, 21 and 28). The omission is still more surprising in view of the fact that Spinoza had discussed the question very interestingly in the *Cogitata Metaphysica* II, 10, which is entitled 'Of Creation'. But an examination of that early work suggests a possible explanation for the silence of the *Ethics*: Spinoza had developed arguments there which *supported* this part of the Creationist theory, *and which he was unable later to refute*. That, at least, is the hypothesis on which this section proceeds. In what follows, I expound the teaching of the *Cogitata Metaphysica*, and try to locate in it the fallacy which eluded Spinoza when he came to write the *Ethics*. The exercise will not merely help us to explain an important lacuna in the mature Spinoza's system, it will also introduce us to the difficult notion of 'eternity', which Spinoza so frequently invokes (*cf.* IX, 3).

In 'Of Creation', Spinoza first takes issue with the claim that

God made the world from nothing ('*ex nihilo*'). He remarks that this form of words implies that ' "nothing" is a material out of which things were produced'. Those who talk in this way 'constantly suppose that when things are being produced there is something antecedent to them from which they come about, and so, when speaking of creation, they could not omit this particle "from" ("*ex*"). . . . Without doubt, rather than considering "nothing" as a negation of all reality, they have supposed or imagined that it is something real' (*CM* II, 10, ii).

The error Spinoza is castigating was parodied in Rochester's lines from *Upon Nothing*:

> Ere time and place were, time and place were not,
> When primitive Nothing something strait begot,
> Then all proceeded from the great united – What.

But Spinoza was unjust to imply that the error was one which believers in the Creation story regularly commit. Aquinas expressly points out that to say that X comes from nothing is only to say that it is *not* the case that X comes from something: we do not mean that there is a non-matter from which X arose, but rather that there was not any matter from which it sprang (*Summa Theologiae* 1a, q. 45, a. 1, ad 3um).

The orthodox have, however, understood the Book of Genesis to reveal that the world was made, not only from nothing, but also a finite time ago, which was usually computed to be about 4004 B.C. Their view conflicted with the teaching of Aristotle, according to whom the world had existed everlastingly (*De Caelo* I, 10–II, 1). Against Aristotle, it was held, first, that natural reason could not settle the question of the everlastingness of the world, and, second, that even if the world were everlasting, it might still be creaturely and dependent. If a foot had remained planted in the dust through an infinite past time, there would always have been a footprint underneath it; yet the footprint would still be the effect of the foot which was positioned there (*Summa Theologiae* 1a, q. 46, a. 2, ad 1um). Like Aristotle, the scholastics believed that time was made by change, most especially by local motion, and that there was no time which 'enfolded' or 'contained' all the times there were, and whose existence could not be fully described in any set of statements which reported only particular changes and motions (*vide* IX, 2). But their theological beliefs forced them to part company with Aristotle when he declared that motion had been everlasting (*Physics* 251b10–15, 18–28). It followed from this denial that the beginning of the world marked the first moment of time, before which no real time had existed. To speak of possible times before that moment was, however, allowed to be meaningful (Aquinas, *In Physicam* VIII, 2, 990; *In Metaphysicam* XII, 5, 2498; *cf.* van Fraasen, p. 19, p. 25).

In the *Cogitata Metaphysica*, Spinoza endorses, and argues for, the substance of this orthodox view. He denies that the world has existed 'from eternity' (that is, as he carefully explains, for an infinite past time: *CM* II, 10, x). The argument depends on the assumption of the irreversibility of an infinitely long completed process. It reads:

> If the world were led back again from this point of time, it would never be able to have endured for so long: therefore the world could not also have arrived at this point from such a beginning. (*cp*. Bacon, *Novum Organum* I, xlviii).

In other words, if it were possible for an infinitely long duration to have elapsed by the present moment, or for an infinitely protracted process to have been completed at this instant, then it would also be possible (as it were) to play back and to complete the sequence, starting from the moment it expired. But however far along the reversal went, the world would have endured only a finite time from the start of the playback, and the process of recapitulation will never have been completed. Since the process is not completely repeatable, it cannot ever have been completed; and so the universe has not endured for an infinite past time to the present.

There is an ambiguity, however, in the idea that 'What can be completed can be completely repeated'. Taken in one way, this is true but innocuous. If a process can have happened, then it must be theoretically possible for a similar process with the very same duration to occur again. But Spinoza needs the stronger thesis that if a process can have happened, then it must be possible for a similar process to *have happened* again. If I can now truly say, 'The world has lasted infinitely long', it must be possible to say the same thing truly at some future date – not because the world has already lasted infinitely long by now, but because it has endured yet another infinite stretch from the time the statement was originally uttered. The weaker version of the crucial thesis implies merely that if the world has just now completed an infinite past, it must be able to persist through an infinite future; and the possibility that the world's future may be infinitely long can safely be allowed. But there is an obvious incoherence in the idea that the world can again *have* completed an infinitely protracted history, reckoning from the present moment onwards.

Spinoza's argument is a good one only if the strong view is granted to him; but what is the justification for that view? Why must it be possible for any process which has already happened to *have* happened again? I cannot see any reason to accept this notion, and without it, the argument fails.

Spinoza's argument might conceivably be repaired by knitting it together with an argument by Jonathan Bennett against the possibility of having performed an infinite task. For Spinoza would insist that the reality of an infinite past implied the possibility of having performed the task of measuring it (*CM* II, 10, v); and if no infinite task can have been completed, then the particular task of having measured an infinite past is impossible to perform. Bennett writes:

> [T]he notion of having performed a series of operations involves that of remembering performing them, possessing that part of one's past. How much I have done or undergone determines how much there is of me now . . . So the idea of having completed an infinite task involves the idea of possessing, now, an infinite stock of memories; and it is plausible to suppose that this cannot coherently be entertained. (*Bennett* (2), p. 122)

Bennett's inference of 'I have now an infinite stock of memories' from 'I have now completed an infinite task' is an uninviting one, since it is apparently mediated by the assumption that if I have performed a task, I must now remember, or be able to remember, performing it – surely not a view which Bennett consideredly holds. But the more tantalising question is why it should be incoherent to suppose that I now have an infinite memory stock. Is the problem that *I* cannot have it (perhaps because if 'How much I have done or undergone determines how much of me there is', I could not then be finite)? Is it that I cannot have it *now* (because there cannot be infinitely many memories available to me *all at once*)? Or is it that I cannot now have infinitely many *memories* of my own past (since the supply of personal memories must have a first member)? Bennett hints at a reason which seems different from any of these: he implies that no-one can be 'infinitely epistemically endowed' (p. 122). It is not so much the fact that the stock is of *memories*, as that it is of *information*, which prevents me from now possessing it. But if that is what Bennett means, he seems to me mistaken: a competent speaker of a language knows of infinitely many sentences that they are syntactically correct; a reasoner with a grasp of elementary arithmetical operations knows of infinitely many formulas that they are true.

So far as I am aware, Spinoza never expressly recants the argument of the *Cogitata Metaphysica*. It is, however, the prevailing view among his commentators that he taught that the Universe has not existed for a merely finite past time. That view seems to me correct (but *vide* IX, 3). However, the commentators have not given good reasons for ascribing the doctrine to Spinoza, and have failed to appreciate the embarrassment which the *Cogitata Metaphysica* argument causes him. Thus Wolf, for example, in elucidating *Ep*. 5, says that 'Oldenburgh cannot get away from the story of the Creation. For Spinoza, of course, things did not begin to be, the Universe or substance being eternal' (Wolf, *The Correspondence of Spinoza*, p. 379). This is too facile. Spinoza recognises a sense of 'eternity' in which what exists eternally is timeless (IX, 3); and in the *Cogitata* he distinguishes the 'eternal' existence which belongs to God, and signifies timelessness, from the existence 'from eternity' which is said to belong to the physical Universe, and which signifies omnitemporality (*CM* II, 10, x). Wolf leaves it unexplained why Spinoza should ride roughshod over distinctions he had helped to perfect.

5 God and free will

Spinoza believes himself, mistakenly as I think, to have proved that intellect and will do not belong to God's essence (*cf.* V, 2). He does, however, allow that intellect belongs to God as an infinite *mode*: *E* I, 22; I, 32C2; *Ep*. 64; *ST* II, 24; *cf.* IX, 4–5. If God does not have a will, or has one only modally, it seems superfluous to argue that He does not have a *free* will. As Spinoza himself remarks, if God has a will only as an infinite mode, then to say He acts from freedom of will is like saying that He acts from freedom of motion-and-rest (*E* I, 32C2). Nevertheless, we discover that Spinoza is anxious to prove this conclusion at length. He may have believed that if it could be shown that *God* was without free will, then it would be easier to convince his readers that *man* was also without it. The exposure of that illusion would in turn create the possibility of gaining such freedom as we *can* have (VIII, 1).

Spinoza's reasons for denying free will to God are twofold. One has to do with the nature of God; the other with the nature of freedom (*vide* V, 6). Let us begin with God.

The theorem at *E* I, 33 reads: 'Things could have been produced by God in no other manner and in no other order than that in which they have been produced'. If it be supposed that things had been produced in some other fashion, Spinoza contends, then a different nature would have to be ascribed to God from that which He actually has, and that in turn would entail that He is not perfect (*E* I, 33S2). Many will reject this opinion as ridiculous, since they are accustomed to attributing freedom of the will to God. God is indeed a free *cause*, as *E* I, 17C2 has shown. But to imagine that he has a free *will* is to set up a great obstacle to science ('magnum obstaculum scientiae'), if only because of the links between this doctrine and the belief in miracles and in providence (*Strauss*, p. 127; p. 131). The demonstrations Spinoza has provided, if they have done their work, will have weakened these prejudices. But for the sake of those who still demur, he will supply a fresh argument, designed to prove that even if will pertains to God's essence, 'it follows nevertheless from His perfection that things could be created in no other mode or order by Him'. If this proof is sound, then Spinoza will truly have crushed the doctrine of Creationism. How does he argue? He says:

> We first consider that which my opponents themselves admit, that it depends upon the decree and will alone of God that each thing should be as it is (*ut unaquaeque res id quod est, sit*); for otherwise God would not be the cause of all things. It is also admitted that all God's decrees have been ratified by God Himself from eternity (*ab aeterno ab ipso Deo sanctia fuerunt*); for otherwise imperfection and inconstancy would be argued against Him. But since in eternity there is no *when* nor *before* nor *after*, it follows from the perfection of God alone that He never can decree nor ever could have (*nec umquam potuisse*) decreed, anything else than that which He has decreed; that is to say, God has not existed before His decrees, and can never exist without them.

The first premiss in this argument, which states that it depends on the will and decree alone of God that each thing should be as it is, can perhaps be expressed as (i) for any '*p*' such that it is the case that *p*, then '*p*' solely because God wills that *p*. This premiss is supposed to be conceded by Spinoza's opponents, and to follow from the claim that God is the universal cause.

The second step, which the opponents also accept, asserts that all God's decrees have been ratified by Him from eternity. Perhaps we can record this as: (ii) for any '*p*' such that God wills that *p*, God wills from eternity that *p*. Premiss (i) made contact with the notion of God's *perfection* by being supported by the view that He is the universal cause; premiss (ii) connects with His perfection by virtue of the fact that His decisions must not be inconstant ('a will ever constant and determined in all things is a perfection': *Ep.* 56).

At the third stage, the interpretation of the proof must fork into two. For as we shall discover (*cf.* IX, 2–3), Spinoza's conception of the nature of eternity is much debated. In general, there are two prevailing views: that by eternity he means timelessness, and that by eternity he means omnitemporality. On the first view, an eternal truth is timelessly true, and cannot meaningfully be said to change in truth-value; on the second, an eternal truth is true now, and at all times before and after now, so that it can meaningfully, but never truly, be said to change from truth to falsity. In saying, then, that in eternity there is no *when*, *before* or *after*, Spinoza may mean either (iii) if from eternity *p*, then timelessly *p*, *or* (iv) if from eternity *p*, that at all times *p*.

The conclusion Spinoza wants to deduce from his three premisses is that 'God never can decree nor ever could have decreed otherwise than He has decreed'. This is a modal proposition, speaking of what can or could have been the case; and it does not directly follow from the assumptions Spinoza has laid down. What follows from (i), (ii) and (iii) is apparently: (v) for any '*p*' such that it is the case that *p*, then timelessly God wills that *p*. And from (i), (ii) and (iv), it seems to follow only that: (vi) for any '*p*' such that *p*, then at all times God wills that *p*. To get from (v) to the conclusion Spinoza wants, he must add an extra premiss: (vii) if timelessly *p*, then it cannot at any time be, and could not at any time have been, that not-*p*. And to reach that conclusion from (vi), he would require: (viii) if at all times *p*, then it cannot at any time be, and could not at any time have been, that not-*p*. Whichever way the reasoning forks, it will then issue in the conclusion: (ix) for any '*p*' such that it is the case that *p*, it cannot at any time be, and could not at any time have been, that God does not will that *p*.

The connection between 'eternity' and 'necessity', codified in (vii) and (viii), may seem a strange one. Nevertheless, it is apparent both in Spinoza (e.g. at *E* II, 44C2D) and in at least some of the opponents he is likely to be arguing against. Aristotle had maintained that eternal things (in the sense of things existing omnitemporally) were also necessary: this registered his acceptance of the so-called Principle of Plentitude (*cf.* Sorabji, p. 60; pp. 128–40). If the sun and stars were *capable* of stopping their everlasting motion, he avers, then given the whole of time, they would at some time stop (*De Interpretatione*, 19a9–18; *Meta-*

physics, 1050b20–30; *De Generatione et Corruptione*, 338a17–b5). But to say that if X is capable of Φing, then at some time it does Φ, implies that if X at no time Φs, then X is incapable of Φing; and that in turn is equivalent to holding that if it is always the case that X does not Φ, then it *must* be the case that X does not Φ. Here the link between omnitemporality and necessity becomes clear. (The connection between *timelessness* and necessity, though not explicitly defended, so far as I am aware, by Spinoza or his sources, can be evolved from the tie between omnitemporality and necessity. For if it is timelessly true that p, then at no time it is *false* that p; and by the Aristotelian equivalences, if it is never false that p then it is *necessary* that p.)

It appears then that Spinoza's proof is valid, that it draws only upon premisses which his scholastic antagonists would have conceded, and that it therefore succeeds in refuting them. He does not, however, seem himself to have been content with it; for he introduces an objection to it, and offers a pair of replies. Let us consider these. The objector is imagined to say:

> Although it be supposed that God had made the nature of things different from that which it is, or that from eternity He had decreed something else about her nature and her order, it would not thence follow that any imperfection exists in God.

And the first reply to him will then run:

> But if this be said, it must at the same time be allowed that God can change His decrees (*Deum posse sua mutare decreta*). For if God had decreed something about nature and her order other than that which He has decreed – that is to say, if He had willed and decreed something else about nature – He would necessarily have had an intellect and a will different from those which He now (*jam*) has. And if it be allowed to assign to God another intellect and another will without any change of His essence and of His perfections, what is the reason why He cannot now change His decrees (*quid causa est, cur jam non possit sua de rebus creatis decreta mutare*) concerning created things and nevertheless remain equally perfect? For His intellect and will regarding created things and their order remain in the same relationship to His essence and perfection (*in respectu suae essentiae et perfectionis, perinde est*) howsoever it be conceived (*quomodocunque concipiatur*).

If I understand this imaginary exchange aright, then the 'opponent' is envisaged as saying that although God cannot *now* change His decrees, He *could have* decreed otherwise than He has concerning the nature and order of things. If so, then the 'opponent's' view corresponds exactly to that of Descartes and differs, it appears, from that of Maimonides: *Wolfson* I, p. 409. For Descartes needs to deny that God can *now* alter His decrees concerning the eternal truths: such a change is ruled out by the fact of His veracity. (If God's veracity cannot be relied on in support of the eternal truths, then we cannot rationally be confident that if we have once clearly and distinctly perceived them, they will still be true; and if we cannot have that confidence, then the work of refuting the sceptic is largely undone.) On the other hand, Descartes also maintains that, even with respect to the necessary and eternal truths, God's freedom and omnipotence imply that He *could have* willed otherwise concerning them. (Like many post-war British philosophers, Descartes is a 'conventionalist' regarding necessary truth. But his conventionalism is theological, not linguistic. The necessity of necessary truth derives not from the fact that men decide to use words according to such-and-such rules, but because God decrees that they be necessary.) If Spinoza's refutation is successful, then he will have driven a wedge between two Cartesian claims: that the eternal truths are cognitively reliable, and that God's freedom and power extend even to the eternal verities (*cp. Caton*, p. 69).

Spinoza's argument against his 'opponent' trades on the assumption, which would surely have been granted him, that God is perfect – indeed, necessarily perfect. For he seems to reason as follows: (x) if God had decreed otherwise concerning the nature and order of things than He has actually done, then He would now possess a different intellect (will) from that which He actually possesses. Further, (xi) if He now had a different intellect (will) from that which He actually possesses, and yet were still perfect, then He would now be able to change His decrees, and nevertheless remain perfect. But (xii) it is impossible that God should now be able to change His decrees, and remain perfect also. So (xiii) God cannot both have a different intellect (will), and remain perfect. Since, however, (xiv) necessarily, God is perfect, it follows that (xv) it is impossible that God should have a different intellect (will) from that which He presently has; and that in turn entails that (xvi) it is impossible that God should have decreed otherwise concerning the order and nature of things.

Spinoza's reasoning seems plausible, but I believe that it commits a subtle fallacy. The error comes in at step (xi). What in fact seems true, and what Spinoza ought to have said, is that if God's intellect and will were different from what they now are, then it is possible that His decrees should have been other than they in fact are. As things are, He has decreed that it is necessary that the lines from the centre to the circumference of a circle should be equal; had His mind been different, it is possible that the decree would not now hold. But it does not follow that if His mind were different, then it would be possible for Him to alter His decrees as they would then have stood, nor does it follow that He would have been able to cause them to change from being true to being untrue. If He had constantly had a different mind, it would not follow that He would also have had an inconstant mind, which could differ from itself at different times. Unfortunately, however, in asserting (xi), Spinoza is making precisely this claim. If (xi) has any plausibility, it borrows it from being confused with a distinct assumption which, though true, does not entail it. If I am right about this, then the effort to drive a wedge into the Cartesian system is a failure.

There remains, however, the second answer to the imaginary objector. That answer goes as follows:

> Moreover, all the philosophers whom I have seen admit that there is no such thing as an intellect existing potentially in God, but only an intellect existing in act (*in actu*). But since His intellect and His will are not distinguishable from His essence, as all admit too, it follows from this also that if God had had another intellect in act and will, His essence too would necessarily have been different; and hence, as I showed at the beginning, if things had been produced by God in a manner different from that in which they now are, God's intellect and will, that is to say His essence (as has been granted), must have been different, which is absurd.

The central step in this argument is, plainly, the identification of God's 'potential' intellect with His intellect 'in act'. The scholium to *E* I, 31 has already made that identification, for finite and infinite intellects alike; but here Spinoza derives it not from his own metaphysics, but from the common consent of those he is refuting. To say that the potential and the actual intellect are the same seems to embrace two connected claims: it entails that the intellect is not a power or faculty distinct from its operations; and it avers that the intellect *can* Φ only if it *is actually* Φing. In holding that God does not have a purely potential intellect, but only one in act, Spinoza is therefore asserting that (xvii) if God *can* understand that *p*, then He does actually understand that *p*. In confirmation, he appeals to the philosophers who, like Maimonides, taught that 'God is an intellect which is always in action, and that there is in Him no potentiality at all' (*Guide for the Perplexed* I, 68; *cf. Wolfson* I, p. 415).

Spinoza next appeals to the consensus in hypothesising that God's intellect and His will are each identical with His essence, and hence with each other. The identity of intellect and will in God will give him what he wants. For it will imply that (xviii) God actually understands that *p* if and only if He actually wills that *p*; and He *can* understand that *p* if and only if He *can* will that *p*. The combination of (xvii) and (xviii) yields (xix): God *can* will that *p* only if He actually wills that *p*. What God does not will, He could not have willed: as was to have been shown. (The proof as he gives it is not quite so straightforward: it proceeds from the identity of will, intellect and essence to the – absurd – conclusion that if God's will had been different, so too would His essence have been. But the substance of the argument is not affected by this simplification.)

This second refutation of the 'opponent' seems to be better than the first. It has, moreover, an important consequence, which Spinoza is swift to point out. This is that all things are perfect, or as perfect in reality as they are in the Divine intellect. 'Since things could have been produced by God in no other manner or order . . . there is no sound reason (*sana ratio*) which can persuade us to believe that God was unwilling to create all things which are in His intellect with the same perfection as that in which they exist in His intellect.' We may call this result, Spinoza's Principle of Perfection.

The Principle of Perfection may have a distributive, an intermediate and a collective form. In its collective form it holds that all things taken together are perfect: the Universe, considered as a whole, could not be more perfect than it is. In its intermediate version, it asserts that each type of thing is as perfect as it can be. And taken distributively, it maintains that each individual thing is as perfect as it can be. Descartes believed that the existence of human error implied the falsity of the Principle in its distributive form: 'I can see indeed that God could easily have brought it about that, while remaining a free agent, and limited in knowledge, I should never in fact go wrong . . . And I readily understand that if God had so made me, then I myself, considered as a complete whole, should have been even more perfect than I am now' (*Fourth Meditation*; A.G., p. 99). But he comes near to endorsing the collective Principle in the next breath: 'I cannot on that account deny that in some way the perfection of the Universe is greater, because some parts of it are not exempt from going wrong and others are, than it would be if all parts were exactly alike' (*ibid.*; *cf. Kenny Letters*, p. 148). And when Spinoza attempts to elucidate the Cartesian view in the *Principles of the Cartesian Philosophy*, he seems to attribute to Descartes a claim which fits in with the intermediate version: 'We cannot say that God has deprived us of a stronger intellect which He could have given us . . . For the nature of a thing cannot demand anything of God . . . God has no more deprived us of a stronger intellect than He has deprived the circle of the properties of a globe' (*PPD* I, 15S). For his own part, however, Spinoza seems to accept the Principle in all three formulations.

The defence of the Principle at *E* I, 33S2 brings to light a further aspect of Spinoza's critique of Creationism. I will conclude this section by noting it. He imagines that his opponents will say that 'there is no perfection nor imperfection in things, but that that which is in them by reason of which they are perfect or imperfect and are said to be good or evil depends upon the will of God alone, and therefore if God had willed He could have brought it about that that which is now perfection should have been the extreme of imperfection, and vice versa'. This, as he now has no difficulty in showing, is worthless: for it has been proved that God could not have willed otherwise than He has done. It follows that He could not have brought it about that what is now perfect or called good should have been imperfect and evil. In other words, just as Descartes was wrong in thinking that the necessity of the eternal truths derived from, and depended on, a contingent decree by God, so it is wrong to think that perfection and imperfection, good and evil, are made so by His will. The truths of ethics, like the laws of logic, *must* be as they are: if they are said to flow from God's will, then that will must itself be a fixed and necessary one (*cp*. I, 1).

Summary

Spinoza has tried to show that even on the traditional picture of God, which credits His essence with a will, it must follow that God could not have created things in any other manner or order. This is established by a proof which seems valid, providing we add to it the assumption that what is eternal is necessary. Spinoza canvasses a possible objection to it, which can be regarded as Cartesian in inspiration. This objection he tries to rebut in a pair of counter-arguments. If he succeeds, then he will expose a serious inconsistency in Cartesianism: between its conventionalism concerning eternal truth and its answer to philosophical scepticism. The first counter-argument is fallacious, but the second appears to work. The refutation spins off a further consequence, in the form of the Principle of Perfection, which also carries anti-Cartesian implications. The new theology, as well as the old, is threatened by Spinoza's metaphysical naturalism.

6 Freedom and necessity

At the start of V, 5, I remarked that Spinoza had two main reasons for denying free will to God, one relating to His nature and perfection, the other to the idea of freedom. We have considered the first of these reason; now let us examine the second.

At *E* I, 32, Spinoza seeks to prove that 'the will cannot be called a free cause, but can only be called necessary'. From this he deduces the corollary that 'God does not act from freedom of the will'. The demonstration of the main theorem asserts that 'in whatever way the will should be conceived, whether as finite or as infinite, it requires a cause by which it may be determined to existence and to action, and therefore (by Definition 7) it cannot be called a free cause, but only necessary or compelled'. Definition 7 of *E* I, reads: 'That thing is called free which exists from the necessity of its own nature alone, and is determined to action by itself alone. That thing, on the other hand, is called necessary, or rather compelled (*necessaria vel potius coacta*), which is determined by another to exist and to act in a certain and determined manner'.

Spinoza's thought on the matter is expressed luminously in a series of letters to and from Hugo Boxel (*Eps.* 54, 55, 56). In these letters, he prises apart a pair of distinguishable contrasts: that between the necessary and the fortuitous on the one hand, and, on the other, that between the free and the compulsory. In the passages I have just quoted from the *Ethics*, these distinctions are made, but not as sharply as they might be: it takes some care to see that Spinoza is *not* equating the necessary with the compulsory, and opposing *both* to the free. *Epistle* 56 lays down very firmly that this is an error: freedom and (a certain type of) necessity are not contradictory, but in fact the same.

In his exchange with Boxel, Spinoza stakes out the claim that:

> Anyone who asserts that the world is the necessary effect of the Divine nature also denies absolutely that the world was made by chance; anyone however who asserts that God could have refrained from creating the world is affirming, albeit in other words, that it was made by chance; since it proceeded from an act of will which need not have occurred. . . . This opinion and this view are thoroughly absurd. (*Ep.* 54)

Briefly and inadequately, the argument seems to be that if God had made the world by an act of free will, then He could have refrained from creating it; but then the creation would have been uncaused; and what is uncaused is fortuitous. But no-one will agree that the world exists by chance; and so we 'must also admit (mark this well) that the world is the necessary effect of the Divine nature'.

That brief epitome will not really do: it conceals a crucial difficulty. For to say that the world is *made* is already to assign a cause for its origin, which is the particular volition of the maker; and hence it cannot be argued that the world is fortuitous and uncaused insofar as it was *made by chance*. What Spinoza must be saying is that if the world originates in a free volition by God, then its cause is itself (absolutely) fortuitous and uncaused; and that the effect of an uncaused cause is itself (in some way, or qualifiedly) uncaused and fortuitous. More fully: Spinoza's argument, which has the form of a *reductio ad absurdum*, must proceed as follows. It will assume, for the purpose of the reduction, that (i) the world began to exist because God freely willed that it should begin. From the notion of 'free will' embedded in (i), we can deduce that (ii) there is (was) no circumstance 'p' such that because p, God willed that the world should begin (*cp. Strauss*, p. 153). To premiss (i) and its corollary will be added a pair of causal assumptions. One will assert that what is uncaused is fortuitous (absolutely); the other will posit that the effect of what is fortuitous is itself fortuitous (qualifiedly). These will be: (iii) for any 'q' such that there is no 'p' such that because p, q, then if q, it is fortuitous (absolutely) that q; (iv) for any 'q' such that it is fortuitous that q, then for any 'r' such that because q, r, it is (qualifiedly) fortuitous that r. From these four theses, it will follow that (v) it is (qualifiedly) fortuitous that the world began to exist. Perhaps the thinkers Spinoza wants to refute would have deemed (v) false or contradictory; if so, then it may be that they would have had to reject (i). It appears to me, however, that the argument we have outlined, while giving Spinoza a *valid* case, does not really give him a *reductio*: for why deny the conclusion which it entails? Perhaps it would have been denied that the beginning of the world was *absolutely* fortuitous; but, as we have noted, the Creationist cannot be forced into that admission if he is careful.

Boxel's answer to Spinoza was, in part, a rejection of the claim that what is uncaused (or, as he joins Spinoza in thinking, unnecessary) is also fortuitous. (That is to attack premiss (iii).) He writes:

A thing is said to have been made fortuitously when it is produced without regard to the aim of its author. When we dig the earth to plant a vine, or to make a pit or a grave, and find a treasure of which we have never had a thought, this is said to happen to chance. But he who, of his own free will, acts in such a way that he can either do so or not, is never said to act by chance, when he does act. For in that case all human actions would happen by chance, which is absurd. Necessary and Free are contraries, but not Necessary and Fortuitous. (*Ep.* 55)

Like Spinoza, Boxel thinks that if X acts from free will, then his act is uncaused and unnecessitated. Unlike Spinoza, he maintains that if X acts from free will, it does *not* follow that X's act is fortuitous. Since he thinks that at least some human acts arise from free will, he must think that at least some uncaused and unnecessitated occurrences are not fortuitous. (That is the denial of (iii).) He defends his viewpoint by arguing that if 'X acted from free will' entailed 'X acted fortuitously', then it would follow that 'all human actions would happen by chance, which is absurd'. Perhaps it is absurd, but why does it follow? It seems to follow only if one assumes that all human acts are free acts; and even the staunchest defender of free will would quail before making that assumption. If Boxel meant only that it would follow that all *free* human acts would be fortuitous, however, then he would not have struck a blow against Spinoza: far from thinking that consequence 'absurd', Spinoza would readily embrace it.

Spinoza's own answer to Boxel runs along rather different lines. He argues that 'necessity' and 'chance' are indeed contradictories, while 'necessity' and 'freedom' are not. (Given the equation, accepted by both parties, of the necessary with the caused, Spinoza's claims are equivalent to saying that 'caused' and 'by chance' are contradictories, 'caused' and 'free' not so.) The first point is purportedly established thus: 'as soon as I realise that the three angles of a triangle are necessarily equal to two rights, I also deny that this is the result of chance. Similarly, as soon as I realise that heat is the necessary effect of fire, I also deny that it occurs by chance' (*Ep.* 56). These instances are of course offered in support of the general claim that if it is necessary that p, then it is not by chance that p. (From that it will follow that if – as Boxel seems also to agree – the world does not exist by chance, then its existence is necessary.) The second point is substantiated as follows: 'No-one can deny that God knows Himself and everything else freely, and yet all are agreed in admitting that God knows Himself necessarily. Thus you seem to me to make no distinction between Coercion or Force, and Necessity. That a man desires to live, to love, and so forth is not a compulsory activity, but it is none the less necessary, and much more so is God's will to be and to know and to act' (*Ep.* 56). Several things are bound up in this. First, and most relevantly to Boxel, Spinoza argues that 'X acts necessarily' does *not* entail 'X does not act freely'. God's self-knowledge is necessary, but it is also free. What 'X acts necessarily' *does* entail is 'X does not act from free will'. (This is because to act from free *will* is to act from no cause, or fortuitously, and hence not of necessity.) The distinction between acting freely (which God does) and acting from free will (which He does not) is alluded to at *E* I, 33S2: some thinkers, Spinoza says, 'are accustomed to attributing to God another freedom, far different from that which we accept – that is, they assume an absolute will'. If Boxel accepts Spinoza's earlier claim that 'necessarily' entails 'not by chance' (which he resists in his letter), and if he is persuaded by the later claim that 'necessarily' does not entail 'not freely', then he will have to admit the possibility of actions which are both necessary and free, but not done from free will.

Spinoza seeks to make acceptance of his views easier by marking a distinction between 'necessity' and 'compulsion'. He admits that 'X acts under compulsion' entails 'X acts necessarily'; but he denies that the converse entailment holds. Accordingly, he can admit that *some* action which is necessitated – that, namely, which is done under compulsion – is unfree, without having to admit that *all* necessitated action is unfree. It is clear from *E* I, Definition 7, that he would expand on this by saying that what was necessary in virtue of being 'other-determined' was compulsory, and so unfree, while what was necessary in virtue of being 'self-determined' was neither compulsory nor unfree, but free.

Let me try to clarify Spinoza's claims in the following equivalences:

E1) Of Necessity= Through a Cause= either through Self-determination or through Other-determination;

E2) By Chance= Not of Necessity= Not through a Cause= Neither through Self-determination nor through Other-determination;

E3) Freely= Necessarily or through a Cause, but not through Other-determination= Through Self-determination;

E4) Under compulsion= Necessarily or through a Cause, but not through Self-determination= Through Other-determination;

E5) Not freely = either by Chance or under Compulsion.

From this it is apparent how complete the rejection of free will is. *If* an act were done from free will, then according to Spinoza, it would not even be free, and would be more like an act done under compulsion. But since Spinoza is a determinist, holding that whatever happens is both caused and necessitated to happen, the possibility of free will is in any case excluded.

There are obviously many points of controversy and of interest in Spinoza's exchange with Boxel. Since I shall be discussing Spinoza's conception of freedom in Chapters VII (8) and VIII (1), I may be excused from commenting here upon the final three equivalences we find in him. (E1) and (E2), however, generate large issues in Spinozism, and we can proceed to them here.

Coincidences and causality

Boxel gave the example of the man who happened upon treasure when planting a vine or digging a grave, in order to show that some acts were both fortuitous and yet caused. If so, then (E2) is false (and, as we observed, the reasoning in *Epistle* 54 will have failed). Is Boxel right? Must things that happen by chance also have causes? More particularly, must *coincidences* have causes? Richard Sorabji has recently discussed this question with reference to Aristotle, and particularly with reference to a difficult passage in *Metaphysics* VI, 3. Aristotle imagines the case of a man who eats some spicy food, gets thirsty, and goes out to a well, where he happens to meet some roughnecks who are passing by, and who set on him and kill him. The murderers did not come to the well for the purpose of finding and killing him, nor did they lure him there. According to Sorabji, Aristotle thinks that the meeting at the well, which of course was coincidental, did not have a cause. There was, it is true, a cause of his going to the well, and of his being there at a certain time: he went because he was thirsty. But his thirst in no way explains, and hence cannot have caused, the fatal meeting at the well. (Sorabji himself accepts and defends the position which he ascribes to Aristotle. I must refer the reader to his lucid and subtle exposition: *Sorabji*, c. 1.) Whether Sorabji is right or not about Aristotle's adherence to the view that coincidences lack causes, it must be admitted to be very plausible in its own right. And if it is correct, then Boxel's objection to Spinoza is unsound.

The trouble is, however, that if (E2) is defended in that way against Boxel's criticism, then Spinoza can no longer consistently maintain the thesis of universal determinism. (It is, in fact, very puzzling that the libertarian Boxel interpreted the case of the chance discovery in a way which did not favour his rejection of determinism; it is even more puzzling that Spinoza failed to see how it menaced determinism.) The dilemma which Spinoza faces is this: either he must deny that events like the discovery of the unexpected treasure are really cases of chance, or he must limit the scope of determinism, so that coincidental events are admitted not to have causes. If he falls upon the first horn, he can keep (E2) and his unqualified determinism, but only at the expense of violent paradox; if he falls upon the second, then (E2) must be given up.

Necessitarianism

What about (E1)? That thesis embodies at least two ideas: that what is necessitated is caused, and that what is caused is necessitated. The first idea might be expressed as: for any 'p' such that it is necessary that p, there is some 'q' such that q, and such that because q, p. Now in the *Cogitata Metaphysica*, Spinoza seems to be registering a distinction between what we might call 'unconditional' and 'conditional' necessity, which had been part of the philosopher's stock in trade since Aristotle (*CM* I, 3, iii; *cf. ST* I, 6; *cp. Prior* (2) pp. 210–11). It would seem that what is necessary unconditionally includes such things as the existence of God, or truths which neither require nor admit of being explained by reference to anything further; while conditional necessity will belong to truths which assert such things as the existence of finite modes. Accordingly, we may divide the thesis that what is necessary is caused, into two parts; for any 'p' such that is unconditionally necessary that p, then p because p (i.e. what is unconditionally necessary is the case because of itself); and for any 'p' such that it is conditionally necessary that p, then for some 'q' which is distinct from 'p', q, and because q, p (i.e. what is conditionally necessary is the case because of something else). Mirroring these theses will be two other theses which emerge from the idea that what is caused is necessary. The first of these will be: for any 'p' such that because p, p, it is unconditionally necessary that p. The second will be: for any 'p' such that there is some 'q', distinct from 'p', such that q and such that p because q, it is conditionally necessary that p. (E1), in other words, unfolds into four separate claims.

The thesis that what is necessary is caused, when elucidated in this manner, is plausible; but the thesis that what is caused is necessary requires some defence. Yet the latter thesis plays an important role in Spinoza's thinking. For by means of it, he is enabled to pass from (what we may call) *Determinism* to (what we may call) *Necessitarianism* (cf. Ayers, pp. 6–7). By a 'determinist', we may understand someone who holds:

D) For any 'p', if p, then for some 'q', q and because q, p.

And by a 'necessitarian', I mean someone who believes:

N) For any 'p', if p, then it is (conditionally or unconditionally) necessary that p.

Spinoza's adherence to (D) is manifested in many places: at *E* I, 11 (Second Demonstration), he writes that 'for the existence or non-existence of anything there must be a cause or reason (*causa seu ratio*)'. It is fair to take this as saying, in part, that whatever *is the case* is caused (which is (D)). It also hints at a distinct principle, which relates not to *causality* but to *explanation*, and which we may name the *Principle of Sufficient Reason*. This may be stated as:

R) For any 'p', if p, then for some 'q', q, and the fact that q explains why it is that p.

Now given (*E1*), is is permissible to deduce (N) from (D). And it is plain that Spinoza accepts (N) with enthusiasm. 'In Nature there is nothing contingent, but all things are determined from the necessity of the Divine nature to exist and act in a certain manner' (*E* I, 29). 'Things could not have been produced by God in any other manner or order than they have been produced' (*E* I, 33). 'Whatever we conceive to be in God's power necessarily exists' (*E* I, 35). 'If men clearly understood the whole of Nature, they would find everything just as necessary as the things treated of in mathematics; but since this is beyond human understanding, we regard certain things as contingent' (*CM* II, 9, ii). Hence it is that Josiah's burning of the idolaters' bones on the altars of Jereboam (II *Kings* 23:15–18), though contingent if anything is, is in fact as necessary as a theorem of geometry (*ibid.*).

If the passage from (D) to (N) is mediated by the claim that what is caused is necessary, we have naturally to ask whether that claim is good. And if (as I think) it is *not* good, we have then to ask whether Spinoza's necessitarianism is defensible. I will conclude this section with some remarks on these two questions.

First then: is what is caused also necessary? Richard Sorabji, in the work to which I have already referred in this chapter, argues that this need not be the case. Following the lead of G.E.M. Anscombe, he describes an example drawn from the scientific literature.

> [A] lump of radioactive material is placed near a bomb, in such a way that if an electron is emitted and hits the triggering device, the bomb will explode. According to most quantum physicists, the rate and route of radioactive emission is undetermined, and it is therefore undetermined whether an electron will hit the trigger. . . . What does require care is selecting the right point in the story as an instance of an unnecessitated effect. We can suppose that a laboratory technician carelessly leaves out a small lump of radioactive material on a laboratory bench. And we may say that the fact of this material being left out is the cause of the electron reaching the trigger. The latter will be an unnecessitated effect, provided that the route taken by the electron is undetermined up to the point of arrival. (If it becomes determined at some earlier point, P, we can simply consider as our unnecessitated effect the arrival of the electron at P). (*Sorabji*, p. 28)

The example seems to me, as it does to Sorabji, to prove that (*E*1) is false.

What then of necessitarianism? If it cannot be defended by deducing it from (*D*) and (*E*1), can it nevertheless be asserted in its own right? The answer is No. In upholding (*E*1), Spinoza assumes, not only that what is caused is necessary, but also that what is necessary is caused; and that is an assumption which seems to be true. Now if (*N*) is also true, it will follow that whatever is the case, has a cause (that is, (*D*)). But I have already maintained, following Aristotle and Sorabji, that (*D*) is false: there are coincidental or chance events, and being coincidental they lack a cause. But if so, then the falsity of (*D*) will attach to (*N*) by virtue of the mediation of (*E*1).

The collapse of (*N*) produces severe strains in the Spinozistic system at other places. For (*N*) is equivalent to the thesis that whatever is (conditionally or unconditionally) possible is also the case; and that is a form of the Principle of Plentitude, which we have seen Spinoza to invoke: V, 5. (The same Principle, as I shall argue later, plays a role in Spinoza's proof of the mind's eternity (IX, 4).) Finally, the idea that whatever happens, happens of necessity, is absolutely indispensable to Spinoza's entire account of the nature of true freedom (VII, 8; VIII, 1).

Spinoza's difficulties over necessitarianism are not yet at an end. Not only can we argue that the falsity of that doctrine is bound up with the falsehood of determinism, and that in any case the derivation of it from determinism is unsound, but we can attack it frontally. To grasp this, however, we have first to observe that necessitarianism can come in quite distinct forms. As it is expressed in (N), it draws upon the distinction between 'conditional' and 'unconditional' necessity. But there is another relevant distinction, which must be kept separate from the conditional/unconditional one, and which in fact cuts across it. That is the distinction between 'logical' and all the other types of necessity. To illustrate the difference between the distinctions, consider Josiah's burning the bones on the altars of Jereboam. If Spinoza is right, this fact has the same sort of necessity as that of a theorem of geometry – that is, logical necessity. But because this fact, unlike the existence of God, is not self-explanatory but only necessary in respect of its cause, Spinoza would also regard it as having at best conditional necessity (*CM* I, 3, iii; *E* I, 24; I, 28: 'that which has a finite and determinate existence cannot be produced from the absolute nature of some attribute of God'). On the other hand, the fact that Josiah burned the idolaters' bones, from the more usual point of view, is not a logical necessity; but if Aristotle is right in thinking that what is past is necessary (in the sense of 'irrevocable'), then that fact has a *kind* of unconditional necessity (*cf. De Interpretatione* 19a23–6; *Sorabji*, p. 22). The logical/non-logical distinction and the unconditional (or 'absolute')/conditional ('relative') distinction are, I think, jammed together in this passage from Curley:

> I think we can most easily come to terms with Spinoza if we represent him as holding the following view. All propositions are either necessarily true or necessarily false. This will hold both for existential and for nonexistential propositions. But, restricting ourselves to truths, not all truths are necessary in the same sense. Some are absolutely necessary, in the Leibnizian sense that their denial is explicitly or implicitly self-contradictory: their truth follows from the essence or definition of the subject. But others are only relatively necessary. Their denial does not involve a contradiction, either explicitly or implicitly. Their truth, rather, is grounded in the fact that they follow logically from other propositions which are true, propositions which give an efficient causal explanation of them. (*Curley* (3), pp. 89–90)

Because of this mistake it is easier for Curley to maintain his view that Spinoza thinks that states of affairs such as Josiah's burning the bones are contingent in the logical sense. For Spinoza would undoubtedly agree that such states were only relatively or conditionally necessary. If we keep the two distinctions apart, however, it becomes far more tempting to say that Spinoza held a strong form of necessitarianism, which can be stated as:

SN) For any 'p', if p, then it is logically necessary that p.

That Spinoza held this strong thesis is asserted by one of his near-contemporaries, Sir Isaac Newton's friend and apologist Samuel Clarke, in a work of 1705 entitled *A Demonstration of the Being and Attributes of God*. Clarke says that Spinoza 'must affirm that it is in itself and in terms a Contradiction, for any thing to be, or to be imagined, in any respect otherwise than it Now is. He must say 'tis a Contradiction, to suppose the Number, or Figure, or Order of the Principal Parts of the World, could possibly have been different from what they Now are' (*Clarke*, pp. 55–6).

Which interpretation of Spinoza is better – Curley's or Clarke's? Curley has demonstrated the power of his interpretation at length, but it is a necessary corrective to see how strongly Spinoza was attracted to the other view. The fact is that, with the derivation of the modes, whether finite or infinite, from the attributes of God, Spinoza has involved himself in consequences whose nature and import he scarcely begins to fathom (*cf.* the splendid page in *Martineau*, I, p. 318). He seems to want to assert that the modes follow from the attributes with strict, deductive necessity; but he havers on the question whether the logical necessity which attaches to God and the attributes does, or does not, attach derivatively to the modes. He seems headed in Clarke's direction when he writes: 'Whatever is, is in God; but God cannot be called a contingent thing, for He exists necessarily and not contingently. Moreover, the modes of the Divine nature have followed from it necessarily and not contingently, and that, too, whether it be considered absolutely, or as determined to action in a certain manner. But God is the cause of these modes, not only insofar as they simply exist, but also insofar as they are considered as determined to any action . . . All things are determined from the necessity of the Divine nature, not only to exist, but to exist and act in a certain manner, and there is nothing contingent' (*E* I, 29D). There is simply no clear, straightforward answer to the question whether he thought that a created fact (finite mode) which stood to another as cause to effect or as ground to consequent was also related to it as theorem to corollary (see also V, 1). Not only is Spinoza's necessitarianism (certainly) unproven and (probably) false – it is not even unambiguously formulated.

Summary

It is time to summarise. I began this section by examining Spinoza's argument with Boxel, in which he sought to demonstrate that God did not make the world by act of free will. This was supposed to have been accomplished by a *reductio*; but I denied that those at whom the proof was aimed would have retreated from the supposedly 'absurd' consequence which was entailed. I then explored certain other issues which arose out of the same correspondence. This led to attributing to Spinoza a set of equivalences, which explained his notions of necessity, chance, freedom and compulsion. Two of these equivalances came up for closer inspection. The first, which encapsulated Spinoza's account of chance, exposed him to a dilemma: he had either to deny the occurrence of chance events, or to abandon his determinism. The second equivalence, when unfolded, emerged as a group of theses concerning necessity and causality. In the light of those theses, we were able to formulate, and to study the relations between, certain characteristic principles of Spinozism, notably determinism and necessitarianism. It was argued that determinism was false; that things could be caused but not necessary; and that necessitarianism was therefore both false and unsupported. Finally, the objections to necessitarianism were pressed further: Spinoza seemed to oscillate between two quite distinct variants of the doctrine.

7 *Final causes*

Spinoza's anxiety to refute the claim that God has free will stems partly from his belief that it creates 'a major obstacle to science'. But an even greater obstacle, he believes, is presented by the related doctrine that God acts for the sake of ends or purposes. The concept of a final cause, he maintains, has no use. It arises out of our ignorance of the real workings of things, and from the fantasy that they are made for our convenience. True science recognises only efficient causes; and in true theology, which is the science of God, He is held to be the efficient, but not the final, cause of the world (*E* I, 16C1; I, 25). The critique of final causes is thus a defence of Galileian and Cartesian science, but it is also an exposure of the anthropocentric delusion fostered by religion.

Descartes had already condemned the appeal to God's

purposes. In the *Fourth Meditation*, he wrote: 'My nature is very weak and limited, whereas the Divine nature is immeasurable, incomprehensible, infinite; this is enough to show me that innumerable things whose causes are unknown to me lie in God's power. For this very reason, I consider the usual inquiries about final causes to be wholly useless in physics; it could not but be rash, I think, for me to investigate the aims of God' (*A.G.*, p. 94). Slyly, under cover of piety, Physics is purged of any reference to God's ends. Descartes felt the purgation to be necessary both for epistemic and for ethical reasons. We can in principle come to discover, and hence *know*, the mechanisms by which a thing orginates; but we can never do more than *conjecture* what purpose God had in fashioning it (*Reply to the Fifth Set of Objections, H.R.* II, p. 223). And he noted the link between the appeal to God's purposes and the presumptuous belief that Creation exists for the sake of man (*Kenny Letters*, p. 222; *cf.* the similar view of Maimonides, *Guide for the Perplexed*, III, 13).

So far Spinoza merely follows Descartes; but Spinoza is more uncompromising. Descartes allows that God is the final as well as the efficient cause of the world (*Kenny Letters*, p. 222). He agrees that God does act for certain purposes, some of which are disclosed to us in Revelation (*Cottingham*, p. 19). He permits us to guess at God's ends for the sake of bettering our conduct (*Replies to the Fifth Set of Objections; H.R.* II, p. 223). He even once concedes that the requirements of ethics comport with encouraging ourselves to believe that God made all things for our sake (*Principles* III, 3; *A.G.*, p. 222). He attributes our ignorance of God's purposes only to our inability, as finite things, to comprehend the infinite (*Principles* I, 25; *H.R.* I, p. 229). Spinoza systematically rejects all these ideas.

In the lengthy and renowned Appendix to *Ethics* I, Spinoza sets out to eradicate the prejudices that 'God Himself directs all things to some certain end' and that 'God made everything for the sake of man, and man that he might worship God'. The God of Spinoza is not the God of Abraham, Isaac and Jacob, the God of Revelation. Just as He does not resemble man (V, 2), so He has no providential care for him. He has not made man to love and worship Him, and He cannot love man in return (*E* V, 17C).

In his Appendix, Spinoza aims to do three things. First, he wishes to explain the *causes* of the origin and persistence of the prejudice that all things in Nature work to some end, which has been pre-appointed by God. Second, he wants to demonstrate the *falsity* of that common belief. And third, he tries to show it has propagated yet *other* prejudices and falsehoods concerning good

GOD OR NATURE

and evil, merit and sin, praise and blame, order, disorder, beauty, deformity.

Spinoza's explanation of why the prejudice arises and lingers is very striking. It rests on the assumptions that man is born ignorant of causes, and that he has a conscious desire to seek that which profits him. Because of his ignorance of causes, he does not know the true springs of his own action, and imagines himself to be free; because of his desire for his own profit, he acts for the sake of an end. When he seeks to explain his actions to himself, therefore, he locates their cause in some end to which he is drawn; and when he attempts to account for the activity of other things, he naturally projects the same pattern of explanation. 'Thus by his own mind he necessarily judges that of another' (as generally in knowledge through the imagination: *E* II, 185; *cf*. III, 2–3). Furthermore, man notices that there are many things which he can put to his own uses, or which contribute to the end of his own profit: his eyes are well adapted for seeing; the plants and animals yield him nourishment; the sun lends him its light. He concludes that these things have been designed, and designed for his own advantage. This leads him to speculate as to the character of the person who has made them (for evidently they are not made by men); and so he advances to the idea of 'some ruler or rulers of Nature' who are 'endowed with human liberty, who have taken care of all things for him, and who have made all things for his use'.[1] He has no knowledge of the mind of these rulers, and so must extrapolate from his 'knowledge' of his own mind; and knowing that he himself is motivated by the thought of his own profit, he affirms that 'the gods direct everything for his advantage, in order that he may be bound to them and hold them in the highest honour'. Man makes God in his own image; and because men's self-images can differ, there arise the many religions, and the wars of jarring sects.

A problem, however, soon made itself felt – the problem of natural evil. 'Amidst so much in Nature that is beneficial, not a few things must have been observed which are injurious, such as storms, earthquakes, diseases.' The solution appeared to be either that man had wronged the gods and provoked their vengeance, or that his manner of worshipping them was unsatisfactory. But the 'solution' was manifestly defective: for it was obvious that 'the beneficial and the injurious were indiscriminately bestowed on the pious and the impious'. The whole flimsy superstructure of

---

[1] '[T]he physician George Chapman in 1705 explained that the Creator made the horse's excrement smell sweet, because he knew that men would often be in its vicinity.' *Lerner*, p. 86.

prejudice and fantasy threatened to collapse. Rather than permit this, men fled to the conclusion that the gods worked in a mysterious way, and that their judgements 'far surpass our comprehension'. Men are like children who blacken a face in play and then recoil in dread and awe from the strange visage (the analogy is Pascal's). And so the human race would have remained in ignorance to all eternity 'if mathematics, which does not deal with ends, but with essences and properties of forms, had not placed before us another rule of truth'.

So much for the sources of the religious hypothesis; but is it demonstrably false? Spinoza thinks so, and refers his readers back to the formal demonstrations at *E* I, 16 and 32. But he goes on to add three further considerations, in the hopes of sealing his case. Let us examine them.

(A) First, he says, the doctrine of final causes 'entirely reverses Nature'. For (i) 'it considers what is really the cause as the effect, and conversely'; (ii) 'it makes what is prior in nature to be posterior'; (iii) 'it renders what is supreme and most perfect, utterly imperfect'. These assertions can perhaps be explicated as follows. (i) In a teleological explanation, we claim that Φ-ing happened in order that it might be the case that *p*. The form of our statement thus intimates that it was due to '*p*' that the Φ-ing took place. But this is to invert the true causal order: if '*p*' arose at all (which may not have happened), then its obtaining is due to the fact that Φ-ing took place, rather than the reverse. (ii) Here Spinoza may mean that God, Who is prior in the order of Nature, becomes (on the finalist view) posterior in the order of discovery. For the finalist doctrine is bound up with the claim that we come to the knowledge of God *a posteriori*: His designs reveal His existence or His character (*cf.* Gassendi, *Fifth Set of Objections*; H.R. II, p. 175). The true order of discovery, however, puts first what comes first in Nature (*E* II, 10CS: 'although the Divine nature ought to be studied first, because it is first in the order of knowledge and in the order of things, (men) think it last'). Alternatively, in asserting (ii), Spinoza may mean no more than what he says, at greater length, in explaining (iii). (iii) The third point rests on the claim that 'that effect is most perfect which is immediately produced by God, and in proportion as intermediate causes are necessary for the production of a thing is it imperfect'. But on the assumption of finalism, the things which follow 'immediately' from God – that is, the infinite modes – exist for the sake of certain finite modes – that is, ourselves – and hence are less perfect than we; which is absurd.

(B) The second main charge against the doctrine of final causes is that it renders God necessitous, and hence imperfect; 'for if God acts for the sake of an end, He necessarily desires something of which He is deprived'. What Spinoza seems to have in mind here is the view, current both in learned and in popular circles, that God created the world in order to display His power and to win adoration for Himself. This – somewhat unedifying – account of the Divine purposes may be found in Calvin's *Institutes of the Christian Religion* (Calvin figures large in Spinoza's thought: *Strauss*, p. 109). 'God has ordained all things to our profit and salvation, and in order to contemplate His power and His grace in ourselves and in the benefits He has conferred upon us, thereby to incite us to trust in him, to call upon Him, to praise and love Him' (*Institutes* I, 14, xxii; quoted by *Wendel*, p. 170). It is true that this mentions God's concern to promote our creaturely benefit, but elsewhere Calvin is less circumspect: 'Although God lacks nothing, still the principal aim He had in creating men was that His name might be glorified in them' (*Treatise on Predestination*, opp. 8 p. 293; cited in *Wendel*, p. 171). For Spinoza, such a description of God's purpose is both contradictory in itself and demeaning to God: contradictory, because God cannot both 'lack nothing' and also want to be glorified; demeaning, because it makes God imperfect, and implies that His service is bondage based on fear (*cp. Strauss*, p. 207).

Spinoza was aware that the theologians had an answer to his charges. He mentions it, and tries to meet it, when he writes:

> Although the Theologians and Metaphysicians distinguish between an end of need (*finis indigentiae*) and an end of assimilation (*finis assimilationis*), they admit nevertheless that God does everything for His own sake, and not for the things to be created, since before Creation nothing can be mentioned, on account of which God should act; and so they are necessarily forced to admit that God lacked those things for whose sake He willed to provide means, and desired them, as is clear in itself. (*E* I, Appendix)

Spinoza seems to be alluding to the work of his contemporary, Heereboord, a Professor of Philosophy at Leyden. (Heereboord is named, and quoted, in *CM* II, 12, xii.) The relevant passage from Heereboord's *Meletemata* has been identified by Gueroult (*Gueroult* I, p. 395), and reads as follows:

> God made everything for His own sake, not because he was in need of the things He made (or if so He would be moved by an

end in the character of a man), but in order that He might cause those creatures to share in His goodness: a fact which the Scholastics articulated in the way – God made everything, not for the sake of the end of need, but of assimilation, as would someone who did not seek his own advantage, but so that he might benefit things outside himself.

Spinoza pinpoints the confusion here: for although Heereboord says that God created the world for the sake of beings other than himself, he also asserts that God made everything for His own sake. But for the rest, Spinoza's criticism of the scholastics' distinction seems unfair. He notes the absurdity in saying:

(1) There were things other than God for whose sake He brought it about that all the things which are other than Himself began to exist.

And he supposes that anyone who maintains that God acts for the end of 'assimilation' is committed to that absurdity. But Heereboord and those whom he follows need not be trapped into that admission. What Heereboord actually says is that God acted in order that He might cause the things that He made to share in His goodness. That is:

(2) God brought it about that there were things other than Himself; and He brought it about that there were things other than Himself in order that the things other than Himself which He was to bring about should share in His goodness.

It does not appear that (2) entails (1); but if not, then (2) is not absurd, and the scholastic distinction can do the work for which it was intended.

(C) The final argument against theological finalism is that it results from, and reinforces, our ignorance of natural causes. His special target here may be Maimonides (so *Wolfson* I, p. 434, citing *The Guide for the Perplexed*, III, 17, 'Second Theory'). But again he may be alluding to Calvin, who taught that 'when we speak of the providence of God, this word does not signify that He, remaining idle in the heavens, watches over what is happening on earth: rather He is like the captain of a ship, holding the helm in order to cope with every event' (*Institutes* I, 16, ii; an eccentric form of this view survives in Berkeley, *The Principles of Human Understanding*, Sections 32, 57, 107, 150). Spinoza argues:

The adherents of this doctrine . . . have introduced a new

species of argument, not the *reductio ad impossible*, but the *reductio ad ignorantiam*, to prove their position; this shows that it had no other mode of defence left. For, by way of example, if a stone has fallen from a roof onto someone's head and killed him, they will demonstrate in this manner that the stone has fallen in order to kill the man. For if it did not fall for that purpose by the will of God, how could so many circumstances concur through chance (and a number often simultaneously do concur)? You will answer, perhaps, that the event happened because the wind blew and the man was passing that way. But, they will urge, why did the wind blow at that time, and why did the man pass that way precisely at the same moment? If you again reply that the wind rose then because the sea on the preceding day began to be stormy, and that the man had been invited by a friend, they will urge again – because there is no end of questioning – But why was the sea agitated? Why was the man invited at that time? And so they will not cease from asking the causes of causes, until at last you fly to the will of God, the asylum for ignorance. (*E* I, Appendix)

What exactly is the issue between Spinoza and his opponents? It seems that they insist that events of a certain type can only be explained in terms of God's will and purposes, while he insists that those events can and must be explained in terms of efficient causes. When the issue is posed in that way, Spinoza must win our sympathy; but we have also to ask – What is the special character of the events in question? From what Spinoza says, it seems that the events are coincidences, the chance concurrence of things which do not usually fall out together. And if that is what he has in mind, it may be that *both* he *and* his opponents are wrong: a chance event can be explained neither by final nor by efficient causes (*cf.* V, 6, *Coincidences and causality*).

When Spinoza indicates the type of explanation for a coincidence which he would regard as satisfactory, he speaks of a set of explanations, each of which is appropriate to some aspect of the coincidence. You explain why a stone falls on a man's head at a certain time by explaining first why the stone fell at that time, and by explaining next why the man was in that place at that time. But is this really an explanation of why the stone fell and the man was under the roof *at the same time*? We do not seem to have a *connected* explanation of the event, but two unconnected explanations for two occurrences which coincide. Richard Sorabji, whose work on this topic we have already mentioned, V, (5), puts the point very effectively:

> [S]uppose that for each of five airliners we have a *separate* explanation of why it crashed on March 1st: the damaged bolt, the drunken pilot, the terrorist bomb, and so on. Does it follow that we have an explanation of why the five crashed *on the same day*? I think that someone who asked for the latter would be looking for a *connected* explanation, such as that a group of terrorists planned all five crashes. There may be such a *connected* explanation, but there may only be five separate explanations of the timing. And if we could give only these, I think the man who asked us to explain the simultaneity would be entitled to feel that we had not answered his question. (*Sorabji*, p. 10)

It is possible, however, that Spinoza picked the example of a coincidence only because it lent itself particularly well to his opponents' needs: since an efficient cause of such an event apparently cannot be found, it is particularly tempting to look for a final cause in God's hidden purposes (*cf. Strauss*, p. 135, on 'vulgar explanation'). And (the theologians may have reasoned) what is true of a seeming accident is true of all events whatsoever: they cannot be explained, or satisfyingly explained, in terms of secondary causes, but only by reference to God's will.

If that is the conclusion to which Spinoza is objecting, then of course his attack upon it has more force. It is fair to characterise the reasoning which leads to that conclusion as an argument *ad ignorantiam*, because it rests upon our ignorance of certain items in a given sequence of causes, which ignorance alone provides the motive for ascribing the outcome of the sequence to God's will. Moreover, not only does that form of reasoning *issue* from ignorance, but it *fosters and confirms* it: it discourages the search for secondary and efficient causes, which alone can give us true knowledge of events; and it stupifies curiosity with pseudo-explanations, appealing to a Divine will whose content can only be identified by reference to the very effects it is invoked to explain (*cf.* Maimonides, *Guide for the Perplexed*, II, 17). The vacuity of 'explanations' which trade on the idea of God's will – or His power – is stressed in the *Tractatus Theologico-Politicus*, where the topic is the cause of prophetic inspiration. Spinoza says:

> As to the particular laws of Nature by which the communications took place, I confess my ignorance. I might indeed say, as others do, that they took place by the power of God; but this

would be mere trifling, and no better than explaining some unique specimen by a transcendental term. *Everything* takes place by the power of God. Nature herself is the power of God under another name, and our ignorance of the power of God is co-extensive with our ignorance of Nature. (*TTP*, c. I; G III, p. 14; *cf.* III, 2).

Concluding observations

Spinoza's critique of theological finalism is the harbinger of the Enlightenment's great onslaught against revealed religion, and through the work of the Enlightenment, it has passed into the modern outlook, and become a fixture in a *Weltanschauung*. Yet his diagnosis of the causes of belief in finalism is unpersuasive, and the arguments by which he assails it, at best inconclusive. To grasp the real significance of his position (and, incidentally, to appreciate the causes of its success), we must fit it into the fabric of moral and political doctrine woven by Spinoza, and not see it merely as a scholastic thesis.

Recall Spinoza's description of the state of mankind before mathematics showed the way out of the *impasse*: prostrated before the gods, terrified of their displeasure, desperate to propitiate them, at the mercy of the natural environment. In this state, ignorance of causes and 'superstition' feed on one another, and 'superstition is engendered, preserved and fostered by *fear*' (*TTP* Preface; G III, p. 6). Now *fear* is a matter of great moment in Spinozism, as it was before in Epicureanism. Spinoza calls it the most powerful of the emotions ('*eoque efficacissimo*': G III, p. 6), and he devotes considerable thought to examining its causes, its uses, and the means of overcoming it. In the Preface to the *TTP*, he discusses the interplay of fear and 'superstition', particularly on the minds of those who 'most greedily desire external goods', and who are contrasted to 'the wise' (G III, p. 5). Although in prosperity fear does not lay a hand on such as these, if reversals of fortune should beset them, their native credulity gives 'superstition' its entry, and 'superstition' in turn stirs up and exacerbates fear. 'If anyone desire an example, let him take Alexander, who only began superstitiously to seek guidance from seers when he first learnt to fear fortune in the passes of Sysis' (G III, p. 6). (Is the choice of Aristotle's most famous pupil for the example an oblique criticism of the 'wisdom' offered by the Peripatetics?) 'Superstition' and fear are conjoined, not only on the level of the individual, but also on that of the collective: 'prophets have most power among the people, and are most formidable to rulers, precisely at those times when the State is in most peril' (*G* III, p. 6).

Now although for the statesman, fear may have its uses, it must nonetheless be contained; and in order to contain it, 'superstition' must be regulated. (In the case of individuals, those who are fitted for the life of reason must regulate it, or eliminate it, in themselves.) 'Superstition' here is identical with revealed religion; it is not, as from *within* the perspective of revealed religion, something *contrasted* to it. (When Spinoza opposes 'superstition' to what *he* calls 'religion', as, e.g., at *G* III, p. 5, he intends a contrast between revealed faith and religion within the limits of reason alone.) Thus the mastery over the passions, and particularly over fear, depends on a critique of revealed religion; and the innermost citadel of such religion is the doctrine of finalism, or the lordship of God over a Nature submissive to His purposes.

Hence the strategic placement of the critique of finalism at the end of *Ethics* I, when the study of the Divine things or *Natura naturans* has been completed, and the study of *natura naturata*, but especially of the human order, is about to begin. The theology and metaphysics of Part I are meant to serve as a *model* for the sciences which follow; they prescribe the correct *method* for those sciences, which is to pursue efficient causes, not final ones; they delineate the proper *objects* for those sciences, stripping Nature of anthropocentric figments, putting 'motion' and 'body' in the place of 'forms', and allowing 'striving' (*conatus*) to occupy the place of purpose; in short, they are like the 'mathematics' which first led men out of ignorance, and put them on the road to 'the true knowledge of things'.

But the critique of finalism does more than simply remove a 'great obstacle to science'; or rather, in doing that it bears directly on the right ordering of life, the right management of the affects. The Appendix to *Ethics* I re-enacts the Epicurean confrontation between the religious and the scientific world view: between 'the world as the work of spontaneously and suddenly appearing, discontinuously willing, working forces, and as such not surveyable by man, causing anguish and confusion' and 'the world as fixed and unchanging eternally identical order, thus in principle within the range of human conceptions, and as such not disquieting but rather offering tranquillity of mind' (*Strauss*, p. 127). How we see the world determines how we respond to it: if as the dominion of arbitrary and hidden will, then with fear and confusion; if as the arena of intelligible drives and forces, then with composure and clarity.

Finally, the critique of God's rulership over Nature carries implications for our political understanding, in the matter of man's rulership over man. The decline of 'superstition' presages the advent of the liberal – that is, the non-confessional – State. Spinoza thinks that the right end of civil society is 'peace and security of life' (*TP* V, 2; *G* III, p. 289): he does not want the world made safe *for* anything, but merely made *safe*. For civil peace to be attained, the erratic forces of religion must be held in check: ' "The mob has no ruler more potent than superstition", as Curtius well says' (*TTP* Preface; *G* III, p. 6). Hence Spinoza proclaims his happiness at living in the Dutch Republic, 'where each may worship God as his conscience dictates' (*G* III, p. 7); for the wise ruler regulates 'superstition' precisely by *not* enforcing it (in the manner of the Ottomans: *ibid.*), but by cordoning it off, by relegating it to the 'private' sphere. In the liberal order, therefore, the religious emotions are deflected away from the public life, and fizzle harmlessly outside its confines. Philosophy is the gainer from this: the same policy which severs religion from the State, necessarily brings in the freedom to theorise (*TTP*, ch. XX).

Both the 'many' and the 'wise' thus profit under Secular Liberalism, though in their respective ways. For those who, (like the 'many' of the Preface to the *TTP*) are greedy for external things (and so peculiarly susceptible to 'superstition') commerce and manufacture take the place of religious strife, and energies wasted in the wars of opinions are diverted into the harmless competition of trade. At the same time, those who (like the narrator of the preamble to the *DIE*) care nothing for honour and riches, but seek an unfailing good, may pursue their project without disturbance, even in the company of their fellow-minded. The religious demand for the unconditional, the infinite, is thus safely canalised: on the one hand, into the service of an insatiable appetite; on the other, into the study of an inexhaustible good. It is true that life under this order becomes more prosaic, more complacent, and is bereft alike of ceremony and of spontaneity. The imagination is turned away hungry, holding an empty bowl: saints and heroes are out of place here, as well as prophets and priests (*cf. MacIntyre* (1), p. 283). But Spinoza is too close to the horror and futility of religious conflict, or too preoccupied with them, to sense these limitations. The discontents and longings of Emma Bovary or the young Marx lie far beyond the horizons of the *Ethics*.

VI

Minds and Bodies

Like much else in his philosophy, Spinoza's theory of the mind is original, speculative, and difficult to understand. It has met with violently differing reactions: some have rejected it outright (e.g. *Froude* I, p. 367); others have found in it the solution to the riddles left by Descartes (e.g. *Jonas*, pp. 262–3). One thing at least is certain: among the great thinkers of the past, Spinoza stands out for insistence that the human mind is a part of Nature, subject to its causal order, and capable of being understood by scientific methods. Human beings imagine themselves to occupy a privileged position, he asserts, likening themselves to a State within the greater State of Nature (*TP*, II), but this is a delusion. Nor is the error confined to the vulgar: learned men and philosophers have maintained that 'man disturbs rather than follows Nature's order, that he has an absolute power over his own actions, that he is altogether self-determined'. But to say this is to make human conduct unintelligible; for 'there must be one and the same method for understanding the nature of all things whatsoever, that is, by the universal laws and rules of Nature'. It follows that the properties of human minds can only be grasped if we adopt a method of studying them which is also fitted for studying the properties of bodies in motion. The teaching of other philosophers has not of course been wholly without value: they 'have written many excellent things about the right conduct of life, and have given mortals counsels full of prudence'. But we must rebuke them for having failed to discover 'the nature and strength of the affects, and what the mind is able to do towards controlling them'. Even Descartes, who attempted to study the soul scientifically, started from these erroneous presuppositions, and so succeeded only in revealing 'the acuteness of his great intellect'. Indeed, the vulgar, false, flattering and destructive picture of human nature appears in its fullest colours in Descartes' work: for he tells us himself that there is 'one thing in us which might give us reason to esteem ourselves, to wit, the use of our free will, and the empire we possess over our wishes . . . This in a certain measure renders us like God in making us masters of ourselves'. Descartes' belief in free will, and his consequent denial that human conduct can be explained in terms of causal laws, may be the most prominent of his errors, but they spring from a deeper source. The basic trouble lies in his account of the mind's relation to the body. Since Spinoza's own theory owed so much to Descartes', it is useful to begin by outlining the Cartesian view. This will enable us to understand more clearly what Spinoza absorbed from his great predecessor, and what he rejected.

1 Cartesian man

The Cartesian theory of the mind has two main parts: one concerned with the distinctness of mind and body, the other with their manner of union and influence upon each other. As Descartes puts it himself, 'there are two facts about the human soul on which depend all the things we can know about its nature. The first is that it thinks, the second is that it is united to the body and can act and be acted upon along with it'. Thus the theory asserts the real or substantial distinction between the human mind and the particular body it consorts with: the mind is held to be a created thinking substance, capable both of existing, and of being conceived to exist, independently of any body. Even those aspects of the mental life which seem most obviously dependent on the workings of a body are not necessarily so: perceiving, dreaming, imagining, the feeling of pleasure or of pain, the experience of passion, inner sensation, or emotion, are all, however confusedly, modes of thought and, as such, properties of the thinking substance alone. Being a substance, the mind is of its very nature indestructible, unless God should otherwise decree; being a substance which thinks, it cannot admit of any corporeal characteristics. The human body, by contrast, is a perishing part of the system of Extension. Unlike the mind, it is not substantial itself, but only a 'mode' or specification of the unitary extended substance (*Williams* (1), pp. 127–8); in its manner of functioning it is to be compared with 'clocks, artificial fountains, mills and similar machines' which are capable of self-initiated motion. Mind and body are thus distinguishable by reference to (i) the ultimate categories of being to which each belongs, (ii) the range of predications each collects, (iii) the span of possible duration allowed to each, (iv) the type of explanation appropriate to the operations in which each engages. So much for their distinctness. On the other hand must be set the evident fact of experience, somehow to be accounted for, that mind and body are not wholly disconnected. The soul is not present in the body as a pilot in a ship; the human being is a unity, not a heap of disconnected parts. Mind and body exert a reciprocal influence upon each other: the ghost can tamper with the controls on the machine; the machine can trap the ghost in its gears and meshes.

In the Cartesian system, then, a form of dualism was wedded to a belief in interactionism. But critics were not slow to question whether such a marriage could last: was dualism, they asked, really compatible with interactionism? Could entities of such radically diverse types really cause changes to happen in one another? In particular, if (as Descartes thought) bodies could only be set in motion by other bodies (putting apart the special case of Divine intervention), how was it possible that the will should exercise any control over the movements of the body and its parts? Descartes had supposed that at the place of interaction in the human brain a swarm of superfine particles had collected, notifying the mind of inner changes in the body, or of the impingement of external stimuli upon it, and responding to the promptings and directives of the will. But that was an obvious fantasy. The 'animal spirits' partook uneasily of the attributes of the two entities they were designed to link: less gross and solid than the subtlest of ordinary bodies, they were yet more material than the unextended soul.

Nor was this the only place at which inconsistency seemed to break out. It was an axiom with Descartes, assumed in his proof of God's existence in *Meditation III*, that a cause had to contain, whether formally or eminently, the reality it imparted to its effect. But Descartes himself provides cases which show that this is untrue: he denies that 'the idea of a sound, which is formed in our consciousness' bears any likeness to 'the trembling of the air which has struck our ears' and so caused the idea to arise; he finds no similarity between the tickling sensation caused by touching the lips of a sleeping child with a feather, and the feather itself (*Traité de la Lumière*, Alquié edition pp. 317–18; *cf. Delahunty*, p. 36). Nor, conversely, can mental causes of effects in the physical world be endowed with physical characters: to suppose so would be to violate another Cartesian axiom, assumed in the proof of the distinctness of mind and body – no thinking thing can possess any extended qualities, no extended thing any mental properties.

Faced with this intra-systemic inconsistency, later Cartesians (among them Spinoza) sought to escape by abandoning interactionism. But it is important to see that this way out was not open to Descartes. For his proof of an external world and his final refutation of scepticism depend on assuming that the mind is acted upon by outer bodies, and hence on the possibility of a causal influence which runs in at least one direction (*cf.* VI, 2, *infra*). And his account of the passions and of our powers over them assumes that the mind or will can give rise to changes in the brain – implying an influence which runs the other way (*cf.* VI, 3, and VII, 2). Cartesian ethics and epistemology, in short, demand two-sided interactionism; Cartesian physics and theology preclude interaction altogether.

Spinoza was perfectly aware of many of these difficulties in Cartesianism. His solution fell into two parts. First, he discarded interactionism, denying that the mental could act upon the physical, or the physical upon the mental. But the truth which lay wrapped up in interactionism – the recognition that the human being is a real, not an artificial, unity – was something he laboured to preserve. Second, he retained dualism, but only in a modified and more plausible form. In the Cartesian scheme, we find a *substantival* dualism: the created world is most basically divisible into a plurality of thinking, immaterial substances on the one hand, and the unique extended substance on the other (itself diversified into a plurality of bodies or modes). But in the Spinozist metaphysics, the essential dualism is *attributival*, not substantival (IV, 4). There is only a single, uncreated, necessarily existing substance, which is Divine; it is characterised or constituted by an infinity of attributes, of which Thought and Extension are alone known to us; and these, though necessarily co-existent in the Divine substance, are really distinct and may be conceived apart from one another (IV, 6). The human mind is a particular 'mode' of Thought, and when considered as such can only be explained by reference to other modes of Thought, similarly considered; and likewise the human body is a mode of Extension, whose workings are to be explained only in a physicalistic manner. Nevertheless, although the mind and the body are to be regarded as modes of distinguishable attributes, they are also in some sense one and the same thing: *eadem res*. The duality of the attributes and of the modes is supposed to have been admitted, without denying the identity of that which permits a dual expression.

There is much that is suggestive in this formulation, much, too, which is obscure. Some of the suggestiveness may be made more explicit, and some of the obscurity dispelled, if we now record a pair of very helpful distinctions (*Barnes* (1) II, p. 191). First note the distinction between saying that the human mind is a substance, a thing capable of existing independently, and the denial of this, which asserts that the mind is insubstantial, dependent or 'adjectival'. Then consider the distinction between the thesis that the mind is (in some fashion) a material thing, and the negative thesis that it is immaterial. The two distinctions cut across each other, giving four possible types of view.

The first view is that the mind is a material substance: a position, I take it, adopted by the early Greek atomists, who identified the mind with a fire (an exhalation or a motion of the air) and later by Thomas Hobbes, who asserted that the self or mind was nothing other than the human body. Second, there is the idea that the mind is a substance, but an immaterial one: the view of Plato and of Descartes. Third, the mind may be said to be non-substantial but material: a view held by certain recent behaviourists and materialists. (In these latter-day presentations, the expression '. . . has a mind' is taken to be an unanalysable predicate, akin to '. . . had a bad temper' rather than to '. . . has a large stamp collection', (*cf. Quine* (2), p. 236). To have a mind, in other words, is a matter of having certain powers or dispositions, nothing more. By itself, this analysis commits one only to non-substantialism, not also to materialism; that facet is added if one holds, as the behaviourists did, that every mental predicate is definable in terms of some array of non-mental predicates, whether categorical or hypothetical or both; it is also added if one maintains, with the materialists, that every instance of a mental quality is identical with some event which can be described in physical terms alone.) Finally, there is the claim that the mind is non-substantial but immaterial: this is the doctrine of Aristotle, who regards having a soul as nothing other than being alive, and having a mind as a condition enabling one to perform certain intellectual feats, but who disagrees with the behaviourists in holding that mental predicates are irreducibly distinct from physical ones, and who differs from the materialists in surmising that not every mental act can be put in correspondence with some change in the body (VI, 4 *infra*).

If we had to find a place in this scheme for Spinoza, we would certainly have to align him with the non-substantialists, and against his great contemporaries Descartes and Hobbes; but for the rest, his theory is curiously Janus-faced, looking backwards to

Aristotle and the Greek past, forwards to modern materialism. On the one hand, he seems to assume the irreducible distinctness of mental predicates from non-mental ones; on the other, he appears to agree that the items in one's mental life can always be entered into correspondence with changes or conditions of the body, and that the connection between suitably paired items from each type will be a necessary one, amounting perhaps to some form of identity. (There is a general difficulty here, concerning whether the view of the mind expounded in Part II of the *Ethics* is consistent with that given in Part V. Part V seems to deny the permanent availability of mental/physical correspondences, Part II to assert it. But for the present let us remain within the orbit of Part II: *vide* IX, 4.) One might hope to give a more precise account, along these lines, of Spinoza's difficult statement that the mind and the body are 'one thing, expressed in diverse modes', but the question of interpretation will have to await its turn. I hope by this brief survey to have indicated the interest and the difficulty of the Spinozist position, and to have exhibited its major points of resemblance to, and difference from, those of other theorists. I want now to explore more adequately its relations with Cartesianism, beginning with the issue of interactionism and then turning to that of dualism.

2 *Interactionism*

In the *Sixth Meditation*, Descartes wrote that 'I am not in my body merely as a pilot is present in a ship; I am most tightly bound to it, and as it were mixed up with it, so that I and it form a unit' (A.G., p. 117). Part at any rate of this claim seems to be that a man is made up of causally interacting factors, and so comprises a unitary thing, as a blade and its handle do, and a blade and a nut do not. But plausible as that seems, it was a view which Descartes found he could maintain only with difficulty. Descartes' royal correspondent, the Princess Elizabeth of Bohemia, brought his attention to one difficulty: mental changes and bodily changes being of such utterly disparate types, how is it possible that a change of one sort can determine a change of the other (*Kenny Letters*, p. 136)? Modern critics have shared her perplexity: Gilbert Ryle, for example, has argued that 'the actual transactions between the episodes of the private <mental> history and those of the public <physical> history remain mysterious, since by definition they can belong to neither series' (*Ryle*, p. 12). Are we forced then to admit, alongside mental and physical occurrences, a series of occurrences which are neither?

Descartes was not unaware of these problems; why then did he feel compelled to defend interactionism in spite of them?

I think we can pinpoint a number of reasons for his defence. The most obvious is that he thought it was a matter of common experience that mind and body acted upon one another. Thus he wrote to Elizabeth that 'people who never philosophise and use only their senses have no doubt that the soul moves the body and that the body acts on the soul . . . Everyone feels that he is a single person with both thought and body so related by nature that the thought can move the body and feel the things which happen to it' (*Kenny Letters*, pp. 141, p. 142; *cp. Kenny Letters*, p. 235).

In addition to this, we can discern less obvious but not less urgent reasons for Descartes to accept interactionism, reasons which are brought about by the pressures and requirements of his other philosophical theories. Take first the vindication in the *Sixth Meditation* of the belief in a world of bodies in external space. Descartes says of that argument: 'I proved the existence of material things not from the fact that we have ideas of them but from the fact that these ideas present themselves in such a way as to make us aware that they are not produced by ourselves but come from elsewhere' (*Kenny Letters*, p. 115). In Spinoza's excellent account of the Cartesian argument (*PPD* I, 21 D), the proof that some of our ideas must be caused by external bodies is divided into two main parts. First, it is assumed that it is *possible* that some of our experiences (pleasure, grief, involuntary sensations) should be caused by body or extended substance. (That this *is* possible, is asserted to be clearly and distinctly perceived.) Second, it is held that no other type of cause (say, God or an angel) can be given to explain these same mental phenomena. (If we tried to fashion such a cause, we would 'at once destroy this clear and distinct concept we have'.) It follows that if these items of consciousness can be explained at all, there must be an extended substance which has the power to affect the mind in several ways. It thus becomes at least highly likely that there is a central mediating body, which has traffic both with the mind and with an outer world, and through which they impinge upon each other.

A similar line of argument is found in Descartes' account of the occurrence of confused and involuntary episodes in the consciousness. In the *Principles* (Part IV, art. 190), Descartes speaks of the passions of love, hate, fear and anger as 'confused thoughts which the mind does not have from itself alone, but because it is intimately united to the body, receiving its impressions therefrom. For there is the greatest difference between these passions and the distinct thought we have of what ought to be loved, chosen or shunned'. The same article notes that the 'natural appetites' of hunger and thirst are 'excited in the mind by means of the nerves of the stomach, fauces, etc. and are entirely different from the will which we have to eat, drink, etc'. The presence of these felt qualities in our experience is attributable only to the very close union of the consciousness with a body. If the mind were in the body less 'connaturally', if it were like a pilot in a ship, then although it would be able to monitor states of the body or external environment, it would perceive pain exactly as a pilot observes, by sight, his vessel's breakages (*A.G.*, p. 117). There is thus a two-fold source and justification for the belief in an extended substance capable of acting upon the body.

First, if we consider our sensory perceptions by themselves, the fact that they come upon us willy-nilly attests to the existence of external bodies which they represent to us; and in a matter like this, where our natural impulse to believe in such a cause is very great, it is not likely that God would permit us to be deceived (II, 1). But second, the fact that our information concerning the external world comes to us suffused with tones of feeling indicates that we stand in an intimate causal relation with a particular part of that world, which we call our own body. Indeed, as Spinoza points out, it is only on the supposition of an especially close union between a mind and its body that Descartes is able to account for the distinction between perceptual states and the other confused or involuntary experiences we undergo: 'among the sensations which . . . must be produced in us by extended substance, we notice a great difference, e.g., the difference between saying that I sense or see a tree, or saying that I am thirsty or grieved . . . Yet I clearly see that I am not able to perceive the cause of this difference unless I first understand that I am closely united to one part of matter, but not to others' (*PPD* I, 21D).

From all this it appears that Descartes' belief in interactionism is deeply motivated, and not a mere decoration on his system. We have next to see why Spinoza disagreed with it, and how he sought to refute it.

3 *The critique of interactionism*

Spinoza's rejection of interactionism is based on a variety of grounds. His most forceful line of attack is found in the early theorems of Part II of the *Ethics*; more special and detailed reasons are given in the Preface to Part V. I will begin by reciting the former.

(A) The crucial proposition here is *Ethics* II, 6. The theorem says that 'The modes of each attribute have God for their cause, insofar only as He is considered under that attribute of which they are modes, and not insofar as He is considered under any other'. The demonstration reads as follows: 'For each attribute is conceived through itself and without another (by *E* I, 10). Thus the modes of each attribute involve the concept of its own attribute, but not however that of another; and so (by *E* I, axiom 4) they have God as cause insofar as He is considered under that attribute of which they are modes, and not insofar as He is considered under any other' (*cp. E* III, 2, D). This is difficult, but the basic idea behind it is familiar – a cause must resemble its effect. Modes of Thought resemble other modes of Thought, but do not resemble modes of Extension; consequently modes of Thought can interact with one another, but can neither act upon nor be acted upon by modes of Extension. The problem which this 'causal likeness principle' poses for interactionism (touched on in VI, 1) was clearly perceived by Bishop Berkeley. 'It is . . . extravagant to say, a thing which . . . is unperceiving, is the cause of our perceptions, without any regard to consistency, or to the old known axiom: Nothing can give to another that which it hath not itself' (*Berkeley*, p. 198). Spinoza's argument is best understood if it is seen as, in substance, the same as that of Berkeley (*cp.* IV, 5).

So construed, the argument depends on the truth of the 'old known axiom' to which Berkeley refers. That 'axiom' can be roughly formulated as:

(1) If X becomes Φ because of Y, then Y is (somehow or in some degree) Φ.

In that form, the idea can be traced back at least as far as Aristotle (*Posterior Analytics* 72a29–30). It has some faint plausibility: if the sugar sweetens the tea, it must itself be sweet; if the machine is ingenious, then so was the artisan (*cf. Delahunty*, pp. 36–7). Jonathan Bennett, however, has conjectured that (1) must be a corollary of a deeper, more basic claim, which he names The Balance Principle. According to him, that Principle says that 'in any fully intelligible causal transaction *something gains what something else loses*' (*Bennett* (2), p. 59; his italics). This crude idea, he asserts, can be spelled out more clearly as either:

(2) If X becomes Φ because of Y, then as Y makes X more Φ,

Y itself becomes less Φ;

or as:

(3) If X becomes Φ because of Y, then X acquires some or all of the very Φ-ness which Y had. (*cf. Bennett* (2), p. 60)

Something like The Balance Principle must underlie the immediate appeal of the great conservation principles in physics: we feel, as Bennett puts it, that Nature must balance her books. And, as he shows with a host of illustrations, the Principle or its corollaries lie behind a great deal of philosophy in the early modern period. Yet (3) is incoherent, and (2) is false. Even (1), which will satisfy the more modest needs of the Spinozist/Berkeleian argument, is scarcely credible. This line of attack on interactionism is a failure; the success it scores is purely *ad hominem*, since Descartes needed (1), or something like it, for his Cosmological Argument.

(B) The piecemeal criticisms of interactionism contained in the Preface to *E* V are overtly *ad hominem*: they are specifically directed against the theory set out in Descartes' *Passions of the Soul* (on which see also VII, 1). Much of the discussion relates to controversies over archaic physiology; but underlying these is a matter of great importance for ethics. For, as Spinoza begins by observing, 'the Stoics thought that the affects depend absolutely on our will, and that we are absolutely masters over them'; and, he points out, 'Descartes much inclines to this opinion'. The real interest of the Preface derives then at least as much from its critique of this Stoic-Cartesian view, as from its objections to interactionism.

Spinoza explains the Cartesian theory of the mind/body union with the epitomising skill and accuracy of which he was a master. He focuses on Descartes' contention that the mind is closely united to the pineal gland in the centre of the brain. This gland was supposedly surrounded by very volatile 'animal spirits', which it could move and by which it could be moved. Descartes had maintained 'that each volition of the mind is united in Nature to a certain motion of the gland' (*E* V, Preface; *cf. Passions*, art. 44); he also averred that 'although each motion of the gland appears to be connected by Nature from the beginning of our life to an individual thought, these motions can nevertheless be connected by habit with other thoughts' (*E* V, Preface; *cf. Passions*, arts 44, 45, 50). Through self-imposed habituation, Descartes concluded, we can acquire absolute control over the passions. 'For passions, as he defines them are "perceptions, or sensations, or emotions of the soul which are related to it especially and which" – note well – "are caused, preserved and strengthened by some motion of the spirits" ' (*E* V, Preface; *cf. Passions*, art. 27). The will can determine itself (*Passions*, art. 17; *Kenny Letters*, p. 226); it can by fixed resolutions cause the pineal gland to move whenever a certain type of volition arises; that glandular movement in turn moves the animal spirits; and the spirits control the effects of the passions.

Spinoza raises several penetrating objections to these views. Two of his criticisms seem to me especially cogent.

(i) Spinoza contends that the Cartesian theory assumes 'an hypothesis more occult than any occult quality'. 'What does he mean by the union of mind and body? What clear and distinct conception has he of a thought united most strictly to a certain small portion of matter? I deeply wish that he had explained this union through its proximate cause.' To say that mind and body are united because each is 'connatural' to the other is to leave us none the wiser; to say on the other hand that the cause of the union is God is, at best, to gesture at its remotest antecedent, leaving the proximate cause unknown.

Spinoza's charge is corroborated by the evidence of Descartes' own *Letters*. In trying to overcome Princess Elizabeth's qualms about interactionism, Descartes asserted that the union of mind and body 'is no more difficult for us to understand than it is for those who believe in accidents to understand how they act on corporeal substances while belonging to a wholly different category'. Illustrating this, he writes:

> When we suppose that heaviness is a real quality of which all
> we know is that it has the power to move the body that
> possesses it towards the centre of the earth, we find no
> difficulty in conceiving how it moves the body nor how it is
> united to it. I think that we misuse this notion when we apply
> it to heaviness, which as I hope to show in my *Physics*, is not
> anything really distinct from body; but it was given us for the
> purpose of conceiving the manner in which the soul moves
> body. (*Kenny Letters*, p. 139)

The more one reflects on this little passage, the more baffling it becomes. Is Descartes making an *ad hominem* argument against 'those who believe in accidents' – presumably, the Aristotelians – by showing that if they accept a certain type of explanation in physics, then they cannot reject the kind of explanation he proposed in psychophysics? Or is his point rather that *all* of us claim to understand how the heaviness of a body can cause it to fall; and although this mode of understanding may be illusory (at least in Physics), nevertheless 'it was given us' (by God?) to help us grasp how mind can move body?

Whichever way we take Descartes' argument, it is astonishingly feeble: if it is directed against the Aristotelians, then it has no force against those who deny the existence or efficacy of 'real accidents'; if it is designedly broader in import, then why should 'volition' do better than 'heaviness' in explaining a body's motion? Spinoza in effect points out that the Cartesian theory fails to meet Descartes' own standards for the intelligibility of an explanation; and in that Spinoza is correct.

(ii) Spinoza also wreaks havoc with the claim that the mind is a source of 'forces' having a common measure with physical forces and capable of moving (or resisting movement from) the pineal gland:

> Next I would wish to know how many degrees (*gradus*) of motion the mind can impress on this pineal gland, and with how great a force it can hold it suspended. For I do not know whether this gland is acted upon by the mind more slowly or more quickly than by the animal spirits, nor whether the movements of the passions which we have tightly bound to firm judgements, cannot be disjoined from them again by corporeal causes; from whence it would follow that although the mind had firmly determined to meet danger, and had joined to this decision the notion of boldness, the sight of danger might cause the gland to be suspended in such a manner that the mind could think of nothing but flight. Indeed, since there is no common measure (*ratio*) between the will and motion, so also no comparison is given between mental and bodily power or forces; and consequently the forces of the body can never be determined by those of the mind.

This is a critique of interactionism, written in a spirit of almost Rylean raillery, but it is also more. Just as Descartes' mistaken notion of the will nurtured the illusion that we could hold ourselves aloof from error (II, 1) so also it encourages the belief that we can gain complete victory over the passions (VII, 2). Spinoza questions Descartes' optimism on both these matters, taking advantage here of the flaws and inconsistencies in the mind-model on which they depend.

Damagingly for his own theory, Descartes admitted that in some cases external bodies can trigger reactions by the body, without – or even against – the choices of the will. If someone suddenly thrusts his hand against my eyes, I cannot prevent them from closing, even if I should wish to; the sudden hand movement, once seen, causes a rush of the animal spirits from the brain into the muscles, shutting the eyes; and this occurs before the will can impress on the pineal gland forces which would so move it that the rush of spirits into the muscles was prevented (*Passions*, art. 13). Spinoza questions, how common a phenomenon is this? Can external stimuli, and the passions they excite in the mind, determine actions and reactions in this reflex-like way, far more frequently than Descartes allows? Descartes asserted that the response from the will which would inhibit an impulse towards (say) flight, can always be made to occur, *quickly* enough and with sufficient *force*, to resist the very rapid and forceful movements of the spirits around the gland, when these are provoked by the sight of danger; and it is only because the will is capable of mustering these contrary forces that the spillage of the spirits into the muscles, causing flight, is obstructed. But what evidence is there that the will, even with practice and habituation, can always dispose of adequate forces soon enough, on the occasions when they are needed? Descartes claims, without much argument, that the will can *usually* generate the necessary resistances: 'if anger causes us to lift our hand to strike, the will can usually hold it back' (*Passions*, art. 46). But he allows that in many cases, unless the will is fortified by practice, it cannot summon up the countervailing force: 'I confess that . . . these movements excited in the blood by the objects of the passions follow so promptly from these single impressions that are made in the brain and from the disposition of the organs . . . that there is no human wisdom capable of resisting them when sufficient preparation is not made . . . In this way those who are naturally much carried away by their dispositions towards emotions of joy or pity, or fear or anger, cannot prevent themselves from fainting, weeping or trembling' (*Passions*, art. 211). Spinoza asks, discouragingly, whether it is always possible to take sufficient preparations. More than that, he points out that if corporeal forces are allowed to exert an influence upon the soul, there is no denying that the passions they excite in it may drive all thought of resistance from the mind, preventing or overcoming the contrary inclination. Figure VI may make the issue clearer (*cp. Passions*, art. 47).

MINDS AND BODIES

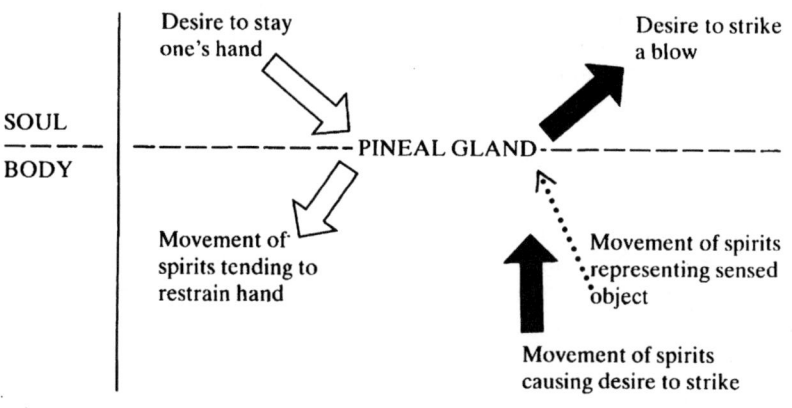

```
                Desire to stay              Desire to strike
                one's hand                  a blow
                        ↘                ↗
SOUL
————   ————————— PINEAL GLAND ——————————
BODY
                        ↙                ↑
                Movement of               Movement of spirits
                spirits tending to        representing sensed
                restrain hand             object

                                          ↑
                                    Movement of spirits
                                    causing desire to strike
```

Figure VI

Imagine that a feeling of anger, the desire to strike someone a blow, has arisen in the soul through external causes: proximately, a movement of the pineal gland; remotely, the agitation of the animal spirits about the gland, which is itself due to the sensed presence of an object of the passion. The will, Descartes claims, can resist this desire, by exercising a pressure of its own on the pineal gland, restraining the animal spirits from flowing into the arm muscles and causing it to come down heavily. But he allows that the forces associated with the anger can impress themselves on the gland so suddenly or with such tremendous strength that the contrary movements arrive too late, too weakly, or not at all. Such a misfortune, he insists, is, however, unusual (no doubt Spinoza would demur), and it lies within our power to prevent it from ever happening. I can magnify the strength of the desire to stay my hand and, with it, the resulting pressure on the pineal gland; and in that manner I can check the flow of spirits into the gland, and thus stem the flow of spirits into the arm. (The magnification of the desire is, for Descartes, itself a complicated business: it involves the effort to remember counsels and precepts, the consequent dispersal of animal spirits to the pores of the brain on which the memory-traces are imprinted, the reflux of the spirits upon the gland, the emergence in the mind of the recognition of the items sought for, and the intensification, by an intra-psychic causality, of the original desire.) But to this Spinoza answers that the forces in the body which throw up the desire to strike may also render it so *strong* that all attempts to inject the contrary desire are short-circuited; the desire to strike may drive every other thought and desire from the mind. There is, on Cartesian principles, no reason to think this impossible, and it is an observed fact of experience, however we explain it, that even sincere resolutions to combat the passions may be ineffectual. The Stoic-Cartesian view that we have, or can have, absolute control over our passions, seemed to Spinoza laughably naive; and he was right.

All of the preceding argument assumes of course that interactionism is true, and that it is fully intelligible to speak of the soul imparting quantities of force to the pineal gland. Against this Spinoza maintains that there is no common measure along which mental and physical 'forces' can both be computed. A decision or a resolution has neither more nor less nor the same quantity of force as a swarm of particles in motion; it cannot impress itself on a specially delicate part of the brain, opposing a determinable amount of resistance to the pressures exerted by subtle bodies converging on that focus. Not only is the Cartesian theory experimentally defective, it is conceptually monstrous. The will's interaction with the body cannot coherently be modelled on the physics of colliding bodies; to suppose so is to spawn a host of Rylean category-mistakes.

4 Dualism

Spinoza's denial of interactionism follows from his denial of dualism. The mind and its body, he says, are 'one and the same thing, but expressed in two modes' (or *ways* – '*modis*'). And their unity is not that of interacting substances falling under distinct attributes: Spinoza is better able than Descartes to assert that the mind is not in the body as a pilot in his ship. The unity of mind and body in man, the microcosm, reflects the unity of Thought and Extension in God or Nature, the macrocosm. As Thought and Extension are really distinct, so are their modes in mind and body; as the attributes are necessarily co-existent, so their modes are bound up together; as the diverse but co-existing attributes express the unique essence of God, so mind and body 'express' one and the same thing.

We have seen, however, that Spinoza's theory of the attributes threatens to collapse under the – arguably inconsistent – demands which he puts upon it (IV, 6–7). If so, we must expect to find a similar breakdown in his theory of the mind. If mind and body are really distinct, then what explains their union? If they are knitted together by conceptual necessity, then how can they be diverse? Spinoza speaks to us here in different and equivocal voices, and it is not remarkable that his readers should have heard various messages in them. There are in fact at least five interpretations of his view which are sold on the philosophical markets: his position is described now as Epiphenomenalism, now as Hylemorphism, now as a Dual Aspect Theory, or again as Parallelism, or as Materialism. Each interpretation catches at the truth, and gets a bigger or smaller piece of it; but each must fail, because the theory is not self-consistent. No doubt the pieces can be fitted together in ways that suggest a better, fuller, more plausible theory than the one we are actually given: but it is vital to mark the place at which exposition stops, and development begins. These judgements will, I fear, seem unconvincing to many: to prove them true, I must review the different interpretations of the theory, and expose the weaknesses of each. That task, thankless in itself, may at least strengthen the conviction that we can explain why no unified and self-consistent interpretation has yet succeeded in winning acceptance.

(A) So far as I am aware, no recent commentator on the *Ethics* has held Spinoza to be an Epiphenomenalist. But in his excellent series of articles on Part II of the *Ethics*, Harold Barker comes within inches of attributing that view to him. '[Spinoza's] argument repeatedly suggests that he is really thinking of the mind as determined by the body, so that, not Parallelism, but Epiphenomenalism, would be the right word to describe the real tendency of his thought'. Barker is of course well aware that this is not Spinoza's conscious, stated position: 'We may say . . . that he is thinking of the mind as merely reflecting what goes on in the body, but the essential point is that he really gives priority or predominance to the body, in spite of his professed doctrine of the complete independence and equality of the attributes' (*Barker*, p. 149). The 'priority' here must be *causal*: the body acts upon, controls, the mind; the mind does not affect the body.

Throughout the *Ethics* there are scattered passages which lend colour to Barker's view. In the Appendix to Part I, Spinoza asserts that 'if the motion by which the nerves are affected by means of objects represented to the eye conduces to well-being, the objects by which it is caused are called beautiful'; he continues, 'these things show that everyone judges things by the constitution of his brain' – then, correcting himself: 'or rather, accepts the affections of his imagination in the place of things'. In *E* III, 59S, where he is trying to pick his way carefully around the traps of interactionist idioms in common speech, he makes one misstep, remarking that 'a disposition of the body' – its state of repletion after a meal – may 'oppose this effort or desire' for more food. A similar slip occurs in *E* IV, 59S, which speaks of a man who, being 'agitated by anger or hatred, is caused to close his fist or move his arm'. But these are, after all, merely trifling inconsistencies; and one is immediately noticed and put right by Spinoza himself.

Barker does not cite much textual evidence in his own support. He declares that the scholium to *E* III, 2 has (i) an 'obvious tendency . . . – in spite of what the proposition itself asserts – . . . to glorify the body at the expense of the mind'. Later, he adds (ii) 'the vehemence of Spinoza's antagonism to any kind of freedom of the will seems to indicate that he is only too ready to misrepresent mental facts in order to make them conform to the laws of the physical order' (p. 150). The first comment is too impressionistic to be of much use; and it misses the point that in this scholium Spinoza is answering one appeal to common 'experience' with another, in the hopes of showing the doubtfulness of interactionism even at this level. The second comment is both irrelevant and unclear. Irrelevant: because Spinoza's anti-libertarian argument derives from his metaphysical determinism, not from the distorting effects of his theory of the mind/body nexus. Unclear: because Barker may be saying that the 'misrepresentations' of the mental consist in viewing the mind as subject to para-mechanical laws, analogous to the laws of physics (which is true but again irrelevant), *or* he may mean that they consist in supposing the mental facts to be themselves part of the physical order, explicable only through changes in matter (which, though pertinent, is expressly denied by Spinoza). Barker seems to have picked out some loose, untidy strands in Spinoza's thinking; he has not uncovered the real pattern within it.

(B) Wolfson has advanced a Hylemorphic interpretation of Spinoza. According to it, 'Spinoza's definition <*sic*> of the mind as the idea of the body . . . is nothing but a new way of restating the Aristotelian definition of the soul as the form of the body'. He enlarges:

> Following the Aristotelian view that it is the form of a thing and not its matter that is identical with the soul, Spinoza says that the first thing which is identical with the actual human mind is the idea of a thing; the term 'idea' here is used by him in the most general sense, comprehending what Aristotle would call the sensible, imaginable and intelligible form of a thing. Since the mind or the soul is identical with the idea, Spinoza sometimes uses the expression 'idea or soul' (*idea, seu anima*). Wolfson II, pp. 47–8)

To get at this we have to grasp the outlines of Aristotle's theory that the soul is the form of the body (for which, see *De*

Anima 412a1–413a10). According to Aristotle, what makes a certain portion of matter or stuff constitute a thing of a given sort is the possession by that matter of a certain *form*. The fact that a pile of stones and timber are arranged or formed in a certain way explains why they make up a *house*; the fact that a packet of tissue has the power to see tells us why it is an *eye*; the endowment of iron and wood with axe-ness explains why they make up an *axe*.

In the case of human beings, it is the fact that a certain organic body has a soul that accounts for its being a living human body, or a *person*; and for that type of body to possess a soul, is simply for it to have certain characteristic powers. 'Having a soul', in general, is nothing more than 'having a certain kind of life'; and 'having a *human* soul' is 'having the kind of life which belongs to a being which has the powers of locomotion, nutrition, sensation, imagination, and thinking'. Though the form of a thing is a causal factor which contributes to the thing's being as it is, the form is not a component or constituent of a thing, part of the stuff of which it is made: you might as well say that the arrangement of the letters in the syllable *AB* enters into the composition of the syllable in the way that the letters *A* and *B* do.

Now Spinoza wanted to explode the scheme of ideas in which 'form' and 'matter' had their place, not to revive it: he denied formal causes any role in scientific explanation. Partly this was due to the fact that they seemed to him idle: what use to say that a body digested because it had a nutritive soul? Partly it was a recognition of the successes, achieved or promised, of a science which dealt only in efficient causes. Partly it reflected his desire to eradicate explanations which accounted for physical processes non-mechanistically in terms of mental conditions, or which posited 'ends' or 'goals'. And partly it was because of the 'looseness' of relation between substantial forms at different levels, which prevented a thorough rationalisation of knowledge (*Farrer*, pp. 95–7). By endowing matter with distinct forms, the theory scuttled any hope of determining how that same matter could enter into a higher organisation, or how it would react when assimilated: you cannot deduce, from the nature of mutton-matter, how it will behave when absorbed into the matter of the dog which devours it. Aristotelian science apparently needed to offer a distinctive account of the relations between each possible pair of different natures; Galileian and Cartesian science, by postulating only bodies in motion, homogeneous in kind, could account for the complex in terms of the simple, the apparently many interactions at the sensible level in terms of relatively few types of interaction at the corpuscular level. The doctrine of substantial forms had 'turned nature into an unmanageable jungle, in which trees, bushes, and parasites of a thousand kinds were wildly interlaced. There was nothing for it, if science was to proceed, but to clear the ground and replant with spruce in rows: to postulate a single uniform nature, of which there should be a single science' (*Farrer*, p. 97).

This hostility to substantial forms, and specifically to souls, is evinced in many places (*vide* III, 2). Thus in the *Cogitata Metaphysica*, he dismisses the Aristotelian thesis that there are three types of soul, vegetative, sensitive and rational, belonging respectively to plants, animals and men (II, 6, i): 'we shall not take many pains to refute this, for as we have already demonstrated, these three souls . . . are nothing but figments, since we have shown that nothing exists in matter other than mechanical structures and operations'. That makes the basic point nicely. The doctrine of souls or forms went hand in hand with a non-mechanistic explanation of natural – and especially of organic – processes. Spinoza's science of body – and so of the living animal or human body – had to be mechanistic. Hence his rejection of Aristotle's theory of the soul (*cp. Caton*, p. 89).

There are, to be sure, structural resemblances between the form/matter or soul/body relation in Aristotle and the mind/body relation in Spinoza. As soul and body are inseparable in Aristotle, so mind and body are in Spinoza; as soul and body are categorially distinct in Aristotle, so mind and body are conceptually distinct in Spinoza. But the resemblances do not amount to an identity: Spinoza did not merely use novel language – he introduced novel ideas. By minimising his originality, Wolfson falsifies his thought.

(C) The 'Dual Aspect' Theory has sometimes been ascribed to Spinoza (as e.g. by *Pap* pp. 278–9) and at other times has been said, more cautiously, to have evolved out of Spinozism (so *Vesey* (1), p. 146). Caution is justified: when the theory is read into Spinoza, the motive may be to make him a whipping-boy. This is clearly the case with Pap, who writes: 'Spinoza is famous for having said that mind and matter are but two aspects ("Attributes") of one and the same substance. But this is the type of cryptic statement which brings fame to metaphysicians, and it is not easy to make out what it means'. On this interpretation, 'the double aspect theory "explains" psycho-physical correlations by saying that one and the same event, which is neither mental or physical, may be apprehended introspectively or perceptively; insofar as it is apprehended in the former way it is mental, insofar as it is apprehended in the latter way, it is physical'.

We need not tarry long over this interpretation: it commits at least three straightforward errors, all of them involving the mistaken 'subjectivist' account of the attributes (*vide* IV, 6). First, in supposing that the attributes are 'aspects', it implies that they depend on being perceived (*Vesey* (1), p. 146); second, it asserts that for Spinoza things in themselves are unknowable (which he denies) and neither mental nor physical (when he holds they are both); third, it takes Spinoza to claim that the 'mental' is the introspectible, and the physical the perceptible (which in Spinoza's terms would be to make the attributes derive from introspecting and perceiving, when these are only *modes* of thought).

There are, of course, forms of the Dual Aspect Theory which are more plausible than Pap's (*cp. Vesey* (1), esp. p. 139; *von Leyden*, pp. 192–5); but if these are offered as accounts *of Spinoza*, then they seem to decompose into one or the other of the two accounts which follow.

(D) Spinoza's theory is perhaps most frequently described as Psycho-Physical Parallelism (as e.g. by *Pollock*, pp. 85–6, p. 193). The nomenclature is not illuminating, but it seems possible to pick out three things that might go under the name. First is the idea that the various psychic *functions* or *capacities* are correlated with separate bodily structures: that memory, let us say, is correlated with a certain portion of the cerebral cortex, in such a way that the one is necessary and sufficient for the other. Second comes the doctrine which asserts a similar correlation between *types* of mental state (perhaps familiar types, like hunger and jealousy, or perhaps types invented by scientific psychology) and general or recurrent types of bodily condition. So the feeling of pain, for instance, might be correlated with the firing of the C-fibres in the body. Third, there is the view that every particular mental state or event is to be correlated with a particular state or event in the body: that is, under a suitable scheme of individuation, an event in the mind's history always accompanies, and is accompanied by, an event in the history of the body. On all forms of Parallelism it will be held that the paired items are really distinct; and there is no question of an item in the one series being taken for a cause, or partial cause, of any item in the other.

The Parallelist interpretation is usually supported by citing the formula from *E* II, 7S which states that the mind and body are one and the same thing, '*sed duobus modis expressa*'. That, however, is ambiguous: it can mean (as the English and French translators render it) 'expressed in two *ways*', or it can mean 'expressed in two *modes*'. Taken the first way, it is consistent with an interpretation which holds mind and body to be not merely parallel, but *identical*; taken the second way, it seems to land Spinoza with *three* things (two modes and whatever it is they 'express'). *Either* translation is embarrassing to the Parallelist view, which needs to find precisely *two* (parallel) things there, not one or three. But the real trouble for it lies in the fact that the attributes (or the corresponding modes in each attribute) cannot, for Spinoza, be *merely* parallel: it is not purely fortuitous, a long run of luck, that modes of Thought and of Extension have always been paired together. Parallelism better describes the views of the Occasionalists, who can always seek cover in the Divine will when asked to explain the uniformities (causal or otherwise) in things; but it will not do for Spinozism, which rightly denies itself such subterfuges.

(E) A fifth view of Spinoza's theory has been advanced by Stuart Hampshire, who characterises it as 'a modified materialism'. This thesis, Hampshire alleges, 'gives the sense, or point, of Spinoza's so-called dual aspect theory of the personality'; and perhaps that remark signals that we are meant to take 'modified materialism' as a development, rather than an exposition, of Spinoza's own view. In any case, it is certainly not Spinozism 'neat'. The doctrine 'asserts that every change in the state of the organism which is a change of thought, is also a change in some bodily state, and usually in the principal instrument of thought, the brain' (*Hampshire* (3), pp. 225–6). But it departs from 'narrow' or 'classical' materialism in holding that 'the order of thoughts can only be adequately explained by the rational and associative connections peculiar to thoughts, and physical states by their connections with other physical states in accordance with the laws of physics . . . The classical materialists are wrong in supposing that the two orders of explanation could properly be reduced to one' ((3), p. 229).

What we have in Spinozism, on this account of it, is materialistic monism combined with dualism of explanatory orders. Mind and body, modes of Thought and modes of Extension, are alike configurations of matter; but considered under 'mentalistic' descriptions, they require a different style of explanation from that demanded by 'physicalistic' descriptions of them. This interpretation does appear to give 'sense' and 'point' to the claim that mind and body are one, and to the qualification that the one thing they are is 'expressed in two ways'. It can accommodate Spinoza's denial of interactionism, seemingly, by treating it as an insistence upon the irreducible distinctness of the two orders of explanation; but it can give full weight to his notion that changes in the mind (body) can be worked by working changes in the body (mind) (*cf.* VIII, 5–6). There are, however, at least three problems in it.

First, if Spinoza believed every change in the mind of the organism to be a change in its body, he believed no less that every change in the body was a change in the mind. He avowedly gives no sort of priority to the material over the mental, and it is as wrong to call him a materialist (even a 'modified' one) as it would be to call him an idealist. Second, if he accepted an identity theory (which seems to be embedded in materialistic monism), then he can scarcely deny interactionism (*Geach* (4)). If a mode of Thought, X, simply *is* the corresponding mode of Extension, Y, then if X is the cause of mental mode Z, it seems to follow that Y is also the cause of Z; and if Y is the cause of extended mode Z, then so must X be. (This is connected with the fact that while '... explains ...' is not referentially transparent, '... causes ...' is arguably so: *Sorabji*, pp. 14–16). Third, while Spinoza does believe that explanations of the mental, *qua* mental, must differ from explanations of the physical, *qua* physical, it is not clear that he thinks that they differ in the way in which Hampshire implies they must. His laws of psychology, though stateable in a different *vocabulary* from his laws of physics, and not reducible to them, do nevertheless have a common *form* with the physical laws: explanations of mental phenomena in terms of rational and associative connections must also be explanations in terms of efficient (mental) causes, and the science of mind *is* for Spinoza a kind of para-mechanics.

The 'materialistic' interpretation, by requiring that mind and body be the same thing as one another, reflects the fact that the attributes are only rationally distinct from substance; the parallelist view, *per contra*, mirrors the real diversity which exists between the attributes. This helps to account for the prevalence, and the appeal, of both interpretations; as also for the difficulty in deciding between them. But it is wrong to pose the issue as a choice: we *cannot* make consistent sense of Spinoza's anti-dualism; we can only try to reform it.

5 *The order and connection of ideas and of things*

Thus far I have been content merely to expound Spinoza's theory of the mind and its relation to the body. But the theory is not a castle built on air; it has argumentative foundations. How solid these foundations are, we must now inquire. For my own part, I think them only shifting sand.

Spinoza's official position is stated at E II, 7, which may well be the most important statement in his book (so *Barker*, p. 123). We read:

> The order and connection of ideas is the same as the order and connection of things. Demonstration. This is evident from Axiom 4 of Part I. For the idea of anything caused depends on the knowledge of the cause of which the thing caused is the effect.

The axiom of Part I to which this refers is: 'The knowledge of an effect depends on the knowledge of the cause and involves it'.

The demonstration seems queerly irrelevant to the theorem it is intended to prove. Why should an axiom which asserts a connection between knowledge of effects and the knowledge of the corresponding causes have any bearing *at all* on a principle which offers to explain the mind/body nexus? The answer, I think, is that E II, 7 runs together three distinct propositions, each of which Spinoza supports, and which need to be picked apart from each other. The crucial importance which belongs to E II, 7 arises largely from the fact that its ambiguity permits Spinoza to put it to many different uses. From this point, his thought radiates outward along several connected but separate lines.

First, then, the proposition asserts what we may call the Postulate of Parallelism. In this sense, it states that there is a precise correspondence or parallelism between the items in the attribute of Thought and those in the attribute of Extension. (Whether this 'parallelism' amounts to identity, and if so, to identity of what sort, is a matter we have just considered.) So much at least is implied by saying that the 'order' of ideas and things is the same; but what is meant by saying that they have the same 'connection'? The point seems to be that if two items in Thought (Extension) are related as cause to effect, then the corresponding items in Extension (Thought) are also related as cause to effect. The scholium at E II, 7 makes all plain: 'Whether we think of Nature under the attribute of Extension, or under the attribute of Thought, we shall discover one and the same order, or one and the same connection of causes; that is to say, in every case the same sequence of things'. That the causal relations between items in the mental series mirror, and are mirrored by, the causal relation between the corresponding items in the physical series, is presupposed at E III, 2S, which deduces that 'the order of actions and passions of our body is coincident with the order of actions and passions of the mind'. Whether a state or condition of X is active or passive is determined by how it was caused to arise: if wholly by another state of X, then active; if not, then passive (*cf.* VII, 2). Hence if the causes of a mental state of X lie outside X's mind, so that the condition is passive, it must follow that the causes of the corresponding bodily state of X lie outside X's body, so that it too will be passive.

In the second place, the theorem puts forward a principle which concerns, not the relation of mental states to bodily conditions, but the relation between thoughts and things. That is, it has to do, not only with the mind/body nexus, but with the mind/world problem, the problem of scepticism. When it takes this form, we may call it the Postulate of Representationalism. A splendid statement of this postulate occurs in Hume:

> Whenever ideas are adequate representations of objects, the relations, contradictions and agreements of the ideas are all applicable to the objects; and this we may in general observe to be the foundation of all human knowledge. (*Treatise of Human Nature*, I, 2, ii; *cp. E* II, 13S)

When Hume wrote this, he stood at the end of a series of developments which originated with Descartes. Cartesian scepticism had prised apart our ideas of things from the things themselves, our conception of how the world is from the world as it is in itself. That scepticism, and the distinction between thought and things which it traded upon, was not arbitrary: it arose, in part, because of a conflict between science and sense: the new physical picture of the world represented things as very different in character from the ways in which they appeared to ordinary perception. Was the world of our senses real – a blaze of light and warmth and colour, a medley of smell and savour and sound? Or was the world of mathematical physics alone real – geometrical forms standing in functionally expressible relations to each other? Some, like Descartes himself, tended to think that the real world was that of the physicist; others, like Berkeley, inclined to the view that it was the world of the man in the street. Both parties were left with problems: the Cartesians, that of accounting for sensory appearances; the Berkeleians, that of honouring the claims of science. The Postulate of Representationalism attempts to rescue the claims of scientific knowledge and to deny total scepticism, not, however, by accrediting *all* of our existing 'ideas', but only such as are 'adequate'. We must, and can, rely on our ideas to give knowledge of a non-subjective reality, but only on those ideas which match the features of the outer reality which are needed for logic and for physics.

Here is Descartes, struggling with the problem of scepticism to which his doctrine of ideas was tied, and offering a form of the Postulate of Representationalism to overcome it:

> We cannot have any knowledge of things except by the ideas we conceive of them; and consequently, we must not judge of them except in accordance with these ideas, and we must even think that whatever conflicts with these ideas is absolutely impossible and involves a contradiction. Thus we have no reason to affirm that there is no mountain without a valley, except that we see that the ideas of the two things cannot be complete when we consider them apart. (*Kenny Letters*, p. 124; cp. *Reply to the Fourth Set of Objections*, Fourth Postulate, H.R. II, p. 54; and Arnauld and Malebranche, cited in *Popkin* (1), p. 212)

The principle that 'we must judge of things in accordance with our ideas' masks a serious confusion: Descartes goes on to deduce from it that atomism is impossible. (Hume's principle also leads to disaster: he uses it to show that a finite extension is not infinitely divisible.) How does the confusion come in?

One problem, particularly acute in Hume, is the tendency to confuse ideas and images, how we think of things with how we picture them to ourselves. (Spinoza explicitly warns against this error: *E* I, 15S; *Ep.* 12; cp. II, 2). ''Tis therefore certain', Hume tells us, 'that the imagination reaches a *minimum*, and may raise up to itself an idea, of which it cannot conceive any sub-division, and which cannot be diminished without a total annihilation' (*Treatise* I, 2, i). But this fact (if it is one) will show that we cannot think of the division of a line proceeding beyond a certain minimum only if it is assumed that what we cannot imagine (that is, form an image of) cannot exist. Another problem, more noticeable in Descartes, is that the principle that 'we must judge of things in accordance with our ideas' hovers uncertainly between banality and falsehood. It is false if it is taken to licence the inference from 'I *must* think of things as being thus-and-so' to 'Thus-and-so is how things are'. It is banal if it means only 'If I must think of things as thus-and-so, then I must think of things as thus-and-so'. It is certain that we cannot have knowledge of things without using ideas, if to have knowledge of them is also to think of them, and to think of them to have ideas of them; but Descartes himself, if he has taught us nothing else, has shown the possibility of our being wrong even about that which we had held most true.

Like Descartes and Hume, Spinoza felt confident that he could read off the character of the objective world from the inner features of (some of) his ideas of it. (So much, I think, is implied by his 'intuitionist' answer to scepticism: *cf.* I, 2). He comes clean in *Ep.* 60:

> I recognise no other difference between a true and an adequate idea than that the word 'true' refers only to an agreement of the idea with its ideatum, while the word 'adequate' refers to the nature of the idea in itself; so that there is really no difference between a true and an adequate idea except this intrinsic relation.

In other words, we can pass validly from the 'adequacy' of an idea (which is a matter of the nature of the idea in itself, its 'intrinsic' quality) to a conclusion that things in the world are as the idea represents them (the idea is 'true', i.e., it has an – 'extrinsic' – correspondence to objective reality).

But why suppose that if Spinoza held this view, it emerges at *E* II, 7? Why gratuitously foist a confusion upon him? The reply is that he himself deploys that theorem in a way which is proper only if it is read as the Postulate of Representationalism. At *E* II, 32, Spinoza lays it down that 'all ideas which are in God always agree with those things of which they are the ideas (by *E* II, 7C) and therefore they are all true (by *E* I, Axiom 6)'. The invocation of *E* II, 7 is fitting only if it can serve to mediate the passage from ideas to the world, from thought to things. Nor is this the only place at which Spinoza exploits the theorem to fasten a connection between our ideas of how things are and the things themselves: it or its corollary is called in for that purpose at *E* II, 9CD; *E* II, 12S; *E* II, 39D and *E* V, 1.

Whether the theorem is read as a Postulate of Parallelism or as a Postulate of Representationalism, however, the demonstration Spinoza gives remains stubbornly irrelevant to it. In fact, it seems to me that the proof of *E* II, 7 only ties in with it at all if we recognise a third sense for that theorem. In this form, I propose to call it the Postulate of the Correspondence of Causal and Demonstrative Orders.

To seize this properly, we need to recall the Aristotelian origins of Spinoza's maxim, 'truly to know is to know through causes (*vere scire est scire per causas*)' (*cf.* I, 1; III, 5). In the *Posterior Analytics*, Aristotle says:

> We consider that we have unqualified knowledge of anything,

as contrasted with the accidental knowledge of the sophist, when we believe that we are aware that the cause from which the fact results is the cause of that fact, and that the fact cannot be otherwise. (71b9 12; Tredennick translation)

Aristotle is giving an account here of the cognitive state which he calls *epistasthai*. This word may be translated either as 'knowledge' (so Tredennick) or 'understanding' (so Barnes). What he seems to mean is that if X knows that p then (and only then) X is aware that p is the case because something (else), namely that q, is the case, and moreover X is aware that it cannot be otherwise than that q (I rely here on *Barnes* (2), esp. pp. 96–7). Aristotle intimates that the type of knowledge which concerns him in this account is *not* the knowledge which consists in the apprehension of primary principles, but rather what might be called *demonstrative* (because inferred) knowledge (*cf*. 71b16; 72a25b3; 72b18–24; 76a16–22). He then considers the marks of the primary principles in a demonstrative science (71b19–22) and asserts that such principles must be (i) true, (ii) primitive, (iii) immediate, (iv) more familiar than, and (v) prior to the conclusion, and (vi) 'causes' of the conclusion. The last three conditions are what most concern us here. 'Greater familiarity' and 'priority' might be explicated (following Barnes) as meaning the same in this context: 'p' is prior to, or more familiar than, 'q', if the knowledge that q requires the knowledge that p, but not conversely. The primary principles must be 'causes' of their conclusions, Aristotle says, 'because we only have knowledge of a thing when we know its cause' (71b30–31; here of course is the source of Spinoza's dictum). This remark may be read as meaning that if X knows that p, and 'p' is not itself a primary principle, then X is aware that q, and aware also that it is the case that p only because it is the case that q. (In general, he seems to regard 'q' as the cause of 'p' if and only if it is true that 'p because q'.)

Bearing this brief analysis of Aristotle in mind, let us glance back at the demonstration of *E* II, 7. The proof turns on *E* I, Axiom 4, of which another statement is given in *Ep*. 7: 'The knowledge *or the idea* of the effect depends on the knowledge *or the idea* of the cause' (I emphasise the two places where the formula differs from that of *Ethics* I). The use of the terms 'idea' and 'dependence' makes this axiom highly volatile. If Spinoza wanted simply to reflect the Aristotelian position, then his axiom would amount to:

(1) X knows that p only if he knows that q (given that it is the case that p because it is the case that q).

But for (1) he asserts (what may be stronger):

(2) X's knowledge that p depends on his knowledge that q.

The move from (1) to (2) is already an invitation to confusion; but it is aggravated by the fact that (in e.g. *Ep.* 72) the 'knowledge' of a cause or effect is treated as identical with the 'idea' of that cause or effect. This equation permits the move from (2) to:

(3) X's idea that p depends on his idea that q.

And now the notion of 'dependence', which *could* signify merely *entailment* (as perhaps in (2)), may instead be taken as expressing causality:

(4) X's idea that p is caused by his idea that q.

What (4) asserts is that the relation which holds between the states 'q' and 'p' themselves (that the former is the cause of the latter) also holds between *the ideas* of those states: the order and connection of *things* is mirrored by the order and connection of *ideas*. It is in this fashion, I believe, that Spinoza arrived at his multiply ambiguous theorem.

If Spinoza, like Aristotle, did no more than to embrace a paradigm of demonstrative science, then he would not have any right to the other, independent assumptions which are ravelled up in *E* II, 7. For that paradigm would commit him only to the following view. In every demonstrative science, there is a set of principles and a set of theorems. Any 'principle' is better known than any 'theorem'; and for any 'theorem', there is a set of 'principles' which 'cause' it, and which are such that, if any one of the 'principles' were removed from that set, the remainder would be unable to 'cause' it. No member of the set of 'theorems' is known to a student unless that student knows, with respect to some set of 'principles', that each member of that set is true, and that the 'principles' of the set 'cause' the 'theorem'. Spinoza seems to believe that in the best sort of discursive reasoning, the mind will proceed in a manner which mirrors this deductive, 'causal' relationship between principles and theorems, passing from what is 'more familiar' and 'prior' to what is 'less familiar' and 'secondary'. It will, in effect, be reproducing in itself the order of priority, and the causal connections, which relate the fact it knows. But nothing yet follows about the causal relations which obtain between the *mental states* (or 'ideas' in the sense employed in (4)) entering into this sequence of reasoning. It certainly does not follow that the successive *mental states* are related in the same ('causal') manner as that in which the *items known* are related. Yet Spinoza treats this result as though it does follow, not only at *E* II, 7D, but also in *Ep.* 37:

> One clear and distinct perception, or several together, can be the *cause* of another clear and distinct perception. Nay rather, all the clear and distinct perceptions which we form can only arise from other clear and distinct perceptions which are in us; they acknowledge no other *cause* outside us.

The same error of supposing that the stages of a process of high-level ratiocination are internally related in the very way that the facts or propositions which occur in that thinking are internally related is found in the *DIE* (*G* II, p. 36):

> As regards the order of our perceptions, and the manner in which they should be arranged and united, it is necessary that as soon as is possible and rational, we should inquire whether there be any being, and if so, what being, that is the cause of all things, so that its objective essence <i.e. the idea of it> may be the cause of all our ideas, and then our mind will to the utmost possible extent reflect Nature. For it will possess it objectively <i.e. as an object of thought> its essence, order and unity.

Finally, Spinoza himself makes explicit, not only at *E* II, 7D, but in the *DIE*, the connection which exists in his mind between the Aristotelian paradigm and his own Postulate of Correspondence, which indeed he mistakenly considers to be the very same thing:

> As regards a true idea, we have shown . . . its objective effects in the soul correspond to (*procedunt ad rationem*) the actual reality (*formalitas*) of its object. This is the same thing (*id quod idem est*) as the saying of the ancients, that a true science proceeds from causes to effect; though the ancients, so far as I know, never formed the conception put forward here, that the soul acts according to fixed laws, and is as it were a spiritual automaton. (*G* II, p. 32)

Sadly, then, Spinoza has not cut the Gordian knot of the mind/body problem. His stroke was more swift than sure; and his aim was distracted by too many other ambitions. The most important proposition of the *Ethics* is not a rigorously demonstrated theorem; it is an article of faith, or rather it is a creed in miniature.

6 Beasts and machines

Cartesianism had left behind a problem about the relation between man's mind and body. It had also left a problem about the relation between men and other natural objects. Both problems were consequences of the way in which Descartes defined the mental. 'The boundaries between mind and body were redrawn by Descartes. Mind, for him, is *res cogitans*, and *cogitatio* includes not only intellectual meditation but also volition, emotion, pain, pleasure, mental images and sensations. For Aquinas, by contrast, the boundary between spirit and nature was not between consciousness and clockwork, it was between intellect and sense' (*Kenny* (4), p. 113). On the pre-Cartesian view, certain functions belonged both to disembodied creatures, such as angels, and to living embodied creatures, such as men: understanding, willing and judging. Other functions belonged both to rational living creatures (men) and to non-rational ones (animals), but not to God or the angels: sense-perception, pleasure and pain, imagination and memory-images. Descartes carved up the functions differently. Some of the attributes which had belonged to living organisms, he now awarded to minds, conceived of as essentially unextended; other attributes of living things were seen as properties of mindless matter. Consider the case of sensation (analysed by *Vendler*, pp. 149–52). On the one hand, Descartes asserts that sensation is a kind of thought, of which, therefore, we are necessarily conscious when it arises; on the other hand, he does not put it on a par with 'pure' thought, of the kind exhibited by conceiving, affirming, denying, doubting or willing. It is, he says, a type of thought which belongs to the soul only because the soul is joined to a body; and it follows that one can conceive the soul in a pure form, existing without sensation. In an illuminating statement of his position (in the *Reply to Objections VI*), he distinguishes three 'grades' of sensation. 'To the first belongs the immediate affection of the bodily organ by external objects.' This is a purely mechanical affair, common to men and the brutes, and not a type of thought. 'The second comprises the immediate mental result . . .; such as the perceptions of pain, of pleasurable stimulation, of thirst, of hunger, of colours, of sound, savour, odour, cold, heat, and the like.' These things are associated, in men at any rate, with corresponding changes in the body, and they count, for Descartes, as kinds of thinking. Finally, 'the third contains all those judgements which, on the occasion of motions occurring in the corporeal organ, we have from our earliest years been accustomed to pass about things external to us' (*H.R.*, II, p. 251). This level is thinking both in a Cartesian and in the ordinary sense. When a man experiences sensation, then he undergoes a physiological change which resembles that which occurs in the lower animals when they are alleged to 'perceive' or 'feel'; but the man, unlike the animal, also enjoys a 'mental result', which may or may not be accompanied by a further activity of the mind in judging. In sensation, then, man performs in two roles – as ghost, and as machine. In analysing dualism (4), we say how Descartes separated what was once united; in considering interactionism (2–3), we saw how he tried to reunite what he had separated.

The sharp Cartesian distinction between mind and body, as I have hinted, necessitated the shifting of two other traditional distinctions: that between the rational and the non-rational, and that between the living and the non-living. Before Descartes, as now (*Bennett* (3), p. 5), rationality was held to be the defining mark of man, distinguishing him from the non-human animals; but both men and the other animals, as against artefacts and machines, fell on the 'living' side of the living/non-living barrier. Descartes changed all that. The animals, not being conscious, were therefore not properly alive. And since they were not alive, their 'cleverness' or 'intelligence' could not be interpreted as akin to our rationality (still less, as Montaigne had suggested, as a superior form of it). What the animals were was, precisely, complex machines (*R. Hall*, p. 198).

Descartes' view soon met with objections. That other keen seventeenth-century observer of brute creation, the poet La Fontaine, taunted him with the foresight of the owl who laid up its captive mice:

> Now let Cartesians, if they can,
> Pronounce this owl a mere machine.
> Could springs originate the plan
> Of maiming mice when taken lean,
> To fatten for his soup-tureen?
> If reason did no service there,
> I do not know it anywhere.

(Elizur Wright translation)

If the provident owl was in some measure rational, it was alive; and if alive, then not a machine – so critics like La Fontaine argued. On the other side, it was possible to argue, as La Mettrie was later to do, that Descartes had erred, not by demoting animals to the level of machines, but by raising men above that level. Descartes had thus to fight a war on two fronts: against the friends of the animals on the one front, and against the partisans of machines on the other.

The arguments against the view that machines could be constructed which were indistinguishable from men were given in Part Five of the *Discourse on Method*. 'If there were machines resembling our bodies, and imitating our actions as far as is morally possible, we should still have two means of telling that, all the same, they were not real men. First, they could never use words or other constructed signs, as we do to declare our thoughts. It is quite conceivable that a machine should be made so as to utter words . . . but not that it should be so made as to arrange words variously in response to the meaning of what is said in its presence, as even the dullest men do. Second, while they might do many things as well as any of us or better, they would infallibly fail in others, revealing that they acted not from knowledge but only from the disposition of their organs' (*A.G.*, pp. 41–2). In a word, his capacities to respond intelligently and appropriately to novel situations distinguishes man from machinery. One capacity is exhibited by his using language in a stimulus-free manner, making his response fit the meaning and context of what he hears; the other is displayed in his ready adaptability to circumstances which are unlike those which he has met with before, and for which he has no special pre-programming. And, Descartes continues, 'in just these two ways we can also recognise the difference between men and brutes'.

The Cartesian view that man is distinguished from other creatures by his possession of language has been revived by Noam Chomsky (*cf.* II, 2). The Chomskian/Cartesian claim has however met with resistance from students both of animal and of machine behaviour. On one side, there are those who claim that animals have actually been taught to speak a human (sign) language: the chimpanzee Washoe was alleged to have first brought off this feat (*cf. Linden*). On the other side are the cyberneticians, some of whom assert that computers can be programmed to understand and use natural languages (*Kenny* (5), p. 45).

The other Cartesian differentia has also been challenged: the contrast he invokes between intelligence and pre-programming (or instinct) has been too sharply drawn. Whatever may be true of machines, animals are not mere bundles of reflexes, nor are men free-floating intelligences, endlessly adaptable. Animal behaviour, whether of a human or of a non-human variety, is very largely a matter of instinct; but not all instinct is 'closed', nor is all instinctive behaviour rigidly stereotyped (*Midgeley* (1), pp. 51-7). Instinct may predispose us to certain patterns of behaviour, without filling in all the details: picturesquely, we could say that the genes set the company policy, but depute its execution to the brain and nervous system (*Dawkins*, p. 63). It may be instinctive in cats to hunt, but in stalking their prey, there is scope for intelligence and adaptability. Of course it is true that animal instinct is, in a sense, 'blind', and can lead to disastrous results. The oyster-catcher will brood over an outsized dummy egg just as it would brood over its own, impervious to the perceptible differences between them: not being keyed to such sensory cues, it takes no account of them (*Midgeley* (1), pp. 262-3; cp. *Lorenz* on deafened turkey hens: p. 112). But it would be wrong to assimilate all non-human behaviour to this model (just as it would be wrong to see all human behaviour as free from such folly): the animals are not locked tightly into their behavioural patterns, nor unable to alter them in the face of novel conditions.

Rather than trying to follow up these latterday controversies, we must look instead at Spinoza's reaction to the Cartesian view. It is plain that he disagrees with Descartes, finding at least two major difficulties in his position. First, he maintains that the animals are alive, that they feel and sense, that they are to some degree rational or 'sagacious'. In many respects, their sagacity even exceeds ours (*E* III, 2S); nor can we doubt that they have sensation – even insects, birds and fish experience lust and appetite, and live contentedly, taking pleasure in their own natures (*ibid.*). Even in his rather Cartesian *Cogitata Metaphysica*, Spinoza remarks that if 'life' is to be ascribed only to things in which a soul ('*anima*') is united to a body, then it will perhaps ('*forte*') have to be attributed to animals (*CM* II, vi, 2). But although the brutes are alive or possessed of a soul ('*anima*'), he seems to deny them a consciousness or mind ('*mens*'): they are not conscious of themselves in the way that men are (III, 5). Second, the Cartesian assimilation of animals, or even men *qua* bodies, to mere clockwork, would also have troubled Spinoza (*Zac*, chapter IV). For clocks imply clockmakers: if men and animals are machines, then they have been designed for a purpose. Descartes seems to admit as much: in discussing the 'men' who form the models or analogues of 'us' in the *Treatise of Man*, he says that each such body is assumed to be 'but a statue, an earthen machine, formed intentionally by God' (*Hall* translation, pp. 2-4). Whether that was Descartes' own view, or a polite bow to convention, the problem created by his analogy remained.

According to Rupert Hall, the biologists of the seventeenth century

> could not believe that the evolution of an organism from an egg or seed could be a completely mechanical process. Only the enlargement of living structures could be mechanical, not the first inception that determined their pattern. And so, as the mechanistic analogy between the Universe and a great clock demanded God the clockmaker to create the Universe, so in biology mechanistic speculation demanded an origin for living forms that was not mechanical. (*R. Hall*, p. 192)

These Cartesian biologists are like the men who 'when they behold the structure of the human body, are amazed; and because they are ignorant of the causes of such art, conclude that the body was made not by mechanical but by a supernatural or Divine art' (*E* I, Appendix).

In relating Spinoza's view to Descartes', the troublesome contrast between 'vitalism' and 'mechanism' may come to mind. Without attaching much importance to the labels, we can say that Spinoza was more of a 'vitalist' than Descartes, in that he sees life-forms lower down on the scale, but more of a 'mechanist', in that he is more anxious to rule out teleological explanations of the inception of those life-forms.

How far down the scale did Spinoza think life extended? At *E* II, 13S, he says that 'all things, although in (on?) different degrees (levels?), are nonetheless animate (*omnia, quamvis diversis gradibus, animata tamen sunt*)'. Is this a form of panpsychism? Some commentators prefer to think it is not: so Donagan explains the passage as meaning merely that every finite mode of Nature 'is conceivable in the mode of Thought' (*Donagan* (2), p. 248). Others (e.g. *Zac*) prefer a less anodyne interpretation. My own belief is that Spinoza is indeed a kind of panpsychist. In this connection, three points need to be made.

(i) In its Spinozistic form, the doctrine is not, *pace* Leibniz, an expression of the implausible belief in a 'world soul'; still less it is the infantile fantasy that each thing possesses a 'psychic double' (*Zac*, pp. 87–93).

(ii) It is possible that Spinoza was convinced that panpsychism was supported by hard empirical data. As a maker of lenses, he was aware of the importance of the microscope, and refers to observations made with them in his scientific correspondence (*Ep.* 36). His fellow countryman, the microscopist and scientist Antony van Leeuwenhoek, was using the instrument to make startling discoveries: 'wherever he turned his microscope, even to seawater, the dust of his gutters baked in the summer sun, or infusions of pepper and spice, it seemed that all organic matter was pullulating with minuscule life' (*R. Hall*, p. 173). It is possible that some of van Leeuwenhoek's research was communicated to Spinoza; Leibniz could have served as intermediary (*Dobell*, p. 113, n. 1).

(iii) Most significantly, Spinoza's own analysis of what life and death consist in implies that whatever is of sufficient complexity to count as a unitary *thing* must be alive. 'By life we understand a force through which things persevere in their own being' (*CM* II, vi, 3): whatever has a *conatus*, i.e. a tendency to maintain the same proportions of motion and rest within its parts, to preserve the same equilibrium, is alive (*cp. Savan*). The same result follows from Spinoza's account in the *Ethics* of the nature of death: if death is disequilibration, and if only what has been alive can die, then life belongs to anything which can suffer a radical change in respect of the proportions of motion and rest within itself. (Perhaps this interpretation is confirmed by the remark in *Ep.* 21 that things, insofar as they depend on God, are not 'dead, corporeal and imperfect': so *Zac*, p. 86). In short, then, I take it that Spinoza had reached a novel view of what life consisted in, identifying it with the tendency to resist certain types of change; he both saw, and accepted, that this theory of life implied that all things above a certain level of complexity were alive.

Spinoza's 'panpsychism', so explained, does not seem to be inconsistent with what I have called his 'mechanism'. We have already noted that, contrary to Descartes, he does not permit any 'seepage' from the will to filter into the body or animal spirits (VI, 3). Nor does he tolerate teleological explanations of the growth, behaviour, structure or origin of living bodies (V, 7). The *human* body in particular is, like any organic body, formed without a conscious purpose; like any other body, it is determined by efficient causes alone, and operates in accordance with purely physical laws. If we like, we can say that it is mechanically explicable; but we ought not to say that it *is* a machine, if machines require designers.

Spinoza's views are in many respects an improvement over Descartes': in particular, it is encouraging to see him returning to the animals many of the features of which Descartes had stripped them. But his attitudes towards the beasts are, if anything, harsher and more exploitative than Descartes' own. Is this an accident, or does it follow from other parts of his system? Curley, who asks this question, points to several aspects of Spinozism which might seem to foster a kindlier attitude towards our fellow creatures: certainly Spinoza strikes at the root of Christian and Cartesian anthropocentrism (*Curley* (4), pp. 21–2). Against this, however, Curley refers to passages such as *E* IV, 37S1: 'the law against killing animals is based upon an empty superstition and womanish tenderness, rather than upon sound reason'. (The reference to 'womanish tendencies' reflects Spinoza's rabid anti-feminism: *TP* XI, 4; *G* III, pp. 353–4.) In fact, as Curley notes, Spinoza gives man a licence to exploit all non-human nature:

> Excepting man, we know no individual thing in Nature in whose mind we can take pleasure, nor anything which we can unite with ourselves in friendship or any kind of intercourse, and therefore regard to our own profit does not demand that we should preserve anything which exists in nature excepting men, but teaches us to preserve it or destroy it in accordance with its varied uses, or to adopt it to our own service in any way whatever. (*E* IV, Appendix, c. xxvi)

Why does Spinoza take this view? Part of the answer may lie in Spinoza's oddly intellectual view of 'friendship or any kind of intercourse'. But Curley also directs attention to two other features of Spinozism: his 'cosmic egalitarianism', and his account of the formation of the State. Spinoza holds that apart from its relation to a comunity, each thing is determined to exist and to act by the laws of its own nature; and whatever it does in accordance with those laws, it does by a sovereign natural right. So it is that the larger fish are determined by Nature to prey upon the smaller; and they act rightly when they do (*TTP*, c. XVI; *Wernham*, p. 125). But in this sense of 'right', X's having the right to have its way with Y does *not* imply that Y must accede, or that Z is not permitted to interfere. To have a right is to have a power; and right runs only as far as power extends. With the formation of the State, however, men renounce their natural right to do whatever they have the power to do, and surrender that right to a new corporate individual which has greater powers, and correspondingly greater rights, than any of them taken singly. Among these rights of the State is the right to command obedience; and since the State can command that its subjects be left alone in certain of their activities, it is now in place to speak of a right held by X which entails that Y and Z may not interfere with him.

Now since animals lack language, they cannot enter into the contract by which the State is formed, and so are left exposed to the continuing depredations of men. The State may in various

MINDS AND BODIES

ways protect them or place restrictions on our treatment of them: it may, for instance, prohibit hunting at certain times or in certain places. But only if the State laid down such prohibitions could the animals be said to have rights against us, i.e., rights that we not interfere with or exploit them. The interest and will of the State – that is of man writ large – is paramount: cosmic egalitarianism leads, by curious pathways, back to anthropocentrism (*Curley*, (4), p. 25; *cp. Midgeley* (2), pp. 37–8, p. 40). In our commerce with the animal kingdom, the lesson in La Fontaine's parable of the wolf and lamb holds good:

> The strongest reasons always yield
> To reasons of the strongest.

VII

Morality and the Emotions

1 *Cartesian passions*

The last three parts of Spinoza's *Ethics* are intended to form a unity, and together comprise his moral psychology and philosophy. Broadly, they deal with three topics: the affects or emotions; the virtues and vices; and the means to acquire freedom and blessedness. The overall plan seems to be signalled near the end of the Preface to Part III (so *Wolfson*, II, p. 185): 'I shall, therefore, pursue the same method in considering (i) the nature and (ii) the strength of the emotions, and (iii) the power of the mind over them, which I followed in the preceding books on God and the Mind, and I shall consider human actions and appetites as if it were a question of lines, planes or bodies'.

Spinoza is conscious of his undoubted originality, but not less of his debts to his predecessors. 'Very eminent men have not been wanting, to whose labour and industry we confess ourselves much indebted, who have written many excellent things about the right conduct of life, and who have given mortals counsels full of prudence; but no-one so far as I know has determined the nature and strength of the emotions, and what the mind is able to do towards controlling them.' In particular, he singles out Descartes: 'I remember, indeed, that the celebrated Descartes, although he believed that the mind is absolute master over its own actions, tried nevertheless to explain by their first causes human emotions, and at the same time to show the way by which the mind could obtain absolute power over them; but in my opinion he has shown nothing but the acuteness of his great intellect.' The work of Descartes to which Spinoza is primarily referring in his *Passions of the Soul,* which grew out of his correspondence with the Princess Elizabeth. (*cf.* VI, 2). In order to understand Spinoza, we must have the outlines of the Cartesian theory of the passions before us. These are readily discerned.

Of the things we experience in ourselves, some, such as heat and movement, can also exist in inanimate bodies, and ought to be ascribed not to the soul, but to the body (art. 4); others, to which the name of 'thoughts' ('*pensées*') should be given, belong only to the soul (*ibid.*). These 'thoughts' fall into two main categories: on the one hand, there are the actions of the soul, that is, our desires ('*volontez*'), which are discovered by experience to come directly from the soul and to depend on it alone; on the other hand, there are the passions of the soul, which are all our perceptions and knowledge ('*perceptions ou connoissances*'). These latter frequently owe their characteristics to things other than the soul, and are received by it from the things they represent (art. 17). The perceptions are sub-divided into two kinds: those which are caused by the soul, and those which are caused by the action of small bodies, the animal spirits, working on the soul (art. 19). The first of these kinds includes the perceptions of our own *voluntez*, and of the imaginations and other *pensées* which depend on the *voluntez*. The second sub-kind is yet further divided into three groups: (i) the perceptions which we refer to bodies without us, e.g. the visual sensation we have of a torch, or the auditory sensation we have of a bell (art. 22); (ii) the perceptions we refer to our own bodies, e.g. hunger and thirst, pains, or heat sensations; (iii) the perceptions we refer to our soul alone, which are the passions in the customary and more specific sense of that term, and which include such feelings as joy and anger. These passions may be either primary or derivative: Descartes lists six as primary (wonder, love, hatred, joy, desire and sadness) (art. 69). The classification is shown in Figure VII.

One comment must be added. In article 147, Descartes mentions certain 'interior emotions' which differ from the passions in that they are only excited by soul itself, without need of the animal spirits. Such emotions, he tells us, accompany the true passions: thus a man may lament his dead wife and weep for her, though all the while he would be annoyed to see her alive again; his heart is oppressed by sadness, but in his soul there arises a secret joy. Again, when reading romances or watching a play, we may be moved to sadness, joy, hatred or love, but along with these emotions we have an intellectual joy in their very excitation. It is mainly upon these inward and intellectual emotions, Descartes says, that our good and harm depend. In his scheme they presumably belong with the perceptions arising from

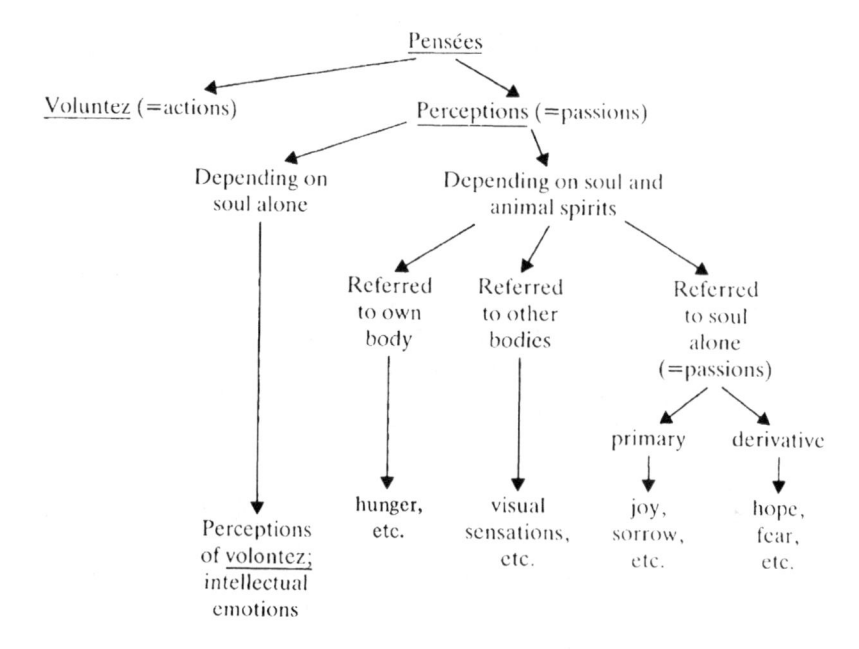

```
                              Pensées
                   ┌─────────────┴─────────────┐
    Voluntez (=actions)              Perceptions (=passions)
         │           ┌──────────────────┼──────────────────┐
    Depending on              Depending on soul and
    soul alone                   animal spirits
         │           ┌──────────────┼──────────────┐
         │         Referred       Referred       Referred
         │         to own         to other       to soul
         │         body           bodies         alone
         │                                       (=passions)
         │                                    ┌─────┴─────┐
         │                                  primary    derivative
         ▼           ▼              ▼           ▼           ▼
    Perceptions    hunger,        visual       joy,       hope,
    of voluntez;   etc.           sensations,  sorrow,    fear,
    intellectual                  etc.         etc.       etc.
    emotions
```

Figure VII

the soul alone, and not with the other emotions.

I agree with Wolfson that the definitions and theorems at the start of *Ethics* II must be understood as criticising these views of Descartes (*Wolfson*, II, p. 187). Spinoza objects to: (i) the Cartesian distinction between action and passion, (ii) Descartes' view of the relation between mind and body (*cf.* VI, 3) and (iii) the detailed treatment of the emotions in Descartes' work. I wish to examine the first of these topics at some length; then I shall go on to consider Spinoza's own account of the emotions.

2 Action and passion

The Cartesian picture represents desires or movements of the will alone as actions, and treats all the emotions, whether intellectual or other, as passions. Spinoza disagrees with this: for him, movements of the will are falsely contrasted with other types of thought, all of which follow the necessary order of Nature; and emotions can be both active and passive. The dispute is not purely terminological, but reflects deeper metaphysical commitments. Jerome Neu puts the point well:

For both, it may be said that actions are 'what I do'. But they

differ in the notion of 'I' involved. Descartes identifies the
person with his thinking element . . . or soul as opposed to his
body. I am my thoughts, but most centrally I am my will, for
that alone is totally within my control and depends only upon
my soul. So only desires can be actions of mine, desires alone
are attributable and ultimately explainable by reference only to
my soul. Spinoza rejects Descartes' crude and unworkable
mind-body dualism. Action, as opposed to passion, is still that
which depends upon me, that which is ultimately explainable
by reference to my nature, but my essence is no longer
restricted to . . . mind. The contrast is no longer between
dependence on my soul and dependence on my body, but
between explanation by reference to my nature as a person (an
individual mind-body) and explanation by reference to causes
in the external world. (*Neu* pp. 79-80)

Apart from the oddness of speaking of the *will* as being under one's control – an oddness almost forced upon one in trying to describe Descartes' view of the will – Neu's handling of this point is exemplary. But, as we shall see, Spinoza's account of the action/passion issue differs from Descartes' not only because of their diverging views on free will and on dualism, but because Spinoza takes far more seriously than Descartes the platitude that the nature of men is to be rational.

Spinoza's theory is founded upon two definitions given at the start of Part III:

Definition I. I name that an adequate cause of which the effect
can be clearly and distinctly perceived through it. I call that
inadequate or partial, of which the effect cannot be understood
through it alone. Definition 2. We then are active, I say, when
something in us or outside us happens, of which we are the
adequate cause, that is (by the previous definition) when from
our nature there follows something in us or outside us which
can be clearly and distinctly understood through it alone. But I
say, on the contrary, that we are passive when something
happens in us, or something follows from our nature, of which
we are at most the partial cause.

Mrs Kneale has called attention to two peculiar features of these definitions. First, the definition of activity and passivity applies only to human beings. This is not because Spinoza thinks that only men can be active or passive, but because his interest in this part of his treatise is with the human soul (*E* III, 3S). Second, both definitions are couched in epistemological terms: an adequate cause is something through which its effect can be *perceived* or *understood*. But this invites the questions: 'How understood? And by whom?'. Kneale writes: 'It seems that the notion of adequate cause, and therefore that of activity, may be understood as relative in the sense that X may be the adequate cause of Y for A but not for B . . . For the psychiatrist a childhood trauma may constitute the adequate cause of an adult breakdown; for the patient's relatives it may not' (*Kneale* (1), p. 217). I am, however, not certain whether she is claiming that the adequacy of a cause is relative to an inquirer's *interest*, or relative to his *conceptual range and skills*. From the example she gives, it would seem that the relatives must not accept the psychiatric explanation of their kinsman's behaviour, not because they are looking for an explanation of another type, but because they do not grasp the technical concepts which the psychiatrist deploys. But if so, then Spinoza could reply that the psychiatrist's judgement does indeed cite a cause which is adequate non-relationally, in the sense that it is valid for everyone; it is simply that not everyone can grasp his description of that cause. I think Spinoza would want to resist the suggestion that explanations could be adequate only relationally: in the Preface to Part III, he underlines his belief that there is only one proper way to study and explain the diverse subject-matter of the different sciences.

Spinoza goes on immediately to fasten the notion of activity, not only to that of being an adequate cause, and to that of following from a thing's nature, but to that of originating from adequate ideas. In the first theorem of Part III, he says: 'Our mind is in certain respects active, but in others passive; that is, insofar as it has adequate ideas, it necessarily is active, and insofar as it has inadequate ideas, it is passive in certain respects'. More fully, he is asserting a set of equivalences, between (i) X is active; (ii) Something in X or outside X happens, of which X is the adequate cause; (iii) Something happens which follows from, and can be explained by, X's nature alone, and apart from external causes, and finally (iv) Something happens because of X's having adequate ideas. To say that something happens because of X's having adequate ideas is, in non-Spinozistic language, to say that X brings something about as a result of having a rational view of his situation, and of making a rational response to it (*Allison*, p. 124; *Parkinson* (4), p. 547). But the last link in the chain extending from activity to rationality, though assumed to have been forged by the demonstration of E II, 1, seems suspiciously weak. Mrs Kneale rightly objects to it:

Proposition 1 cannot follow from Definitions I and II without an extraordinary change in the meanings of words, for it is not the case that it is only the having of adequate ideas which makes events in human life intelligible. We can see this by thinking again of the psychiatric patient. His reactions may be quite intelligible to the psychiatrist and to himself in terms of his apprehension of the situation, but this does not mean that this apprehension consists in adequate ideas. According to Definition II, the psychiatric patient is active, and perhaps to a greater degree than a normal person, because his reactions may be entirely explicable in terms of his own state, with little reference to the environment; but according to Proposition 1, he must be passive because his ideas are inadequate. (*Kneale* (1), p. 218)

This is well said: Spinoza cannot pass from (ii) to (iv) without changing the meanings of words intolerably. But his passage is mediated by (iii), and we must pause over that. In a weak and non-metaphysical sense of 'nature' – the sense Mrs Kneale invokes in saying that the patient's reactions are explained in terms of 'his own state' – the move from (ii) to (iii) is unexceptionable, the move from (iii) to (iv) dubious. But in a metaphysically loaded sense of 'nature', to explain my condition in terms of my nature alone is to account for it in terms of the working out of rational beliefs, desires and purposes. If (Spinoza seems to think) it is platitudinous that my nature is to be rational, then I am acting according to my nature (and only thus, in strictness, 'acting') when I am acting rationally. This conception of 'nature' underlies the shift from (iii) to (iv), although it makes the previous deduction problematic.

We can see Spinoza's special, metaphysical view of what our nature consists in at work in other places. Consider what he says about the suicide (a case strangely like that of Mrs Kneale's psychiatric patient): 'no-one neglects to desire what is useful to himself and to preserve his being unless he is overcome by external causes and those contrary to his nature. No-one, I say, from the necessity of his nature, but driven by external causes, turns away from taking food, or commits suicide . . . (though) latent external causes may so dispose his imagination and so affect his body, that it may assume a nature contrary to its former one' (*E* IV, 20S) *cf.* IV, 18S). Here the distinction 'determined by one's nature/determined by external causes' is made to fall on exactly the same line as 'rational/irrational'. Spinoza certainly does not want to claim that a suicide cannot be accounted for by analysing the victim's state of mind, investigating his obsessions, fears, fantasies and so on; in fact, he explicitly tells us that we must consider his imagination, and the external causes which have affected it. The impossibility of attributing his death to his own nature is simply that it is the kind of thing which he could not possibly have done for good reasons.

The difficulty which has just been brought out is connected with another. Can Spinoza consistently allow that we are *ever* other than passive (*cf.* VII, 8)? To be passive, he says, is to be at best a partial cause; but at *E* I, 28, he has proved that every finite mode is determined from outside, both in respect of its existence and its operation (*ad operandum*) by another finite cause, and that by another, to infinity. And in *E* IV, 2 and 4, he holds that 'We are passive insofar as we are part of Nature' and that 'It cannot happen that man should not be part of Nature, and should not suffer changes save those which can be understood through his own nature, and of which he is the adequate cause'. Whatever we do or undergo, then, we must be affected by, and dependent on, other things; and hence we can never be other than partial causes of what happens in us or outside us. (This is apparently true of us even when it is a matter of our thinking clearly and consecutively (*E* V 40S; *cf. Bidney*, p. 38).)

Parkinson, who (correctly) sees this as a difficuty, not only as to how we can be active, but as to how we can act freely, proposes a solution based on Definition 2 of Part III. He writes: 'Spinoza may be saying that we can explain the action of a man through its external causes: to do this would be to view it as a scientist might do – e.g. in terms of some physical science, such as neurophysiology, or in terms that might belong to psychology. But we can also assess the action in terms of its rationality; we can say, for example, that the man has understood (or failed to understand) the situation in which he finds himself. It is the same action which is assessed in each case, but in a different way; and insofar as the act is rational, it is the act of a free man' (*Parkinson* (4), pp. 546–7).

Parkinson's suggestion is attractive, and may be the best that can be done on Spinoza's behalf; but there are at least two problems with it. First of all, it will continue to hold true that whatever we do or undergo is passive; for all our behaviour and experience can be looked at scientifically and, so viewed, must be seen as the product of many causes in addition to ourselves. Second, Parkinson comes close to saying that Spinoza relies on a basic distinction between two types of explanation, one in terms of causes, and the other in terms of reasons. This distinction is an ancient and honourable one, hearkening back to Socrates in *The*

Phaedo; but it is surely not one which would recommend itself to a philosopher as thoroughly naturalistic as Spinoza, or to one so deeply committed to explaining human action as if it were a question of lines, planes and bodies (*cp.* V, 7; VI, 6).

Perhaps we could try to improve on Parkinson, as follows. Spinoza, let us say, envisaged the possibility of a psychology at once thoroughly scientific and yet capable of referring to an agent's beliefs, emotions, and desires. (Indeed, his own project in Part III is probably intended to outline such a subject.) To the extent that the beliefs and affective states which featured in the explanations of someone's behaviour were rational, he could be said to be active, or to act freely. There would thus be only one type of psychological explanation, which straddled the distinction between reasons and causes, and not two types, a 'rational' and a 'causal' one. But this suggestion brings us round again to the problem we ran up against earlier: why should only those explanations which attributed *adequate ideas* to an agent, involve treating him as an *adequate cause*? Rather than looking to Definition II for a solution, as Parkinson does, we should reject it as the source of our difficulty. For it is clear that Proposition 1, not Definition II, dominates Spinoza's thinking.

3 *The concept of endeavour*

Descartes' distinction between action and passion, as we have seen, was drawn with reference to the will. Rejecting that Cartesian basis, Spinoza sought to recast the distinction, locating it instead in the difference between adequate and inadequate ideas. At the start of Part III, then, we see him embarking on the project of trying to create a psychology which will explain thought, emotion and activity without using the notion of the will. For that project to stand a chance of success, Spinoza must try to find a principle which will fit into the space left vacant by the exit of the will, and do better at explaining why it is we act (*Allison*, p. 124). The concept which he shapes to fill the void is that of *conatus*, or 'endeavour'.

The *conatus* of a thing is simply its effort or endeavour to maintain itself and preserve its being. This endeavour, which is exhibited by all finite modes, is called *appetitus* (appetite or, in Broad's phrase, *vital impulse*) when it is found in human beings (*E* III, 9S; *Broad* (2), p. 22). It has both a mental and a bodily expression. Conceived physically, it is a tendency of the human organism to maintain the proportions of motion and rest existing within itself, to preserve its characteristic state in the face of other things acting upon it. On its mental side, it is the tendency of the mind to preserve its characteristic unity and individuality. In this aspect, Spinoza calls it *voluntas* (will or, as Broad prefers, *mental self-maintenance*). Appetite, Spinoza argues, 'is nothing other than the very essence of man, from the nature of which those things follow necessarily which promote his preservation; and thus he is determined to do those things. Hence there is no difference between Appetite and Desire (*Cupiditas*), save that Desire is generally related to men insofar as they are conscious of appetite; and therefore it may be defined as Appetite together with the consciousness of it'. From all this, it seems we can assemble the following scheme:

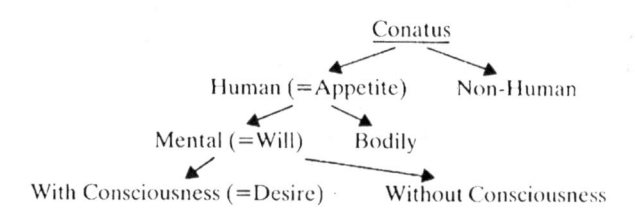

```
                        Conatus
                       ↙       ↘
            Human (=Appetite)   Non-Human
              ↙        ↘
        Mental (=Will)   Bodily
          ↙        ↘
With Consciousness (=Desire)   Without Consciousness
```

There are some problems. Spinoza seems to use 'desire' both in a broader sense, so that it covers the same ground as 'appetite', and a narrower sense, in which it does not. Worse, he seems committed by his remarks at *E* II, 21 to holding that men can have no appetites of which they are not conscious (for discussion, see *Neu*, pp. 74-6). But whatever he may think elsewhere, it seems plain enough that in Part III he recognises the possibility of unconscious appetites: 'whether or not a man be conscious of his appetite', he writes, 'it remains one and the same appetite' (*E* III, Definition of the Affects I, Explanation) – clearly implying that there can be appetites of which we are not conscious.

Spinoza's view that the essence of man is to endeavour to persist in his own being entails that we are continually striving for *self*-preservation and *self*-maintenance, and for nothing else. The desire for self-preservation becomes, as in Hobbes, the basic, or rather the only motive in human behaviour. On the instinctual level, we pursue self-preservation blindly; as we grow more rational, we seek it with greater insight and deliberation (*Broad* (2), p. 35). This astonishing claim about human nature is of course not based on any investigation of the facts; it is demonstrated *a priori*, from principles alleged to govern the behaviour of all bodies.

The demonstration proceeds as follows. First, it is taken to be self-evident that 'nothing can be destroyed, except by a cause external to itself' (*E* III, 4). It appears that this is an application of the principle of inertia for bodies in motion or at rest, and amounts to a denial of the possibility of spontaneous change. Since a physical thing is nothing other than a certain proportion of motion and rest, and thus cannot suffer a change in that proportion without being destroyed, no thing can destroy itself, for that would be to alter the proportion which it, quite simply, *is*. Hence destruction can only come from an external cause, and 'insofar as one thing can destroy another,... they cannot exist in the same subject' (*E* III, 5). But then, this inertial force or resistance comes to be conceived positively, as actual endeavour (*Allison*, p. 125). As Martineau puts its, vigorously if rather floridly: 'To exclude a cause of destruction is not to provide a cause of fresh phenomena, and secure the development of a determinate history; and it is nothing less than this that Spinoza lays upon the shoulders of his *conatus*, when he plants it and sets it to work in our human nature. It is not content with offering a dead weight against non-existence: it keeps at a distance whatever would reduce, and selects and appropriates whatever may increase, the scope of the nature which it guards' (*Martineau* v.I, p. 339). Because nothing internal to a thing can encompass its destruction, and because it is naturally resistant to anything which would disturb or undo it, Spinoza concludes that 'each thing, insofar as it is in itself, endeavours to persevere in its being' (*E* III, 6). Since the essence of a thing is that which, being given, the thing is given, and which, being removed, the thing is removed (*E* II, Definition II), and since the *conatus* answers precisely to this specification, the *conatus* of a thing must be its essence (*E* III, 7). As its essence, the *conatus* must remain with the thing throughout the thing's existence, and cannot impose a limited or determinate duration upon the thing (*E* III, 8).

What holds with unrestricted generality for all things must of course hold good for the mind; hence 'the mind, both insofar as it has clear and distinct ideas, and insofar as it has confused ideas, endeavours to persevere in its being for an indefinite time' (*E* III, 9). All our thoughts, emotions and volitions, then, are expressions of our *conatus*, our fundamental tendency to maintain ourselves and preserve our existence. From this two important consequences follow. First, disinterested action is impossible. It is simply not in our power to act in ways which we perceive to imperil our existence, and so impossible to subordinate our life and safety to the end of promoting another's welfare (or illfare). And second, 'we neither strive for, wish, seek, nor desire anything because we think it to be good, but on the contrary, we adjudge a thing to be good because we strive for, wish, seek or desire it' (*E* III, 9S). Let us linger over these points in the following two sections.

4 Egoism

In his *Brief Life* of Thomas Hobbes, Aubrey recounts that the philosopher, when asked to explain his charity towards a beggar in the Strand, answered: 'Because I was in paine to consider the miserable condition of the old man; and now my almes, giving him some reliefe, doth also ease me'. Hobbes, who had beheld the man 'with eies of pitty and compassion', did himself an injustice. The egoist will characteristically distort the motives from which we act, seeing the impulse towards self-preservation everywhere, when in fact it is only rarely and intermittently that this desire moves us. In saying '*I* gave alms in order to relieve *him*', it may appear that my motive is at least as much self-regarding as other-regarding; and it may also be true that I would not have made the sacrifice unless I had wanted to. But it does not follow that I acted purely to satisfy my own wants, or to put myself at ease: when I look at the facts of the matter, I must recognise that it is *his* wants, not mine, which are to the fore of my consciousness.

To see this, consider the following thought-experiment. Suppose that, pained by the sight of the beggar's misery, I am given the choice between (i) not actually giving him alms, but being unshakeably convinced that I have, and (ii) giving him alms, but being convinced that I have not. If my motive could *only* be to prevent myself from feeling distress, I would be drawn irresistibly to the first choice; but as things are, I might well make the second. Nor will it do to say that, if the second choice is really possible, that is only because I project myself into the position of the beggar, and identify myself with him. For first, the identification is *vicarious*: I do not actually think myself to *be* the beggar, nor even that our roles are *likely* to be reversed. And second, my interest in, and care for, another may spring as much from the recognition of our *differences*, as from perceiving that we are *alike*.

The truth is that the capacity to act non-egoistically runs deep in animal nature. 'Many creatures take great trouble over rearing their young, and also defend them vigorously, sometimes getting killed in the process. Many also defend and rescue young that are not their own; some will adopt orphans. Some (for example, dolphins and elephants) also help and rescue adults of their species in difficulties, and some, such as wild dogs, will also feed sick and injured adults' (*Midgeley* (1), p. 131). These are all cases which may naturally be described as showing disinterested benevolence; and those who reject that description should ask themselves whether they would be more willing to accept the existence of disinterested cruelty or malice. (It is remarkable that many who deny the reality of altruism will agree that there can be selfless maleficence.) Indeed, the range and extent of non-egoistic motives is immense. The motives of shame and glory, of revenge, of desire for knowledge or amusement, are all liable to outweigh a cool, prudent concern for what we perceive to be our interest. One of the chief claims which egoists like Hobbes and Spinoza make is that we would be much better off if we pursued self-preservation more single-mindedly. 'If people attended better to their own interests instead of showing off, they would avoid doing many of the terrible things they do; in particular, they would give up waging wars of religion. The humbug of chivalry was therefore Hobbes' prime target, and the *Leviathan* is, among others things, the *Catch-22* of its day' (*Midgeley* (1), p. 123; contrast V, 7, *ad fin.*).

Like Hobbes, Spinoza is acutely aware of the pervasiveness of the desire for glory, and of the horrors which it is always liable to unleash: ambition, or the immoderate desire for glory, 'is a desire which increases and strengthens all the affects, and that is the reason why it can hardly be kept under control. For so long as a man is possessed by any desire, he is possessed by this. Every nobleman, Cicero says, is led by glory, and even the philosophers who write books about despising glory place their names on the title page' (*E* III, Definition of the Affects xliv; but *vide E* V, 10S). Mary Midgeley, from whose account I have borrowed freely here, believes that Egoism is best conceived as an effort to *reform* humankind rather than to describe it: 'People, in fact, are not very prudent, even emotionally. And Egoism is not a report of existing psychological facts, but a reforming doctrine, an attempt to do something about a wasteful habit. Philosophers such as Spinoza want individuals to take themselves more seriously, to *be* themselves, to assert their independence and refuse to be lost or merged into tribes or families' (*Midgeley* (1), p. 356).

Before one acclaims Hobbes' and Spinoza's 'reform', however, one should reflect on some of the questions it raises. When 'tribes' and 'families' are taken away, then what remains but (as Burke was to put it) 'the dust and powder of individuality'? The 'autonomous' will, positioned outside any concrete historical context, seems, the more one looks for it, to be a non-entity: just as the Cartesian 'mind' is a negation (whatever is *not* body), so the Liberal 'will' is conceived as the self so far as it is *not* subject to social roles, status, expectations, unelected norms, imposed loyalties. (That is why it always appears as an author engaged in search of a character.) Furthermore, this impoverished concept of the self sustains a radically defective account of the virtues (*MacIntyre* (2), pp. 204–7) – here, notably, the virtue of courage. For Hobbes, courage is a 'passion' which 'enclineth men to private Revenges, and sometimes to endeavour the unsettling of the Publique Peace' (*Leviathan*, Review and Conclusion). That Aristotle had already diagnosed *this* 'passion' as *pugnacity*, had pointed out that those it leads 'do not act for honour's sake', and had clearly differentiated it from *courage*, wholly escapes Hobbes' notice (*Nichomachean Ethics*, 1117a5–10). *Martial* courage in particular, insofar as it implies a willingness to face death in battle (for the sake, nearly always, of 'tribes' and 'families'), must seem, not virtuous, but strictly *incomprehensible* on this view (*cf. E* IV, 20S); for if the civil order is *founded* on the 'Feare of Death' (together with the 'Desire of such things as are necessary to commodious living, and a Hope by . . . Industry to obtain them'), then what can motivate a man to risk death for the sake of the good of (unknown) others (*Leviathan*, I, c. 13; *cp. TP* II, Section 15)? Spinoza, who advocated an unpaid civilian army, thought that its soldiers would be induced to fight for the sake of individual liberty: 'in the civil State, all the citizens together are to be considered as a man in the state of Nature; and, therefore, when all fight on behalf of the State, are all defending themselves, and engaged on their own business (*sibique vacant*)' (*TP* VII, Section 22; *G* III, p. 310). We shall examine this alleged convergence of selfish and public-spirited motives at a later place (VIII, 3); but to a generation which has brooded over Yossarian's exchange in *Catch-22* with Major Major Major Major, Spinoza's explanation must seem enormously unconvincing (*Heller*, p. 107).

Spinoza's theory is in any case incoherent even on his *own* premises. Shortly before explaining what will make an unpaid soldiery take the field, he asserts that the Commonwealth will not have the power (and so will lack the right) to cause its citizens 'not to strive to avoid death' (*TP* III, Section 8; *G* III, p. 281). Spinoza's contradictory view reflects the transitional period in which he wrote: it looks forward to the Liberal capitalist order, backward to the ideal of the Greek city or Roman republic, when the State appeared as the citizens' handiwork, and the free man's life found meaning in the larger life of the polity (*Lukács*, pp. 46–7; pp. 50–1).

Egoism reconsidered

Spinoza's doctrine of Egoism has come under attack for yet other reasons. The charge is that he has advanced two distinct and inconsistent theories under the cover of a single, self-consistent one (*Savan*, p. 199; contrast *Zac*, p. 101; *Allison*, pp. 126–7). The problem is this: on the one hand, Spinoza insists that each thing endeavours to persevere in its being, and has no other motive for what it does; on the other hand, he regularly assumes that things seek to *increase* their power of acting, and resist what threatens to *lessen* it. How can things be striving single-mindedly to keep their power constant, when they are also bent on increasing it? But really, there is no inconsistency here. Hobbes, who also asserts the primacy of self-preservation, pointed out why it should involve the power-drive: 'I put for a general inclination of all mankind, a perpetual and restless desire of power after power, that ceaseth only in death. And the cause of this is not always that a man hopes for a more intensive delight than he has already attained to; or that he cannot be content with a moderate power; but because he cannot assure the power and means to live well, which he hath at present, without the acquisition of more' (*Leviathan*, I, c. xi). Anxious for our own safety, we seek ever more insurance; and since the possible threats to us are continual, we must continually strive to enlarge our power to resist them. Neither Hobbes' man nor Spinoza's is a power-crazed psychopath: they value power as a means to security, not as an end in itself.

All the same, there *is* a good reason to find Spinoza's theory inconsistent at this point also. In his view, man's power does not consist in being able to dominate other things and people, to keep them under his control; rather, 'human power must be judged by strength of mind rather than by vigour of body', and hence those whose reason is most powerful are themselves most powerful (*TP* II, Section 11; *Wernham* trans., p. 275). Now this power is augmented by perfecting the intellect as far as may be, that is, by understanding God's attributes and actions (*E* IV, Appendix, c. iv); and in this effort, we are immeasurably assisted by the cooperation of our fellows (*TP* II, Section 15). 'When each seeks most what is profitable to himself, then are men most profitable to one another' (*E* IV, 35C2). But the kind of power we must be after if we want to stay alive in a hostile world does not seem to be the power which consists in, or follows from, an enlarged understanding. A cool, controlling type of man, or a man who bows before every change in the wind, has at least as good a chance of survival as a dedicated thinker or scientist: who would reckon the odds on Spinoza to be better than those, say, on Cromwell? It is not so much that Spinoza goes wrong in saying that we must pursue more and more power in order to survive, as that he misdescribes the *sort* of power we must have more and more of (*cf. Santayana*, p. 148). At *E* IV, 21D, he equates 'the desire to preserve one's own being' with 'the desire to live blessedly and well', implying that the means to fulfill these desires are identical; but surely the power that is necessary to our staying alive is not all that is necessary to our flourishing?

The truth seems to be that Spinoza is ultimately not concerned with self-preservation, in the banal sense of prolonging temporal existence; why else would he say that the wise man (i.e. the one who understands what is at stake in preserving his existence) is also the least afraid of death (*E* IV, 67)? In the last analysis, it is not mere life, but *activity*, that matters to Spinoza, 'The interest in self-preservation is interest in self-determination' (*Strauss*, p. 218; *vide* VIII, 3).

5 Value

Let us turn now to the second corollary of Spinoza's position, which announces that 'we adjudge a thing to be good because we strive for, wish, seek or desire it'. In part, Spinoza's comment may be aimed against Descartes' claim in the *Passions* that desire originates from the judgements of good or evil, and is inherently prospective in character (*Passions*, art. 57). In seeking to deny this, Spinoza may be making a point about the causality of human action: we are not determined *a fronte*, by future goods or ills which we first see and then try to realise or avert — that thought is incoherent. Rather, we are determined *a tergo*, by desires which were themselves mechanically caused by antecedent factors, and which comprise the mechanical causes of what we do (*Joachim* (2), p. 229). But it is also illuminating to set Spinoza's statement against this claim by Aristotle: 'We desire the object because it seems good to us, rather than the object's seeming good to us because we desire it' (*Metaphysics*, 1072a29). Spinoza seems to have stood Aristotle on his head: our judgements of value do not determine our desires, they are determined by them.

David Wiggins has recently offered to adjudicate this controversy between Aristotle and Spinoza (*Wiggins*, (2) esp. pp. 348–9). 'Maybe it is the beginning of real wisdom to see that we have to side against both Aristotle and Spinoza here and ask: "Why should the *because* not hold both ways round?".' Wiggins defends this interesting idea by suggesting that Moore and his followers were right to compare value-judgements with judgements of colour. We see a pillar box as red because it is red. But pillar boxes count as red only because we have a perceptual apparatus which so functions as to discriminate, and to learn to group together, just those things which are red. Not every animal has this type of perceptual organisation, and consequently few or no animals see things as red: it is an 'anthropocentric category'. But for all that, redness is not a relational property: 'red pillar box' does not mean 'red-to-humans pillar box'. Nor are colour-terms unique in these respects. We laugh at things or are repelled by them, because they are funny or disgusting; but unless we had a mental set which disposed us to laugh or be repelled, we would have no use for those concepts. So, arguably, it is with our notions of value. Spinoza is right, if he wishes to call attention to the fact that the notions of goodness and badness have a covert reference to the desires and needs of human beings: if we were all the size of Lilliputians, we would not call good the ships and buildings which we now call good. But Aristotle is also right, if his point is that the goodness of a ship or of a building does not depend on whether we choose or desire it. On the contrary, it is our belief that these things are good which calls forth our attraction towards them: take away that belief, and the desire is dissipated.

It is, however, unfair to Spinoza to represent him, as Wiggins does, as disagreeing flatly with Aristotle. In the *Short Treatise*, he is prepared to say that desire is a consequence, not the cause, of the belief that something is good: 'it cannot be found to have come upon any one except for an apparent good (*sub specie boni*). It is therefore clear that Desire . . . is the outcome of the first kind of knowledge. For if anyone has heard that a certain thing is good, he feels a longing or an inclination for the same, as may be seen in the case of the invalid who, through hearing the doctor say that such and such a remedy is good for his ailment, at once longs for the same, and feels a desire for it' (*ST* II, 3; *Wolf* translation, p. 73). Again, in the *Ethics* he emphatically does not believe that one can read off the goodness of a thing from the fact that it is desired, and allows that there is a standpoint from which we may judge our desires to be directed to bad and harmful objects (*E* IV, 17S, quoting Ovid, *Metamorphoses*, VII, 20). But more importantly of all, his aim in writing the *Ethics* is, in large part, to provide a remedy for the passions which afflict us, by describing how they damage us, how they arise and can be removed, and what a sane and healthy life would consist in. And while he does not exaggerate the efficacy of the bare knowledge of good and evil to re-shape our desires (*E* IV, 15; 17S), he clearly hopes that we, like the patient to whom a nostrum is offered, may be willing to take it. The goodness of things, being determined by their usefulness to us (*E* IV, Definition, I), is thus in a manner objective, and independent of our desires; and the life of the man who obeys the 'dictates of reason' provides an external standard against which to measure ourselves. Such judgements of value do of course depend on the fact that we are creatures with a special type of nature, needs and goals, but that does not imperil their objectivity (contrast *Unger*, pp. 49–53, in criticism of the Liberal 'Morality of Desire', with which he associates Spinoza).

We can go a step further in the direction of reconciling Aristotle and Spinoza. In *E* II, 49D, he asserts that 'in the mind there exists no absolute faculty of willing or not willing. Only individual volitions exist, that is to say, this and that affirmation and this and that negation'. And a bit later he writes: 'The Will and the Intellect are one and the same. The Will and the Intellect are nothing but the individual volitions and ideas themselves' (II, Section 2). Now these remarks invite two questions: what are individual volitions affirmations or negations *of*? And how are they related to desires? To the first question, the answer is presumably that they are affirmations of *value*: to will that *p* is to affirm that it is or would be good that *p* (or perhaps, to affirm that it would be better that *p* than that any feasible alternative should hold). And any such individual affirmation might be held simply to *be* a desire that *p*: volitions are desires, desires volitions (*cp. Duff*, p. 92). Hence there could be no kind of causal priority of a particular desire for a thing over the thought that the thing was good: the desire would, so to speak, already come intellectualised, the thought affectivised. It may be that this account of the relation between volition and desire lies behind Spinoza's claim that the knowledge of good is itself an affect (*E* IV, 8); and it seems confirmed by his identification of 'the decrees of the mind' with 'appetites' at *E* III, 25.

This reading of Spinoza appears to clash with his own statement about the nature of *conatus* (*E* III, 9S) and with an interpretation of the doctrine commonly based upon it. In the Explanation to Definition I of the Affects at the end of Part III,

Spinoza writes that 'whether a man be conscious of his appetite or not, it remains one and the same appetite'; and this, taken in conjunction with the claim that we judge something good because we desire or strive after it, has led to the view that Spinoza, like Schopenhauer or Freud, regarded man as a plaything of unconscious impulses. Writing in 1903, R.A. Duff asserted that 'the usual interpretation of this language is, that the *conatus* which works in man is a blind unconscious force, a will-to-live which makes use of man as its instrument, and which he is powerless to resist or to change. Consciousness is but an accident of its operation, an epi-phenomenon of its activity in a human body' (*Duff*, p. 78). C.D. Broad seems to have adopted a similar view when he interpreted Spinoza as follows: 'The presence or absence of consciousness makes no difference whatever to the impulse or its consequences. The decision and the action are completely determined by the impulses, whether we are aware of them or not; and the process of deliberating or deciding, if it be present, is a mere idle accompaniment to a *fait accompli*, as the King does when he gives his assent to an Act of Parliament' (*Broad* (2), p. 24).

What Spinoza actually says, however, implies only that our desires may not be conscious, and that if we are conscious of them, the fact will not *of itself* alter them. It does not follow that conscious reflection upon our desires and their objects cannot modify them, nor that deliberation is as idle and ceremonious as the Royal Assent. It is not Spinoza's purpose to liken us to sleepwalkers, unconscious of their movements, nor even to neurotics compulsively spilling ink or washing hands, whose conscious explanations have nothing to do with the desires which underlie such performances. On the contrary, he believes that we (most of us) are at least partly responsive to the pressures of Reason, and experience desires which can be changed as our picture of the world becomes truer. Even when I am most at the mercy of passive emotions, conscious deliberations will normally make a difference to my conduct: my craving for revenge conflicts with my desire for safety, and so I postpone gratifying it until I can strike with less danger to myself (*E* III, 39D). In *any* type of planning, I must take conflicting inclinations into account, and calculate the costs and benefits of immediate or complete, as opposed to deferred or partial, satisfaction of each of them. I may exhibit rationality to a high degree in formulating or in acting upon such a plan, even where the impulses involved are damaging and irrational ones. But it is not only in this way that desires and impulses can be brought into some kind of order, or subjected to conscious control.

Unlike Hume, Spinoza does not think that Reason is, and ought only to be, the slave of the passions. Spinoza recognises the intentionality of desire, at least when we are conscious of it: I cannot desire a thing without bringing it under some concept (*E* II, Axiom III; *Neu*, p. 86). (Indeed, as I have suggested, he may have wished to go further, in holding that we cannot desire a thing without also regarding it as in some way good or valuable: desire just *is* the affirmation of value.) But if my desire is bound up with beliefs about the character of its object, then as those beliefs alter or are corrected, the desire is inherently liable to be changed. If I come to see something as useful to me, or as augmenting my power, I will be drawn to it; if I see it as obstructive or debilitating, I will grow averse to it. The true view of things, and of their goodness or badness, may force itself upon me only in the face of great resistances; and when I have achieved it, it may be only imperfect, fragmentary or intermittent. But to the extent that I have it steadily before me, to that extent my desires must be ordered and directed to what is truly my good (*vide* VII, 9, *infra*).

6 *The passions*

Our findings suggest that we should see the conception of the good presented in the *Ethics* as undergoing progressive clarification and deepening. Beginning as the idea that the good is whatever satisfies desire (where no account is taken of the nature of the desire), it is transformed into the view that the true good for man consists in fulfilling his desires as a rational being, achieving his highest virtue and power of mind in understanding things by the third form of knowledge (*E* V, 25D). The end of all our action is to satisfy appetite; but when we think through how best to satisfy it, and to insure our own preservation, we shall see that it most profits us to live with our fellows in peace and concord, to join them in the pursuit of an inexhaustible and non-competitive good, and to develop our powers of mind in the understanding of nature. The main obstacle to our achieving a clear view of what our good lies in, and the main impediment to acting on that view when we have attained it, is that we are gripped by passions which set us at odds with ourselves and with other men. They disturb the orderly working of our thought, and distract us from our proper goals; they are painful in themselves, or else productive of pain; and they feed on one another, making it ever harder to break out of their hold. The first thing to do in

MORALITY AND THE EMOTIONS

order to liberate ourselves from them is to try to understand and define them; and this task chiefly occupies Spinoza for the remainder of Part III.

In opposition to Descartes, who admitted six primary passions, Spinoza recognises only three: Joy (*Laetitia*), Sorrow (*Tristitia*), and Desire (*Cupiditas*), which presupposes the other two (*E* III, 11S). Joy and Sorrow are defined by (indirect) reference to the *conatus*: Joy is the transition from a lesser to a greater perfection (or power), Sorrow the transition from a greater to a lesser. Joy is divided into two kinds: titillation or localised pleasure, and a more diffuse sense of well-being called cheerfulness (*hilaritas*); Sorrow is correspondingly divided into (local) pain (*dolor*) and melancholy. From these three primary emotions, all other emotions arise, either by being *composed* of them (like jealousy and other 'vacillations of the mind'), or by being *derived* from them, that is, by being forms of Joy, or of Sorrow, or of Desire which 'pass under names varying as their relations and external signs vary' (*E* III, Definitions of the Affects, after Definition XLVIII). Spinoza lists a total of 48 passions, consisting in (i) the three primary ones; (ii) Admiration and Contempt, which Descartes mentions but which Spinoza does not consider to be truly passions; (iii) the derivatives of Joy and of Sorrow; (iv) the derivatives of Desire, amongst the last three of which is a special sub-group (Ambition, Luxuriousness, Drunkenness, Avarice and Lust) distinguished by the fact that they possess no contraries (*cf. Wolfson* II, pp. 208–10). Schematically:

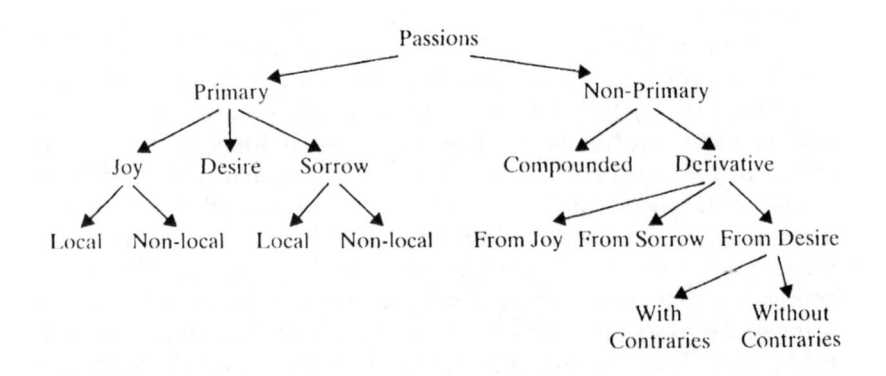

```
                           Passions
                    ↙                  ↘
              Primary                    Non-Primary
             ↙  ↓  ↘                    ↙         ↘
         Joy  Desire  Sorrow      Compounded    Derivative
         ↙ ↘          ↙ ↘                     ↙    ↓    ↘
     Local Non-local Local Non-local    From Joy From Sorrow From Desire
                                                          ↙         ↘
                                                       With        Without
                                                     Contraries   Contraries
```

The diagram is, however, incomplete in one important respect: it takes no account of the fact that there are *active* emotions as well as passive ones (*E* III, 58; 59). These are the emotions which 'are related to a man insofar as he acts', i.e. emotions of which a man's nature is the adequate cause, or which spring from his adequate ideas. Spinoza ascribes the behaviour which follows from the active emotions to Strength of Soul (*Fortitudo*), which is, he says, expressed in two types of desire: Firmness (*Animositas*), or the rational desire for self-preservation, and Generosity or Large-Mindedness (*Generositas*), which is the rational desire to live with and assist others (*E* III, 59S).

As Jerome Neu has pointed out, there are serious problems about which emotions are to count as active, which as passive (*Neu*, pp. 97–8). One problem turns on Spinoza's claim that active states can be explained wholly by reference to the nature of the thing which has them. For Spinoza clearly wants to allow that pleasure can be an active emotion (*E* IV, 59D). But if I am pleased because of some external object (fine clothes, say, or a handsome horse), then surely the explanation of my pleasure must refer to that object; and hence I cannot myself be the adequate cause of it. It is however true that the emotion of joy will differ, not only in accordance with the nature of the person who feels it (*E* IV, 57S), but also in accordance with the nature of the object to which it is directed (so that delight in one's children differs from delight in one's wife: *E* IV, 56 and scholium); and it may be that Spinoza would deny that joy in anything other than God or the mind itself could be an active emotion (at *E* 58D, he describes the mind's joy at contemplating its own adequate ideas). If that is his view, then by his own admissions even a passive emotion may be unfailingly good (which seems strange): for at *E* IV, 42, he claims to prove that cheerfulness can never be excessive, but is always good – and 'cheerfulness' surely includes joys directed to other objects than the mind or God. Nor can the difficulty about the external causes of active emotions be got round by pointing out that for Spinoza all perception of external bodies reveals the constitution of the perceiver's body; for if this is the basis for saying that my joy at an external cause must ultimately be referred to my nature alone, then it will follow that *all* joy of this sort must be active – which Spinoza of course does not believe (*E* IV, 44S).

A second and nastier problem concerns those emotions which arise from a clear perception of possible evils or harms – say, the fear of a mob which is after me, and the desire to escape from it. Is this fear active or passive? In one way, it seems that Spinoza regards it as active, since it is founded upon a rational concern for my own life, and springs from an adequate conception of the danger and of the means to avert it. Thus at *E* III, 59S, Spinoza says that 'presence of mind in the face of dangers' is a species of firmness, which implies that it is an active emotion; and at *E* IV, 69C, flight at the proper time is cited as exhibiting firmness. Thus the fear which moves me to flee a mob seems to count as an active emotion. On the other hand, Spinoza maintains that 'he who is led by fear, and does what is good in order to avoid what is evil, is not led by reason' (*E* IV, 63). Thus, if an invalid eats what he dislikes because of the fear of death, his desire is rather that of not dying than of remaining alive; that is, he seeks to avoid an evil rather than to pursue a good, and so it springs, not from Reason, but from a fear which in this case is a type of sorrow (*E* IV, 63CS). Is it the same with the fear of the mob, and the desire to flee from it?

Before we can attempt to resolve the puzzle, we must take account of a complication in the case of the invalid. Spinoza recognises two kinds of fear: one which he calls *Metus*, and defines as an inconstant sorrow (*E* III, Definition of the Affects, xiii), and one which he names *Timor*, defined as 'the desire of avoiding the greater of two dreaded evils by the less' (*E* III, Definition of the Affects, xxxix). Now the discussion of the case of the invalid is headlined by a contrast between those who are led by Reason and those who are led by fear in the sense of *metus* ('Qui *metu* ducitur . . .'). This implies that the invalid is experiencing a form of sorrow, and hence that his emotion is certain to be passive. On the other hand, in scholium itself Spinoza characterises the invalid as being gripped by fear in the sense of *timor* ('Comedit aeger id, quod aversatur, *timore mortis*'); and it is plausible to say that the invalid acts from a desire to avoid the greater of two evils (death) by choosing the lesser (food he dislikes). If so, he is actuated by an affect which – thus far – may be either active or passive. And in another passage, Spinoza says that if a man goes after what he sees to be the lesser evil in a case where a greater evil is the alternative, then that man will be desiring something which must, in the circumstances, be accounted a good; and so he will be acting according to the guidance of Reason (*E* IV, 65D and C). Looked at in this way, the invalid's fear (*timor*) is an active emotion; he is guided by the knowledge of good, and so the case fails utterly to illustrate the contrast between being guided by fear and being guided by reason.

The invalid is himself opposed to the healthy man who

'delights in his food, and who enjoys life more than if he feared (*timeret*) death, and desired directly to avoid it'. And both cases are meant to confirm the theorem that 'By a desire which arises from reason, we directly follow the good, and indirectly flee the bad' (*E* IV, 63C). It seems then that the healthy man *directly* desires some good (presumably, life), and only *indirectly* (if at all) flees some correlative evil (death). Conversely, then, the invalid *directly* desires to avoid an evil (death), and only *indirectly* desires to secure the correlative good (life), if he desires that at all. The healthy man's direct desire must then, by the demonstration at *E* IV, 63C, spring from Reason, i.e. from an active emotion of joy, or from the knowledge of good, whereas the invalid's direct desire must arise from sorrow (*tristitia*), or from the knowledge of evil. But since the invalid's desire to avert death plainly originates in his fear (*timor*), it seems that the emotion is being treated, at least in the example, as a form of sorrow, not differing specifically from *metus*, and hence as itself a passive emotion. The later definition of *timor* is irrelevant to the case.

This discussion may help to clarify the example from which we started – the case in which I am fleeing from an angry mob. If my flight is motivated by the direct desire to stay alive, and not by the direct desire to avert death, then that desire will have sprung from Reason, that is, from joy and the knowledge of good, which are active emotions. But if I flee from the direct desire to avoid death, then my desire will have sprung from a passive emotion, which Spinoza presumably would characterise as 'fear' (*metus* or *timor*). Thus in the case in which my emotion was active, I could not properly be said to have 'feared' the mob; rather, my flight revealed 'firmness' and 'presence of mind'.

The analysis I am proposing has four difficulties. (i) It forces us to assume that Spinoza uses the term '*timor*' inconsistently. (ii) It involves him in a distinction between '*directly*' desiring a good (evil) and '*indirectly*' desiring the correlative evil (good); and this is a distinction which is both elusive and unexplained. (iii) It finds in him a contrast between 'the knowledge of good' and 'the knowledge of evil' which is problematic. For he follows Aristotle (*Nicomachean Ethics*, 1129a12) in asserting that the knowledge of good and the knowledge of evil are correlative; but since they are correlative, and since the knowledge of evil consists in inadequate ideas (*E* IV, 64), it seems that the knowledge of good must also be inadequate (as *E* IV, 68D seems to admit). How then can emotions and affects which spring from the knowledge of good be rational and active? (iv) Finally, if fear is inherently passive, then there seems to be no place in Spinoza's scheme for prudent, rational or justified fears.

These four difficulties seem to me to tell, not so much against my reading of Spinoza, as against Spinoza himself. The truth is that his treatment of the 'active/passive' distinction within the emotions is a terrible tangle. I have tried to unknot some of the puzzles here; and I shall deal with certain others later (*vide* VII, 8).

7 *The laws of feeling*

Let us now consider how Spinoza supposes the non-primary emotions to be formed. His explanations rely on the assumption of two basic Laws of Feeling, which Wolfson usefully designates 'The Law of Association of the Emotions' and 'The Law of the Imitation of the Emotions' (*Wolfson*, II, p. 213; p. 215). The first law may be explained as follows. Suppose that a human body has been affected by two external objects on a given occasion, of which one object has increased or diminished that body's power, whilst the other has left it unaltered. If on a later occasion the second object (or one sufficiently like it) acts alone upon the body, the body will tend to be affected as it was on the earlier occasion, when the two objects acted together. If, say, the body previously underwent a lowering of its vitality, so that the mind felt an emotion of sadness, the perception of an object only accidentally associated with its past sadness will tend to make that emotion recur (*E* III, 15). Thus an object previously affectless or neutral may come to awaken sorrow in the mind, and so come to be hated by it. Wolfson argues interestingly that Spinoza follows Aristotle in holding that two objects are 'accidentally' associated if either they are like each other, or unlike, or contiguous (*cf.* Wolfson, II, pp. 213–4, and *De Memoria* 451b19–20). Example: at *E* III, 16, Spinoza seems to be saying that if I normally take pleasure in X because it is Φ, then if I imagine Y to resemble X in some respect Ψ I will love Y whether or not is it Φ.

Spinoza attaches great importance to this first law, since it enables him to explain many phenomena which otherwise seem baffling. 'We now understand why we love or hate certain things from no cause which is known to us, but merely from sympathy or antipathy, as people say . . . I know indeed that the writers who first introduced the words "Sympathy" and "Antipathy" desired thereby to signify certain occult qualities of things, but nevertheless I believe that we shall be permitted to understand by those names qualities which are plain and well known' (*E* III, 15CDS, *cp. Kenny Letters*, pp. 224–5). More generally, the law is invoked in order to account for emotional conflicts, both within and between individuals. Thus in *E* II, 17 and 18, Spinoza is describing three sorts of 'fluctuation of the mind' arising from the association of the emotions. (i) In the first case, he says that if X normally affects us with a certain emotion, then if Y, which affects us with the contrary emotion, is imagined to resemble X, our response to Y will tend to become a mixture of the two contrary feelings. (ii) A second type of case comes from the fact that the same object can affect different parts of the body in different ways, or even the same part in different ways, and so become the self-same cause of contrary emotions. (iii) The third case is illustrated by reactions such as hope or fear, which are 'inconstant' emotions (of joy and of sorrow respectively) arising from the image of a past or future thing of which we are in doubt. If I hope for a certain outcome, I take joy in the thought that it has or will come to pass; but remembering its likeness to other outcomes, which either did not occur or proved to be disappointing, I will also experience sorrow when I consider the prospect. Interpersonal conflicts, on the other hand, may arise because the bodies of men, and so too their minds, have acquired different habits of responding to external objects, and different emotional reactions with them. If I associate X with something I hate, I will hate X too, and strive to destroy it; if you associate X with something you love, you will love and strive to preserve X (*E* III, 28). Again, the law will explain many forms of prejudice and intolerance: 'if anyone has been affected with joy or sorrow by someone who belongs to a class or nation other than his own, and if this joy or sorrow is accompanied by the idea of this person as its cause, under the name of his class or nation, he will not hate him merely, but the whole of the class or nation to which he belongs' (*E* III, 46).

Spinoza's second law in part counteracts the bad results of the first, and in part intensifies them (*Wernham* Introduction, pp. 7–8). According to it, if we imagine that a person or thing like ourselves is affected by some emotion, then we ourselves will tend to feel the same emotion (*E* III, 27). This holds true if our attitude towards the person in question is neutral; if it is someone we love, then his feeling of joy or sorrow will be transferred to us in greater measure than if we had no feelings towards him, and will be proportioned to the strength of the joy or sorrow imputed to him (*E* III, 21); if on the other hand, it is someone we hate, then if he is imagined to feel joy, we shall feel sorrow, and if he is imagined to feel sorrow, we shall feel joy, again in proportion to the strength of the contrary affects imputed to him (*E* III, 23). In the case in which a hated thing feels pain, however, my joy at his displeasure will be interlaced with sorrow: for whenever something like me sorrows, my perception of its feeling will induce sorrow in me too; similarly, the joy a hated thing is imagined to feel must tend to induce joy in me as well, thus causing my sorrow to be complicated by the presence of the contrary impulse (E III, 23S). The pleasure and pain caused in the things we love and hate also influence our reactions to the causes of those emotions in them: what causes joy in a thing I love will itself tend to be loved, what causes sorrow in it will tend to be hated (E III, 22): this fact explains the emotions of favour and of indignation (E III, 22S). And whatever causes joy in a thing I hate will tend to evoke hatred in me, just as whatever causes sorrow in a hated thing will tend to be loved (E III, 24) – reactions which are related to the passion of envy (E III, 24S). Because we have a built-in tendency to affirm only what will cause joy in ourselves and in what we love, we are naturally disposed to excesses such as pride (in ourselves) and overestimation (of others); and because we affirm what will cause sorrow in the things we hate, we are chronically liable to think too little of them, which is contempt (E III, 26S).

The Law of the Imitation of the Emotions underlies many of our social sentiments. If we witness the suffering of another, then unless we hate him we shall feel unmixed sorrow ourselves; and this emotion, which is pity, will move us to try to suppress the cause of that other's suffering. (Like Hobbes, Spinoza seriously misrepresents pity. He treats it as primarily a matter of relieving one's own sorrow, not another's; and so he leaves it unexplained why we should not adopt more straightforward methods of extinguishing the discomfort in ourselves than those which involve destroying the cause of the other's misery. Moreover, since the thing pitied is the cause of sorrow in us, we should have some tendency to hate it, which he denies: E III, 27C2D.) Again, since the joy we imagine in others will tend, if we do not hate them, to produce joy in us, and the sorrow they feel, sorrow, we are disposed to do those things which will cause them joy, and avoid those things which will cause them sorrow – hence ambition and, less damagingly, humanity (E III, 29 and scholium).

These beneficial effects of the second law are offset by its workings in other spheres. If someone else loves what I love, or hates what I hate, my original feelings towards that object will be reinforced; but if he loves what I hate, or hates what I love, my emotions towards that object will become complicated by the contrary feeling, and I will suffer fluctuation of mind. This personal conflict in me will tend to provoke a conflict with those who do not share my affects: for I will endeavour to make them love what I love and hate what I hate. 'Each person by nature desires that other persons should live according to his way of thinking; but if everyone does this, then all are a hindrance to one another' (*E* III, 31C). Envy too arises from the operation of the second law: if I imagine that someone else is enjoying a thing which only one person can possess, the sight of his enjoyment will suffice to cause me to love and desire that thing; but then his possession of it will present an obstacle to my fulfilling my desire, and I will endeavour to take it from him (*E* III, 32). So it comes about that 'from the same property of human nature from which it follows that men pity one another it also follows that they are envious and ambitious' (*E* III, 32S).

The workings of Spinoza's Laws, both salutary and destructive, can be illustrated from other passions. Consider sexual love. Since I feel joy in the joy of the person I love, and since the cause of joy is itself loved by the person to whom it is imparted, I will endeavour to cause joy to the beloved and so to be loved in return (*E* III, 33D). The more successful I am in this endeavour, the greater will be my self-exaltation (*E* III, 34). I will thus strive to 'unite the beloved as closely as possible' to myself, that is, I will try to make myself the sole cause of his or her joy. If someone else should desire my beloved, this fact will enhance my own joy in possession, and stimulate my effort to gratify the beloved as much as possible; but if my beloved's joy is caused, not by me, but by my rival, my self-exaltation will be diminished, and I will be pained. Both rival and beloved then, being causes of pain, will tend to be hated. 'This hatred towards a beloved object when joined with Envy is called Jealousy, which is therefore nothing but a fluctuation of the mind springing from the love and hatred both felt together, and attended with the idea of another person whom we envy. Moreover, this hatred towards the beloved will be greater in proportion to the joy with which the jealous man has usually been affected by the reciprocal love between him and his beloved, and also in proportion to the emotion with which he had been affected towards the person who is imagined to unite himself to the beloved' (*E* III, 35S). Having hated my rival, I will come to hate my beloved for causing joy to a hated thing, and for being associated in my mind with that rival's image. This last thought, Spinoza says, is generally encountered ('*plerumque locum habet*') in the love for a woman. (The text is ambiguous: he could mean that in general, where sexual love is found, this jealous thought will occur, or that this thought is generally restricted to cases of sexual, rather than other, forms of love.)

Here Spinoza's restraint gives way, and he breaks into language of uncharacteristic coarseness and violence: 'The man who imagines that the woman he loves prostitutes herself to another is not merely saddened because his appetite is frustrated, but he turns away from her because he is forced to join the image of the beloved to the genitals and excretions of another' (*E* III, 35S; we shall have occasion to return later to Spinoza's jittery attitude towards love between the sexes (*vide* VIII, 2, *Love*)). The general point is clear: just as pity traces its origin back to the same source as envy and ambition, so mutual love and the pleasures which attend it grow from the same root as jealousy and all its agonies.

I think that enough has been said to indicate the scope and ingenuity of Spinoza's effort to raise up a complete theory of the passions on the narrow foundation of two laws and three primary affects. Yet it is clear that the attempted *tour de force* does not finally succeed. Critics have noted the weaknesses in, for example, the Law of the Imitation of the Emotions (*Broad* (2), pp. 37–8). In arguing for that Law, Spinoza assumes that X's perception of the physical state of his fellow human Y will give rise to a modification in X's body similar to that in Y's; hence if Y's physical state is correlated with a certain emotion, X, whose body will have entered into a similar physical state, must feel a similar emotion (*E* III, 27D). He supports these contentions empirically: 'if we wish to consult experience, we shall find that it teaches all these things, especially if we should attend to our earliest years. For we find that children, because their body is, as it were, continually in equilibrium, laugh and cry merely because they see others do the same' (*E* III 32S).

But this will not really do. For first, it is not generally true that adult bodies tend to mimic the overt behaviour of other human bodies they perceive; but it is not less true of adults than of children that they respond sympathetically to other people's emotions. To socialise a child is very largely a matter of making it aware of the emotions of others, and of feeling sympathy for them.

Second, the outward *signs* or *expressions* of an emotion are at best a small part of that emotion's physical correlate; the residue, which is the more important part, is normally unobservable. Joy, for example, if its physical correlate is not simply the internal transition of the body to a greater perfection, is correlated with physical expression such as laughter, or with physical signs like quicker breathing. Only such expressions or signs are observed by other witnesses; the changes within the body of the man who feels joy normally go unnoticed. It follows that even if the sound of someone else's laughter, or the sight of his faster breathing, produced similar responses in me, I would on that account feel only a tiny part or pale reflection of his joy. (Nor would my sympathetic joy be increased if – as happens in rare experimental conditions – I was aware of the accompanying *internal* changes in his body.) Indeed, Spinoza makes things worse for himself by remarking that 'the external affections of the body which are observed in the affects, such as trembling, paleness, sobbing, laughter and the like . . . belong to the body alone without any relationship to the mind' (*E* III, 59S). This may mean that the relationship between laughter (say) and joy is purely contingent and non-conceptual. If so, it becomes wholly inexplicable why the sound of *Y*'s laughter should tend to cause joy (rather than sorrow or irritation) in the mind of *X*, who hears it.

8 Of human bondage

Part IV of Spinoza's *Ethics* offers a grim and sobering assessment of the condition of mankind. In its detachment, realism and astringency, it rivals, and perhaps excels, the pictures of human life created by the other great moralists of the seventeenth century – by La Rochefoucauld, La Bruyère, La Fontaine, Pascal. Man, says Spinoza, is born into bondage (*E* IV, 68S). He is at the mercy of external forces which continually threaten to destroy him; he is swept by emotions whose origin he does not understand, and whose terrible force he cannot mitigate or control. For much of his existence, he is in the condition of the brutes, goaded by bestial appetites (*E* IV, 68S; *E* III, 27). Even the knowledge of his true good may be powerless to save him from overmastering passions and inexpugnable fantasies (*E* IV, 17S). Yet these dismaying thoughts should not cause us to despair: 'I say them because it is necessary for us to know both the strength and the weakness of our nature' (*E* IV, 17S). Spinoza's object is not to rail at vice, but to teach virtue (*E* IV, 63S). If Reason is weak, it is not entirely impotent: there is some hope of escape. The myths of the Fall and the Redemption convey, in mythical forms, the truth concerning our natural depravity, and the means we have to overcome it. 'We are told that God forbad free man to eat of the tree of the knowledge of good and evil, and warned him that as soon as he ate of it he would immediately dread death rather than desire to live.

Afterwards we are told that when man found a wife who agreed entirely with his nature, he saw that there could be nothing in nature which could be more profitable to him than his wife. But when he came to believe that the brutes were like himself, he immediately began to imitate their affects and to lose his liberty, which the Patriarchs afterwards recovered, being led by the spirit of Christ, that is to say, by the idea of God, which alone can make a man free, and cause him to desire for other men the good he desires for himself' (*E* IV, 68S). Spinoza's thought may be reflected in these pregnant epigrams from Wittgenstein's *Notebooks* of 1914–16:

> How can man be happy at all, since he cannot ward off the misery of this world?
>
> Through the life of knowledge.
>
> The life of knowledge is the life that is happy in spite of the misery of the world. (edited and translated by G.E.M. Anscombe, p. 81e)

How then can enslavement to the passive emotions be brought to an end? Spinoza does not minimise the difficulties. In the first place, he notes that we are inescapably parts of Nature, and subject to its common order; from that it follows that external causes, which surpass us in power, are always liable to bring about changes in us of which we are ourselves only partly the cause; but then any such changes will be passivities in us, since they cannot be understood by reference to the laws of our nature alone (*E* IV, 2; 4). 'Hence it follows that a man is necessarily always subject to passions, and that he follows and abets the common order of Nature, accommodating himself to it as far as the nature of things requires' (*E* IV, 4C). (As an argument, this is not impressive, since it seems to move from a more general sense of 'passivity', in which it simply means 'what we undergo', to a narrower sense in which it means 'passive emotion'. But let that pass.) Second, Spinoza contends that truth in itself does not expel false or inadequate ideas and imaginations, nor therefore the passions which are attached to them. Even if I know that the sun is at a vast distance from the earth, my sensory state when I look at it will remain the same as it was – that is to say, it will continue to look to me as if the sun were 200 feet distant. And similarly, 'we know that when we groundlessly fear any evil, the fear vanishes when we hear correct intelligence; but we also know, on the other hand, that when we fear an evil that will actually come upon us, the fear vanishes when we hear false intelligence, so that imaginations do not disappear with the presence of truth' (*E* IV, 1S). Two points may be deduced from this: (i) it is not the truth or the falsehood of a report *as such* which brings about an alteration in the emotions; and (ii) the emotions are as likely to be changed by hearsay knowledge as by knowledge of higher grades. Later on, however, Spinoza seems to assert that *knowledge* as such – without regard to grade – can work no change in the affects. In particular, he denies that knowledge of good and evil, or the knowledge of where our own best interests lie, can of itself redirect our emotions, causing us to pursue the useful and to eschew the harmful (*E* IV, 14; *E* IV, Definition I and II). Behind this lies the claim that 'an affect cannot be restrained or removed unless by a contrary and stronger affect' (*E* IV, 7; *cp.* Nietzsche, *Beyond Good and Evil*, Section 117). The demonstration of this important theorem depends on the assumption that a state of the body will persist unchanged unless the body is acted upon by another force. The reasoning is that an affect is by definition the idea of an affection of the body; a given affection of the body will persist unless counteracted by a stronger and contrary affection of that body; to any such affection, there will correspond an idea, which will itself be an affect; and that affect will be contrary to the original affect, exactly as the affection to which it relates is contrary to the original affection (*E* IV, 7D).

It might now be said that Spinoza has shown, not merely that escape from bondage is very difficult, but that it is impossible without extraordinary good fortune. The problem is brought out by A.E. Taylor. 'We should expect [Spinoza] . . . to teach a doctrine of intellectual conversion, making escape from the passions consequent on the attainment of adequate ideas. But if he is to take that line consistently, he must be prepared to hold that truth, at least truth about the good, as truth, has an inherent attractive power which can master the emotions.' But this cannot be, as Taylor observes, for Spinoza insists that truth and knowledge as such cannot get a hold over our passionate nature. 'Thus it seems in the end to be an accident, dependent on those circumstances of our environment which Spinoza tells us are, taken together, so much more powerful than ourselves, whether we ever escape out of our bondage or not, though the object of the whole *Ethics* has been to show us how we may compass our own deliverance' (*Taylor* (1) p. 295). The answer Spinoza would give to this objection is that it assumes a false distinction between ideas and affects: the knowledge of good and evil is a second-order idea, corresponding to affects of the first order (specifically, joy and sorrow) which are themselves ideas of affections of the body; but these second-order ideas are only notionally distinct from the corresponding affects, being united to them in the way in which the idea of the body is united to the body; and hence the knowledge of good and evil may itself be considered as an affect (*E* IV, 8D). When it is considered in this guise, it can be said to oppose other affects, and the desires which spring from it can fight against the desires associated with those other affects. 'From the true knowledge of good and evil, *insofar as this is an affect*, necessarily arises desire, which is greater in proportion as the affect from which it springs is greater. But this desire, because it springs from our understanding something truly, follows therefore in us insofar as we act, and therefore must be understood through our essence alone, and consequently its strength and increase must be limited by human power alone' (*E* IV, 15D). Thus the attainment of true knowledge of good and evil will of itself generate active emotions, by which the passions may be restrained. And insofar as the attainment of true ideas lies in our power, we are finally able to encompass our own salvation.

Does this rebut Taylor's objection? I think not. First of all, Spinoza admits that the strength of a desire is proportioned to the power of the cause from which it originates. But since the desires which spring from a true understanding of good and evil reflect human power alone, while the desires which oppose them reflect the power of external causes, which is always liable to exceed our own, there can be no guarantee that rational, inwardly determined desires will be able to combat and overcome irrational, externally induced ones (*E* IV, 15D). 'The force and increase of any passion and its perseverance in existence are limited by the power of an external cause compared with our own power, and therefore may surpass the power of man'; consequently, 'the other actions or power of a man may be so far surpassed by the force of some passion or affect, that the affect may obstinately cling to him' (*E* IV, 6 and Dem.) Hence we are always at the mercy of external forces when it comes to working out our emancipation from the passions; by Spinoza's own admissions, as Taylor points out, our becoming free is a matter of good fortune and fortuitous circumstance, and not otherwise within our power. (In theological terms, it is as if Spinoza had seemed to side with the Pelagians, holding that salvation could come through good works alone, but then had adopted the Augustinian view that an arbitrarily given grace was necessary for that end.)

Second, the answer I have assigned to Spinoza is inconsistent with what he says elsewhere. For that answer assumed that the knowledge of good and evil consisted in adequate ideas, from which active emotions could arise. But at *E* IV, 64, Spinoza asserts that the knowledge of evil consists in inadequate ideas; and at *E* IV, 68D he writes that 'he who is born free has no other than adequate ideas, and therefore has no conception of evil, nor consequently of good, as good and evil are correlative'. The inconsistency is due, I think, to the fact that the 'knowledge of good and evil' is made to do double duty – part of the time, it refers to an affect, the mental or *felt* side of changes within the body to a greater or lesser vitality, and part of the time it relates to an item of knowledge or belief concerning what is useful or harmful to us. Taken in the first way, as an affect or emotion, this 'knowledge' can be *neither* adequate nor inadequate; taken in the other way, it admits of truth and falsehood, and may be *either* adequate or inadequate.

This latter difficulty must be pursued further; indeed, I think that when it is fully spelled out, it will reveal a deep incoherence in Spinoza's thinking. To begin with, let us mark the distinction between (i) the affects of joy and sorrow, which are the 'ideas' correlative to certain changes in, or affections of, the body; (ii) the reflective ideas of these affects, or the consciousness of them, which Spinoza holds to be only notionally distinct from them; (iii) the knowledge of good and evil, that is, the knowledge that certain states or things are useful to us, and others harmful. Now I claim that Spinoza tended to conflate (i) with (ii) and (ii) with (iii). The slide is very evident in a passage from Joachim's commentary, which faithfully reproduces Spinoza's thought, including the confusions in it.

Joachim writes: 'So far as we feel pleasure or pain, and so far as we desire, we can also be aware of these our feelings and desires: for consciousness in man can always be turned upon itself, and become self-consciousness. Hence an emotion of pleasure or pain may carry with it the reflective idea of that emotion; and the "knowledge of good and evil" is simply an emotional state of which we are reflectively conscious'. In this remark, which is closely based on *E* IV, 8D, we can see the tendency to identify (i) with (ii); the reference in the final clause to 'the knowledge of good and evil' points us forward to the equation of (ii) with (iii), which soon follows. 'Here, then, we seem to have a remedy to check or suppress the overmastering passions. We have a reflective idea as to our good and evil which may become a true knowledge, i.e. a reflective idea of what is really good and bad for us.' In calling this 'idea' *reflective*, Joachim links it to (ii); in describing it as knowledge *of what is really good and bad for us*, he hitches it to (iii). The final move, which completes the circle by joining (iii) to (i), comes in his conclusion: 'And this knowledge is on one side of itself an emotional state, and therefore capable of fighting against the passive emotions' (*Joachim* (2), pp. 258–9).

The confusion is not superficial; it signals a deeper problem. On the one hand, Spinoza wants to say that the affects can be checked by knowledge or belief as such. His own example at *E* IV, 1S, which describes the removal of fear by well- and ill-founded reports, reveals how this can happen. More generally, however, he wishes to argue that reasoned belief or knowledge concerning the passions, their nature and tendency, usefulness or harm, can be effective in controlling them. Thus it is that 'in proportion as we know an affect better, it is more within our control, and the less does the mind suffer from it' (*E* V, 3C). A third type of case in which reason can combat the passions is illustrated by *E* V, 10S, which shows how knowledge of good and evil, in the form of right rules and sure maxims, can be used to extirpate emotions such as hatred, fear or ambition. (Example: if I constantly bear it in mind that hatred is to be conquered by love and generosity, I shall render myself less susceptible to being moved by hate.) When he is advocating these remedies for the passions, Spinoza is opposing item (iii) to affects on the level of those mentioned in (i). On the other hand, because he believes that an affect can only be resisted by another affect, he must *deny* the possibility of conflicts of the types just described, unless item (iii) can be reduced to the level of (i). This he accomplishes by treating (i) as (ii) and (ii) as (iii). The step from (i) to (ii) had already been taken by Descartes, when he made self-reflectiveness the mark of the mental: it is built into the structure of the *Cogito* that one cannot have a thought without being conscious that one is having that particular thought (*Kenny* (4), p. 119). (At the same time, Descartes was forced to distinguish between thoughts and the accompanying consciousness of them: thus he says that the perception of a pain, but not the pain itself, may have the properties of being clear and distinct (*Kenny* (4), p. 124).) The additional step, from (ii) to (iii), seems to have been Spinoza's own contribution, encouraged perhaps by a nominalistic identification of 'knowing the nature of good and evil' with 'knowing things which are good and evil'.

If I am right in finding these errors in Spinoza, then the 'remedy' which Joachim describes is not one which Spinoza can consistently offer (*cf. Bidney*, p. 252, for confirmation of the charge of inconsistency). Certainly, he does sometimes say that we can win ourselves from the passive emotions by rational means – by forming adequate ideas, by gaining a steady, unclouded view of our good and evil. But by his own showing, this sort of remedy is unobtainable. The 'knowledge of good and evil' proves on examination to be nothing more than the affects of joy and sorrow themselves; and the noxious passions will be mastered only if circumstance favours us, and does not prevent joy (or rather cheerfulness) from arising in us with sufficient strength to expel less wholesome emotions. To invoke Taylor's contrast again – Spinoza must declare that liberation from the passions, if it comes at all, can only be 'emotional' in character; but his own truer instincts lead him to think that we can free ourselves by 'intellectual' means. With these thoughts in the background, let us approach Part V of the *Ethics*, in which Spinoza's cure for the passions is more fully set forth.

9 The conquest of the passions

In the first 20 propositions of Part V, Spinoza considers the power of the mind over the passive emotions, and prescribes means by which it may control them. These remedies may be grouped under at least seven general headings, which we must now examine (Spinoza lists *five* cures for the emotions at *E* V, 20S; Wolfson detects *six*, Broad *four*).

(i) First of all, we can form clear and distinct ideas of the affections of our body (*E* V, 4) and of the passions which are associated with them; and when we form a clear and distinct idea of a passion, we thereby extinguish it (*E* V, 3). Thus, for example, insofar as we form a clear and distinct idea of sorrow or of pain – that is, insofar as we come to understand its *causes* – the pain will cease to be a passion – that is, it will cease altogether (*E* V, 18CS). It is chiefly these propositions, I think, which have led certain writers on Spinoza to compare his work to that of Freud. So we find Hampshire saying that 'for Spinoza no less than for Freud, moral praise and blame of the objects of our particular desires, and of the sources of our pleasure, are irrelevant superstitions; we can free ourselves only by an understanding of the true causes of our desires, which must then change their direction'. Or again: for both Spinoza and Freud 'there can in principle be only one way of achieving sanity and happiness; the way is to come to understand the causes of our own states of mind' (*Hampshire* (2), p. 141, p. 142).

The comparison with the psychoanalytic search for causes is in many ways illuminating; but we should notice one crucial point of difference, in which Freud's view is immeasurably superior to

Spinoza's. Spinoza has to represent it as a *necessary truth* that a passion will be eliminated once we clearly and distinctly understand it by recognising its cause; but while it is often true that the passions will yield themselves to this treatment, it is not always or necessarily true. A dentist may have a perfectly clear idea of the causes of his toothache; this knowledge may itself delight him, and serve to mitigate his pain, or distract his attention from it, but it will scarcely cause the pain to go away. Again, if it is proved to me that I love a squint-eyed woman because her features remind me of a girl I knew in my childhood, my affection for her need not therefore cease to exist.

This objection to Spinoza, at once so banal and so conclusive, has been stiffly resisted by several of his expositors (see, most recently, *Allison*, p. 153). They do Spinoza the injustice, however, of not basing their defence on the demonstration which he actually gives. That demonstration asserts that a passion is a confused idea (sc. of a state of the body); but since it is only notionally distinct from the idea which consists in the accompanying consciousness of itself, it can be rendered clear and distinct if the idea of it is made clear and distinct. In coming to be clear and distinct, however, it ceases to be confused, and hence is transformed into something other than a passion (*E* V, 3D). The argument plainly assumes the identity of an affect with the second-order consciousness of that affect; and it asserts the transferability of the properties of clarity and distinctness to affective states, such as pain (which seems absurd).

Caird, who sees clearly enough the inadequacy of the reasoning, purports to 'strip' it of 'its technical form' and explain its 'drift' instead. (This, he thinks, will immunise it from our objection.) He writes:

> When it is asserted that by the knowledge of our passions we gain the mastery over them . . . it is obviously not meant that to have a theoretical knowledge of passion is to be exempt from its control, which would be as absurd as to say that the diagnosis of a disease is equivalent to its cure . . . But what he means is, that when we gain the point of view of true knowledge, passion loses its hold over us. . . . [T]he attitude of purely individual feeling, in which things are good or evil only as they contribute to the satisfaction of our appetites and passions, vanishes away when we rise to that higher attitude in which we identify ourselves with universal interests, and look on our particular pleasures and pains in the light of that universal order of which we are but an insignificant part. So

viewed, our satisfactions lose their deceptive importance. They become no more to us, or to reason in us, than those of other individuals . . . Thus, regarded from the point of view of reason, the passions cease to exist for us except insofar as they are functions of the universal, or forms under which reason itself is realised. (*Caird*, pp. 276–7)

Caird seems to be taking Spinoza to have said that, in forming a clear and distinct idea of a passion, we are regarding it as something which, simply because it is our own, we have no more reason to indulge than the passion of any other creature. Insofar as we are rational, we must adopt a wholly impersonal attitude towards our own wants and passive emotions; and in taking up that stance, we shall be detaching ourselves from them – we shall no more suffer them than we would suffer the passions of another individual. This seems to me impossible as a construal of Spinoza's remarks at *E* V, 3 and *E* V, 18CS; but it may describe a view he would endorse on other grounds. If so, there are at least two problems in it. First, is it so obvious that I cannot give 'because it is mine' as a reason for preferring something? Is love for a soccer team, a college, a country, a nation, simply *because it is one's own*, necessarily to be accounted a form of irrationality? Hirschman has argued interestingly that at least some such loyalties are 'most functional' when in fact they *look* 'most irrational'. Loyalty to a small group for which close 'substitutes' are readily available – his example is a football club – may create an 'exit barrier', and help prevent the large-scale deterioration in the group's performance which might follow if small-scale deterioration sent members scurrying to the alternative (*Hirschman* (2), p. 81). Second, it is not at all obvious that the adoption of an impersonal standpoint will in fact eliminate the affects. Even if I regard my own hunger impersonally, and concede that there is no more justification to ease it rather than the hunger of any other, the hunger will remain with me: fine philosophy does not fill a belly. The craving for food, even if it 'is no more to *reason* in us', is not therefore 'no more to *us*'. What is true of bodily sensation seems to be true of emotions as well: even if I agree that, from an absolute standpoint, my own survival matters no more than that of any other, my fears for myself may continue unabated. The 'remedy' which Caird thinks Spinoza to be recommending is no more efficacious than the 'remedy' we have already criticised.

(ii) Spinoza's second nostrum for the passions involves correcting certain common beliefs about causality. He reminds us that he has already proved that 'the affect towards an object which we imagine to be free is greater than towards one which is necessary', and that 'to imagine an object as free can be nothing else than to imagine it *simpliciter*, while we do not know the causes by which it was determined to action' (*E* V, 5D). But when we realise that agents, including human ones, are not free and undetermined, but are necessitated to behave as they do, then our reactions towards them must alter – we can no longer see them as proper objects of hatred, resentment, gratitude, or many other attitudes and emotions. (For more on this, *vide* VIII, 2 *infra*.) To the extent to which we can come to understand all things as necessary outcomes of causes, we shall have a greater power over the affects, and suffer less from them (*E* V, 6). Experience itself, Spinoza claims, testifies to this metaphysical truth: we observe that a man's sorrow over the loss of some good is mitigated when he realises that the loss was inevitable, or again we see that no-one pities an infant child because, as is unavoidable, it does not know how to speak, walk or reason (*E* V, 6S). (He does not consider it possible that one might, like Hardy or Housman, damn the scheme of things entire, even while believing that it unfolded in a necessary pattern.) Furthermore, Spinoza notes that, far from having a *single* cause, the events which happen in Nature have a multitude of causes, and result from the concurrent operation of many factors at the same time, as from a chain of causes stretching backwards indefinitely in the past. 'That affect by which the mind is determined to the contemplation of a number of objects at the same time is less injurious than another equally great affect which holds the mind in the sole contemplation of one or a few objects' (*E* V, 9D). In coming to view someone, therefore, not as *the* cause of some good or evil, but merely as *a* cause of it, we will no longer be able to react towards him with the same uninformed and violent passions (*cp*. VIII, 2).

Spinoza's view may be elucidated by comparison with that of a more recent moralist, writing on the subject of remorse. In her essay 'Pleasure and Happiness', Jean Austin says:

> We all make mistakes and we most of us do things we know we ought not to have done. It is laudable to feel distress at the consequences of such acts, but wrongly egocentric to dwell upon the fact it should be *oneself* who was responsible for these. The disaster, if it was one, must be *regretted in itself*, but *remorse*, though it may function as a useful deterrent to future wrong doing, contains an element of self-indulgence that if

again one can sufficiently objectify, one can to that extent rightly diminish. (*Austin*, p. 249)

Spinoza would certainly disagree that it was ever laudable to feel distress at the consequences of one's mistakes, but he would concur that it was bad to 'dwell on' one's responsibility for them. On the other hand, his reason for thinking it bad seems to be subtly different from Austin's: it is not so much that that reaction involves 'self-indulgence' or 'wrongful egocentricity', as that it implies treating oneself as a *free* cause, and perhaps *the main* cause, of what has ensued. (Of course, such a false estimate of oneself may reflect, and contribute to, wrongful egocentricity.) The thought I must put to myself in overcoming remorse is not so much 'It does not matter that these things have come about through *me*' as '*I* did not matter in the coming about of these things' (*vide* VIII, 2). But both in Spinoza and in Austin, the obtrusive thought of the self nourishes the emotion of remorse; and to the extent that that thought recedes, the emotion is weakened.

(iii) Spinoza's first two methods for dissipating the passions are closely related to a third. According to him, clear and distinct ideas, and so the active emotions allied to them, have a tendency to propagate themselves, and hence to 'crowd out' the passions (*cf. Joachim* (2), p. 287). But, he claims, we can always form clear and distinct ideas of the affections of the body (*E* V, 4), and by extension of the passions of which they are the physical expressions. These clear and distinct ideas will give rise to certain affects in the mind, which will themselves be clear and distinct ideas (*E* V, 4S); and the mind will take pleasure in this development of its power, which will in turn lead it to form still other clear ideas, and so to enlarge its power further still. This right ordering of ideas in the mind is, so to say, a natural tendency, which the mind will follow unless impeded by external obstacles; and in following it, it will necessarily dispose the affections of the body in a sane and proper order (*E* V, 10D).

(iv) Our knowledge of our appetites and emotions, as it is enlarged, can alter them in yet another way. Consider the passion of ambition, which is a perverted form of the desire that other men should live conformably to our own way of thinking (*E* V, 4S; *E* III, 31C). This desire is inherent in all of us, since it follows from the workings of the Law of the Imitation of the Emotions. In its irrational form, this desire to akin to pride, and causes contention among men; but if a man lives according to the dictates of reason, and has seen that the best and surest way to win over his fellows is by love and generosity (*E* IV, Appendix xi), then that same desire is an active emotion, which is called Piety (*E* III, 37, D2, and S1; *E* V, 4CS). The remedy which transforms a passive emotion into an active one by means of this sort of knowledge is, Spinoza says, the most excellent which lies in our power (*E* V, 4CS).

(v) Fifth, Spinoza asserts that 'the affects which spring from reason or which are excited by it, if time be taken into account, are more powerful than those which are related to individual objects which we contemplate as absent' (*E* V, 7). That is, the intellectual emotion which arises, say, from contemplating the beauty of a proof in mathematics or philosophy, while less intense than a passive emotion such as longing, will prove in the long run to outlast it, and to exert a greater influence over the mind. For unless the external cause of a passive emotion be actually present, the emotion will tend to fade; but an intellectual emotion can always be revived, since nothing can exist which excludes the present existence of its causes. Hence the intellectual emotions will fortify us against the passions, and the passions will gradually be forced to accommodate themselves to these steadier and more permanent feelings (*E* V, 7D; *Broad* (2), p. 33).

(vi) Spinoza also takes note of 'the multitude of causes by which the affections which are related to the common properties of things or to God are nourished' (*E* V, 20S). What he means, I think, is this: whatever objects the mind may think of, it can relate either to universal and necessary laws, or to God. If it thinks, say, of some episode which has caused remorse or grief, it can view that event as an instance of such laws, or as an effect of the Divine nature. In taking that view, it will evoke in itself the active emotions which are bound up with the contemplation of scientific and philosophical truth. Hence we can always summon up the active emotions, and deploy them to combat feelings like remorse or grief.

(vii) Seventh and last, Spinoza proposes a remedy which is homespun and commonplace, but no less effective for that. It is offered as an antidote which can be used even before we have acquired a perfect knowledge of the emotions. It is 'to conceive a right rule of life, or sure maxims of life, – to commit these latter to memory, and constantly to apply them to the particular cases which frequently meet us in life, so that our imagination may be widely affected by them, and they may always be ready to hand'. Consider, he says, the precept that hatred is to be conquered by love or generosity, and not repaid by hatred. 'In order that we may always have this precept of reason in readiness whenever it will be of service, we must think over and often meditate upon the common injuries inflicted by men, and consider how and in what way they may best be repelled by generosity; for thus we shall connect the image of injury with the imagination of this maxim, and it will be at hand whenever an injury is offered to us' (*E* V, 10S). He might well have added that a constant re-reading of the demonstration in his *Ethics*, which purports to prove that hatred can never be good (*E* IV, 45), would perhaps do more to fix the precept in our minds, and to convince us of its truth, than merely taking it as a rule of thumb, and reciting it over and again to ourselves.

Concluding observations

A word now in retrospect. Spinoza's theory of the passions, and his strategy for conquering them, comprise a remarkable achievement, meriting the praises which have been lavished upon them. In my account, I have tried to bring some of their inadequacies into sharper relief, and I have stressed his indebtedness to Descartes; but I do not mean to tarnish either his accomplishment or his originality.

Spinoza has seized, perhaps more clearly than any philosopher since, the horror and futility of the passive emotions, and the urgency of guarding ourselves against them. He recognised that they are frequently distressing and devitalising in themselves; that they set men at odds with each other; that they threaten the unity and integrity of the individual soul; that they encourage a lopsided, and hence unhappy, personal development. But chiefly he deserves credit for observing their power to cloud our practical judgements, to cause us to put mistaken values on the things we want or loathe, to disregard or to miscalculate the consequences of our choices – in short, their power to cause us to make choices we later regret, or would regret with the benefit of fuller knowledge (on these matters, *cf. von Wright*, (2) p. 147, p. 150). It may be objected that in emphasising these points, he exaggerates, for it seems too extreme to say that *all* the passions are noxious, that they *must* have detrimental influences, that they can *never* be useful to us. (Is not fear, for instance, helpful, in that it induces us to take precautions when otherwise we might court disaster (*von Wright*, (2) p. 150)?) But even to this Spinoza has an answer: to all the actions to which we are determined by a passion, we may be determined, without the passion, by reason and the active emotions (*E* IV, 59; *cf. Neu* p. 98). Perhaps that answer is not adequate or consistent; certainly Spinoza has impressed some of his readers as oscillating between the advocacy of a life governed by calm and steady emotions, and a life which is God-like in its freedom from *all* the affects save intellectual love (*Neu,* p. 81). I shall return to some of these topics in the next chapter; but for now, it is right to salute Spinoza's permanent contribution to our understanding.

VIII

Freedom and Reason

Part IV of the *Ethics* presents a picture of the life of the Spinozist sage, the 'free man'. The character Spinoza portrays is 'free' both in that he has overcome his passions so far as may be (*E* IV, 1S) and in that his actions are to the greatest possible extent self-determined. The picture we are given is as beautiful and as impressive as anything of its kind in philosophy; it can be compared with Aristotle's study of the 'great-souled man', which it seems intended to rival (*Nicomachean Ethics*, IV, Section 3). For Spinoza, the idea of freedom is indissolubly linked with that of Reason: the free man is led by Reason (*E* IV, 73) and lives by its dictates (*E* IV, 67). The present chapter explores Spinoza's handling of these ideas.

1 Liberation through knowledge

If one had to distinguish what is living and what is dead in Spinozism, then undoubtedly one would find that the most vital part of his philosophy among us is the thesis that Reason – or more exactly, knowledge – liberates. But it has not always been noticed that this thesis, as Spinoza explains it, harbours an inner tension. The Stoics had taught that men were like dogs tied to a cart: they will be dragged along willy-nilly; but if they *consent* to being dragged, then they are free. This Stoical view is uppermost in Spinoza's thought when he seems to equate freedom with acquiescence in a world-order we have come to understand: the free man, being led by Reason, will accordingly contemplate all things as necessary (*E* II, 44), and so be reconciled to his fate, recognising that it flows from the eternal decree of God (*E* II, 49); indeed, he will actively desire that things should be as they are (*E* IV, Appendix, xxxii; *cf. Strauss*, pp. 210–11). Thus it happens that the more one knows by Reason, the less one dreads death, and the more reconciled to it one becomes (*E* V, 38).

Now this Stoical tendency in Spinoza is counteracted by another one, which perhaps holds more interest for *us*. On this other view, knowledge brings freedom, not because it *reconciles* us to our fates, but because it empowers us to *shape* them (*cf.* VII, 9). No student of Spinoza has done more to illuminate this area of his thinking than Sir Isaiah Berlin; and the right starting point for our inquiry into it is Berlin's eloquent essay, 'From Hope and Fear set Free'.

Berlin points out that the slogan, 'Knowledge always liberates', is not very helpful. One might try to improve on it by saying 'Knowledge never impedes, always increases, the sum total of human freedom' (*Berlin*, p. 195), but even that slogan veers off into unintelligibility. For how are amounts of freedom to be computed? If attending a university will permit me to become a barrister but prevent me from becoming a ballet dancer, is my overall freedom greater, less or the same? Berlin waives that difficulty, however, in order to press another: there seem to be cases in which acquiring greater knowledge will *deprive* one of the power, or the freedom, to do what one previously was able to do. 'If I am a singer', he says, 'self-consciousness, the child of knowledge, may inhibit the spontaneity that may be a necessary condition of my performance'. Or again, a creative writer may refuse to subject herself to psychoanalysis, fearing that the sources of her imaginative powers will evaporate if exposed to the dry light of self-knowledge. 'One door opens', as Berlin puts it, 'and as a result of this another shuts.'

Faced with this difficulty, the defender of the thesis may give way a little. He may maintain that whilst an accession of knowledge may diminish freedom in one respect, it will necessarily also add to it in another, yielding a net gain. Or, admitting that we cannot intelligibly speak of 'sum totals' of freedom, he may say that whenever knowledge involves the loss of some freedom, it also carries with it a freedom which is more valuable. But this again is dubious. Would a novelist forego the capacity to imagine, in return for the self-knowledge which relieved a minor facial tic? Knowledge might reduce someone to utter paralysis of the will, robbing him of the freedom to perform the most simple routines: if I learn that an only child has died in a motor accident, I may simply be unable to 'cope'. By no reckoning will that knowledge make me freer or more powerful.

Despite these difficulties, Berlin claims to discern a truth, or rather a modest truism, hidden within the thesis. There is, he says, 'a clear but platitudinous sense in which all knowledge increases freedom in some respect: if I know that I am liable to epileptic fits, or feelings of class-consciousness, or the spellbinding effects of certain kinds of music, I can – in some sense of "can" – plan my life accordingly; whereas if I do not know this, I cannot do so; I gain some increase in power and, to that extent, in freedom' (pp. 175–6). In other words, I take it, if I know that I am liable to some condition, or prone to some pattern of behaviour, then the bare possession of that knowledge will put me in a position to try to change myself, if I should think change desirable; whereas without that knowledge, I would not be in a position to instigate a change. In this (thin) sense of 'can', I can do something about the way I am if I know how I am, and cannot do anything if I do not know. But, as Berlin points out, this gain in freedom and in power necessarily consequent upon a gain in self-knowledge may be offset by a loss of freedom in other spheres. If I recognise the signs of an imminent epileptic fit, then while I can now try to prepare myself for it, I may be quite unable to continue to write about Spinoza, to enjoy a recording of *Parsifal*, or to contemplate the jacarandas through my window.

More importantly, Berlin observes that whilst my increased knowledge puts me in a position to try to affect my conduct, I may still not be able to exploit that position, i.e. to give effect to the changes I desire to make in it, to shape or control it as I would wish. Knowing myself subject to epileptic fits, I may still be unable to avoid them; knowing that I am easily embarrassed, I may continue to blush frequently; knowing that I am class-conscious, I may remain unable to react to a certain accent with anything other than distaste. I may be aware, not only of my tendency to act or react in these ways, but also of the causes of that tendency; I may strongly desire not to behave in such a manner; and yet the coupling of knowledge with desire may not be able to eradicate, or even to modify, the pattern of my conduct. Although I may be said to be in a position to control myself, or at any rate to attempt to do so, it is true in a deeper and more interesting sense that I cannot help but do what I am prone to do.

When he turns to criticism specifically of Spinoza, Berlin wants both to unearth the (implausible) assumption which lies beneath the thesis, and to expose its (unacceptable) divergence from the common moral outlook. On Spinoza's theory, Berlin says, an agent's freedom 'consists in the fact that he will not be acted upon by causes whose existence he does not know or the nature of whose influences he does not understand. But that is all. Given Spinoza's premises . . . the notion of choice turns out to depend on the deficiencies of knowledge, the degree of ignorance. There is only one correct answer to any problem of conduct, as to any problem of theory. The correct answer having been discovered, the rational man logically cannot but act in accordance with it: the notion of free choice between alternatives no longer has application' (p. 185).

This formulation is not entirely happy. In saying that 'the notion of choice depends on the deficiencies of knowledge', Berlin may be taking Spinoza to hold either (a) that he would not have the experience which we characterise as a 'free choice' unless we were ignorant in such situations of the 'correct answer' to our practical problem, or (b) that we would not impute 'free choice' to ourselves unless we were ignorant of the causes which determined our action. Both of these theses seem to be Spinozistic (*cf. TP* II, Section 1, *Wernham* pp. 272–3, which lends colour to the first of these claims, and *E* II, 34S, which affirms the second.) But Berlin's words also carry a hint of the idea (c) that we never actually chose between alternatives at all, but merely seem to do so; and it is gratuitous to assign this bizarre claim to Spinoza.

Berlin maintains that it is only on a special understanding of 'freedom' that the thesis 'Knowledge always liberates' appears to follow. 'It is this conception that underlies the notion that an increase in knowledge is *eo ipso* always an increase in freedom, i.e. an escape from being at the mercy of what is not understood. Once something is understood or known (and only then), it is, on this view, conceptually impossible to describe oneself as being at the mercy of it. Unless this maximalist assumption is made, it does not seem to me to follow that more knowledge necessarily entails an increase in the total sum of freedom' (*ibid.*). Berlin, if I have understood him, interprets Spinoza to have held (i) that every practical problem has a uniquely correct solution; (ii) that a response to the problem is free only if it embodies that solution; and (iii) that the correct response will occur only if it is brought about by the agent's knowledge of his own nature, power and requirements, of the situation in which he acts, and of the causal order of the world. And in taking issue with Spinoza, Berlin focuses the disagreement on step (ii), which incorporates the special concept of freedom on which the 'Knowledge always liberates' thesis relies.

Berlin wants to snap the link which this reasoning fastens between freedom and knowledge. He argues that if one's perception of the 'correct' solution to his problem imposes a certain response, or drives one ineluctably to a certain action, then it is wrong to say that that action is chosen freely. The choice is a free one only if another alternative, however irrational, remains within the agent's power: if I am forced to choose an action as I may be forced to accept a mathematical deduction, then the eventual decision was in no sense freely made. 'Knowledge will only render us freer, if in fact there is freedom of choice . . . if I have no freedom to begin with, knowledge will not increase it' (p. 184).

The argument which Berlin attributes to Spinoza is vulnerable at more than one place. A difficulty in the premiss (i) that every practical problem has a unique solution, is acknowledged by Spinoza himself at *E* II, 49S, which discusses the 'ass of Buridanus' (*vide* II, 2, *supra*). That case is scarcely exceptional; it stands in for countless others. (What, e.g., is *the* correct opening move in any given game of chess?) Spinoza's answer to these questions – that no choice would be made at all – is unsatisfactory, as he almost seems to recognise. But to concede that a choice would occur in the absence of a controlling reason (or, in physical terms, that a body should move without the action of an external force) would be to admit the existence of a will capable of inducing bodily motions. This, of course Spinoza cannot do. Berlin in effect wants to drive Spinoza into the same predicament as this; but he comes at him from a different direction, which goes by way of (ii).

In rejecting the 'special' Spinozist notion of freedom, Berlin claims to side with ordinary opinion. On the common view, he assumes, it can happen that the necessary conditions both of my Φing and of my not-Φing are present, and yet that neither outcome is wholly determined by antecedent circumstances. Only if the outcome is partly undetermined will the agent have the free choice whether to Φ or not. Hence in particular, only if the agent is not determined by his own adequate ideas and active emotions will he be choosing freely.

What is at stake in the contest between this concept of freedom, and the concept explained by Spinoza? According to Berlin, if we accept the truth of determinism, we must abandon the common understanding of freedom; and the consequences for our conceptual framework and form of life would be momentous. 'It would alter our conceptual framework far more radically than the discoveries of the physicists of the seventeenth or twentieth century, or of the biologists of the nineteenth, have changed it . . . The entire vocabulary of human relations would suffer radical change . . . The entire language of the criticism and assessment of one's own and others' conduct, would undergo a sharp transformation' (pp. 188–9). Of course this is not to say, nor does Berlin think it follows, that determinism is false. If so radical – and impoverishing – a change in our self-understanding is conceivable, then we must reckon on the possibility that the advance of knowledge will cause it to happen. But it may be doubted whether determinism *does* demand such changes in attitude, and whether, if it does, it is really thinkable that they should occur. The Libertarian, epitomised by Berlin, denies that we can rationally continue to assess and react to each other in many of the ways we currently do, if once we admit that human behaviour is the effect of causes. In his celebrated lecture 'Freedom and Resentment', Sir Peter Strawson disputes this pessimistic conclusion, and takes a line midway between Berlin and Spinoza. Strawson's claims bear directly on some of the most fundamental issues in Spinozism, and we do well to consider them in some detail.

2 *Freedom and resentment*

Central to Strawson's position is a distinction between 'objective' and 'reactive' attitudes to other persons. He notes 'the very great importance we attach to the attitudes and intentions towards us of other human beings, and the great extent to which our personal feeling and reactions depend upon, or involve, our beliefs about these attitudes and intentions' (*Strawson*, p. 5). If, for instance, someone treads painfully on my hand, it will generally make a difference to my reaction whether I believe him to have acted negligently or malevolently, or with the intention of showing good will. 'Even a dog distinguishes between being stumbled over and being kicked' (*Holmes*, p. 7). Where our natural reactions to others depend upon the good will, ill will or indifference we take them to display in *their* actions and attitudes, Strawson proposes to speak of the 'reactive attitudes'. They include resentment, gratitude, forgiveness, anger and certain forms of reciprocal love (*Strawson*, p. 9). Broadly, he divides them into two sorts: 'personal' or 'participant' reactive attitudes, and 'generalised' or 'vicarious' reactive attitudes. Where a reactive attitude is personal, it rests on, and reflects, a demand that one's own interest be considered, or at least not injured, by others; where it is vicarious, the same demand is present in a generalised form (pp. 14–15); it is of course possible to react disinterestedly to an injury done to, or benefit conferred on, oneself. Further, 'just as there are personal and vicarious reactive attitudes associated with demands on others for oneself and demands on others for others, so there are self-reactive attitudes associated with demands on oneself for others', such as feelings of compunction, guilt, remorse or shame (p. 15). Contrasted with all of these are the 'objective attitudes'. 'To adopt the objective attitude to another human being is to see him, perhaps, as an object of social policy; as a subject for what . . . might be called treatment; as something certainly to be taken account, perhaps precautionary account, of; to be managed or handled or cured or trained . . . The objective attitude may be emotionally toned in many ways, but not in all ways; it may include repulsion or fear, it may include pity or even love, though not all kinds of love. But it cannot include the range of reactive attitudes which belong to involvement or participation with others in inter-personal human relationships' (p. 9).

It is apparent that the objective and the reactive attitudes, while not exclusive of each other, are *opposed* to each other (p. 9). No doubt we can switch from one to the other, even with respect to the same action of the same person; but it seems impossible at once, e.g., to *resent* someone's conduct, or to feel *indignation* at it, and yet to regard it as calling for a *cure*. Strawson does not do much to explain the sources of this opposition; but Jonathan Bennett, in developing Strawson's work, suggests two possible explanations for it. First, Bennett says, 'viewing someone as a natural object involves seeing him as an analysed complex, whereas taking a reactive attitude to him seems to involve seeing him as a unitary whole' (*Bennett* (2), p. 207). I take it that Bennett means that 'objective' attitudes involve seeing another person as a node in the causal order, an item which other things work *through*. Viewed in this light, a man's behaviour will be seen as the outcome of the workings of circumstance upon character, exactly as the behaviour of a piece of iron or copper is to be explained in terms of its internal structure and of the external influences which act upon it. An intelligent agent, regarded in this manner, can be said to 'act' only in sense or way in which an inanimate substance 'acts'. Bennett's second explanation of the opposition is less satisfactory. He says, 'One's reactive attitudes, I suggest, refer essentially to oneself . . . If I resent or am grateful for what you did, I have a picture in which *I* loom very large; whereas if my attitude to your action is an objective one, my picture of the situation will not be dominated by myself, except perhaps in the role – which is only accidentally *mine* – of someone to whom you relate in such and such ways' (pp. 207–8).

But this is to overlook the *vicarious* reactive attitudes, which do not refer essentially to the person who feels them.

Strawson's distinction figures importantly in his effort to resolve the apparent conflict between determinism and morality. In his view, the resistance to the project of reconciling determinism with our present vocabulary and practice arises in the following way.

> When [the pessimist's] opponent . . . undertakes to show that the truth of determinism would not shake the foundation of the concept of moral responsibility and of the practices of moral condemnation and punishment, he typically refers . . . to the efficacy of these practices in regulating behaviour in socially desirable ways. These practices are represented solely as instruments of policy, as methods of individual treatment and social control. . . . The picture painted by the optimists (i.e. those who advocate the reconciling project) is painted in a style appropriate to a situation envisaged as wholly dominated by objectivity of attitude . . . But a thoroughgoing objectivity of attitude, excluding as it does the moral reactive attitudes, excludes at the same time essential elements in the concepts of *moral* condemnation and *moral* responsibility. This is the reason for the conceptual shock. The deeper emotional shock is a reaction, not simply to inadequate conceptual analysis, but to the suggestion of a change in our world. (pp. 20–1)

The pessimist's reaction is partly right, but more profoundly mistaken. He is right to say that there is more in our practice of punishment and reward than manipulation, treatment and control. He may be right in thinking that the disappearance of the reactive attitudes, and the substitution for them of a consistently objective attitude, would be a deplorable and dehumanising loss. But his panic at the prospect of such a loss, his fear that determinism will entail it, and his clutching at the talisman of 'contra-causal' freedom are, Strawson thinks, wholly groundless.

First of all, it is simply untrue that when we set aside our reactive attitudes in particular cases, and view ourselves and others in an 'objective' light, we do so out of a conviction that determinism is the truth. Our reasons in such cases, though multifarious, are of a much more specialised, less abstract and philosophical, character. We inhibit resentment, say, and adopt an attitude of detached curiosity, because we believe that the potential agent did not understand the nature of his act, or was out of character, or (more radically) because we cannot explain his conduct in terms of his conscious purposes, or regard his conception of the world as an insane delusion, or find him lacking in a moral sense. None of these reasons for the switch from a reactive to an objective attitude can be presented as a consequence or corollary of determinism (p. 18).

Second, 'we cannot take seriously the thought that theoretical conviction of such a general thesis would lead to the total decay of the . . . reactive attitudes' (p. 18). Our commitment to personal relationships of a sort to which these attitudes are indispensable is 'part of the general framework of human life, not something that can come up for review as particular cases can come up for review within this general framework' (p. 13). The (optimist's) suggestions that objective attitudes do, or should, dominate our personal relationships, and the (pessimist's) fear that this might come to happen, are alike illusory.

Third, to the question whether it is *rational*, given an acceptance of determinism, not to suspend the reactive attitudes altogether, Strawson's answer is: 'it is *useless* to ask whether it would not be rational for us to do what it is not in our nature to (be able to) do' (p. 18). Being as we are, we cannot give up the framework in which these attitudes feature, any more than we can abandon the 'original, natural, non-rational (but not irrational)' tendency to form inductively-based beliefs (p. 23, note).

Fourth and finally, the attempt to supply a metaphysical justification of this framework, like the effort to justify the practice of induction, meets with inevitable failure. Challenged to produce the justification, the Libertarian 'finds it as difficult to state coherently and with intelligible relevance as its determinist contradictory. Even when a formula has been found ("contra-causal" freedom or something of the kind) there still seems to remain a gap between its applicability in particular cases and its supposed moral consequences' (p. 24). 'Why does freedom in this sense justify blame?' (p. 4).

In all of this, Strawson's opposition to a Libertarian view of the type espoused by Berlin is very evident. Berlin writes as though he finds a certain (allegedly metaphysical) notion of freedom wholly intelligible, and links the ideas of praise and blame firmly to it. Further, he seems to think that we have an option whether to retain or to give up our existing moral attitudes; and he appears to believe that it would be rational to alter them radically if determinism were proved to be true. Spinoza's view partly accords with Strawson's, and partly with Berlin's. Like Strawson, Spinoza finds the idea of 'contra-causal freedom' to be false, perhaps unintelligible. But unlike Strawson, and like Berlin, he thinks that our ordinary views of accountability are bound up with that notion; and he considers that it is both possible and rational systematically to root out the reactive attitudes, certainly in our personal lives, and conceivably in our general culture. In maintaining that a *rational* man would be free from the reactive attitudes, Spinoza is guilty – or so Bennett claims – of a mistake. Let us look at the charge.

According to Bennett, 'the policy (of eschewing reactive attitudes altogether) has been urged. Spinoza held a view which could be expressed in the form: "Because the facts always permit the teleological, objective attitude, they always forbid reactive attitudes". Strawson's work . . . enables us to explain Spinoza's mistake' (*Bennett* (2), p. 207). The particular point in Strawson's work which Bennett thinks relevant is the claim that reactive attitudes and the objective attitude oppose each other. '[R]eactive and objective attitudes do conflict psychologically, and that fact has explanatory value. Presumably, Spinoza noticed that a clear view of X as a natural object or event would not cohabit in his mind with a reactive attitude towards X, and he wrongly thought that this was a propositional conflict; from which he inferred that because everything is a natural object or event, reactive attitudes are infected with falsity. He was helped in this direction by the fact that instead of "reactive attitudes" he spoke instead of "freedom" and of "blame" ' (p. 208).

If Spinoza has made a mistake here, it is not, I think, the one which Bennett imputes to him. As Bennett clearly explains, reactive attitudes do embody propositional contents: if I resent X, say, then I must believe that X has somehow manifested ill-will, or at best indifference, to me, or that he has intentionally tried to injure or insult me in some way. Now Spinoza would claim, I think, that the reactive attitudes typically, and perhaps always, encapsulated beliefs which were inadequate ideas. For example, in resenting X's conduct towards me, I may believe him to be *the* cause of some injury. I thus overlook the fact that many causes combined together to produce this effect, and the fact that X's role is played out within an infinite sequence of past causes, the earlier items in which irreversibly fixed the outcome which absorbs me. Or again, in feeling anger with X, I assume 'He could have helped himself', neglecting to consider that in the sense I think this true, it is false. Spinoza is not, *pace* Bennett, misled by speaking of 'freedom' here; he speaks of freedom because, as he sees it, the reactive attitudes presuppose that we are free. In general, Spinoza would surely claim that the reactive attitudes, insofar as they involve seeing people as 'unitary wholes', necessarily impose a false view upon us. To see X as a unitary whole is, I suggest, to see him as a sovereign and self-determining will; whereas to see him as an 'analysable complex' is to see him as a natural object whose behaviour, like that of inanimate agents, is a function purely of his inner constitution and external surroundings. If this is right, then Spinoza did *not* confuse a psychological conflict with a logical inconsistency. His error – if it *is* an error – was to suppose that the reactive attitudes incorporated beliefs which were metaphysically false. He did not reason: 'Because the facts always *permit* the teleological, objective attitudes, they always forbid the reactive ones', but: 'Because the facts always *demand* the objective attitudes, they always forbid the reactive ones'. The objective attitude, to men as to other objects in Nature, is the uniquely correct one: it is as fatuous to be angry with a clumsy man as with a tile that has fallen from its place (*E* I, Appendix). Towards all natural objects, our concern should be partly contemplative, partly practical: we should delight in the knowledge of their nature and properties and, possessed of such knowledge, control and manipulate them for our wisest ends. To engage with them in hate or anger, fear or pity, love or resentment, is to remain ensnared by the imagination, and all the delusions it casts up. These imaginative delusions may be articulated and systematised by the Libertarian metaphysician, but they are found, in an implicit form, in our uncorrected thoughts and reactions: 'contra-causal' freedom is not an invention of the philosopher, but the creation of the plain man. It is, for all that, a phantasm. 'Personality is an illusion to be accepted on weekdays for working purposes. We are cosmic ganglia' (Holmes, quoted in *Noonan*, p. 106).

Even apart from the falsity which he believes to infect the reactive attitudes, Spinoza thinks that it would be rational to eschew them. Suppose 'the possibility of a godlike choice' were offered to us, so that we could decide whether or not to purge ourselves of the reactive attitudes. (The description of the choice is Strawson's: p. 18. Spinoza, of course, considers the choice to be – limitedly – a *human* possibility.) Would it be rational to choose to be without them? Strawson touches briefly on the question: 'Quite apart from the issue of determinism might it not be said that we should be nearer to being purely rational creatures in proportion as our relation to others was in fact dominated by the objective attitude? I think this might be said; only it would have to be added, once more, that if such a choice were possible, it would not necessarily be rational to choose to be more rational than we are' (p. 13, note). Why not? The answer is as much for the literary artist as for the philosopher to give: where we are offered pictures of the forms of life of such unmitigatedly rational, manipulative, cold-blooded creatures, void alike of love and hate, we recoil from them. (Think of Swift's Houyhnhnms.) But Spinoza holds up the model of such a society as a humanly ideal one. The reactive attitudes are, in his view, characteristically harmful, distracting, devitalising, wasteful. It is no more self-interestedly rational to prefer a life which contains them over one which does not, than it would be to prefer a life troubled by fever or chills to one without them.

Love

Consider here Spinoza's treatment of love, a passion which he one-sidedly studies only in its morbid forms, and which he nearly always condemns. Speaking of the pursuit of riches, fame and sensual pleasure (the only kind of love he recognises, apart from the intellectual love of God), Spinoza writes: 'there are innumerable cases of men, who have hastened their death through over-indulgences in sensual pleasure. All these evils seem to have arisen from the fact that happiness or unhappiness is made wholly to depend on the quality of the object we love. When a thing is not loved, no quarrels will arise concerning it – no sadness will be felt if it perishes – no envy if it is possessed by another – no fear, no hatred, in short no disturbances of the mind. All these arise from the love of what is perishable . . . But love towards a thing eternal and infinite feeds the mind wholly with joy, and is itself unmingled with any sadness, wherefore it is greatly to be desired and sought for with all our strength' (*DIE*, G II, p. 7).

No positive value is found in purely human love and affection; no difference noted between 'sensual pleasure' and the emotions which may grow out of it. Spinoza can see only what is debilitating, distressing, noxious in the passion; he does not consider that, with all the risk it involves, it is necessary to fullness and richness of life. Because he exaggerates the value of 'tranquillity of mind', making it alone the measure of what is good, he thinks it rational to exclude from life any of the elements which might jeopardise it (*cp.* von Dunin-Burkoski in *Strauss*, p. 211).

Since love is always liable to disturb our composure, creating as it does the possibility of grief and of loss (*E* V, 20S), Spinoza consistently repudiates it, holding it to have no place in the life led according to the dictates of Reason. His condemnations sound a note of anxiety, otherwise rare in his writing: 'We see men sometimes so affected by one object, that although it is not present, they believe it to be before them; and if this happens to a man who is not asleep, we say that he is delirious or mad. Nor are those believed to be less mad who are inflamed by love, dreaming about nothing but a mistress or harlot day and night, for they excite our laughter' (*E* III, 44S). 'The love of a harlot, that is to say, the love of sexual intercourse, which arises from beauty (*forma*), and in general all love which has any other cause than the freedom of the mind, easily passes into hate; unless – which is worse – it is a species of delirium, and then discord is cherished rather than concord' (*E* IV, c. 19). 'As for marriage, it is certain that it accords with Reason if the desire to mingle bodies is not engendered by beauty alone, but also by the love of begetting children and of educating them wisely; and if besides the love of each for the other (that is, of man and woman) does not have beauty alone as its cause, but chiefly freedom of mind' (*E* IV, c. 20; *cf.* also *E* V, 10S, with which should be compared La Rochefoucauld, *Maximes*, 1664 edition, n. 107).

There is surely something missing in this account of married love, which sees it as essentially a device for promoting intellectual development and for rearing children. Between this cool compact, and 'the love of a harlot', Spinoza discerns no varieties of relationship; or if he discerns them, he holds them to include harmful and irrational affectivity. Spinoza's fascination with the pathological forms of love, and his consequent inability to find a proper place for it in the scheme of human life, is a distortion which must have its cause in some private mischance; and yet it is merely an extreme, not the unique, instance of his condemnation of the reactive attitudes. The man who lives according to the dictates of Reason, he says, can 'hate no-one, be angry with no-one, can neither envy, nor be indignant with, nor despise anybody, and can least of all be proud' (*E* IV, 73S). These attitudes, or some of them, inherently involve a lessening of our vital power; and since it is the mark of rationality to try to extend our power as far as may be, we should strive to purge our minds of them.

Summary

The boldness, and the strangeness, of Spinoza's claim can scarcely be exaggerated; I know of no other great philosopher who has so forthrightly advocated that we recondition ourselves to think of one another without any shade of praise, blame, pride, shame, anger, envy, resentment, love, hatred, or indignation. It is an even stranger view than we might have expected it to be, since it is not accompanied by any cynical recommendations that we treat one another as things to be exploited or misused; on the contrary, Spinoza believes that a clear view of our own best interest will cause us to enlist the willing co-operation of others, and to show them all possible gentleness, honesty, and forms of respect. But is it a true view? The charges that the reactive attitudes are, by and large, irrational, is based on two grounds: first, that they import the false metaphysics of Libertarianism; and second, that they typically weaken and devitalise us, and constitute a threat to the overriding good of tranquillity of mind. The first reason, as we have seen, has been disputed; and I think that the dispute has not yet been conclusively settled. But the second reason seems to me uncompelling. It depends upon a particular psychology of the emotions of the type described in Part III of the *Ethics*, and it seems also to rest upon a scheme of values which is eccentric and unbalanced. Tranquillity of mind, blessedness, and intellectual love of God – these may be great goods, but they are neither the sole, nor perhaps even the supreme, goods. Lives in which they are found may be thin, impoverished and insipid in many other respects; lives in which they are rare may contain many compensating forms of value.

3 Virtue

The 'Life of Reason', as Spinoza describes it, has exercised a powerful fascination on many of his readers. The attractiveness of the ideal seems to lie chiefly in the fact that it embodies a paradox: it is a life which holds together both virtue and selfishness. The doctrine of egoism (*vide* VII, 4), though coupled with the adoption of an 'objective attitude' towards all others (VIII, 2), does not lead Spinoza to the conclusion that we ought to treat our fellows cynically and manipulatively – to see them as opportunities or obstacles only, which one should exploit when they are useful, guard against when they are harmful, and disregard when they are neither. On the contrary, he maintains, just as Kant did, that in transacting with another, I must not seek to treat him solely as a means, by taking him for 'a mere instrument of *my* will, without any regard to *his* rationality' (*MacIntyre* (2), p. 44). Only insofar as I try to influence another by offering reasons for him to accept or reject, and eschew all duress, bad faith, or irrational suasion, will *my own* best interests, rightly conceived, be forwarded. The 'paradox' purports to represent the solution to a problem which has beset philosophers from Plato onwards (*Republic* 360bc). And yet one wonders: can so fine a flower spring from such arid soil? The argument of this section is that the ideal seems tenable only because Spinoza implicitly identifies the *man* with the *intellect*.

Spinoza tells us that 'according to the laws of his own nature each person necessarily desires that which he considers to be good, and avoids that which he considers to be evil' (*E* IV, 19). This remark gives rise to certain problems. One problem is that it seems to suggest that our desires are formed by our view of the goodness or badness of things, whereas Spinoza asserts that it is our desires which form our views (*E* III, 9S). I have already tried to deal with this difficulty, suggesting that Spinoza is not really inconsistent (*cf.* VII, 5). A second problem is this: Spinoza defines *good* as 'what we certainly know to be useful to us', and *evil* as 'what we certainly know hinders us from possessing anything that is good' (*E* IV, Definitions I and II). From these definitions, in combination with the theorem at *E* IV, 19, it will plainly follow that every man desires what he knows to be useful to him, and will avoid what he knows to be hindering. And by speaking of what is 'useful' or 'hindering', Spinoza seems to mean 'what is useful to promoting our own life and power, or what hinders our efforts to promote that end'. Now this suggests that Spinoza's man will have only the very limited goal of living, or of living healthily and pleasantly. And in fact there are certain passages which might seem to support that view. At *E* IV, 24, for instance, Spinoza describes 'acting absolutely in conformity with virtue' as 'nothing but acting, living, and preserving our being (these three things have the same meaning) as Reason directs, from the ground of seeking our own profit'. If the *free* man perfectly embodies the life of virtue, then all his actions must be directed to these ends – which seem to comprise a paltry ideal.

Other statements of Spinoza's, however, contradict this notion forcibly. Thus at *E* IV, 72, he tries to prove that a free man never ('*nunquam*') practices fraud, but always acts honourably ('*cum fide*'); and in the scholium which is attached to this proposition, he makes it clear that the free man will not use deceit even if his life depends upon it. (The argument which Spinoza gives is rather Kantian: the free man must obey the counsels of Reason, which are the same for all men; and Reason could not consistently counsel all men to exempt themselves from the common law against deceit if their lives could only be saved by a fraud.) Again, at *E* IV, 26, Spinoza contends that 'the mind, insofar as it uses reason, judges nothing to be profitable to itself excepting that which conduces to understanding'. This proposition is echoed at *E* V 9D: 'An affect is bad or injurious only insofar as it hinders

FREEDOM AND REASON

the mind from thinking'. Finally, at *E* IV, 28, he writes, 'The highest good of the mind is the knowledge of God, and the highest virtue of the mind is to know God'. In short, Spinoza takes rational egoism as the source of virtue, endorses its directives, and sets up the self-interested life as a goal; but he also maintains that the exercise of mental power, especially in the intellectual love of God (which is science and metaphysics), is the highest human virtue; and he demands that the virtuous man should be willing to lose his life rather than to tell a lie. From postulating an instinct for self-preservation, he has derived an ideal of truthfulness, disinterested inquiry, and self-sacrifice.

The result can only be explained, I think, on the assumption that Spinoza implicitly *identified* human beings with their minds, or more precisely with part of their minds, the intellect. On the assumption of their identity, and not otherwise, it makes sense to suppose that the good for man consists in what is good for the intellect, i.e. in thinking both wisely and efficiently (*cp. Nicomachean Ethics*, 1178a 1–8). Hence we find Spinoza saying that 'we know nothing certainly to be good or evil, save such things as really conduce to understanding, or such as are able to hinder us from understanding' (*E* IV, 27). Spinoza's view has been described as 'the complete intellectualisation of virtue'; but it is that only because it proceeds from 'the complete intellectualisation of man'.

Spinoza's adherence to the primacy of the intellect comes out in his discussion of sensuous and aesthetic values, i.e. values connected with the imagination. In a famous passage, he writes:

> It is the part of a wise man, I say, to refresh and invigorate himself with moderate and pleasant eating and drinking, with sweet scents and the beauty of green plants, with ornament, with music, with sports, with the theatre, and with all things of this kind which one man can enjoy without hurting another.

What seems not to have attracted notice, however, is that these pursuits are recommended solely because they render the body fitter, and hence reinforce the mind's powers of understanding:

> For the human body is composed of a great number of parts of diverse nature, which constantly need new and varied nourishment, in order that the whole of the body may be equally fit for everything which can follow from its nature, and consequently that the mind may be equally fit to understand many things at once. (*E* IV, 45, C2S; *cp. E* IV, Appendix, c.xxvii; *Nicomachean Ethics*, 1176b 34–5)

In a similar spirit, Spinoza appears to find value in ordinary social and civic virtues only because they contribute to the power of the intellect. The problem he faces here also arose for Aristotle. If the pursuit of science and philosophy is the highest expression of man's nature, and provides the life which is fittest for him, what place is to be found for the virtues of character (*Williams* (2), p. 60; *MacIntyre* (2), p. 148)? These virtues demand the performance of roles and activities which fall to us as citizens, as members of a family, as persons belonging to a certain profession, rank or class. Yet they encroach upon our freedom to study and to speculate, and distract us from our intellectual tasks. Spinoza does not seem to deal directly with this difficulty, but an answer may be pieced together from his words, 'Things are good only insofar as they assist man to enjoy that life which is determined by intelligence' (*E* IV, Appendix, v). Peace and a common law are needed to prevent aggression, to hold the worst passions in check, and to release the mind for abstract thought. Every man should strive to educate his fellows, to purify them of envy and hate, to make them more honest, friendly and co-operative, because thus they can join forces in the search for knowledge, exchanging ideas and opinions freely (*E* IV, Appendix, iv, ix, xii).

I have been arguing that Spinoza bridges the chasm between rational egoism and virtue by identifying the human being with the intellect, and by interpreting self-preservation to mean the development of adequate ideas. It may seem that this does an injustice to him. For he does try to *argue* that if men are led by a clear-sighted view of their own interest, they will naturally tend to live on peaceful terms with one another, and to help each other. The weaknesses of his proof are, however, insuperable. He summarises the reasoning at *E* IV, 35C2, which endeavours to show that 'when each man seeks most that which is profitable to himself, then are men most profitable to one another'. The proof seems to rest upon three main assumptions: (i) when men agree most in nature ('*maxime natura conveniunt*'), then they are most profitable to one another; (ii) men most agree in nature when they live under the guidance of Reason; (iii) men live under the guidance of Reason when each seeks what is useful to himself.

It is hard to know what to make of this little argument; but first let us take it on its own terms. Premiss (i) is backed up by a set of considerations originally introduced at *E* IV, 29. This ancillary argument maintains that objects can act causally on one another (and so affect each other for good or ill) only if they have something in common, or do not disagree in nature – that is, as a minimum, only if they can be conceived under a common attribute. Things have the more in common, or agree more in nature, the more positive properties they have (*E* IV, 32S). The more things have in common, the more ways there are in which they can affect one another; and so the more good *or ill* they can do to each other – so we should *expect* Spinoza to continue. But in fact he shifts ground at this point, arguing instead that the more they agree in nature, the more *profitable* to each other they are, i.e. the more *good* (alone) they can do (*E* IV, 31 and D). The shift is accomplished by a *reductio*: 'if any object were evil to us through that which it possesses in common with us, it could lessen or restrain what it possesses in common with us, which is absurd' (*E* IV, 30D). The *reductio* seems to assume: (iv) that if X makes Y worse, i.e. does evil to Y, then there is some respect Φ in which X has made Y less Φ, and has done so through, or by virtue of, its own Φness; and (iv) it is impossible that there should be some character Φ such that X makes Y less Φ by virtue of its being Φ itself. Since Spinoza is thinking of human beings and their emotions here, it may be that he would appeal in support of these contentions to the Law of the Imitation of the Emotions: if, say, Y is affected by X's hatred, then Y will himself feel some inclination to hate, and so will be made worse; but being affected by X's hatred cannot make Y more loving.

There is some faint plausibility in this, but it runs up against counter-instances. Your calmness may serve, not to tranquillise, but to excite and agitate me; your anxiety and nervousness may call forth resolution on my part; your hatred might call forth my love. The beliefs about causality which underlie (i) are accordingly false; and the reasoning in which (i) figures is inconclusive.

At a deeper level, however, the argument at *E* IV, 35 may be, like Adam Smith's 'invisible hand' argument (*The Wealth of Nations*, Book IV, c. 2), an attempt to prove the coincidence of private and collective interests (*see Hirschman* (1), p. 16, n.). (Smith, be it noted, was aware that the coincidence was not perfect: he pointed out that the erection and maintenance of 'certain public works and certain public institutions', along with the national defence and the costs of administering justice, would 'never repay the expense to any individual or small number of individuals', although they might 'much more than repay it to a greater society': Book IV, c. 9, *ad fin.*) There is no doubt that such an attempt must fail, if one assumes, as Spinoza intermittently *seems* to do, that rational self-interest requires the pursuit or protection of one's own life, health, security and satisfaction without reference to other people's (*E* III, 6; *E* IV, 8; *E* IV, 20S;

E IV, 22C; *E* IV, 24).

It is worth examining briefly *why* the attempt must fail. The answer, which I can only adumbrate here, begins by reflecting on such important discoveries of game theory as 'The Prisoner's Dilemma', which in one form demonstrates that two people may harm each other more than they help themselves if each makes a rational, self-interested choice (*R. Hardin*, c. 2, c. 9). The 'Tragedy of the Commons', a multi-person variant of the same motivational structure, is perhaps a more compelling case: it illustrates very beautifully the situation in which people pursuing their individual interests would collectively (and even individually) be better off if they could be dissuaded from such actions, even though none of them would gain from unilateral self-restraint.

Imagine a seventeenth-century English common, where each of the local villagers may graze as many of his sheep as he pleases. The amount of forage which each sheep can get will be reduced as more sheep are set out to graze: as the numbers grow, the sheep will tend to eat and crowd each other out. But so long as there is any profit for a villager in grazing a sheep on the common, he will have an incentive to put one out. Assume 100 villagers, each owning three sheep. It might be true that the pasture will hold all 300 sheep, but no more; that the sum totals of meat and wool for the village would be *greater* if only 200 sheep were pastured there rather than 300; that if each villager was allowed to put only two of his sheep there, *his* total yield of meat and wool from the fatter and healthier sheep would exceed his total yield from the three underfed and sickly ones. The villager is, however, assumedly unconcerned with the sum totals *for the village*; and he may observe that if he withdrew one of his three sheep whilst not everyone else did the same, he could well be worse off with two sheep rather than three. (For an excellent analysis of the problem and its ramifications, see *Schelling*, pp. 110–15, p. 231.) What cases like this show is that there are many situations in which, if we *all* act as rational, self-interested agents, we shall all be *worse off* than we need to be – worse off than we would be if some motive other than self-interest actuated a sufficient number of us, or than we would be if some external agent entered in who, like Hobbes' sovereign, lifted self-interest into a different trajectory.

While Spinoza did not see (as Adam Smith did) that unrestricted self-interest would lead to a dearth of public goods, and while he most assuredly did not see (unlike the game theorists) that self-interest, universally pursued, can be self-defeating, his apparent oversights become far more comprehensible if he is taken to be operating with different notions of 'self' and 'interest' ('*utile*') from those assumed in the later writers (*Hirschman* (1), pp. 32–3, pp. 43–4). The theorem that 'when each man seeks most that which is most profitable to himself, then are men most profitable to one another' becomes vastly more plausible if read as a comment about the acquisition of knowledge (*cp. Nicomachean Ethics*, 1177b1). The real meaning of Spinoza's theorem is that the interests of men *conceived of as thinkers or as intellects* are collectively best served if each of them pursues his own interest as determinedly as possible. Thus we circle back again on the conclusion that Spinoza reconciles virtue with selfishness only by equating persons with intellects.

If persons are essentially intellects, so that the good for man becomes identical with the good of the intellect, then it is explicable why Spinoza should think that each man's pursuit of his good should not obstruct the attainment of the best possible outcome for all. In *E* IV, 36S, Spinoza raises the question, 'What if the highest good of those who pursue virtue (=self-interest) should not be common to all?'. His answer is that 'it is not a matter of accident, but it arises through the nature of Reason alone, that the highest good of man is common'; and he adds that this result 'is deduced from the essence of man itself (*ex ipsa humana essentia*) insofar as it is defined by Reason'. The point is that if man is viewed as an intellect, then his highest good will consist in a good which is intellectual; and an intellectual good is one which is necessarily 'common to all'. This claim about the character of the highest good for man affirms the *DIE*, which implies that the supreme good must be something which can be loved, but which also (unlike finite and time-bound objects of love) does not give rise to dispute ('*litis*'), sadness, envy, fear or hate (*G* II, p. 7; *cp. Nicomachean Ethics*, 1169a21, on the 'competitive goods'). And when at *E* V, 20D, he describes the supreme good, which he identifies as science (or 'the intellectual love of God'), he says that it 'is common to all men, and we desire that all men enjoy it. It cannot therefore be sullied by the affect of envy, nor by that of jealousy, but on the contrary must be all the more strengthened the more people we imagine to rejoice in it'. Because man is essentially intellect, what is good for each can be 'common to all' in that (i) all are capable of enjoying that good; (ii) none can be excluded from possessing it; (iii) one person's enjoyment of it does not diminish another's; and (iv) one person's enjoyment of it tends to magnify another's. Scientific knowledge is the supreme good for man/intellect; and it is not indefensible to say that knowledge is a good 'common to all' in these four respects. But that being so, then self-interest and the common interest cannot diverge.

The paradox which gives the ideal of 'The Life of Reason' so much of its fascination is thus dispelled. Spinoza does not draw sociability out of egoism, virtue out of rational self-interest; he shows, at best, the convergence in aims of badly truncated selves. The judgement we made at the end of the previous section can be reaffirmed: Spinoza's view of the human good is partial, because his view of the human self is partial.

4 *The contemplative life*

In the Tenth Book of the *Nicomachean Ethics*, after having warned us that 'we must not follow those who advise us, being men, to think of human things, and, being mortal, of mortal things' (1177b30), Aristotle declares that 'the activity of God, which surpasses all others in blessedness, must be contemplative; and of human activities, therefore, that which is most akin to this must be most of the nature of happiness' (1178b21). For all his other disagreements with Aristotle, Spinoza affirms that the life which is primarily devoted to contemplation is the most blessed and the best: the most useful thing in life, he says, is to perfect Reason so far as we can, for in this consists the highest happiness or blessedness for man; for blessedness is nothing other than the quietude ('*acquiescentia*') of the spirit which arises from the intuitive knowledge of God (*E* IV, Appendix, c. iv).

We have already seen that this conception of the good for man threatens to clash with the doctrine of rational egoism; here we must observe that it creates tension within his system at other places as well. Roughly, how can he attribute such value to having adequate ideas, when ideas of value are themselves not adequate? The difficulty has been put this way by Santayana:

> I cannot think that Spinoza meant to present in the second portion of his work more than one of those ideals of human life which may become the standards of good and evil; he cannot have pretended that his choice of understanding as the chief good would commend itself to everyone. He explains the arbitrary character of all ideals too plainly and forcibly to assert that his own ideal is not arbitrary. All that he means to do is to describe a type which to him was the most attractive – the type of the man overwhelmed with a sense of the unity and reality of things, the sense of unity contributing a mystical, the sense of reality a scientific element, in short, the man of adequate

ideas. The tendency of a man's mind commonly determines what ideal he shall adopt; and if he is strenuous and single-minded, as Spinoza was, he will do much towards realising that ideal in his own person; therefore we need not be surprised at the strong likeness between Spinoza's ideal and himself. (*Santayana*, pp. 148-9)

As a description of Spinoza's *intentions*, this is surely wrong; for as Santayana goes on (too sceptically) to admit, 'it is not impossible that he convinced himself that it followed from the first part of his system'. There is no place, in an *Ethics demonstrated in the geometrical order*, for the projection of a personal and arbitrary ideal. The attempt at a strict proof based on unassailable axioms may be no more than 'the masquerade of a sick recluse' (Nietzsche, *Beyond Good and Evil*, Section 5); but it is not a conscious and intended masquerade.

Santayana, however, is right to see a problem here. For one thing, if value is subjective, as Spinoza (arguably) maintains, then how can he claim to *know* the superiority of one ideal of life over all others? (The issue of the subjectivity of value, considered in VII, 5, will not be pursued here.) That general question apart, Santayana seems also to be asking: How can a philosopher who expressly asserts that everyone judges what good or evil is according to his dominant passion (*E* III, 39S), presume to lay down one ideal as inherently best? 'The covetous man thinks plenty of money to be the best thing and poverty the worst. The ambitious man desires nothing like glory, and on the other hand dreads nothing like shame' – so Spinoza. But equally, the theorist reckons contemplation of the eternal order to be the chief good, inducing blessedness; and what entitles him to say that the other goods are either specious or secondary? 'Adequate ideas may make me blessed, but I may prefer to be rich; they may even make me immortal, but I may prefer to be merry and die' (*Santayana*, p. 149).

Spinoza was not unaware of this problem, and has a measured answer to it. (The fact that he *does* try to resolve the difficulty undercuts Santayana's notion that he *knew* his ideal to be idiosyncratic.) Spinoza says: 'Although each individual lives contented with its own nature and delights in it, nevertheless the life with which it is contented and its joy are nothing but the idea or soul of that individual, and so the joy of one differs in character from the joy of another as much as the essence of one differs from the essence of another' (*E* III, 57S). 'The joy by which the drunkard is enslaved is altogether different from the joy which is the portion of the philosopher' – just as the lust felt by a horse differs from the lust felt by a man (*E* III, 57S; *cp. Nicomachean Ethics*, 1176a5–10).

Spinoza's reasons for thinking that the philosophical delight in contemplation is superior to other joys seem to follow Aristotle's closely. The activity of contemplation is best because it exercises the best part of us on the best knowable objects; it is more continuous than other activities; it afford pleasures 'marvellous for their purity and enduringness'; and the one who pursues it is the most self-sufficient, the least dependent for his pleasure on other persons or things (*Nicomachean Ethics*, 1177a19–b1). To this Spinoza would add that contemplation brought relief from all perturbances of mind (*G* II, p. 7), and left us at one with our fellows (*E* V, 20D).

The basic strategy in arguing along these lines is to appeal to criteria on which all (even Santayana's hedonist) can agree, or which are implicit in their choices; and then to show that one type of activity is better *on those criteria*. In Spinoza's terms, the intention would be to show that insofar as we *have* adequate ideas, we can be brought to see the *value* of having adequate ideas. Even a drunkard can see that if one activity is followed by sorrow, and another not, then the latter is (so far) superior, or that if one enjoyment eases anxiety, while another arouses it, then the first is (so far) better than the second. From such beginnings one might persuade the drunkard that his characteristic enjoyments are inferior to others, and perhaps even that one joy outshines all the rest.

Whether or not such reasoning could establish that a philosopher's joy is better than a drunkard's, or (more ambitiously) that a *life* dominated by intellectual love is better than one given over to sensual pleasure, it does *not* follow that knowledge should never be sacrificed for another good, nor that the life focused on the *single* good of contemplation excels a life which encompasses *many* goods, sensual pleasure among them; and even if we take knowledge alone as the lodestar, we need not accept Aristotle's (and Spinoza's) view that 'those who know will pass their time more pleasantly than those who inquire' (*Nicomachean Ethics*, 1177a27; *cp. E* V, 33S). The *search* for knowledge may be as valuable as the reposeful *contemplation* of it; and we rightly accept 'the pain and labour of the negative'. But in any case knowledge does not stand alone in the pantheon of values (*Finnis*, c. IV).

Consider for example the good which is *play*. In many kinds of play, the delights we experience exhibit many of the features which Spinoza and Aristotle find in the pleasures of knowledge: they can be enjoyed uninterruptedly for long periods; they are unmixed with pain or regret; (they cause no harm to others,) but unite us more closely to them; they ease anxiety and sickness of mind; they may not even require other persons or things (e.g. when we race against a record, rather than against another competitor). Moreover, the value of play does not derive solely from the fact that it renders us fitter for abstract thinking; apart from such consequences, play is sought for its own sake. Finally, although play may interfere with study (I may have to choose between a game of tennis and reading Spinoza), it is not always rational to prefer the study to the play.

Of course it might still be true that a *life* spent largely in play would be trivial, as a life spent in study would not be: 'it would be strange indeed if the end were amusement', as Aristotle observed (*Nicomachean Ethics*, 1176b28). But lives can have several centres (like an ellipse) or a single centre (like a circle); and a life which brought together a balanced diversity of goods could be as valuable as a life which hinged on a single dominant good, even if that good was contemplation. If we have to compare *only* single-centred lives with one another, then it might emerge that the contemplative life was best, because dominated by a good which excelled any other; but that conclusion might not hold if we compared single-centred lives with *many-centred* ones. (If French cooking is better than any other, it may still be true that a varied diet of French, Chinese and Italian cooking is superior to a diet of French cuisine alone.) The philosopher's estimate of the philosophical life need not be dismissed as arbitrary or self-serving. But Life is satisfyingly painted in colours other than Reason's monochrome.

At the start of this section, we mentioned Aristotle's warning not to follow those who would distract us from contemplation by reminding us that we are mortal. For contemplation itself, he says, can render us god-like and immortal: 'so far as we can, we must make ourselves immortal, and strain every nerve to live in accordance with the best thing in us' (1177b33). That immortality follows from contemplation may also be Spinoza's view (*vide* VIII, 5); and those thoughts on immortality form the subject of our concluding chapter.

IX

Eternity and Immortality

1 Immortal longings

The immortality of the human soul concerned Spinoza from the first stages of his thinking. In his *Life of Spinoza*, Lucas reports that Spinoza scandalised the Jews of Amsterdam by declaring, as a young man, that the Scriptures did not teach human immortality: 'with regard to the soul, wherever Scripture speaks of it the word Soul is used simply to express Life, or anything that is living' (*Lucas*, p. 46; *Wolfson* II, p. 324). As Wolfson points out, this early belief may echo the views of Uriel Acosta, whose teaching on the subject has been preserved for us in a treatise published in 1623 by his opponent Samuel da Silva (*Wolfson* II, p. 323; *Strauss*, pp. 56–63). Acosta denied that the soul was separable from the body, and maintained that 'it cannot be proven from the Law that the human soul is immortal'. (For a similar view, see Hobbes's *Leviathan*, IV, c. 44: 'The Soule in Scripture, signifieth alwaies, either the Life, or the Living Creature; and the Body and Soule jointly, the Body alive'.) The extent of Acosta's influence upon the young Spinoza is questionable (*cf. Popkin* (2), pp. 177–8); but it seems fair to take Lucas' account at face value.

If Spinoza held the reported view, however, he soon came to change his mind. In the *Short Treatise* (II, 23), he argues that the soul may be so united with God as to come to share in His immutability, and to be immortal. The form of immortality which he describes has several notable features (*Taylor* (2), pp. 146–7). First, it seems to be a type of existence which may be entered into during the present life, not something for which we must wait until death. Second, it is not, as in Christian belief, something inherent in all men, but is to be acquired by each; and those who succeed in acquiring it may possess it in different degrees. Finally, it can be obtained by regulating our thoughts, and by forming adequate ideas. As we shall see, these conceptions survive even in the *Ethics*, albeit with significant changes. The most obvious differences between Spinoza's first and last discussions are twofold: the *Ethics* speaks of *minds*, not of *souls*, and it holds out the hope, not of *immortality*, but of *eternity*. Yet the underlying consistency of Spinoza's approach is remarkable. At no time does he seem to have been drawn to the Platonic and Cartesian view that the soul or mind is a substance, capable of existing independently of the body (*cf.* VI, 1); still less he was attracted to the Christian dogma of survival in a resurrected body (*Harris*, pp. 670–1; *Hampshire* (2), pp. 171–2).

Spinoza's discussion of the mind's eternity in the *Ethics* is emphatically marked off from what has preceded it. At the end of the long scholium to *E* V, 20, he declares that he has concluded all that he had to say relating to the present life, and announces that he will pass 'to the consideration of those matters which pertain to the duration of the mind without relation to the body (*quae ad Mentis durationem sine relatione ad Corpus pertinent*)'. Shortly afterwards, he states his most important result: 'The human mind cannot be absolutely destroyed with the body, but something of it remains, which is eternal' (*E* V, 23). This theorem, and the demonstration which is attached to it, raise baffling and vexatious problems. Let me mention three of them.

First, by *E* II, 7, the order and connection of ideas is the same as the order and connection of things. From this it is inferred that the human mind is the idea of the body; and it seems to follow in turn that there should be an eternally existing idea of a non-existent body. If mind and body are the same, or even parallel in their careers, how can one exist when the other has perished? Nor is the difficulty evaded by saying that Spinoza claims eternity for only a *part* of the mind. For that part must be an idea, and hence must correspond to something bodily; but since what is physical is perishable, so must its mental correspondent be.

Second, Spinoza ascribes eternity solely to that in which essence and existence are the same (*E* I, Definition 8); but essence and existence are united only in God (*E* I, 20), not in created things (*E* I, 24); hence only God can be eternal. Yet he also says that the infinite immediate modes are eternal (*E* I, 21); and of course he ascribes eternity to some part of the human mind (*E* V, 23). The eternity of the infinite modes can perhaps be reconciled with the requirement that eternity belongs to God alone

(*Steinberg*, pp. 161–2; *Curley* (3), p. 72), for these modes follow by necessity from the Divine attributes; but it is not clear that these means of overcoming the difficulty will apply to the human mind, which follows from God only insofar as He is qualified by another finite mode (*E* I, 28).

Third, the mind, or part of it, is stated to be eternal; more generally, it is said that we feel and experience *ourselves* to be eternal (*E* V, 23S: '*Sentimus experimurque, nos eternos esse*'), Now 'eternity' is defined in *E* I in such a way as to imply that what is eternal is timeless (rather than omnitemporal, or real at all times); and this seems confirmed by *E* V, 23S, which asserts that 'eternity cannot be defined (or: limited – *definiri*) by time, nor can it have any relation to time' (*cp.* V, 4). Similarly, *E* V, 34S may be warning us against the vulgar error of confounding the eternity of the mind with its continuing-to-endure. On the other hand, there are passages in the *Ethics* which seem to imply that the existence of both the mind and the infinite modes is not timeless, but omnitemporal. Thus (a) it is said at *E* I, 21 that the infinite modes must exist 'always' or 'at all times' ('*semper*') (*cf.* Donagan (2), p. 245); (b) the immediate infinite mode of Extension is motion-and-rest (*Ep.* 64); but it is nonsensical to think that motion-and-rest could be timeless (*Donagan* (2), p. 246); (c) Spinoza claims that something of the mind *remains* (*E* V, 23), which suggests that the 'eternal' part continues to endure or exist; (d) at *E* V, 20S, Spinoza writes that he has finished with what relates to the *present* life (by contrast, seemingly, with the *future* life), and that he will be discussing those matters which pertain to the *duration* of the mind without the body (which suggests that the disembodied mind *endures*).

Faced with this third problem, the commentators disagree. Martha Kneale believes that Spinoza invokes the non-temporal notion of eternity in Part I of the *Ethics*, but has an omnitemporal notion in view in Part V; Alan Donagan takes him to mean 'omnitemporality' by 'eternity' throughout the *Ethics* (*Kneale* (2), *Donagan* (2)). Both Kneale and Donagan think that the contrast Spinoza makes between 'eternity' and 'duration' is meant to mark the difference between what is unconditionally necessary and what is contingent; in their favour is that fact that Spinoza seems to use 'necessity' and 'eternity' interchangeably (e.g. at *E* II, 44C2, D). Joachim and Hampshire, on the other hand, believe that Spinozistic eternity is timeless existence; and they have been followed by recent critics of the Kneale/Donagan interpretation, such as Hardin and Steinberg. Taylor desperately attempts to solder the two inconsistent interpretations together: he writes that 'though for Spinoza duration is no part of the definition of eternity and cannot of itself constitute it, yet eternity does and must entail as a consequence some kind of endless duration' (*Taylor* (2), p. 149).

These, then, are some of the dfificulties which cluster about Spinoza's view of the mind's eternity. Let us try to unravel them, beginning with the nature of eternity.

2 Eternity

The starting point for any discussion of the notion of eternity must be Wolfson's magistral study of the career of that concept in Classical and Medieval thought (*Wolfson* I, c. 10). In particular, it is essential to note his distinction between 'Platonic' and 'Aristotelian' conceptions of eternity. Wolfson writes: 'Briefly stated, the difference between the two meanings is this. To Plato eternity is the antithesis of time and it means the exclusion of any kind of temporal relations. To Aristotle eternity is only endless time' (*Wolfson* I, p. 358). Wolfson's account, developed with enormous erudition, has been embellished by Mrs Kneale. She points out that Plato implies in the *Timaeos* (37e6–38a6) that what is eternal (*aionios*) cannot properly be described by the use of past or future tenses: of such a thing, we can only say that it *is*, i.e. that it is timeless (*Kneale* (2), pp. 228–9). But 'timelessness' is not the only quality which Mrs Kneale believes to have been associated with 'eternity'. Besides the Aristotelian sense of 'omnitemporality', she finds it to have been linked on the one hand to the idea of *life*, on the other to the notion of *necessity*. Indeed, she claims that 'the extra connotation of life which is conveyed by the Greek words *aion* and *aionios* . . . undoubtedly make it easier for later theologians to regard God as the unique eternal object' (p. 230). Enlarging on the last point, she continues: 'Boethius . . . introduces the notion (sc. of life) into his definition of eternity: *Aeternitas est interminabilis vitae tota simul et perfecta possessio* ('Eternity is the endless and perfect possession of all life all at once'). This definition is defended by St Thomas in Part I, Quaestio X, Art. 1 of the *Summa Theologica*, although, in his own statement, he does not use any word equivalent to 'life' but insists simply that eternity is *tota simul* (all at once)' (p. 230).

Kneale is critical of Aquinas, not least because he attempts misguidedly to wed the Platonic and the Aristotelian notions of eternity. She argues that the Thomistic contrast between time and eternity is incoherent: it is self-defeating to say that the eternal is *tota simul*, for 'simultaneity' is itself a temporal notion. 'Things in time happen either successively or together (*simul*) and to say that the parts of time, past, present and future happen together is to deny the necessary condition of simultaneity' (p. 230). From this and other considerations she deduces that 'timlessness as the *totum simul* of time is a self-contradictory notion and we must either find a different meaning for it or identify it with necessity' (p. 231). She adds that to call a truth 'timeless' is simply to say that 'there *is no point* in asking when two and two are four in the way that there is a point in asking when the daffodils are in bloom' (p. 231). But the pointlessness of such questions or assertions does not prove them to be meaningless: 'this does not mean that it is not the case that two and two are four today, that they were four yesterday and that they will be four tomorrow. These statements are not meaningless or untrue, but simply so obvious as to be pointless. I would go so far as to say that it is true that today two and two have been four for a day longer than they were yesterday and similarly that, if God exists, he has existed a day longer than he had existed yesterday' (*ibid.*). And she accuses Spinoza of arguing fallaciously from the pointlessness of such utterances to their meaninglessness (referring, apparently, to *CM* II, c. 1). The charge reads as follows:

> The argument which led Spinoza and has led many others to deny that an eternal object exists at a given time is of a type which has seemed to some very modern. It was much favoured by the late Professor Austin and its general form is: 'There are no conceivable circumstances in which it would be pointful to utter the sentence S. Therefore the sentence S is meaningless'. Using this kind of argument, Austin denies in effect that 'He sat down intentionally' in normal circumstances expresses any proposition at all, let alone a true proposition. It seems to me that this type of argument has been sufficiently dealt with by Professor J.R. Searle in his paper 'Aberrations and Assertions'. As he remarks, it depends on confusing the conditions under which it is correct (conventionally or socially) to assert that-P with the conditions under which it is true that-P. It is very rarely, if ever, socially correct to assert that two and two are four on Wednesdays, because this suggests that they might be something else on other days. (p. 232)

This diagnosis, while essentially sound, may not do complete justice to Spinoza (*vide* VIII, 3, *infra*); but for the moment it suffices to note how widespread the error was. Wolfson assures us that *whatever* Jewish or Christian sources Spinoza consulted, he would have found that 'eternity', at least as applied to God, did not merely mean endless time. Wolfson contends furthermore that Spinoza was following the lead of his predecessors when he defined 'eternity' in *E* I as 'existence itself, so far as it is conceived necessarily to follow from the definition alone of the eternal thing'. Referring to the 'Explanation' attached to this, Wolfson comments: 'eternity is not merely beginningless and endless time or duration. "It cannot therefore be explained by duration and time, even if duration be conceived without beginning or end" ' (*Wolfson* I, p. 366).

Wolfson's interpretation is standard; it is accepted even by those who, like Kneale, make an exception from it for Part V of the *Ethics*. But the received wisdom has been challenged by Alan Donagan in an important and stimulating article. Donagan argues that, in the *Ethics* at any rate, Spinoza consistently identifies 'eternity' with 'omnitemporality', and that he credits both God and the human mind with existence at all times. I do not agree with Donagan, and accept the orthodox view that Spinozistic eternity is timelessness; but Donagan's case is so impressive that it must be answered in detail. The issue is the focus of our next section.

3 Omnitemporality

For convenience, we can divide the relevant texts into four groups: those from the *Cogitata Metaphysica*; those from the earlier parts of the *Ethics*; the celebrated *Epistle 12*; and Part V of the *Ethics*.

(A) The *Cogitata Metaphysica* is early and unreliable; it may reflect Descartes' views as much as, or even more than, the views which Spinoza eventually adopted. Nevertheless it is a valuable source. We have already seen that it argues – fallaciously, in Mrs Kneale's opinion – that necessary truth, including truths about God, are timeless, and cannot be said to admit of temporal variation (Section 2). The argument which Mrs Kneale appears to be criticising reads as follows:

> Those who do attribute duration to God separate His existence from His essence. Indeed, there are those who ask whether God has existed any longer now than at the time when He created Adam; and since this seems sufficiently clear to them, they accordingly decide that duration must in no way be removed from God. Truly, such people beg the question, because they suppose that the essence of God is distinct from His existence. For they ask whether God, who existed up to

the time of Adam, has not from the time of Adam's creation until now added additional time to His existence. On this basis, they attribute to God a duration increased by each passing day, and suppose that He is, as it were, continually created by Himself. If they did not distinguish the existence of God from His essence, they would not attribute duration to Him, since duration absolutely cannot pertain to the essence of things. Surely, no one will ever say that the essence of a circle or triangle, as an eternal truth, has endured longer now than in the time of Adam. Moreover, since duration is thought of as greater and less, as though it consisted of parts, clearly it follows that no duration can be attributed to God: for since his being is eternal – that is, since there can be in it nothing of before or after – we can never attribute duration to it without at the same time destroying the true concept we have of God, since by attributing duration to the being of God we divide into parts that which is infinite in its own nature and which can never be thought of except as infinite. (*CM* II, 2, ii)

Kneale's analysis of this passage seems to me correct: she has picked out its main argument, and exposed the fallacy in it (for a different view, see *Steinberg*, pp. 165–7). Where her account goes wrong, however, is in purporting to be complete. For there is a second, subordinate argument in the passage which she has overlooked. This argument, to which Spinoza came to attach importance, is stated in the last full sentence of the paragraph (beginning with 'Moreover').

Briefly, Spinoza is contending that if God could be said to endure (for a greater period of time, or for longer than He had since creating Adam), then His existence would be made up of parts (or phases); but that is ruled out by the fact the He is infinite in His own nature. As it stands, this reasoning is unpersuasive; but its point is not unintelligible. Spinoza thinks that 'something infinite cannot have even two parts: if the parts were both finite, then so must the whole be; but if at least one were infinite, then one infinite (the whole) would be greater than another (a part)' – which he rejects as absurd (*Bennett* (2), p. 44). This same assumption underlies the argument at *E* I, 15S, where Spinoza tries to show that the infinity of Extension excludes its divisibility (and thus qualifies Extension to be an attribute of God); it occurs here, as also in *Epistle 12*, in support of the claim that an eternal and infinite being cannot have a temporally-phased existence.

For the rest, the *Cogitata Metaphysica* sharply separates

ETERNITY AND IMMORTALITY

duration and eternity: at II, 2, iii, it repudiates the notion that eternity is a species of duration (even, it seems, everlasting duration); and at II, 10, v, it announces that duration (together with time) begins and ends with the beginning or ending of created things. The point is neatly explained by Wolfson: 'Duration is a mode of existence, and time is a mode of duration. It is analogous to the successive relations between time, motion and body in Aristotle. Motion, according to the medieval Aristotelian phraseology, is an accident of the body and time is an accident of motion. Substitute the terms duration and existence respectively for motion and body and the term mode for accident and you get a perfect analogy' (*Wolfson* I, p. 354). Duration presupposes change in 'created' things, of finite things whose existence is not implied by their essence; and time, conceived of as an abstract quantity, presupposes duration, of which it is the measure. Unlike duration, time (in the relevant sense) is merely a 'mode of thought', i.e. mind-dependent: if there were no men to take measurements, then the measure of duration would not exist (*CM* II, 10, v; *cp.* Aristotle, *Physics* 223a 16–17, 21–9).

(B) The fact that Spinoza uses 'time' only to signify a measure of duration, and not to speak of temporal *passage*, has been exploited by Donagan in support of his reading of the *Ethics*. Donagan writes:

> He himself used the Latin synonym for 'time' ('*tempus*') in a deliberately restricted sense. The one passage I know of in the *Ethics* that throws light on this sense is little more than an allusion: 'Besides, nobody doubts that the way in which we imagine time is this: we imagine some bodies to be moved, with respect to others, more slowly, or more quickly, or equally quickly' (*E* II, 44C1S). This echoes the following analysis in his *Cogitata Metaphysica*, which a letter of April 20, 1663, to Lewis Meyer, shows to have expressed his own view.
>
> '[I]n order that (a quantity of duration) be determined (*determinetur*), we compare it with the duration of other things which have a certain and determinate motion (*motus*), and this comparison is called time' (*CM* I, 4).
>
> This analysis tells us what *a* time is: namely, an interval of duration measurable by a clock. It analyses the sense of 'time' in which it is said that *the* time Michelangelo took to paint the ceiling of the Sistine Chapel was four and a half years. (*Donagan* (2), pp. 242–3)

Relying on this distinction, Donagan can construe several passages in a sense which favours his case. Thus, when Spinoza asserts that 'eternity cannot be defined by time' (*E* V, 23S), Donagan takes him to mean that 'endless time is not definable by any measurable interval of duration' (p. 243). On this reading, the statement is consistent with the Aristotelian view that eternity is endless time; whereas if 'time' signified temporal passage, it would not be. Spinoza is not saying that eternity categorically excludes measurement; he is saying only that we cannot assign any (finite) measure, however great, to it.

On this basis, Donagan offers to explain the refractory accounts of 'duration' and 'eternity' embedded in the definitions of *E* I. He says:

> [Spinoza's] definitions of duration and eternity are only indirectly related to time in the sense of temporal passage. 'Duration (he wrote) is indefinite continuation of existing (*existendi continuatio*). *Explicatio*. I say "indefinite", because (such continuation) can by no means be limited (*determinari*) by the nature itself of the existing thing, or even by its efficient cause, which indeed necessarily posits (*ponit*) the existence of the thing, but does not take it away (*tollit*)' (*E* II, Definition 5). Here enduring existents are differentiated from nonenduring ones as being existents whose continuation can possibly have a limit. What existents are excluded by this differentia? In view of Spinoza's definition of eternity, it is natural to say that they are eternal existents.
>
> 'By "eternity" (he wrote) I mean existence (*existentiam*) itself, inasmuch as it is conceived to follow solely from the definition of an eternal thing. *Explicatio*. For such existence, like the essence of a thing, is conceived as an eternal truth; and therefore cannot be explained through duration or time, although a duration may be conceived to lack a beginning or an end' (*E* I, Definition 8).
>
> Taken in conjunction with his definition of duration, as its *explicatio* invites us to take it, this definition contrasts eternity with duration, as existence which, being necessary, cannot have temporal limit – whether a beginning or an end – with existence which, being contingent, can have such a limit. In effect, it treats eternity as necessary continuation of existing. (*Donagan* (2), pp. 243–4)

Two objections might be made to this. It could be said that in treating eternal existence as a matter of necessary truth, Spinoza is willy-nilly committed to claiming that it is timeless. Donagan answers this by referring to Kneale's argument that it is meaningful to speak of necessary truths as being true at or over

ETERNITY AND IMMORTALITY

times. (Even so, Spinoza may not have seen the fallaciousness of the reasoning he employed in the *Cogitata Metaphysica*: the error is a subtle one, and there is no explicit repudiation of it.) Second, it could be contended that if Spinoza had not thought of eternal existence as timeless, he would have defined it in *E* I, Definition 8 as continuation of existence without beginning or end. Donagan replies that 'in referring to eternity, Spinoza shunned the word "*continuatio*", presumably because it presupposes a point of reference from which existence "continues" before or after; for he held that no moment in eternity is privileged. It is therefore closer to his usage to say that eternity, as he conceived it, is equivalent to necessarily omnitemporal existence, understanding "omnitemporal" as meaning "at all moments in the passage of time" ' (*Donagan* (2), p. 244). But it is not clear to me why defining 'eternity' in terms of 'continuation' should imply that some moment of time is *privileged*: if an eternal thing is something that continues in existence without start or finish, then at *any* moment you pick, that thing will be continuing to be. Furthermore, it is odd that Spinoza's account of eternity should have to be explicated in terms of a notion which he does not have a word for, and which is (at best) recessive in his writing – the notion of 'temporal passage'.

Following on from his analysis of the definitions in Part I, Donagan tries to disarm other passages in that book which appear to conflict with his interpretation. He attends particularly to *E* I, 33S2:

> Furthermore, all God's ordinances (*decreta*) have been ratified from eternity (*ab aeterno*) by God Himself. For that it should be otherwise would argue imperfection and inconstancy. But since in eternity (*in aeterno*) there is no when, before or after, it follows solely from God's perfection that God can never ordain anything else (*aliud*), nor ever could have; and that God did not exist before His ordinances, nor can exist without them. (Donagan's translation)

Commenting on this, he writes:

> Here Spinoza shows that God cannot ordain at one time what he does not ordain at another, by pointing out that what is true of an eternal thing is true at all times: such questions as 'When was this true of it?' 'Was this true of it before that?' and 'Will this be true of it before that?' are all inapplicable to an eternal thing. What is being repudiated is inconstancy; and to deny that something is inconstant suggests, not that it is timeless, but

that it is at all times the same. (p. 246)

As Donagan construes Spinoza, the argument here is in all relevant respects identical with that of *Cogitata Metaphysica* II, 2, which it plainly echoes. (The statement that 'in eternity there is no when, before or after', is another reminiscence of the *CM* II, 1, ii). If, as we have thus far assumed, the earlier argument concluded to the timelessness of the eternal, then it is astonishing that Spinoza should repeat it, and even make use of similar forms of words, in order to reach a different and incompatible conclusion elsewhere. If on the other hand the reasoning in the *CM* was designed to reach the very conclusion which Donagan discerns here in the *Ethics*, then why does Spinoza go to such lengths in the earlier book to deny that eternity is any 'species of duration'? Why does he explicitly distinguish a sense in which 'from eternity' (*ab aeterno*) signifies beginninglessness in time, from the (timeless) sense it carries when applied to God (*CM* II, 10, x)? Furthermore, Donagan is in effect ascribing to Spinoza an argument which is still worse than that given him by Mrs Kneale. From (i) 'It is pointless to ask "Was this true of God before that?" or "Will this be true of God before that?" ' it might seem to follow that (ii) 'God does not continue to exist, and temporal determinations cannot be asserted of Him'. But it scarcely seems natural to infer (iii) 'God exists at all times'. If He existed at *all* times, questions of the forms mentioned in (i) would surely be agreed to make sense: omnitemporality does not imply changelessness, but timelessness does.

(C) Donagan seeks to draw further support for his view from outside the *Ethics*. He quotes a section of the long *Epistle* 12 (which Spinoza thought important enough to deserve a special title of its own: *The Letter on the Nature of the Infinite*). In his own translation, it reads:

> I call the states (*affectiones*) of substance modes; and their definition, inasmuch as it is not the definition itself of substance, can involve no existence. From this it follows that, although they exist, we can conceive them as not existing. From this, in turn, it follows that we, when we attend solely to the essence of modes, and not to the order of the whole of nature (*totius naturae*), cannot conclude from the fact that they now exist (*existant*), either that they will exist (*extituros*) hereafter or that they will not, or that they have existed (*extitisse*) herebefore or that they have not. From this it plainly appears that we conceive the existence of substance as *toto genere* different from the existence of modes. And from this

arises the difference between *eternity* and *duration*. For through duration we can explain only the existence of modes; (we can explain the existence) of substance, however, through eternity, that is, (through) infinite enjoyment of existing (*fruitionem . . . existendi*), or, in strained Latin, *essendi*.

Of this, Donagan says:

> Here what distinguishes eternity, the existence of substance, from duration, the existence of finite modes, is not timelessness as opposed to omnitemporality, but necessity of existence as opposed to its merely contingent continuation. (p. 245)

If that is right, the passage may be *consistent* with Donagan's overall position, but it does not *imply* it. If the substance/mode contrast is anchored in the necessary/contingent one, and not in the timeless/durational one, it does not follow that substance has everlasting existence, unless it can be shown that necessary existence *entails* temporality. Further, the passage stresses that the eternal character of the existence of substance consists in its *infinite* enjoyment of being; and as we have seen, Spinoza argues in the *CM* that the infinite existence of God excludes the possibility of division into phases — whence His timelessness follows. The impossibility of marking real divisions in an infinite substance is emphasised in the paragraph of *Epistle* 12 which comes immediately after that quoted by Donagan:

> From all this it is clear that we can at will determine the existence and duration of modes and conceive it as greater or less, and divide it into parts, when, as most frequently happens, we are considering their essence only and not the order of Nature. Indeed we can do so without thereby in any way destroying the conception we have of them. But Eternity and Substance, since they cannot be conceived as other than infinite, cannot be treated thus without our destroying our conception of them at the same time.

Spinoza goes on to infer (as at E I, 15S), that Extended Substance, as infinite, must be lacking in real parts; and its indivisibility into spatial bits is surely to be matched by indivisibility into temporal stretches (or, *a fortiori*, instants). Once again, then, we have found that Spinoza's views tally with those he recorded in the *Cogitata Metaphysica*.

(D) Finally, we come to *Ethics* V. Donagan honestly faces up to the difficult task of trying to fit in the difficult passage at E V, 23S; his account of it is interesting. The context of the passage is set by the proof of the eternity of some part of the mind, which has just been given; that theorem seems to carry the consequence that just as something 'survives' the body's death, so also it must have existed 'before' the body's birth. Spinoza tries to disinfect this consequence: he wants to deny that there can be any recollection of our prenatal condition. He writes (Donagan's rendering):

> [I]t cannot happen that we recollect that we have existed before the body, because no traces of it are to be found in the body, and eternity can neither be defined by time nor have any relation to time.

It looks as if Spinoza had reasoned: (i) the part of the mind which is eternal is timeless; (ii) what is timeless can have no relation to what exists, or happens, in time; (iii) in particular, what is timeless cannot cause changes in bodies which endure in time; so (iv) the eternal part of the mind cannot leave traces in the human body with which it is associated; so (v) there cannot be recollection that we existed before birth.

Donagan, who admits this to be a possible reading of the paragraph, points out that it is hard to reconcile with other passages in the *Ethics*. For God is paradigmatically the eternal thing; yet Spinoza holds that God is qualified by certain finite modifications existing in time (*E* I, 28D), and that He is the immanent cause of finite and enduring things (*E* II, 45S). Hence Spinoza must allow that an eternal being can stand in certain relations to time, and even that it can be causally connected to changes taking place in time. 'He must therefore have intended his remark that eternity cannot have any relation to time to be understood as qualified. His text indeed suggests such a qualification, and only one: namely, '*sub specie aeternitatis*'. Accordingly, I submit that his remark should be understood as meaning that eternity, *qua* eternity (or an eternal thing, *sub specie aeternitatis*), cannot have any relation to time' (Donagan (2), p. 247).

How then is *E* V, 23S to be explained? It comes, Donagan says, to this:

> The eternal part of man cannot, *sub specie aeternitatis*, leave traces in his body; for leaving such traces would be an event in time. But it does not follow that the eternal part of man may not be related to time by forming part of a human mind actually existing for a time. All that follows is that, if something eternal forms part of something existing for a time,

then it does not do so *sub specie aeternitatis*, that it is, by the necessity of its eternal nature. (p. 247)

I am uncertain how well I understand this. It appears that Donagan is saying that an eternal thing, *qua* eternal, cannot enter into (causal) relations with things existing in time; but also that an eternal thing, regarded in some other light, *can* enter into such relations, and form part of a mind which is bound up with a temporally persisting body. But if an eternal thing (though not *qua* eternal) can be so related to a body, why can it not (though not *qua* eternal) leave traces in a body? If an eternal thing, *sub specie durationis*, can unite with and act upon a body, then it can, *sub specie durationis*, cause events in time within that body. I do not see how Donagan meets that critical issue: if some part of the mind literally existed in time before the birth of the body – as, of course, on his account it must – then why should it be impossible to have some recollection of its existence during that time? It is no good to say that a 'necessary' and 'omnitemporal' being cannot affect things or processes in time: Aquinas held that the sun was a necessary thing in this sense; but he also attributed to it effects on animal generation (*cf. Kenny* (6), pp. 42–4). Donagan, it seems to me, is in effect conceding the timelessness of eternal beings by asserting that, *as* eternal, they have no relation to time.

All the same, it remains a problem for the alternative interpretation to explain how, in *E* I, God can be said to be qualified by modes in time, and to be their immanent cause. For this seems ruled out by step (ii) in Spinoza's argument. I can only plead that Spinoza's accounts of the relation of the eternal God to the world, or of the eternal part of the mind to the rest of the mind and the body, are extremely puzzling in any case. Nor does Donagan seem to be in a better position to handle these difficulties than his opponents. For if God's eternity consists in everlastingness, then why is it necessary that God should be related to finite and enduring modes only as qualified by such a mode? Why should it be true that the eternal can have none but qualified relations to time? If it is puzzling to see how a timeless thing can have commerce with things in time, it is no less puzzling that the commerce between an (ever-) enduring thing and other temporal existents should be found problematic.

I conclude, then, that the best and most natural construction of the texts which Donagan cites has them contradict the view that Spinozistic eternity is omnitemporality. His efforts to square them with that reading, although ingenious and instructive, are finally unsuccessful. But there are also texts which seem to tell strongly in *favour* of his view, and which we must accordingly try to neutralise, on pain of finding Spinoza inconsistent.

Perhaps the easiest passages to reconcile with the orthodox view of Spinoza are those found in *E* V, 20S. Spinoza says there that he will proceed to 'those matters which pertain to the duration of the mind without the body'. But this need not imply that he thinks that the disembodied mind has duration. His remark can be paraphrased: 'I shall now pass to the consideration of whether the mind might be said to endure without relation to the body' (*Hardin*, p. 137). This suggestion is reinforced by the fact when he sums up the discussion at *E* V, 40S, he makes no mention of the 'duration' of the mind, and claims to have shown that it is an 'eternal' mode of thought. Again, when he says at *E* V, 20S that he has concluded his treatment of the *present* life, he may not be indicating a contrast with a *future* life. It is possible that when he criticises the vulgar for confounding the eternity of the mind with duration (*E* V, 34CS), he is implying that the common view of our posthumous state as lying in a future is grossly mistaken (but *cf. Taylor* (2), p. 162). Furthermore, the 'present' life he speaks of may be contrasted, not with a putative 'future' existence, but with the mode of ideal or possible existence which is distinguished from our 'present actual existence' at *E* V, 29 (*Hardin*, pp. 136–7).

Another passage which is easily disposed of is *E* V, 23, where it is said that something of the mind 'remains (*remanet*)'. Harris has suggested that we take 'remains' in the sense of 'is a remainder' in arithmetic or 'is a residue' in chemistry: it need not have a specifically temporal meaning (*Harris*, p. 673; endorsed by *Hardin*, p. 136).

More refractory is the passage at *E* I, 21. It reads: 'All things which follow from the absolute nature of some attribute of God must (*debuerunt*) have existed always (*semper*) and as infinite, i.e. (*sive*) through the same attribute are eternal and infinite'. Gueroult seems to see no problem here, taking Spinoza to have timelessness in mind (*Gueroult* I, p. 326); and Hardin, who admits the difficulty, insists that the passage 'cannot by itself be decisive' (*Hardin*, p. 130).

Perhaps one can do slightly better. First, we must note that the demonstration comes on the heels of a corollary which asserts that the attributes of God are immutable (*E* I, 20C2). We should expect then that the immutability of the things (the infinite immediate modes) which 'follow' from the absolute nature of the attributes should share in this immutability; and if the 'eternity' ascribed to them at *E* I, 21 is timelessness, then that expectation will have been met. (I have claimed earlier in this section that timelessness does, and omnitemporality does not, imply immutability.) Second, Spinoza unpacks the statement that these modes must have existed always – it means, he explains, that they are eternal. The shift from the perfect tense to the present, and from 'always' to 'eternal', may be intended as a *corrective* to the suggestion that the modes endure forever. If that reading is even *possible*, then the text cannot be quoted as unequivocally favouring the view Donagan defends.

The most persuasive point in Donagan's case, as Hardin admits, arises from the fact that the infinite immediate mode of Extension is motion-and-rest; and it seems unintelligible to regard this as timeless (*Hardin*, p. 130; *Donagan* (2), p. 246). But the nettle must be grasped: Spinoza does *not* regard temporal passage as an intersubjective feature of the world, but only as an 'appearance', akin to colour, heat or sound (*Hardin*, pp. 130–2). What we take for the awareness of temporal passage is a confused idea of the timeless causal order of the world: 'our mind can be said to endure, and its existence to be limited by a definite time only insofar as it involves the actual existence of the body; and thus far alone has it the power to determine temporally the existence of things, and to conceive them *sub duratione*' (*E* V 23S). It is only because we are *embodied* creatures, endowed with sense, memory and imagination, that we can see things as really past, present or future; change and becoming are illusory from an absolute standpoint. That is why Spinoza can say that it is of the nature of reason to conceive things 'without any relation to time, but under a certain form of eternity' (*E* II, 44C2D). That also is why he claims that a man, insofar as he forms his ideas under the dictate of Reason, will not be glad that an evil is past rather than present or future, nor desire an (equal) good which is present more than one which is future (*E* IV, 62D): from an absolute point of view, the pastness of an evil, the presentness or futurity of a good, are not real characters of those things. Spinoza's God does not know what has happened, or is happening now, or is to happen, in any other way than as timelessly present. But death can bring us release from these illusions, and the anxieties which fester through them; and it is even possible that, at moments in and out of time, we can ourselves see things *sub specie aeternitatis*.

Spinoza, then, on the view I advocate, must not only agree that motion-and-rest is timeless; he must deny the fundamental reality of all temporal passage. This is an heroic view, if also a mad one: 'Even if my distinction between past, present and future aspects of physical things is a fragmentary misperception of changeless realities, it remains true that I have various and uncombinable illusions as to which realities are present. I must therefore have these illusions not simultaneously but one after another; and then there is after all real time and real change' (*Geach* (2), p. 305). Spinoza's error about Time and Eternity runs like a great, hidden fault-line through the whole extent of his system.

4 The proof of the mind's eternity

Spinoza's proof that some part of the mind is eternal is set forth at *E* V, 23:

> In God there necessarily exists a conception or idea which expresses the essence of the human body (V, 22). This conception or idea is therefore necessarily something which pertains to the essence of the human mind (II, 13). But we ascribe to the human mind no duration which can be limited by time, unless insofar as it expresses the actual existence of the body, which is manifested through duration, and which can be limited by time, that is to say (II, 8C), we cannot ascribe duration to the mind except while the body exists. But nevertheless, since this something is that which is conceived by a certain eternal necessity through the essence itself of God (V, 22), this something which pertains to the essence of the mind will necessarily be eternal – Q.E.D.

Central to this argument is the identification of a certain part of the human mind with an idea which exists in God, viz., with 'an idea which expresses the essence of this or that body under the form of eternity' (*E* V, 22). This idea, unlike the other ideas which comprise the human mind, does not take the body or any state of the body as its object. Its object is the *essence* of a particular body. And here, as Donagan rightly observes, we need to note a distinction which Spinoza draws between 'formal essence' and 'actual essence'. As Spinoza uses the term, it appears that the 'formal essence' of a particular thing is, simply, a possible object. (Descartes seems also to admit the reality of merely possible objects when he distinguishes, at the start of the *Fifth Meditation*, between the idea of a triangle, the actual triangle – which exists if and only if something in the physical world is triangular – and the 'form' or 'essence' of a triangle. On the basis of this and other passages, he has been credited with holding that there are 'Meinongian Pure Objects', or unactualised possibilities which are in some sense or manner real (*Kenny* (1), pp. 147–6).

Spinoza appears to have held the same 'Meinongian' view.) The 'formal essence' of X, unlike the idea of X, is not mind-dependent; on the contrary, Spinoza regards it as something eternal (*CM* I, 2, iv). But since the 'formal essence' of X, unlike God, does not 'exist in itself', and since, unlike enduring finite modes, it has not been 'created', it cannot be said to exist in actuality (*CM* I, 2, iv). They are eternally real; but although they are uncreated, their existence is derivative and depends upon their being 'contained' in the divine essence (*CM* I, 2, iv). What then is an 'actual essence'? We must remember that not every possibility is or becomes actual, i.e. a part of the order of things in the actual world. 'Things are conceived by us as actual in two ways: either insofar as we conceive them to exist with relation to a fixed time and place, or insofar as we conceive them to be contained in God, and to follow from the necessity of the Divine nature' (*E* V, 29D). The latter type of 'actuality' recognised here belongs to 'formal essences'; we may call it *subsistence*. The former kind of 'actuality' belong to those possible things which form part of the world-order: we may call it, simply, *actuality*. The *real* is co-extensive with the *subsistent*; what *subsists*, may or may nor be *actual*. To speak of the 'actual essence' of X is thus to speak of X's 'formal essence' *as actualised*.

Now since Spinoza equates the eternal part of the mind with an idea expressing the essence of a particular body, it may seem that the eternity of that idea is not different from the eternity of the essence to which it corresponds. And some of Spinoza's commentators seem to have taken him in this sense. Pollock (who mentions but disagrees with the view) expresses it by saying that at first sight 'it looks as if too much had been proved, though not stated; as if what is asserted of the human mind were by implication asserted of all things whatever. Spinoza would then be saying aloud: "The human mind is in a certain sense eternal" – and adding in a whisper, for the few who could penetrate his secret – "and everything else too" ' (*Pollock*, p. 295). The mind would be 'eternal' only in being a permanent possibility.

Donagan suggests a way out of the difficulty. In effect, he attributes to Spinoza an extension of the *Postulate of Parallelism* which was laid down at *E* II, 7 (VI, 5). Not only must we say that the order and connection of ideas corresponds to the order and connection of things; we must accept that to every possibility or formal essence contained in the attribute of Extension, there corresponds an idea of that essence in the attribute of Thought. And (here his interpretation is extremely novel) the idea of any such essence must have a different mode of existence from the essence to which it corresponds. 'What, in the attribute of Thought, corresponds to a mere possibility in the attribute of Extension, must be more than a mere possibility' (*Donagan* (2), p. 254). These ideas do not merely subsist; they are *actual*.

Why suppose that Spinoza placed the ideas and their corresponding essences on a different footing? Donagan refers us back to *E* II, 8 (to which Spinoza also alludes in his proof at *E* V, 23). At that place, Spinoza says, 'the ideas of non-existent individual things or modes are comprehended in the infinite idea of God, in the same way that the formal essences of individual things or modes are contained in the attributes of God'. And in the appended corollary, he writes: 'Hence it follows that when individual things do not exist unless insofar as they are comprehended in the attributes of God, their objective being or ideas do not exist unless insofar as the infinite idea of God exists; and when individual things are said to exist, not only insofar as they are included in God's attributes, but insofar as they are said to have duration, their ideas involve the existence through which they are said to have duration'. The point is this. The essence of a non-existing body is real only in that it is 'contained' or implicit in the attribute of Extension. But the idea which corresponds to it is real, not (only) in that it is 'contained' in the attribute of Thought, but in that it is included in the infinite intellect of God. And the infinite intellect of God is a mediate infinite mode, part of *Natura naturata*, and itself an enduring thing (*Donagan* (2), pp. 254–5; *Steinberg*, pp. 172–3).

From here, the rest of the proof seems easy. Donagan explains it lucidly:

> Once it has been grasped that the identity of the order of ideas and the order of things not only does not forbid that there should be actual ideas of the formal essences of non-existent things, but on the contrary demands it, Spinoza's proof of immortality is simple. . . . When a living human body is destroyed, the corresponding mind, as non-derivative idea of that body actually existing, perishes with it; for they are the same mode in two distinct attributes. However, that mind, as actual essence, had as a part the idea of the formal essence of that body. And the idea of that formal essence belongs to God *sub specie aeternitatis*: it is part of the infinite idea of God, which is an eternal mode of God in the attribute of Thought. Therefore the part of a man's mind which consists in the idea of the formal essence of his body must be eternal: it must have

pre-existed in his body, and cannot be destroyed with it. Q.E.D. (*Donagan* (2), p. 255)

The proof, as Donagan expounds it, accords with his view that the eternity of (a part of) the mind consists in existence at all times. For the idea which comprises that part of the mind belongs to the infinite intellect of God; and the intellect of God, being produced from the attribute of Thought, part of *Natura naturata*, not *Natura naturans* (*E* I, 31). Since its status is creaturely, therefore, the intellect of God would seem to exist only durationally; and hence the ideas which are present in it would seem also to be durational (*Steinberg*, p. 174).

We are now in a position to attempt a solution to two major problems (*cf.* IX, 1). 'Why are human minds said to partake of eternity, when only God is strictly eternal?' The answer must be that what 'survives' is the idea of the formal essence of this or that body; and that idea 'involves the eternal and infinite essence of God' (*E* V, 39S). In other words, that idea, like the formal essence to which it corresponds, is 'in' God in such a way as to be able to share His eternity. As with the formal essences, its mode of existence must be at once derivative (in that it 'follows from' the nature of God) and yet not exhaustible by a finite duration. 'How then can the mind/body parallelism of *E* II, 7 be maintained?'. It can be maintained because it is not the mind, but only a part of it, which remains; and that part answers, not to the body or to any transient state or part of it, but to its formal essence.

The merits of Donagan's interpretation of the proof are manifest; indeed, I do not think it possible to find a better account of the matter. But if that is how Spinoza reasoned, he is snarled up in a tangle of difficulties. The crucial assumption needed for the proof is that the existential status of the ideas of singular non-existents *differ* from that of the formal essences of particulars in the Divine attributes. This, allegedly, is laid down at *E* II, 8. But in fact that theorem seems to assert that the 'formal essence/attribute' relation is the *same* as the 'idea/infinite intellect' one. The supposed difference in status only results if we add the consideration that the infinite intellect, but not the attributes, is part of *Natura naturata*. Taking *E* II, 8 by itself, we seem forced to say *either* that the idea of a non-existing thing is no more actual than the formal essence to which it corresponds, *or* that the corresponding formal essence endures and is actual, exactly like the idea in the Divine mind. In the first case, it would be necessary to admit that the idea existed eternally only as any merely possible object exists eternally: like the critics Pollock mentions, we could accuse Spinoza of making *everything* (or every *possible* thing) eternal. In this second case, where the idea itself is actual, and does not merely subsist, we should have to say that the essence or possibility which corresponds to it is also actual. Assuming that for every possible item in Extension there is a corresponding idea in Thought, it would follow that all the possible items in Extension were actual. There could not, strictly, be ideas of non-existing things; because wherever a formal essence was the object of an idea, that formal essence would share in its idea's actuality. Hence either everything, whether possible or actual, is eternal, and the eternity of the human mind does not differentiate it from the other possible beings; or everything possible is also actual – and it is the Principle of Plentitude which guarantees the mind's everlastingness (*cp.* V, 5).

Let me try to spell out the problem more fully. Assume – what of course is not the case – that Edward VIII and the Duchess of Windsor had had an eldest son. We might infer that there is a (merely) possible object, the eldest son of that couple. To say that there is such a possible object is to say, in Spinoza's language, that there is a formal essence contained in the attributes. But by the Postulate of Parallelism, there must also be an idea of that formal essence in the infinite intellect. Now if we follow out the line of reasoning expounded by Donagan, we must say that the idea of the eldest son of Edward VIII and his Duchess is part of *Natura naturata*, like the intellect which contains it; that that idea accordingly has durational actuality; and that a part of the mind of the King's eldest son is eternal, in the sense of everlasting. On this showing, then, the eternity which Spinoza holds out to mankind is a superabundantly common. And of course Spinoza would recoil from such bizarre generosity. He himself tells us, in the first application of *E* II, 8, that the ideas of non-existing things do *not* have duration and *cannot* be said to exist (i.e. to be actual): *E* II, 11D. But if he rejects a necessary consequence of the line of reasoning which Donagan imputes to him, then he is committed to discarding one of the premisses in it. Which one? It seems that it can only be the assumption that there is such a possible object as the eldest son of the King and Duchess. But how can the rejection of this plausible premiss be justified? Only, it seems, by declaring that since the imaginary son of the Windsors was at no time actual, he cannot even have been possible. The general form of this claim expresses adherence to the Principle of Plentitude: if X is at no time actual, then X is not possible (*cf.* V, 5). That Principle must be lying in the background if the proof of the mind's eternity, in the construal given it by

Donagan, is to go through.

Now there are other reasons to think that Spinoza embraced the Principle of Plentitude, and so it is not unwarrantable to invoke it in support of (Donagan's reading of) the proof. But there are also indications that Spinoza would *not* have accepted the Principle in the extremely strong form which is required here – a form which rules out the reality of all objects other than the actual. For at E II, 8 and 10, and in the proof itself at E V, 23, he certainly appears to imply that there *are* non-actual possibles. Nor is the fact that the proof needs supplementation the only difficulty with Donagan's version of it. If strict parallelism between mind and body is to be maintained, then the actuality of the idea of the body's essence must carry with it the actuality of that essence itself; and E II, 8 cannot be deployed to fight against this consequence. (On the contrary, as we have seen, it lends support to the identity of existential status of essences and ideas.) But then Spinoza is involved in the unwelcome conclusion that (some part of) the body is as everlasting as the human mind. Furthermore, unless Part V of the *Ethics* stands quite apart from the rest of Spinoza's work, the 'eternity' which is ascribed to the mind at E V, 23, cannot be infinite duration (*cf.* IX, 3). If it is said that by assigning the appropriate part of the mind to the infinite intellect, Spinoza is perforce treating it as omnitemporal, the answer must be that he is guilty of self-contradiction.

The fact of the matter is that the 'proof' of the mind's eternity is a botched job. It involves Spinoza in wanting both to retain and to repudiate the Principle of Plentitude; it jeopardises his loyalty to the Postulate of Parallelism, and the non-dualist, non-interactionist theory of the mind which is developed from it; and it lands him in the inconsistency of ascribing duration to what he regards as timeless. (We shall shortly see that the difficulties it caused him are not yet at an end.) Is there not some sign that he felt uneasy himself when he wrote at E V, 41: 'Even if we did not know that our mind is eternal, we should still consider as of the first importance Piety and Religion, and absolutely everything which in Part IV we have shown to be related to strength of mind and generosity'?

5 The survival of the fittest

Preachers and theologians have sometimes taught that men can be saved by good works. Spinoza writes as if he accepted a demythologised form of that view. He speaks as if a greater or lesser part of the mind could be rendered eternal, and he suggests

ETERNITY AND IMMORTALITY

that the means to securing the survival of a greater part lie in our power. At *E* V, 38D, he says: 'The essence of the mind consists in knowledge. The more things, therefore, the mind knows by the second and third kinds of knowledge, the greater is that part which abides'. Since the 'first' kind of knowledge is not really knowledge at all (III, 1), he must mean that the more we know, the more of us survives. And at *E* V, 39, he makes clear that our survival-prospects are brighter, the more fit our bodies become: 'He who possesses a body fit for many things possesses a mind of which the greater part is eternal'. Yet these views are decidedly odd when set against the demonstration at *E* V, 23. For that proof entails that the eternal part of the mind is the idea which takes the formal essence of an individual as its object; and how can that idea become greater or less in response to our activities? If the 'formal essence' of X is simply X regarded as a pure possibility, then that essence should be changeless, and incapable of being affected by what X does; and since its object is unalterable, the idea which corresponds to it should be equally unable to be magnified or reduced. Can we overcome this difficulty? I think we can, although the solution I propose must be regarded as highly conjectural. It appears to me that in addition to the formal proof of the mind's eternity there is a separate, latent line of thought, which results in contradictory conclusions.

In the scholium to *E* V, 23, Spinoza says that we feel and experience our own eternity (*'sentimus experimurque nos aeternos esse'*). The state of mind he is describing might be thought to be a mystical one, surpassing the ordinary modes of consciousness; but in fact his meaning seems to be less exalted. For he tells us that the state of mind is like sensing, or more specifically like seeing, and that it arises from following deductive proofs: demonstrations are the *eyes* of the mind. What he is referring to, then, is a state of mind which arises in, or through, sound reasoning. Now when we form adequate ideas, and fix their deductive relations to each other and to the rest of our beliefs, we are bringing it about that our own minds reproduce the order which ideas have in the infinite intellect of God. Our minds, when we think and reason rightly, come to mirror the Divine intellect; and the further our adequate knowledge extends, the more god-like our minds become. It is but a small step to take if we say that our minds become in some sense *identical* with the infinite intellect, and do not merely 'mirror' or 'reflect' it. In this very connection, Spinoza speaks of the 'union' of the mind with God, and is willing to transfer some of the properties of the object of knowledge to the ideas by which it is known: 'This true knowledge varies with the objects that come before it: the better the object is with which it happens to unite itself, so much the better also is this knowledge. And, for this reason, he is the most perfect man who is united with God' (*ST* II, 4; *cp*. *ST* II, 26, vii–viii). This assimilation of the knower to the known is made easier if we conceive of the infinite intellect, not as a conscious mind, but as an impersonal body of knowledge, which can be displayed in the form of an axiomatised deductive system. Our own minds then can be conceived of as, in part, fragments or subsystems of this comprehensive order of ideas, selectively incorporating some of their axioms, and setting out the consequences with the proper deductive connections. Mrs Kneale has attributed some such view to Spinoza: she maintains that the Divine knowledge 'in the case of each human body *is* the corresponding human mind, or at least that part of it which is eternal'; and she adds, 'A given mind . . . is that system of knowledge which has the existence of God as its first premiss (this is common to all), the existence of other parts of the Universe as intermediate premisses, and the existence of its own body as conclusion. Thus every human mind is in a way the same system of knowledge as every other human mind, but it is the system arranged in a different way' (*Kneale* (2), p. 239).

Now given this picture, certain remarkable consequences follow. For we *can* form adequate ideas, and deduce theorems from them; and to the extent that this is possible, we can conform our minds to, or identify them with, the intellect of God. Moreover, the greater the number of adequate ideas we possess, the greater is the part of the mind which is identical with the Divine mind. Hence it is that the more we know by the second and third kinds of knowledge, the greater is the part of our mind which is eternal. And because our capacity to form adequate ideas is bound up with the health and sensitivity of our bodies, the fitter our bodies become, the larger the portion of our mind which enjoys eternity.

This interpretation of Spinoza helps to clear up other puzzles that have surrounded his treatment of the mind's eternity. For example, it has been much disputed whether Spinozistic survival is personal or not. Hampshire puts the negative side:

> The possible eternity of the human mind cannot therefore be intended by Spinoza to mean that I literally survive, as a distinguishable individual, insofar as I attain genuine knowledge, for insofar as I do attain genuine knowledge, my individuality as a particular thing disappears and my mind

becomes so far united with God or Nature conceived under the attribute of thought. (*Hampshire* (2), p. 275)

Mrs Kneale, however, followed by Donagan, rejects that notion bluntly:

> Hampshire's view that *qua* eternal the human mind is lost in the Divine consciousness must be wrong; for the premiss to the argument for the eternity of the mind reads . . . 'There exists necessarily, however, in God an idea which expresses the essence of *this and that* body under the form of eternity.' It is the eternity of the idea of *this and that* body, i.e. of *this and that* human mind which is precisely in question. (*Kneale* (2), pp. 237–8; *cp. Donagan* (2), p. 252)

Wolfson seems unhappily torn between the two views: he writes that, for Spinoza, 'immortality is in a certain sense personal and individual' (*Wolfson* II, p. 318); but four pages later we find him saying that the proof *denies* that 'the soul continues to exist after death in its entirety and as an individual entity'.

What has happened, I submit, is that the commentators have failed to disentangle the two different and incompatible strands of thought which are knotted together by Spinoza in *Ethics* V. The overt line of reasoning, analysed in the previous section, is set out in the demonstration of the theorem at *E* V, 23, to which Mrs Kneale refers in defence of her view. That line issues, as she says, in the conclusion that what survives is in some way personal or individual; it also issues, as we have noticed, in the conclusion that the 'eternal' part cannot be made greater by our exertions nor lesser by our inadequacies. If 'salvation' is personal, it must come from God, not from works. The other, latent line of thinking, picked out in the present section, underlies the theorems at *E* V, 38 and 39.[1] It favours Hampshire's view that what survives is impersonal, absorbed without individuality into God. 'Impersonal', because what survives is not a mind but a body of knowledge; 'absorbed', because that knowledge cannot be differentiated from the other 'minds' or bodies of knowledge which coincide with it in propositional content, nor from the comprehensive body of knowledge which forms the Divine 'mind'. In short, the apparent disagreement of the commentators reflects a real inconsistency in Spinoza.

The hypothesis I am proposing will illuminate other controversial matters. Donagan, for instance, finds Mrs Kneale to be

---

[1] The 'Magian' dualism of 'soul' and 'spirit' which Spengler discerns in Spinoza may surface at this point: *Spengler* I, pp. 305–7.

'mistaken in attributing to [Spinoza] the hideous hypothesis of universal salvation' (*Donagan* (2), p. 257; *Kneale* (2), p. 239). He adduces two considerations: first, that Spinoza teaches that an undeveloped mind, snuffed out by a premature death, will know almost nothing of God, itself or things, and hence cannot attain blessedness (*E* V, 39S); second, that the destiny of the wicked, because it will involve understanding and love of God, must embroil them in continual frustration (*Donagan* (2), pp. 257–8). (It seems to me that Donagan's two considerations are at cross-purposes: because the infant's mind lacks adequate ideas, its *survival* (and not its *blessedness*) is rendered doubtful, since we survive in proportion to the number of adequate ideas we possess; but the prevalence of inadequate ideas in the minds of the damned is assumed to lead, not to their *extinction*, but to their *wretchedness*. See also *ST* II, 35, which denies the existence of devils.) Whether we regard Spinoza as a 'universalist' or not will largely depend, I suggest, on which line of thought we emphasise in him. The 'official' proof at *E* V, 23 inclines one to the view that the eternal condition is the same for all men: if survival comes from God, then it is universal. The 'latent' reasoning intimated at *E* V, 39 (which provides Donagan's main textual support) points rather to the conclusion that a mind nearly void of adequate ideas – as many minds are – can survive in, at best, an attenuated form: if salvation is from works, then few will be blessed.

I have argued that Spinoza's 'explicit' line of thought is hopelessly confused; is the 'latent' reasoning any better? Not at all. In describing the mind's union with God, Spinoza speaks as if a miraculous intervention had been taking place, suspending the normal, bodily conditioned workings of the mind. So Spinoza's partisan, Theophilus, in his dialogue with Erasmus, says that the human understanding is an 'immediate' creation brought forth from the Divine attributes, and participates for that reason in their eternity: it is not formed by God *as qualified* by the mediation of any finite mode. This indicates a manner of creation for the human intellect which distinguishes it from all other finite modes, and which is strictly impossible on Spinoza's own assumptions (*cf. The Short Treatise*, Second Dialogue, *G* I, pp. 33–4; *Wolf*, pp. 38–9; contrast *E* II, 6C and 9). When demythologised, all talk of the mind's greater life and blessedness resulting from a more intimate union with God, means only that the mind attains eternal existence by undertaking to transform itself from a personal and transient consciousness into an impersonal and timeless body of knowledge. Now such a 'transformation' is more than miraculous: it is incoherent. Only to the mystical vision, not to the discursive understanding, can the knower and the known be one. Spinoza's formulas in the latter part of the *Ethics*, deriving as they do from the hallowed language of religion, retain much of their evocative power; nor is it possible to question the depth and the sincerity of the emotion they express. But his literal meaning cannot satisfy the religious consciousness, whose 'vulgar' demands he so haughtily despises; it clashes with the naturalistic elements of his own outlook; it does not measure up to the exacting standards of philosophical rigour which he set for himself.

Yet if the reasoner fails, the mystic will always command love and admiration; and it is fitting that the mystic should have the final word. For 'reasoning is not the principal thing in us, but only like a staircase by which we can climb up to the desired place' (*ST*, 26: 'Of True Freedom').

Bibliography

(This bibliography lists only works directly referred to or quoted in the text; it does not include every authority used in the writing or preparation of this book; and it omits reference to classics of philosophy except when there is need to identify a particular edition or translation.)

R.M. Adams, 'Where Do Our Ideas Come from?' in Stich (ed.), below, pp. 71–88.
H.E. Allison, *Benedict de Spinoza*, Boston, Mass., 1975.
G.E.M. Anscombe (1), 'Aristotle', in *Three Philosophers*, by G.E.M. Anscombe and P. Geach, Ithaca, N.Y., 1961.
G.E.M. Anscombe (2), *An Introduction to Wittgenstein's Tractatus*, 3rd edn, London, 1967.
D.M. Armstrong (ed.), *Berkeley's Philosophical Writings*, London, 1965.
J. Austin, 'Pleasure and Happiness', in Schneewind (ed.), below, pp. 234–50.
M.R. Ayers, *The Refutation of Determinism*, London, 1968.
H. Barker, 'Notes on the Second Part of Spinoza's Ethics', in three parts, reprinted in Kashap (ed.), below, pp. 101–68.
J. Barnes (1), *The Presocratic Philosophers*, vols I and II, London, 1979.
J. Barnes (2), *Aristotle's Posterior Analytics*, Oxford, 1975.
D. Bell, *Frege's Theory of Judgement*, Oxford, 1979.
J. Bennett (1), *Kant's Analytic*, Cambridge, 1966.
J. Bennett (2), *Kant's Dialectic*, Cambridge, 1974.
J. Bennett (3), *Rationality*, London, 1964.
G. Berkeley, in Armstrong (ed.), above.
I. Berlin, *Concepts and Categories*, H. Hardy (ed.), New York, 1979.
D. Bidney, *The Psychology and Ethics of Spinoza*, (reprint), New York, 1962.
F. Brentano, *The True and The Evident*, ed. and trans. R.M. Chisholm, I. Politzer, K. Fischer, London, 1966.
C.D. Broad (1), *The Mind and its Place in Nature*, paperback edn, New York, 1960.

BIBLIOGRAPHY

C.D. Broad (2), *Five Types of Ethical Theory*, London, 1930.
G. Buchdahl, *Metaphysics and the Philosophy of Science*, Oxford, 1969.
R. Butler (ed.), *Cartesian Studies*, Oxford, 1972.
E. Caird, *Spinoza*, Edinburgh, 1910.
S. Carr, 'Spinoza's Distinction between Rational and Intuitive Knowledge', in *The Philosophical Review*, vol. 87, 1978, pp. 241–52.
H. Caton, *The Origin of Subjectivity*, New Haven, Conn., 1973.
R.M. Chisholm, *The Problem of the Criterion*, Milwaukee, Wis., 1973.
S. Clarke, *A Demonstration of the Being and Attributes of God*, London, 1705.
R.G. Collingwood, *The Idea of Nature*, Oxford, 1945.
Z. Cowen and P.B. Carter, *Essays on the Law of Evidence*, Oxford, 1956.
E.M. Curley (1), 'Descartes, Spinoza and The Ethics of Belief', in Mandelbaum and Freiman (eds), below, pp. 159–90.
E.M. Curley (2), 'Experience in Spinoza's Theory of Knowledge', in Grene (ed.), below, pp. 25–59.
E.M. Curley (3), *Spinoza's Metaphysics*, Cambridge, Mass., 1969.
E.M. Curley (4), 'Man and Nature in Spinoza', in Wetlesen (ed.), below, pp. 19–26.
R. Dawkins, *The Selfish Gene*, Essex, 1978.
R.J. Delahunty, 'Descartes' Cosmological Argument', in *The Philosophical Quarterly*, vol. 30, 1980, pp. 34–46.
J. Dewey, 'The Pantheism of Spinoza', in *The Journal of Speculative Philosophy*, vol. XVI, 1887, pp. 249–57.
E.J. Dijksterhuis, *The Mechanization of the World Picture*, trans. C. Dikshoorn, Oxford, 1969.
C. Dobell (ed.), *Antony van Leeuwenhoek and His 'Little Animals'*, paperpack edn, New York, 1960.
A. Donagan (1), 'Essence and the Distinction of Attributes in Spinoza's Metaphysics', in Grene (ed.), below, pp. 164–81.
A. Donagan (2), 'Spinoza's Proof of Immortality', in Grene (ed.), below, pp. 241–58.
W. Doney, 'Spinoza on Philosophical Scepticism', in *The Monist*, vol. 55, 1971, pp. 617–35.
R.A. Duff, *Spinoza's Political and Ethical Philosophy*, Glasgow, 1903.
J.L. Evans, 'Error and the Will', in *Philosophy*, vol. 38, 1963, pp. 136–48.
A. Farrer, *Reflective Faith*, ed C. Conti, London, 1972.
P. Feyerabend, *Against Method*, New York, 1975.
J. Finnis, *Natural Law and Natural Rights*, Oxford, 1980.
G. Fløistad, 'Spinoza's Theory of Knowledge Applied to the Ethics', in *Inquiry*, vol. 12, 1969, pp. 41–67.
H. Frankfurt (ed.), *Leibniz*, Garden City, N.Y., 1972.
H. Froude, *Short Studies on Great Subjects*, vol. I, London, 1903.
R. Garrigou-Lagrange, *The One God*, trans. Dom Bede Rose, O.S.B., St Louis, Mo., 1943.
P. Geach (1), *The Virtues*, Cambridge, 1973.

BIBLIOGRAPHY

P. Geach (2), *Logic Matters*, Oxford, 1972.
P. Geach (3), *Reference and Generality*, Ithaca, N.Y., 1962.
P. Geach (4), 'Spinoza and the Divine Attributes', in Vesey (2), ed., below.
M. Grene (ed.), *Spinoza: A Collection of Critical Essays*, Garden City, N.Y., 1973.
M. Gueroult, *Spinoza*, in two vols: vol. I, Paris, 1968; vol. II, Paris, 1974.
I. Hacking, 'Individual Substance', in Frankfurt (ed.), above pp. 137–54.
R. Hall, *From Galileo to Newton*, paperback edn, London 1970.
T.S. Hall, *René Descartes: Treatise of Man*, Cambridge, Mass., 1972.
H.G. Hallett, *Benedict de Spinoza: The Elements of His Philosophy*, London, 1957.
S. Hampshire (1), *Thought and Action*, New York, 1959.
S. Hampshire (2), *Spinoza*, Baltimore, Md., 1962.
S. Hampshire (3), *Freedom of Mind*, Oxford, 1972.
C.L. Hardin, 'Spinoza on Immortality and Time', in Shahan and Biro (eds), below, pp. 129–38.
R. Hardin, *Collective Action*, Baltimore, Md., 1982.
E. Harris, 'Spinoza's Theory of Human Immortality', in *The Monist*, vol. 55, 1971, pp. 668–85.
J. Heller, *Catch-22*, New York, 1961.
K.J. Hintikka (1), 'A Discourse on Descartes' Method', in Hooker (ed.), below, pp. 74–88.
K.J. Hintikka (2), *Knowledge and Belief*, Ithaca, N.Y., 1962.
A.O. Hirschman (1), *The Passions and The Interests*, Princeton, N.J., 1977.
A.O. Hirschman (2), *Exit, Voice and Loyalty: Responses to Decline in Firms, Organizations, and States*, Cambridge, Mass., 1970.
T. Hobbes, in Peters (ed.), below.
O.W. Holmes, Jr., *The Common Law*, ed M. DeW. Howe, Boston, Mass., 1963.
M. Hooker (ed.), *Descartes: Critical and Interpretive Essays*, Baltimore, Md., 1978.
E. Husserl, *The Crisis of European Science*, trans. D. Carr, Evanston, Ill., 1970.
H. Joachim (1), *Spinoza's Tractatus de Intellectus Emendatione*, Oxford, 1940.
H. Joachim (2), *A Study of the Ethics of Spinoza*, Oxford, 1901.
H. Joachim (3), *The Nature of Truth*, Oxford, 1948.
H. Jonas, 'Spinoza and the Theory of Organism', in Grene (ed.), above, pp. 259–78.
S.P. Kashap (ed.), *Spinoza*, Berkeley, Calif., 1972.
S.V. Keeling, *Descartes*, 2nd edn, Oxford, 1968.
N. Kemp Smith (ed. and trans.), *Descartes' Philosophical Writings*, London, 1958.
A.J.P. Kenny (1), 'Descartes on the Will', in Butler (ed.), above, pp. 1–31.

BIBLIOGRAPHY

A.J.P. Kenny (2), *Descartes: A Study of His Philosophy*, New York, 1968.
A.J.P. Kenny (3), *The God of the Philosophers*, Oxford, 1979.
A.J.P. Kenny (4), *The Anatomy of the Soul*, Oxford, 1973.
A.J.P. Kenny (5), 'Determinism and Mind', in *The Nature of Mind*, by Kenny and others, The Gifford Lectures, Edinburgh, 1972.
A.J.P. Kenny (6), *The Five Ways*, London, 1969.
W. Kessler, 'A Note on the Attributes', in *The Monist*, vol. 55, 1971, pp. 636–9.
M. Kneale (1), 'Leibniz and Spinoza on Activity', in Frankfurt (ed.), above, pp. 215–38.
M. Kneale (2), 'Eternity and Sempiternity', in Grene (ed.), above, pp. 227–40.
P. Lachièze-Rey, *Les Origines cartésiennes du Dieu de Spinoza*, Paris, 1950.
D. Lachtermann, 'The Physics of Spinoza's Ethics', in Shahan and Biro (eds), below, pp. 71–112.
L. Lafuma (ed.), *Opuscules et Lettres de Pascal*, Paris, 1955.
I. Lakatos, *Mathematics, Science and Epistemology*, vol. II, ed J. Worrall and G. Currie, Cambridge, 1978.
G. Leibniz, in Loemker (ed.), below.
L. Lerner, 'Shards and Burnt Hieroglyphs: Seventeenth Century Studies', in *Encounter*, vol. LXI, 1983, pp. 83–89.
E. Linden, *Apes, Men and Language*, New York, 1976.
L. Loemker (ed.), *Leibniz: Philosophical Papers and Letters*, Chicago, 1956.
K. Lorenz, *On Aggression*, trans. M. Kerr Wilson, paperback edn, New York, 1971.
J. Lucas, *The Oldest Biography of Spinoza*, ed, trans., and annot. by A. Wolf, Port Washington, N.Y., 1970.
G. Lukács, *The Young Hegel*, trans. R. Livingstone, London, 1975.
J.J. MacIntosh, 'Spinoza's Epistemological Views', in Vesey (2), ed., below.
A. MacIntyre (1), *Against the Self-Images of the Age*, London, 1971.
A. MacIntyre (2), *After Virtue*, Notre Dame, Ind., 1981.
M. Mandelbaum and E. Freiman (eds), *Spinoza: Essays in Interpretation*, LaSalle, Ill., 1975.
J. Martineau, *Types of Ethical Theory*, 3rd edn, vol. I, Oxford, 1898.
W. Matson, 'Spinoza's Theory of Mind', in *The Monist*, vol. 55, 1971, pp. 567–78.
R. McKeon, *The Philosophy of Spinoza*, New York, 1928.
M. Midgeley (1), *Beast and Man*, Sussex, 1978.
M. Midgeley (2), 'Duties Concerning Islands', in *Encounter*, vol. LX, 1983, pp. 36–43.
J. Neu, *Emotion, Thought and Therapy*, London, 1977.
J.T. Noonan, Jr., *Persons and Masks of the Law*, New York, 1976.
R. Nozick, *Philosophical Explanations*, Cambridge, Mass., 1981.
J. Offenberg, 'A Newly Found Letter from Spinoza', in *Philosophia*,

BIBLIOGRAPHY

vol. 7, 1977, pp. 1–15.
A. Pap, *The Elements of Analytical Philosophy*, New York, 1972.
G.H.R. Parkinson (1), *Spinoza's Theory of Knowledge*, Oxford, 1954.
G.H.R. Parkinson (2), 'Truth is its own Standard: Aspects of Spinoza's Theory of Truth', in Shahan and Biro (eds), below, pp. 35–56.
G.H.R. Parkinson (3), 'Being and Knowledge in Spinoza', in van der Bend (ed.), below, pp. 24–40.
G.H.R. Parkinson (4), 'Spinoza on the Power and Freedom of Man', in *The Monist*, vol. 55, 1971, pp. 527–53.
B. Pascal (1), 'De l'esprit géometrique', in Lafuma (ed.), above.
B. Pascal (2), *Pensées*, bilingual edn, ed and trans. H.F. Stewart, New York, n.d.
R.S. Peters (ed.), *Body, Man and Citizen: Selections from Thomas Hobbes*, New York, 1962.
F. Pollock, *Spinoza*, London, 1880.
R. Popkin (1), *The History of Scepticism from Erasmus to Descartes*, revised edn, New York, 1964.
R. Popkin (2), 'Spinoza and LaPeyrere', in Shahan and Biro (eds), below, pp. 177–96.
K. Popper, *Conjectures and Refutations*, 4th edn, London, 1972.
A. Prior (1), *The Doctrine of Propositions and Terms*, eds A. Kenny and P. Geach, London, 1976.
A. Prior (2), *Formal Logic*, 2nd edn, Oxford, 1962.
W.V.O. Quine (1), *From a Logical Point of View*, 2nd edn, New York, 1963.
W.V.O. Quine (2), *Word and Object*, Cambridge, Mass., 1960.
N. Rescher (1), *The Coherence Theory of Truth*, Oxford, 1973.
N. Rescher (2), *Essays in Philosophical Analysis*, Pittsburgh, 1969.
R. Robinson, *Definition*, Oxford, 1950.
B. Russell, *A History of Western Philosophy*, London, 1961.
G. Ryle, *The Concept of Mind*, New York, 1949.
G. Santayana, 'The Ethical Doctrine of Spinoza', in *The Harvard Monthly*, 1886, pp. 144–52.
D. Savan, 'Spinoza on Death and the Emotions', in Wetlesen (ed.), below, pp. 192–203.
T. Schelling, *Micromotives and Macrobehavior*, New York, 1978.
J. Schneewind (ed.), *Mill: A Collection of Critical Essays*, Garden City, N.Y., 1968.
R.W. Shahan and J.I. Biro (eds), *Spinoza: New Perspectives*, Norman, Okla., 1978.
R. Sorabji, *Necessity, Cause and Blame*, London, 1980.
O. Spengler, *The Decline of the West*, one vol. edn, trans. C.F. Atkinson, London, 1932.
D. Steinberg, *Spinoza's Theory of the Mind*, Ph.D. Thesis, The University of Illinois at Urbana Champaigne, 1977.
S. Stich (ed.), *Innate Ideas*, Berkeley and Los Angeles, Calif. 1975.
L. Strauss, *Spinoza's Critique of Religion*, New York, 1965.
P.F. Strawson, *Freedom and Resentment*, London, 1974.

BIBLIOGRAPHY

A.E. Taylor (1), 'Some Incoherences in Spinozism', in two parts, in Kashap (ed.), above, pp. 189–211; pp. 289–309.
A.E. Taylor (2), 'The Conception of Immortality in Spinoza's Ethics', in *Mind*, vol. 5, 1896, pp. 145–66.
R.M. Unger, *Knowledge and Politics*, New York, 1975.
J.G. van der Bend (ed.), *Spinoza on Knowing, Being and Freedom*, Assen, 1974.
B. van Fraasen, *An Introduction to the Philosophy of Time and Space*, New York, 1970.
Z. Vendler, *Res Cogitans*, Ithaca, N.Y., 1972.
G. Vesey (1), 'Agent and Spectator: the Dual Aspect Theory', in *The Royal Institute of Philosophy Lectures*, vol. 1, 1966–7, pp. 139–59.
G. Vesey (2) (ed.), *The Royal Institute of Philosophy Lectures: Reason and Reality*, vol. 5, 1971–2.
W. von Leyden, *Seventeenth Century Metaphysics*, London, 1968.
G.H. von Wright (1), 'Wittgenstein On Certainty', in *Problems in the Theory of Knowledge*, ed. von Wright, The Hague, 1972, pp. 47–60.
G.H. von Wright (2), *The Varieties of Goodness*, London, 1963.
F. Waismann, *How I See Philosophy*, London, 1968.
A. Wedberg, *A History of Philosophy*, vol. II, Oxford, 1982.
F. Wendel, *Calvin*, trans. P. Mairet, London, 1963.
J. Wetlesen (ed.), *Spinoza's Philosophy of Man*, Oslo, 1978.
D. Wiggins, 'Truth, Invention and The Meaning of Life', in *The Proceedings of the British Academy*, vol. 72, 1976, pp. 331–78.
J. Wild, 'Introduction' to *Spinoza Selections*, ed. J. Wild, New York, 1930.
B. Williams (1), *Descartes: The Project of Pure Enquiry*, Sussex, 1978.
B. Williams (2), *Morality*, New York, 1972.
M.D. Wilson, *Descartes*, London, 1978.
H.A. Wolfson, *The Philosophy of Spinoza*, in two vols, paperback edn, New York, 1969.
S. Zac, *L'Idée de vie dans la philosophie de Spinoza*, Paris, 1963.

Index

Acosta, Uriel, 279
action: and endeavour, 222–3, 227; and passion, 215–20, 230–1, 233–6, 253
affections, 243–6, 248–52; and substance, 112–14
alteration and substance, 99–100
analysis in Descartes' method, 10
animals: Descartes' view of, 206–8; Spinoza's view of, 208–12
anti-scepticism in reply to the *diallelus*, 15–18, 21–2
appetite, 221, 230
Aquinas, St Thomas, 137, 139, 144, 282–3
Aristotle: on coincidence and causality, 159; on the contemplative life, 275; and desire, 227–9; and eternity, 144, 149–50, 286–7; on knowledge from causes, 201–2; and the mind, 180; *Nichomachean Ethics* compared to Spinoza's *Ethics*, 5–8; and the soul, 192–4; and substance, 96–7, 101–2, 106
assent: and assertion, 39; Spinoza's account of, 33–5, 39–40, 42–3
assertion, 33–5, 44; and assent, 39
attitudes, objective and reactive, 260–8
attributes: defined, 91, 102; Divine, 85, 86–7, 117–18, 119–20, 123–4, 130, 132, 136, 164, 293–4; modes and, 103–5, 114, 121; and necessity, 164; Spinoza's doctrine of, 116–22, 190, 198; substance and, 89, 102–14, 118–24
Austin, Jean, 250–1

Bacon, 67, 68, 70, 71, 116
Balance Principle, The, 184–5
Barker, Harold, 191–2
behaviourism, and the mind, 180
belief: and error, 48–9; suspension of, 42–3
Bennett, Jonathan, 97–100, 146, 184–5, 261, 264
Berkeley, G., 184
Berlin, Sir Isaiah, 256–60, 263–4
blessedness, spiritual: and knowledge, 5, 56, 57–8, 304; and reason, 275–6
body: Laws of Feeling and, 236–7, 240–1; mind and, 177–99, 204–6, 280
bondage, human, 241–3
Boxel, Hugo, 156–7, 159–60
Broad, C.D., 230
'Buridanus, the ass of', 44–5, 259

Caird, E., 248–9
Calvin, 169, 170
Carr, S., 80–2
cause: and activity, 216–17, 218–20, 233; and coincidence, 159, 162, 171–2; dependence of effects on, 10; and emotions, 233–4, 236–9, 242, 247, 252; final, 165–74; God as, of the Universe, 127–8, 129–31, 132–5, 148–9, 156, 165–73; knowledge advancing from, 48, 81, 201–4; knowledge of, 198; mental, and physical effects, 178–9, 184, 191–2; and necessity, 158–9, 160–3; physical, and mental effects, 191–2; of substance, 111–12, 114–15

312

INDEX

Chisholm, R.M., 15
Chomsky, Noam, 38, 207
Clarke, Samuel, 164
coincidences and causality, 159, 162, 171–2
Collingwood, R.G., 120
common notions and knowledge, 74–8, 83–4
compatibility and the attributes, 118, 121
contemplation, 275–8
contingency: in Spinoza's axioms, 19–20; of the Universe, 131–2, 161
Creationism: Descartes and, 166; Spinoza and, 127, 131–2, 136, 143–7, 148–56, 166–71
criterion of truth, scepticism and, 13–18, 22–4
Curley, E.M., 130, 163–4, 210–12

definitions, Spinoza's, 91–6, 101
Descartes: affinity between Spinoza and, 2; on attributes and modes, 103–4, 106, 107–8, 118–19; and the body, 177–9, 181–3, 186–90, 205–6; classification of ideas, 24; confusing images and ideas, 36–9; confusing words and ideas, 39; differences between Spinoza and, 32, 33, 35–46, 58, 183–5, 208; and doubt, 27–8, 29, 31–2, 39–40; and error, 31–3, 35, 48; and geometrical method, 9–11; and God, 126, 134, 136–7, 151, 165–6; on infinity, 65; and knowledge, 7–8, 32, 58; and the mind, 31–2, 43, 176–9, 181–3, 185–90, 205–9; particularism of, 16–17, 18; and the passions, 182–3, 213–16, 227; on the Principle of Perfection, 153–4; and scepticism, 29, 31, 199–200; and substance, 89, 103–4, 109, 113, 118–19, 120; and suspension of belief, 42–3; and the will, 32–3, 35–6, 37, 40–6, 177, 179, 215–16
desire, 221, 222–3, 230–3, 244, 251–2; and reason, 230–1, 235, 269; and value, 227–31, 269
determinism: Spinoza's, 159–60, 161, 163, 259–60; Strawson on, 262–3, 265
diallelus, the, 12–19, 21–4
Donagan, Alan, 209, 281, 284, 286–94

passim, 296–304 *passim*
doubt: Descartes and, 27–8, 29, 31–2, 39–40; Spinoza's view of, 25–30, 39–40
dualism: and attributes, 105; and mind and body, 178–9, 190–7, 206
Duff, R.A., 230

effect: dependence on cause, 10; knowledge advancing to, 48, 81, 202–3; knowledge of, 198; mental, and physical cause, 191–2; physical, and mental cause, 178–9, 184, 191–2; the world as, of the Divine nature, 156
egoism, 223–7, 268, 270–5
emotions (*see also* passions), 232–47; Descartes on the, 213–15; and endeavour, 222, 230; and knowledge, 241–8, 251–2; morality and the, 213; reason and, 230, 234–5, 246–53, 266–7
empiricism: in Descartes' classification of ideas, 24; in reply to the *diallelus*, 15; and substance, 90
endeavour, 220–2, 226, 229–30
envy, 4, 238, 239
error: and common notions, 76; Descartes' account of, 31–3, 35, 48; knowledge and, 47–54, 59; nature of, 46; Spinoza's view of, 33, 35, 46–54
eternity: God's will and, 148–50, 154, 288; and necessity, 149–51, 154, 282; Spinoza's view of, 147, 149, 280–1, 287–304
ethics, 5–8, 55
Ethics: compared to Aristotle's *Nichomachean Ethics*, 5–8; experience and knowledge in, 73; style of, 3–4, 8–9, 11, 19; truth of, 18–21
existence: eternal, 287–8, 290–304; God's, 129, 289–90, 293; of substance, 289–90
existence-changes and substance, 99–100
experience and knowledge, 57, 64, 67–74
explanation and coincidence, 171–2
Extension, 86–7, 105; body as, 177, 179; common notions and, 75, 77; and God, 117, 119, 126; in relation

313

INDEX

to Thought, 121–3, 178–9, 182, 184, 198, 205

fear, 173–4, 233–6, 237
feeling: faculty of, 41–2; Laws of, 236–40
final causes, doctrine of, 165–74
freedom: of action, 219–20; and necessity, 155–9, 162; and reason, 155–65, 168–9; of the will, 35–6, 37–46, (God's, 136, 147–58, 165–7, 169–73)

Geach, Peter, 33–4
generalisations, 6–7, 69–70
geometrical method, 3–4, 8–12
God: attributes of, 117–18, 119–20, 123–4, 130, 132, 136, 164, 293–4; deceptive, and doubt, 27, 28–30, 32; the Divine mind, 131–6, 138–9, 147, 150–3, 297–8, 301–4; and eternity, 280–1, 282, 284–5, 288–94, 295, 298; and free will, 131–2, 136, 147–58, 165–7, 169–73; idea of, and knowledge, 31, 82; infinity and, 65, 119, 123–4, 285, 290, 293, 297–8; knowledge of, 61, 83, 270, 274, 275; and Nature, 125–31, 161, 166–9, 172–4; omnipotence of, 136–43

Hall, R., 209
Hampshire, Stuart, 196, 247, 281, 302–3
hate, 237–9, 252–3
hearsay, knowledge from, 59–62
Heereboord, 169–70
Hintikka, Jaakko, 52–3
Hobbes, T., 9, 62, 106, 108, 117, 223–4, 225, 226
hope, 237
Hume, D., 65, 90, 106, 199–200

ideas: and activity, 217–18, 220, 233; classification of, 24; and common notions, 74–5; and emotions, 233–4, 239, 243–5, 247, 248–51; and error, 47–8, 50–4, 69–70; and eternity, 296–304; and immortality, 280; innate, 24; and knowledge, 57, 63, 74–5, 199–201, 203–4, 275–6; order and connection of, 198, 203–4, 280, 296–7; Spinoza's account of assent and, 34–5; Spinoza's views on, 36–9, 201; and the understanding, 127–8; words and, 39, 63, 64–6
images, ideas confused with, 36–9, 63, 200
imagination: and body, 205; and delusions, 265; and error, 49–54, 70; and knowledge, 57, 58–9, 242–3; Maimonides' view of, 58–9; and truth, 242–3
imagining as mode of perceiving, 41
immortality, 279–80, 297, 303
incompatibility and the attributes, 118
infinity, 65; and existence of the world, 144–7; God and, 65, 119, 123–4, 285, 290, 293, 297–8; of substance and attributes, 119, 123–4, 290
innatism, Descartes', 24
instinct, Descartes' view of, 207–8
intellect, the: and attributes, 116–17, 122; Descartes' view of, 32, 35, 41–2, 43; Divine, 131–6, 138–9, 147, 150–4, 297–8, 301–4; and emotions, 252; and endeavour, 226–7; and experience, 71; and free will, 38; and its ideas, 127–8; Maimonides' view of, 58–9; purification of, 5; refutation of scepticism and, 31; Spinoza's 'tool analogy', 21–4; Spinoza's view of, 41–2, 229; and virtue, 270–1, 274
intelligence, Descartes' view of, 207–8
interactionism and mind and body, 178–9, 181–90, 191–2, 196–7, 206
intuition, 78–87
intuitionism, Spinoza's, 19–21, 23, 201
intuitionistic theory of truth, 18–21, 23
intuitive science, Spinoza's, 57

jealousy, 239–40
Joachim, H., 12, 46–7, 51, 245–6, 281
joy, 232–3, 237–9, 240–1, 276–7

Kant, Immanuel, 99–100
Kneale, Martha, 216–17, 217–18, 281–3, 285–6, 302–4
knowledge: from causes, 48, 81, 201–4; of causes and effects, 198, 202–3; Descartes' view of, 32, 58, 199–201; and doubt, 26–30, 31; and emotions, 235–6, 241–8, 251–2; and error, 47–54, 59; and eternity,

INDEX

301–4; of God, 61, 83, 270, 274, 275; grades of, 26; joy of, 276–7; liberation through, 255–60, 263, 271, 274; Maimonides' view of, 58–9; and reason, 6–8, 57, 68, 72, 74–5, 78–9; Spinoza's theory of, 52, 55–88; truth of, 15–23, 44, 51; varieties of, 56–7

language-use: and freedom of will, 38–9; man distinguished by, 207
Laws of Feeling, 236–40
Leibniz, G., 2–3, 3–4, 106
liberation through knowledge, 255–60, 263
Libertarianism and attitudes to others, 260, 263, 268
life: Descartes' view of, 206–8; and eternity, 282; Spinoza's view of, 208–9
love, 237–40; intellectual, of God, 266, 270, 274, (and knowledge, 57–8); Spinoza's view of, 4, 266–7

machine, man as a, 206–7, 208
Maimonides, 58, 117, 152
Martineau, J., 222
materialism, 125, 180–1
method: Aristotle and, 8; Descartes', 9–10 (of doubt, 31–2); Spinoza's geometrical, 3–4, 8–9, 10–12
methodism in reply to the *diallelus*, 15–16, 23
Midgeley, Mary, 224
mind: attributes and, 116–17, 120–1, 123; and body, 176–99, 204–6, 280; Descartes' view of the, 31–2, 43, 176–9, 181–3, 185–90, 205–9; the Divine, 131–6, 138–9, 147, 150–3; and error, 51–2; and eternity, 280–1, 291–304; science of the human, 77, 127, 197; and soul, 77, 177; Spinoza's view of the, 33, 34, 37–8, 42–4, 176, 179–81, 183–99, 204, 280; and virtue, 270
mode: body as a, 177; defined, 91, 101; eternity and, 280–1, 289–90, 293–4; mind as a, 179; and necessity, 164; and substance and attribute, 102–5, 114, 121
monism, 105–8, 115–16, 123–4
Montaigne, 12
moralists' attitude to human nature, 4

morality: Aristotle and, 6, 8; and the emotions, 213; Spinoza and, 2, 6–7; Strawson on, 262

naturalism, Spinoza's, 131, 155
Nature: God and, 125–31, 161, 166–9, 172–4; human mind and, 176
nature, human: changing, 4; rationality and, 218–19, 221–2, 269; understanding of, 4–5, 176–7, 271
Necessitarianism, 140, 160–4
necessity: and cause, 158–9, 160–3, 168–9; and eternity, 149–51, 154, 282, 290, 295; freedom and, 155–9
Negativism and the Divine attributes, 117
Neu, Jerome, 215–16, 233
Nominalism and the Divine attributes, 117, 135–6

Oldenburgh, Henry, 109
omnipotence, God's, 136–43
omnitemporality, 284–93; and eternity, 281, 284, 288
opinion, as knowledge, 57, 59

panpsychism, Spinoza's, 209–10
pantheism, Spinoza's, 125–31
Pap, A., 194–5
Parkinson, G.H.R., 102, 103, 219–20
particularism, 15–18, 21–2
passions, the (see also emotions), 231–47; action and, 215–20, 230–1, 233–6, 253; conquest of, 247–53; and knowledge, 57–8, 229, 241–8, 251–2; the mind and, 213–14, 217, 237; religion and, 174; and thought, 182–3, 185–6, 187–90
perceiving: knowledge acquired by, 57; modes of, 41–2
perceptions, sensory: and emotions, 236; and interaction of mind and body, 182–3, 205–6; and the soul, 214–15
pity, 4, 238, 240
pluralism, 105–8
politics, Spinoza and, 2, 55, 175
Pollock, Sir F., 296
Postulate of the Correspondence of Causal and Demonstrative Orders, 201–2, 204
Postulate of Parallelism, 198, 201, 296, 299–300

INDEX

Postulate of Representationalism, 199–201
power: egoism and, 226–7; knowledge and, 256–7
pride, 4, 238
Principle of Perfection, Spinoza's, 153–4
Principle of Plentitude, 162, 299–300
Principle of Sufficient Reason, 161
psychology, Spinoza's, 76–8, 126, 197, 220

Quine, W.V.O., 85–6

rationalists' reply to the *diallelus*, 15
rationality: and attitudes to others, 260, 263–8; of man, 206, 216, 217–20, 230, 249; and virtue, 270–4
Reason: Aristotle's conventionality in respect of, 8; and desires, 230–1, 235, 269; and emotions, 230, 234–6, 246–53, 266–7; freedom and, 255–65, 268–9; and intuition, 78–85; and knowledge, 6–8, 57, 68, 72, 74–5, 78–85; Spinoza's loyalty to, 1; Spinoza's radicalism in respect of, 8; and virtue, 271–8
religion, Spinoza and, 55, 61–2, 132, 167–8, 173–5, 305
Robinson, Richard, 91
Russell, Lord B., 90
Ryle, Gilbert, 181

Santayana, G., 275–6
scepticism: Descartes' view of, 29, 31, 199–200; the *diallelus*, 12–19, 21–2, 25; Spinoza's view of, 25, 26–30, 199, 201
secondary qualities, ideas of, 24
sensations, and mind/body interaction, 205–6
sensory perceptions: and emotions, 236; and interaction of mind and body, 182–3, 205–6; and the soul, 214–15
sensory qualities, Spinoza's theory of knowledge and, 55–6
signs, knowledge from, 59, 62–4
simplicity: and the attributes, 121–2; Divine, 118, 123
Sorabji, Richard, 161–2, 171–2
sorrow, 232, 234–5, 237–8
soul: animals and, 208–9; immortality of, 279–80; mind and, 77, 177, 192–4, 205; the passions and, 213–16, 233, 276
State, the, Spinoza's view of, 211–12, 225–6
Stoical view of freedom, 255–6
Strawson, Sir Peter, 260–4, 265
substance: and affections, 112–14; and attributes, 89, 102–14, 118–24; cause of, 111–12, 114–15; defined, 89–91, 94, 101; and eternity, 189–90; infinity of, 290; the mind as, 177, 180; and modes, 104–5, 114; notions of, 96–101, 109–11
subjectivism, and the attributes, 116
superstition, 173–4, 175
Swinburne, 126
synthesis: in Descartes' method, 10–11; of reason/intuition views, 83–5

Taylor, A.E., 243, 281–2
theology, Spinoza and, 131–7, 155, 165, 169
Theophilus, 129–30
Thought, 105: common notions and, 76; and God, 117, 119; ideas as modification of, 24; and immortality, 280; the mind and, 178–9, 205; and Nature, 126; and the passions, 182–3; in relation to Extension, 121–3, 178–9, 184, 198, 205
time: and eternity, 281–95, 300; since the world began, 144–7
truth: of common notions, 76; criterion of, scepticism and, 13–18, 22–4; and doubt, 26–30, 31, 40; and error, 51; eternal, 40, 68, 149, 151, 284–5, 287–9; intuitionistic theory of, 18–20; the mind and, 31–2, 44; necessary, 287–8; and passions, 242–5, 247–8; of Spinoza's axioms, 19–21, 24; timelessness of, 284–5, 287–9; and virtue, 270

understanding: and assent by the will, 41; body and, 205; and freedom, 258; and ideas, 127–8; and the passions, 247–8, 254; and virtue, 270, 275
universals, theory of concrete, 85–7

INDEX

value, 227–30, 269, 275–6
virtue, 268–78

Wheel, The, *see diallelus*
Wiggins, David, 228
will, the, 43–4; Descartes' concept of, 32–3, 35–6, 37, 40–6, 177, 179; Divine, 131–2, 136, 147–58, 165–7, 169–73; and motion of the body, 178, 187–90, 259; necessity and, 155–9; and the passions, 186, 187–90, 215, 220; Spinoza's view of, 33, 35–6, 37–46, 229
Williams, Bernard, 45
Wittgenstein, L., 20–1, 29–30, 242
Wolfson, H.A., 128–9, 192, 236, 282, 283–4, 286, 303
words: ideas confused with, 39, 63; Spinoza on, 64–7